STUDIES IN EARLY MODERN CULTURAL,
POLITICAL AND SOCIAL HISTORY
Volume 45

URBAN GOVERNMENT AND
THE EARLY STUART STATE

Studies in Early Modern Cultural, Political and Social History

ISSN: 1476–9107

Series editors

Tim Harris – Brown University
Stephen Taylor – Durham University
Andy Wood – Durham University

Previously published titles in the series
are listed at the back of this volume

URBAN GOVERNMENT AND THE EARLY STUART STATE

PROVINCIAL TOWNS, CORPORATE LIBERTIES, AND ROYAL AUTHORITY IN ENGLAND, 1603–1640

Catherine F. Patterson

THE BOYDELL PRESS

© Catherine F. Patterson 2022

All Rights Reserved. Except as permitted under current legislation no part of this work may be photocopied, stored in a retrieval system, published, performed in public, adapted, broadcast, transmitted, recorded or reproduced in any form or by any means, without the prior permission of the copyright owner

The right of Catherine F. Patterson to be identified as the author of this work has been asserted in accordance with sections 77 and 78 of the Copyright, Designs and Patents Act 1988

First published 2022
The Boydell Press, Woodbridge

ISBN 978-1-78327-687-5

The Boydell Press is an imprint of Boydell & Brewer Ltd
PO Box 9, Woodbridge, Suffolk IP12 3DF, UK
and of Boydell & Brewer Inc.
668 Mt Hope Avenue, Rochester, NY 14620–2731, USA
website: www.boydellandbrewer.com

A catalogue record for this book is available
from the British Library

The publisher has no responsibility for the continued existence or accuracy of URLs for external or third-party internet websites referred to in this book, and does not guarantee that any content on such websites is, or will remain, accurate or appropriate

This publication is printed on acid-free paper

For David and Charlie

Contents

List of Figures	viii
Acknowledgments	ix
Editorial Conventions and Abbreviations	xi
Location Map	xii

Introduction	1

Part 1. Governing Corporate Towns

1 Shaping the Body Politic: Charters of Incorporation and Early Stuart Government	13
2 Challenging Charters: Borough Corporations and Quo Warranto	50
3 Managing Division: Borough Government, Central Authority, and Municipal Elections	78

Part 2. Corporate Towns and the Business of Government

4 Governing Poverty and Disorder: Corporate Towns and Social Policy	111
5 Promoting Peace and Plenty: Corporate Towns and Trade	146
6 Paying the Price: Corporate Towns and the Burdens of the State	181
7 Defining Church and Corporation: Corporate Towns and Religious Policy	220
Conclusion	255

Bibliography	265
Index	287

Figures

Maps

Location Map of English, Welsh and Irish Towns Frequently Referenced   xii

1.1   Incorporations and Reincorporations of Provincial Towns and
Cities in England and Wales, Reign of James I (1603–25)   22

1.2   Incorporations and Reincorporations of Provincial Towns and
Cities in England and Wales, Reign of Charles I (1625–41)   23

Tables

3.1   Municipal Election Disputes Heard by the Privy
Council, 1604–40   105

Acknowledgments

This book began its gestation when I was a new mother and came to fruition during the Covid-19 pandemic. The years in between found me, for a lengthy period, in administrative roles. All of this is to say that its path has been longer and less direct than originally intended, making my intellectual and personal debts all the greater.

My academic debts are many. Research for this book has taken me to archives and libraries in towns and cities all over England, and my thanks are due to archivists and staff members who made those records available and answered my frequent questions about the materials – and sometimes about where to get a good meal. I am also grateful to have had access to the library of the Institute for Historical Research in London and its extraordinary local history collection, and the Folger Shakespeare Library in Washington, DC. The staff of the University of Houston Libraries – particularly those in Interlibrary Loan – have been immeasurably helpful over the years. Joe Goetz and Sue Garrison at Rice University's Fondren Library kindly helped me with access to a key database during the pandemic, when entrance to the library was restricted. Completing a book during the pandemic has meant reliance on electronic resources, web versions of reference works, and e-books. For this reason, readers may notice more URLs in the footnotes than typical. I am grateful that the expansion of digitization allowed me to complete the project even when libraries around the world were closed.

I have profited from many scholarly conversations about towns, corporations, charters, and early modern Britain in general with colleagues over the years, including those who commented on conference papers arising from this project. They include Mary Sarah Bilder, Tom Cogswell, Paul Halliday, Simon Healy, Richard Hoyle, the late Mark Kishlansky, Muriel McClendon, Marjorie McIntosh, Robert Palmer, David Chan Smith, Phil Stern, Bob Tittler, Joe Ward, and Phil Withington. I greatly benefitted from the intellectual stimulation of the Folger Shakespeare Library's 2019 seminar, "The Corporation in Early Modern Political Thought," led splendidly by Phil Stern; my thanks are due to him and the other participants of this seminar.

Special thanks go to Quentin Adams, Tom Cogswell, Carrie Euler, Sarah Fishman, Phil Stern, and Joe Ward, who read parts or all of the manuscript in draft and provided insightful comments. In addition, Tim Harris's comments as series editor at Boydell, as well as those of anonymous reviewers for the press, provided vital feedback. I am particularly grateful for the generosity of these scholars, who read and commented on the manuscript in the midst of the global pandemic, when all of us were stretched thin, both personally and professionally. Their input has been invaluable; any remaining errors or infelicities are entirely my own. The task of completing the manuscript and getting it

ACKNOWLEDGMENTS

to press has been made easier by the assistance of Peter Sowden at Boydell and Brewer, whose constructive guidance has been critical along the way. I would also like to recognize the expert assistance of David Wood in creating the maps in this book.

I acknowledge with thanks the financial support I have received for this project. A Summer Stipend from the National Endowment for the Humanities and a Fellowship Research Grant from the Earhart Foundation supported my research at the earliest stages of this project. I especially appreciate the ongoing support of the University of Houston. Small Grants from the Division of Research and a Research Progress Grant from the College of Liberal Arts and Social Sciences funded visits to archives and libraries in the UK as well as production assistance for the book; Faculty Development Leave allowed me to develop and advance the project. A small grant from the Cullen Chair of History and Business (as well personal encouragement from the holder of that chair, Joe Pratt) helped to keep the project moving. Thanks are also due to two deans of the College of Liberal Arts and Social Sciences with whom I worked, John Roberts and Antonio Tillis, who provided opportunities of time and resources for my scholarship during and after my sojourn in administration.

I am happy to acknowledge the journals that have published articles from which portions of the present work are drawn, and for permission to use them here. Parts of Chapter 2 have appeared as "Quo Warranto and Borough Corporations in Early Stuart England: Royal Prerogative and Local Privileges in the Central Courts," *English Historical Review* 120 (2005), 879-906. Parts of Chapter 7 have appeared as "Corporations, Cathedrals, and the Crown: Local Dispute and Royal Interest in Early Stuart England," *History* 85 (2000), 546-71.

My personal debts are also many. Current and former colleagues at the University of Houston have provided a positive professional and social environment. In particular, Sarah Fishman, Anadeli Bencomo, Landon Storrs, Nancy Young, and Ann Christensen have been scholarly encouragers as well as good friends. My parents Joy and Duane Patterson have been unfailingly supportive, as have my siblings Liz Patterson and Tom Patterson, who have shared in many family responsibilities, especially in the last few years. I only wish my father had lived to see the finished book. My deepest gratitude goes to my husband and my son, David and Charlie Wood. They have lived with this project for a long time and have carried a variety of loads so that I had the time and space to complete it. This book is for them.

Editorial Conventions and Abbreviations

Spelling from manuscript sources has been modernized. Dates are in Old Style, with the year taken to begin on January 1. The term "Privy Council" is capitalized throughout, to ensure distinction from the common councils and other councils typical in many towns.

Add.	Additional Manuscripts, British Library
APC	*Acts of the Privy Council of England*
BL	British Library, London
Bodl. Lib.	Bodleian Library, Oxford
CambA	Cambridgeshire Archives, Ely
CCRO	Chester City Record Office
CovA	Coventry Archives
CSPD	*Calendar of State Papers, Domestic*
CSP Ireland	*Calendar of State Papers, Ireland*
DALS	Devon Archives and Local Studies, Exeter
ESRO	East Sussex Record Office, Brighton
GA	Gloucestershire Archives, Gloucester
HALS	Hertfordshire Archives and Library Service, Hertford
Harl.	Harleian Manuscripts, British Library
HHC	Hull History Centre
HMC	Historical Manuscripts Commission
HoP 1604–29	*History of Parliament Online, House of Commons 1604–1629*
HRO	Hampshire Record Office, Winchester
KHLC	Kent History and Library Centre, Maidstone
KLTH	King's Lynn Town Hall
LA	Lincolnshire Archives, Lincoln
NRO	Norfolk Record Office, Norwich
ODNB	*Oxford Dictionary of National Biography (online edn 2004–)*
P in P	*Proceedings in Parliament*
RBL	*Records of the Borough of Leicester*
RBNott	*Records of the Borough of Nottingham*
ROLLR	Record Office for Leicestershire, Leicester and Rutland, Leicester
SA/I	Suffolk Archives, Ipswich
SRRC	Shropshire Records and Research Centre, Shrewsbury
TNA	The National Archives, London
VCH	*Victoria County History*
WAAS	Worcestershire Archive and Archaeological Service, Worcester
WSHC	Wiltshire and Swindon History Centre, Chippenham
YCA	York City Archives

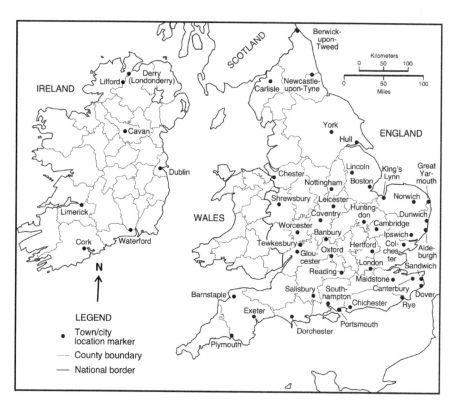

Location Map of English, Welsh, and Irish Towns Frequently Referenced

Introduction

The relationship between center and localities has fascinated historians of early modern England for decades. For an era that descended into civil war and eventual revolution, understanding how subjects related to royal government and responded to its demands remains a critical subject of inquiry. Questions about alienation or connection, division or consensus, have animated lively debates about the coming of the conflict at mid-century. Increasingly, historians have looked beyond identifying seeds of discord, examining instead the ways that local people governed themselves and interacted with central authority. In doing so they seek to reveal how early modern government worked, in all its strengths and weaknesses. This book investigates these critical questions through the lens of urban governance – in particular, provincial corporate towns – to explore how early Stuart government worked and how it changed over time.

Provincial towns, until relatively recently, have garnered less attention among scholars of the early modern period than county and parish communities. Relative to other parts of Europe, England (and Ireland, Scotland, and Wales) were curiously un-urban, except for the great metropolis of London and a handful of smaller regional or national capitals. Nothing comparable to the independent city-states of Italy or the Hanse towns of Germany and the Low Countries existed in England; even the cities with ancient liberties, like London or Bristol, operated under the king's authority. London has attracted more attention, as the metropolis far outran every other urban place in terms of population, economic power, and political pull.[1] Its economic primacy, political significance, and proximity to the royal court gave it a unique place in the early Stuart state. Yet as this book reinforces, provincial towns served a vital role; they, rather than London, are the focus of this inquiry. Provincial towns supported the crown's governance and security in many ways, and they bore a relatively heavy burden for the realm, particularly in times of trade depression, plague, and war. Their concerns linked local problems with national issues;

---

[1] Christopher Friedrichs, *The Early Modern City 1450–1750* (London, 1995); Sybil Jack, *Towns in Tudor and Stuart Britain* (New York, 1996); Valerie Pearl, *London and the Outbreak of the Puritan Revolution: City Government and National Politics 1625–43* (London, 1961); Robert Ashton, *The City and the Court, 1603–1643* (Cambridge, 1979); Ian Archer, *The Pursuit of Stability: Social Relations in Elizabethan London* (Cambridge, 1991); Joseph P. Ward, *Metropolitan Communities: Trade Guilds, Identity, and Change in Early Modern London* (Stanford, CA, 1997); Eliza Hartrich, *Politics and the Urban Sector in Fifteenth-Century England, 1413–1471* (Oxford, 2019); Peter Clark and Paul Slack (eds), *Crisis and Order in English Towns 1500–1700: Essays in Urban History* (Toronto, 1972).

1

their corporate charters linked them directly to the prerogative authority of the crown. Both the corporate nature of their governance and the urban features of their situation – commercial economy, dense population, unique political culture – shaped the experience of the towns within the early modern state. The view from the provincial towns offers a distinctive perspective from which to investigate the workings of the state and the nature of relations between center and provinces in the early Stuart period.

In most studies of the relationship of central authority and local communities, the county has been the unit of analysis. Works on the "county community," going back to Alan Everitt's *The Community of Kent and the Great Rebellion*, have been central to interpretations of England's polity in the early Stuart period. His book took the provincial perspective, believing that too much emphasis had been placed on parliament and high politics. Other county studies followed, including Anthony Fletcher on Sussex, David Underdown on Somerset, and John Morrill on Cheshire.[2] While the counties differed, as did the approaches and periodization taken by the authors, a common theme of strong localism emerged, pitting an intrusive state against an inward-looking gentry community. Subsequent studies, while focusing on the county unit, challenged the ideas both of a coherent and consistent gentry community and an essential disconnect between center and peripheries. Ann Hughes's study of Warwickshire, among others, uncovered a less homogeneous gentry whose relationship with central authority and national concerns was far more complex than that revealed in earlier studies.[3] Research on particular gentry and noble families found similarly multidimensional and multidirectional relations.[4] While many of these works touch on towns within their county studies, the urban dimension is peripheral to their analysis.

Likewise, investigations of the state more broadly focus on communities and institutions other than corporate towns as they study questions of connection and autonomy. Anthony Fletcher's *Reform in the Provinces*, exploring the consequences to government of social and economic change, made a case for the local authority of early Stuart justices of the peace and deputy lieutenants, who routinely sidestepped central intervention. Steve Hindle's *The State and Social*

---

[2] Alan Everitt, *The Community of Kent and the Great Rebellion* (Leicester, 1966); Anthony Fletcher, *A County Community in Peace and War: Sussex 1600–1660* (London and New York, 1975); David Underdown, *Somerset in the Civil War and Interregnum* (Newton Abbott, 1973); John Morrill, *Cheshire, 1630–1660: County Government and Society during the English Revolution* (London, 1974). See also Thomas G. Barnes, *Somerset 1625–1640, a County's Government during the "Personal Rule"* (Cambridge, MA, 1961).

[3] Ann Hughes, *Politics, Society, and Civil War in Warwickshire, 1620–1660* (Cambridge, 1987); Clive Holmes, "The County Community in English Historiography," *Journal of British Studies* 19 (1980), 54–73.

[4] Thomas Cogswell, *Home Divisions: Aristocracy, the State, and Provincial Conflict* (Manchester, 1998); Jacqueline Eales, *Puritans and Roundheads: the Harleys of Brampton Bryan and the Outbreak of the English Civil War* (Cambridge, 1990).

INTRODUCTION

Change, in contrast, argued both for the agency of local people - and indeed parish-level inhabitants below gentry status - in effecting social change through institutions of the state, and for the importance to central authorities of having the cooperation of those local leaders. Michael Braddick's *State Formation in Early Modern England*, while examining "the impersonal forces which shape the uses of political power," emphasized the importance of local office-holders to the nature and formation of the state's authority, which relied on local input and not just centralizing power.[5] As Mark Goldie has argued, "Governance was not something done from on high to passive recipients of authority, but something actively engaged in by the lesser agents of government."[6] All of these works offer insightful analysis of the interpenetration of national and local concerns, and perhaps more importantly, the significance of actors from the parish and county levels in shaping the business of the state in the early modern period.

While most of the treatment of central and local relations has focused on county and parish, towns and cities are increasingly receiving their due. Older narratives of the period, influenced by royalists in the Civil War who criticized urban governments and corporations, often portrayed towns and cities as fundamentally antagonistic to central authority. Thomas Hobbes famously declared corporate bodies to be like worms in the entrails of sovereign national authority, while Edward Hyde, earl of Clarendon, condemned the "natural malignity" of the "great towns and corporations" in 1642.[7] Modern historians, while not comparing them to parasites, have nevertheless long pointed out the tendency of cities and towns to obtain increasing self-governance from their gentle or noble landlords, seeking rights to hold their own courts, lease their own lands, regulate and punish their own people, preside over their own markets, and manage their own affairs. With charters of incorporation, towns sought a legal basis on which to secure authority and conduct business. This pattern fits neatly into the historiography of localism that was so influential in some interpretations of early modern government. Town leaders, like those of the English counties, turned inward to focus on local matters, unhappy with the increasing demands of the central government and eager to exclude or ignore forces that bound the locality to the larger polity. Individual town studies, like that of Exeter by Wallace MacCaffrey, stressed the city's drive for independence

---

[5] Anthony Fletcher, *Reform in the Provinces: The Government of Stuart England* (New Haven, CT and London, 1986); Steve Hindle, *The State and Social Change in Early Modern England, c. 1550–1640* (Basingstoke, 2000); Michael J. Braddick, *State Formation in Early Modern England, c. 1550–1700* (Cambridge, 2000).

[6] Mark Goldie, "The Unacknowledged Republic: Officeholding in Early Modern England," in Tim Harris (ed.), *The Politics of the Excluded, c. 1500–1850* (Basingstoke, 2001), p. 155. See also Patrick Collinson, "The Monarchical Republic of Queen Elizabeth I," *Bulletin of the John Rylands Library* 69 (1987), 394–424.

[7] Thomas Hobbes, *Leviathan, or the Matter, Forme, & Power of a Common-wealth Ecclesiastical and Civill* (London, 1651), p. 174; Edward, Earl of Clarendon, *The History of the Rebellion and Civil Wars in England*, vol. 1 (Oxford, 1843), p. 273.

3

URBAN GOVERNMENT AND THE EARLY STUART STATE

and its fierce focus on local interests. John Evans's work on Norwich, while acknowledging an important connection between leading magistrates and the crown, nevertheless described that city as a "world in itself," at least in the reigns of Elizabeth and James I. Peter Clark's depiction of Gloucester showed a city deeply unhappy with, and ideologically distanced from, royal government.[8] The town's business was paramount, and external forces – whether interfering gentry or invasive officers of central government – resisted, or at least minimized.

That narrative of independence and exclusion has a good deal of power, but other historians have emphasized the ways that center and localities interacted. Robert Tittler's important book, *The Reformation and the Towns*, charted the evolving relationship of provincial towns and their governors with the crown across the sixteenth and into the seventeenth century. As the forces released by the Reformation freed up land and resources within many urban spaces, the governors of England's provincial towns gained political authority and greater autonomy. In the process, town magistrates increasingly forged a relationship with central government to bolster their local power, a process that changed the political culture of provincial towns. Phil Withington's wide-ranging book *The Politics of Commonwealth* argued for the centrality of urban places and civic ideals to early modern England's economy as well as its politics and political culture; the discourse and practices of "city commonwealths" were leading change agents that helped shape the national polity. My own earlier book demonstrated how patronage functioned as a connective tissue between center and locality, binding towns to elite individuals and authorities beyond their own borders. David Underdown's book on Dorchester and David Harris Sacks's on Bristol both reveal vital links between urban places and the business of the realm more broadly. It would have been impossible for the men of Bristol to achieve their ends of stability and prosperity had they rejected a relationship with the state, and in turn the economic and political interests of Bristol contributed to the development of policies affecting trade and commerce throughout the realm.[9] It was not simply the townsmen reaching outward (or upward), but the crown, too, needed these connections to maintain security and order over its provinces.

---

[8] Wallace MacCaffrey, *Exeter 1540–1640: The Growth of an English County Town* (Cambridge, MA, 1958); J.T. Evans, *Seventeenth-Century Norwich: Politics, Religion, and Government, 1620–1690* (Oxford, 1979), p. 63; Peter Clark, "'The Ramoth-Gilead of the Good': Urban Change and Political Radicalism at Gloucester, 1540–1640," in P. Clark, A.G.R. Smith and N. Tyacke (eds), *The English Commonwealth 1547–1640: Essays in Politics and Society Presented to Joel Hurstfield* (Leicester, 1979), pp. 167–87.

[9] Robert Tittler, *The Reformation and the Towns in England: Politics and Political Culture, c. 1540–1640* (Oxford, 1998); Phil Withington, *The Politics of Commonwealth: Citizens and Freemen in Early Modern England* (Cambridge, 2005); Catherine F. Patterson, *Urban Patronage in Early Modern England: Corporate Boroughs, the Landed Elite, and the Crown, c. 1590–1640* (Stanford, CA, 1999); David Underdown, *Fire from Heaven: Life in an English Town in the Seventeenth Century* (New Haven, CT and London, 1992); David Harris Sacks, *The Widening Gate: Bristol and the Atlantic Economy 1450–1700* (Berkeley and Los Angeles, CA, 1991).

INTRODUCTION

Building on these themes, this book takes a fresh look at the nature of relations between center and locality in the early Stuart period, with provincial corporate towns at the center of the inquiry. While certainly the processes of change unfolded over a longer period of time across the sixteenth and seventeenth centuries (as the work of Tittler, Withington, and Braddick shows), concentration on the reigns of James I and Charles I allows closer attention to the impact of changing royal policy in this critical period. The early Stuarts' interest in urban and corporate governance as a means of state-building – and indeed empire – is notable in Britain as well as in its efforts at colonization abroad. In addition to incorporating and reincorporating England's towns, the early Stuarts planted new towns and controlled established ones in Ireland. They also planned to shape the Virginia colony in an English pattern of corporate towns with rural hinterlands, as Paul Musselwhite has shown. Though ultimately unsuccessful, attempts at urbanization in Ulster and Virginia indicate the early Stuart crown's focus on towns as critical elements of governance as well as civilization in places considered disorderly. The pattern set early in the seventeenth century would propagate throughout England's young empire in the later seventeenth and early eighteenth centuries, as chartered corporate towns would be established, whether by royal grant or other forms, in places as far-flung as Madras, Tangier, Philadelphia, and Norfolk.[10] Towns, and particularly the corporate form, offered the early Stuart crown a means of order, control, and in some cases Protestantization across its ever-expanding territories as well as at home.

Yet this interest in civic forms as constitutive of good order stood in tension with less consistently positive attitudes toward urbanity. On the flip side of the civilizing and order-producing elements of urban government lay the potential for "popularity" about which the early Stuarts had increasingly grave concerns. Both James and Charles harbored doubts about the disorder of borough governments where participation of a broader sector of the populace was the norm. As one commentator put it in 1623, "the populer goverment doth directlie take away the power of the monarchie."[11] Trends toward narrower, more oligarchical urban government can be seen during both reigns, though Charles, in particular, made his antipathy to popular government well known.[12]

---

[10] Paul Musselwhite, *Urban Dreams, Rural Commonwealth: The Rise of Plantation Society in the Chesapeake* (Chicago, IL and London, 2019); Philip Stern, "The Corporation and the Global Seventeenth-Century English Empire: A Tale of Three Cities," *Early American Studies* 16 (2018), 41–63; P. Musselwhite, "'This Infant Borough': The Corporate Political Identity of Eighteenth-Century Norfolk," *Early American Studies* 15 (2017), 801–34.

[11] Susan M. Kingsbury (ed.), *The Records of the Virginia Company of London*, vol. 4 (Washington, DC, 1935), p. 223 (Capt. John Bargrave to Lord Treasurer Middlesex, June 9(?), 1623). See also Musselwhite, *Urban Dreams*, p. 51. The comment referred to borough corporations in the Virginia colony, but the concern about boroughs and popularity was a broader one.

[12] Richard Cust, "Charles I and Popularity," in T. Cogswell, R. Cust and P. Lake (eds), *Politics,*

URBAN GOVERNMENT AND THE EARLY STUART STATE

In exploring these themes, this book focuses squarely on matters of governance and order, the "points of contact" where borough authorities connected with the institutions of the state. It tracks the relationship of corporate towns and their officers with central authority across a variety of dimensions, from corporate charters to poor relief to ecclesiastical jurisdiction. Recent work on trading companies and the origins of empire has emphasized the importance and the flexibility of corporations as a tool for government and state formation;[13] the corporate governments of provincial towns likewise played a significant role. As bodies that held their privileges of self-government from the crown through their charters, borough corporations had a direct bond with the monarch. Their officers viewed themselves as the king's immediate deputies, identified with monarchical authority. While protective of local privileges, corporations also understood themselves as part of the larger state; the corporation of Hertford, for instance, sought review and confirmation of its bylaws by central authorities in both 1607 and 1636, to ensure that all were "agreeable with the king's laws" and therefore enforceable.[14] Borough magistrates, of more prominent provincial towns and cities but even smaller and more lowly ones, communicated with and petitioned the Privy Council and the king regularly, seeking to make their voices heard.[15] This communication ran in both directions; orders and policies flowed down from Whitehall, but likewise information and lobbying efforts flowed up from borough corporations in attempts to influence decision-making at the center. Corporate towns were increasingly bound into the workings of the state.

Those workings were not a simple duality of center and locality. The overlapping jurisdictions that characterized the early modern state meant that borough corporations also regularly interacted, and sometimes clashed, with other actors and authorities, whether county JPs, assize judges, lord and deputy lieutenants, ecclesiastical authorities, regional councils, the courts, or royal patentees. The negotiation of governance through this complicated institutional structure, with the king at its head, is a major focus of the book. Readers will notice that while parliament makes appearances in these pages, it is not the

---

Religion, and Popularity in Early Stuart Britain: Essays in Honour of Conrad Russell (Cambridge, 2002), pp. 235–58.

[13] See Philip J. Stern, *The Company-State: Corporate Sovereignty and the Early Modern Foundations of the British Empire in India* (Oxford, 2011); P. Stern, "'Bundles of Hyphens': Corporations as Legal Communities in the Early Modern British Empire," in L. Benton and R. Ross (eds), *Legal Pluralism and Empires, 1500–1850* (New York, 2013), pp. 21–48; Rupali Mishra, *A Business of State: Commerce, Politics, and the Birth of the East India Company* (Cambridge, MA, 2018); Edmond Smith, "Governance," in W. Pettigrew and D. Veevers (eds), *The Corporation as a Protagonist in Global History, 1550–1750* (Leiden and Boston, MA, 2019), pp. 163–86.

[14] HALS, Hertford Borough Records, vol. 20, fol. 82, vol. 30, p. 98. Corporate bylaws could not be "repugnant" to the laws of the nation and were open to legal review; see Mary Sarah Bilder, "The Corporate Origins of Judicial Review," *Yale Law Journal* 116 (2006), 502–66.

[15] On the importance and political meaning of petitioning, see David Zaret, *Origins of Democratic Culture: Printing, Petitions, and the Public Sphere in Early-Modern England* (Princeton, NJ, 2000), pp. 68, 81–6.

INTRODUCTION

main event. Even when parliament was in session – infrequently across the early Stuart period, except in the 1620s – most of the business of governing happened at the local level, in meetings of corporations in the many towns and cities, county quarter sessions, and parish structures, as well as in the courts, regional councils, and Privy Council. The intent here is not to diminish the significance of parliament, on which so much scholarly attention has focused, but rather to shine a light elsewhere, on the regular practices and exchanges of government and administration. It was through these interactions that much of governance was accomplished by authorities at all levels, and where the interests of locality and center routinely connected, or chafed.

This book argues that England's corporate towns actively engaged with the early Stuart state and were important in shaping it, seeking connection to the crown as a key means of securing their own authority and prosperity; this connection, however, remained in constant tension both with borough corporations' own sense of autonomy and privileges, and with the crown's increasing interventions and suspicions about urban government and religious politics. Across the early Stuart period, corporate boroughs consistently looked outward, seeking to extend and secure their liberties by connecting them to the crown and the broader activities of the state. A dogged concern for their privileges animated much of the interaction between towns and the various layers of government, from county JPs to the monarchs themselves, but this did not equate to simple localism or an inward focus. Towns and cities of differing sizes and experiences maintained a regular stream of communication with central government, seeking reinforcement, relief, and renewal of liberties. They saw local concerns within the context of the larger interests of the state, and they regularly reached out to king and Privy Council to achieve their ends. Central government likewise could see the value of securing corporate liberties as a means of maintaining order in the towns, strengthening the authority in the hands of borough governors as deputies of the king. A dynamic push and pull characterized relations between towns and crown, as borough corporations negotiated their position within the state.

The relationship of crown and towns was neither static nor uncompli-cated, and more discordant forces paralleled those of connection, a trend that accelerated across time. What was seen as a particularly urban proclivity for "popularity" sparked distrust on the part of central authorities throughout the early Stuart period, but especially under King Charles. James, eager to forge good relations with reliable men in the localities, continued the pattern set in the sixteenth century in providing privileges to the towns and giving borough governors greater authority relative to their powerful neighbors, both lay and clerical, as well as over their own inhabitants. Charles proved warier of the towns, viewing many of them as predisposed to faction and popularity, as well as religiously suspect. Throughout his reign, but notably during the Personal Rule, King Charles and his Privy Council sought to apply ideals of political and religious order into which corporate boroughs did not always fit, disrupting older patterns. Charles's government adopted a nascent and diffuse, but still identifiable "urban policy" that checked borough liberties in various ways, and which the towns could find difficult to negotiate. Many elements of connection remained, but signs of friction, and at times alienation, can be seen in some corporate towns in response to royal policy, particularly over matters of religion and liberties.

Woven throughout this analysis is a second thread, the question of the ability of the state to support its own needs. While some historians have looked to the "functional breakdown" of the state as a major contributor to political conflict that ultimately helped spark civil war, others have argued that the early Stuart state was often inefficient but not dysfunctional.[16] As this book will show, borough corporations had a significant stake in the success of the state to meet its obligations, and indeed in trying to convince the state what its obligations were. Corporate boroughs were on the one hand "little commonwealths" focused on their own concerns, but as governing bodies they were also deeply implicated in the interests of the state at large, through trade, policies of social and moral control, matters of security and defense, as well as taxation and military obligations. Towns contributed significantly to the peace and prosperity of the state, but they expected the state to offer benefits in return. Negotiating for these benefits constituted much of the communication between towns and the crown in this period; the outcome was not simply dictated by central mandates, but by the persistent engagement of borough governors to convince the crown of national obligations for things like infrastructure, defensive works, and security against enemies. The feeling among borough governors – particularly those of port towns – that their localities bore a heavier-than-fair burden and the crown's often-unsatisfactory response created strains that in some cases gave rise to stands in support of liberties. How local problems became matters of national interest, and how provincial towns negotiated financial responsibilities for concerns that were at once local and national, will be a recurring theme.

The chapters that follow explore key aspects of relations between the crown and corporate towns, interrogating both the nature of their interactions and how they changed over the course of the early Stuart period. The chapters in Part 1 focus on corporate charters and the interaction between corporations and the crown over order, internal governance, and liberties. Chapter 1 examines the patterns of corporate charters, tracing how charters shaped borough government and the relationship between the early Stuart monarchs and the towns. Urban magistrates gained increased authority and privileges through charters, but the crown also used incorporation, in England as well as Ireland, to imprint particular, and changing, ideals of order. Legal challenges to urban

---

[16] Conrad Russell, *Parliaments and English Politics, 1621–1629* (Oxford, 1979), pp. 64–70; C. Russell, *Causes of the English Civil War* (Oxford, 1990), pp. 168–84; Cogswell, *Home Divisions*, pp. 180–4; T. Cogswell, "Ten Demi-Culverins for Aldeburgh: Whitehall, the Dunkirkers, and a Suffolk Fishing Community, 1625–1630," *Journal of British Studies* 58 (2019), 318, 335–6.

INTRODUCTION

government and corporate liberties are the focus of Chapter 2. Through quo warranto, the crown exerted prerogative power to shape and sometimes curb borough governments, especially under King Charles. At the same time, the process of quo warranto could also be used by local actors to gain their own ends and to serve as a means of negotiation between town and crown. Chapter 3 looks at the internal order of borough government, analyzing municipal elections to reveal the ways corporate towns engaged with central authority in resolving problems of division and belonging. It also shows the crown's increasing interest in maintaining hierarchical order in the face of "popularity" in urban government.

Part 2 turns outward, examining how corporate towns fit into the main components of the early modern state's work. According to Braddick, the early modern state used its power "to preserve social order; to enforce and protect established religion; to protect the territorial and trading base of government; and to secure the financial, administrative and military resources to do these things."[17] Chapters 4–7 loosely follow these four themes to analyze how corporate towns helped shape royal policy, as well as being shaped by it. All of these arenas involved regular interaction and negotiation between towns, the crown (most often embodied in the Privy Council), and the other elements making up the early Stuart state, but some, like trade and social policy, proved more amenable to concord than others, like fiscal and religious policy. Social and moral order are the focus of Chapter 4. The towns' long experience in dealing with problems of poverty, disease, and drink placed them at the forefront of national policy on these matters. Programs for poor relief and alehouse regulation, among others, drove increasing connection between borough government and the state; town magistrates were not simply recipients of top-down policy, but active participants in the maintenance of social order, a critical underpinning of their corporate privileges. Chapter 5 examines provincial towns and trade, as both borough magistrates and central government engaged to advance the peace and prosperity of the realm. Borough corporations were key regulators of trade, with economic liberties defined in their charters. But trade required interaction – with other towns, London merchants, markets abroad – and the infrastructure and security necessary to support it. Town officials negotiated both to protect local business and further the state's interests, as provincial townsmen helped shape national conversations.

Chapters 6 and 7 turn to topics that generated connection but also controversy between corporate boroughs and the early Stuart crown. The highly charged subject of the military and fiscal demands of the state is the focus of Chapter 6. Burdens like militia troops and training, fortifications and defense, billeting, and ship money impacted corporate towns in distinct ways, affecting chartered liberties as well as pocketbooks. Negotiating these costs both tied corporate towns into the state and stirred antagonisms, especially under pressure

[17] Braddick, *State Formation*, p. 48.

9

of war. Finally, Chapter 7 examines religion, which was deeply enmeshed in the corporate life and government of provincial boroughs. Increasingly stringent royal policy, particularly during the Personal Rule, reshaped corporate liberties and redefined the boundaries of ecclesiastical and civic jurisdiction within the state. While relations between towns and the crown over religion were complex, Caroline government's privileging of the church over corporate liberties, and its enforcement of new religious policies that, among other things, curtailed godly preaching, generated anxiety in many towns, and in some, alienation. The book's Conclusion gathers these themes of connection and distance together and looks briefly ahead to the experience of provincial towns in the critical period of 1639-42.

No single work can hope to capture all of the many dimensions of interaction between locality and center, towns and the crown. What follows necessarily focuses on only a selection of the many issues that confronted government in this period, but those that do appear shed light on the nature of relations within the state more broadly. Nor can it hope to comprehend all of the great diversity between different types and sizes and interests of towns, each of which had its own chronicles and characteristics, personalities and problems. The cathedral city of Salisbury had jurisdictional concerns not shared by a small market town like Congleton. Gloucester, a major clothing center, experienced shifts in trade policy differently than the small fishing town of Aldeburgh. Port towns such as Great Yarmouth and Plymouth bore certain burdens not felt by inland boroughs like Northampton or Leicester – at least not until the mid-1630s. No town, large or small, was monolithic in outlook; magistrates might be fairly unified or sharply divided over certain issues. And the borough governors who are the main focus of this book had always to contend with their own freemen and general inhabitants, whose views could (and sometimes did) differ substantially from the magistrates. The goal of the book is not to try to create a single model that fits all cases, but rather to identify and analyze broad patterns of interaction that reveal how provincial towns fit into and helped shape the early Stuart state. It also shows the ways these patterns changed across the period, exposing the networks of connection, but also the cracks and fissures present in that state by the late 1630s.

Part 1

Governing Corporate Towns

1

Shaping the Body Politic: Charters of Incorporation and Early Stuart Government

A borough's charter of incorporation was a nearly mystical thing. Through the will and words of the sovereign, it made a disparate group of men into a single corporate person. While enumerating and validating the rights and privileges of a corporate town to govern itself and to carry on its business, a charter also defined a borough relative to the monarch and to other institutions and individuals in the realm. Incorporation, articulated and embodied in the material charters that towns treasured, made corporate boroughs different from most other forms of local government in England. A charter provided a town a measure of autonomy, yet it also deeply bound the borough that requested it to the crown that granted it, strengthening the monarchical state.

We know that the early Stuart monarchs, like their Tudor predecessors, promoted this form for urban government, granting large numbers of charters of incorporation and reincorporation to towns and cities large and small. Less clear is the sort of relationship between borough and crown a charter was intended to create. Historians of England's trading companies have increasingly focused on the complex ways that those corporations functioned within the imperial state, but there has been somewhat less focus on how borough corporations functioned in the monarchical state.[1] Robert Tittler has documented the crown's extensive incorporation of provincial boroughs from 1540 forward. He highlights the bond between central authority and urban governments forged in the wake of the Reformation, characterizing this development in the context of

---

[1] Philip Stern's work on the legal and theoretical ideas of corporations has illuminated how both trading companies and other types of incorporations functioned as part of a pluralistic constitution containing overlapping jurisdictions, leading to negotiation and dynamic relations among elements of the early modern state. P. Stern, '"Bundles of Hyphens': Corporations as Legal Communities in the Early Modern British Empire," in L. Benton and R. Ross (eds), *Legal Pluralism and Empires, 1500–1850* (New York, 2015), pp. 21–47; P. Stern, *The Company State: Corporate Sovereignty and the Early Modern Foundations of the British Empire in India* (Oxford, 2011). See also Rupali Mishra, *A Business of State: Commerce, Politics, and the Birth of the East India Company* (Cambridge, MA, 2018). Daniel C. Beaver, "Sovereignty by the Book: English Corporations, Atlantic Plantations and Literate Order, 1557–1650," in C. Kyle and J. Peacey (eds), *Connecting Centre and Locality: Political Communication in Early Modern England* (Manchester, 2020), pp. 157–73, offers a cultural analysis of corporate charters and their integrative effects. For the later seventeenth century, Paul Halliday, *Dismembering the Body Politic: Partisan Politics in England's Towns, 1650–1730* (Cambridge, 1998) argues for the critical connection between towns and the monarchy through charters of incorporation.

URBAN GOVERNMENT AND THE EARLY STUART STATE

a "drive for local autonomy," particularly regarding control of towns lands and relations with neighboring gentry. Phil Withington has described a "corporate system" that developed under the Tudors and early Stuarts, integrating the local and the national.[2] Some of the scholarship on particular towns has emphasized a sense of independence that charters allegedly conveyed; enjoying and protecting their liberties, townsmen focused inward. Central authorities were distant, intervening at moments of disruption, when the interaction was likely unwelcome. For instance, one historian has emphasized Chester's "independent nature" and the "continuing alienation of local from central government" in the early Stuart period.[3] At the same time, some suggest that while borough liberties were vitally important to local residents, the crown was less interested in them. One scholar has said that English monarchs had "no real wish to assume a permanent direct role in urban management";[4] charters put boroughs and their responsibilities at a distance. Yet incorporation created an inherent link between towns and the crown, in what they said, the way they were obtained, and how the liberties contained in them were maintained.

This chapter explores borough charters and their significance in governance in the early seventeenth century. Subsequent chapters will investigate the ways that borough governments balanced their chartered liberties with their responsibilities to the state in various dimensions, but here the focus is on the charters themselves and the relationship they forged between sovereign and corporation. Through charters, monarchs extended royal authority into urban communities, while boroughs attempted to expand their control over their people and their prosperity, a goal that the early Stuart kings largely supported. The process for obtaining a charter provided a venue for negotiating jurisdiction and authority; boroughs pressed for privileges that the crown carefully weighed. The early Stuarts used incorporation and charters strategically to promote orderly government in England as well as Ireland. Yet the crown's approach to charters was not static. Caroline government intervened more aggressively with charters to promote its vision of order, particularly in the 1630s. The corporate charter served as a point of contact between towns and the crown under the early Stuarts, but as a document of royal prerogative, it could also be a tool of royal policy.

---

[2] Robert Tittler, *The Reformation and the Towns in England: Politics and Political Culture, c. 1540–1640* (Oxford, 1998), pp. 87–96, 161–76; Phil Withington, *The Politics of Commonwealth: Citizens and Freemen in Early Modern England* (Cambridge, 2005), pp. 16–48.

[3] A.M. Johnson, "Politics in Chester during the Civil Wars and Interregnum 1640–62," in P. Clark and P. Slack (eds), *Crisis and Order in English Towns 1500–1700: Essays in Urban History* (Toronto, 1972), p. 205. See also Wallace MacCaffrey, *Exeter, 1540–1640: The Growth of an English County Town* (Cambridge, MA, 1958), and J.T. Evans, *Seventeenth-Century Norwich: Politics, Religion, and Government, 1620–1690* (Oxford, 1979).

[4] Sybil Jack, *Towns in Tudor and Stuart Britain* (New York, 1996), p. 74.

The language of charters

We generally think of incorporation in the early modern sense as an act of sovereign grace enacted by the monarch. By the king's "special grace, certain knowledge, and mere motion," incorporation granted fictitious personhood to a group or entity and conveyed particular liberties, franchises, and privileges. For most English boroughs, a royal charter from the monarch constituted the means by which they formalized their corporate status. The monarch's prerogative power gave the charter life and made the corporation. But at the same time, most boroughs had a host of customary privileges that existed long before royal incorporation by the Tudors and Stuarts. With a charter, the monarch "ratified" and "confirmed" ancient privileges but also granted new ones and fixed "defects" or vagueness in the old. By the early modern period, even prescriptive privileges were understood to have been granted to boroughs by ancient royal charters, now lost.[5] Yet an ambiguity remained between borough as ancient community with its own customary legal existence and borough corporation as a creation of the monarch, with its liberties and government tied directly to the crown. This ambiguity shaped many of the interactions between towns and the crown. Town governors sought both to protect their corporate liberties and to connect themselves closely to the monarch. King and Privy Council both trusted borough magistrates with concentrated authority and at times pressed prerogative power to constrain borough liberties and "popular" tendencies.

Contemporary legal experts averred that incorporation could take a number of forms. Sir Edward Coke, in his Report on the case of Sutton's Hospital (which involved an eleemosynary incorporation), declared that corporations could be created in four ways: by common law, by authority of parliament, by royal charter, and by prescription.[6] William Sheppard reiterated and expanded upon this understanding in his 1659 legal guide *Of Corporations, Fraternities, and Guilds*.[7] Of common law and prescriptive corporations Sheppard said little, except to imply that prescriptive corporations, while good at law, have difficulty proving their privileges in the absence of a charter clearly articulating them. Sheppard also alluded to the idea that corporations may be made by act

---

[5] William Sheppard, *Of Corporations, Fraternities, and Guilds ... With Forms and Presidents of Charters of Corporation* (London, 1659), p. 7; William Blackstone, *Commentaries on the Laws of England*, vol. 1 (Philadelphia, PA, 1893), p. 471. See also W.S. Holdsworth, "English Corporation Law in the 16th and 17th Centuries," *Yale Law Review* 31 (1922), 382–407, for a thorough discussion of legal understanding of corporations in the early modern period.

[6] Sir Edward Coke, *Reports*, Pt. 10, in S. Sheppard (ed.), *The Selected Writings and Speeches of Sir Edward Coke*, vol. 1 (Indianapolis, IN, 2003), p. 363. Coke gives no further explanation of these four methods or their origins.

[7] Sheppard, *Of Corporations*, pp. 6–9.

URBAN GOVERNMENT AND THE EARLY STUART STATE

of Parliament.[8] But "most of the Corporations have been made," he said, by charter or letters patent from the sovereign.[9]

Whatever the law may have said about parliament, common law, and prescription making good corporations, many early modern boroughs sought validation of their privileges through formal incorporation by royal charter. Prescriptive liberties had the authority of antiquity, but they were open to challenge, absent a written document.[10] A charter granted by the monarch formalized the incorporation and clearly outlined the mode of government, extent of jurisdiction, and economic privileges of a borough, securing a town's ability to defend itself against threats both internal and external. It also provided a strong link between town and crown. A royal charter established the corporation's officers as the king's deputies in the locality and identified the town with the monarch. The leading men of Salisbury captured this sense when they appealed to King James in 1603 to incorporate their city, which was still a prescriptive borough under the lordship of the bishop. They hoped for incorporation "so that this city may hereafter be your highnesses city and so called."[11] Historians of towns and cities have often emphasized the autonomy that charters conveyed, but it should also be remembered that incorporation bound a borough directly to the crown even as it conveyed elements of self-government.[12] Borough leaders sought out the prerogative authority of the crown through charters of incorporation as a way to establish their place in the state and the legal and physical boundaries of their jurisdiction.

The connection between borough and monarch was often spelled out in the text of a charter, especially in the preamble. The body of a charter laid out in dry legalese the rights and privileges of the corporation - perpetual succession, to

---

[8] Some boroughs contemplated parliamentary confirmation of chartered privileges, though not actual incorporation, during this period. Winchester and Shrewsbury discussed it but did not act on it; Southampton, Berwick upon Tweed, and the Cinque Ports took their case to the Commons; Southampton (4 Jac. I, c. 10) and Berwick (1 Jac. 1 c. 28) actually achieved it. HRO, W/B1/4 (Winchester Ordinance Book, 15 James-23 Charles), fol. 35v; Shrewsbury Constituency Report, *HoP 1604-29*, www.historyofparliamentonline.org/volume/1604-1629/constituencies/shrewsbury; W.J. Connor (ed.), *The Southampton Mayor's Book of 1606-1608*, Southampton Records Series, vol. 21 (Southampton, 1978), pp. 70, 71, 91, 92-3; M.S. Giuseppi (ed.), *Calendar of the Manuscripts of the Most Honourable Marquess of Salisbury*, vol. 19 (London, 1965), p. 475; ESRO, Rye Corporation Records, RYE 47/97; TNA, SP14/160, fols 79-80, 83-4; *Statutes of the Realm*, vol. 4, pt. 2, pp. 1148-9, 1057-8.

[9] Sheppard, *Of Corporations*, p. 8. For Sheppard, writing in 1659, that sovereign was the Lord Protector, not the monarch.

[10] Sheppard, *Of Corporations*, p. 7; Blackstone, *Commentaries*, vol. 1, p. 471. See also Holdsworth, "English Corporation Law."

[11] WSHC, Salisbury City Archives, G23/1/3, fol. 174v.

[12] MacCaffrey, *Exeter*, for example, emphasizes the self-sufficient and semi-autonomous nature of that city, while Tittler, *The Reformation and the Towns*, pp. 149-50, stresses the drive for local autonomy that motivated incorporation in the sixteenth century particularly. To be sure, neither author argues that towns sought actual independence.

SHAPING THE BODY POLITIC

sue and be sued, to purchase land, and the like. The preamble, however, allowed for reflection on the character or situation of the place being incorporated and on the relationship of sovereign and borough. Penzance's 1614 charter drew attention to the town's importance to defense in Cornwall and its great expenses in fortifications, repair of piers, and protecting against pirates as reasons for King James to incorporate it.[13] Preambles signaled key concepts such as the ancientness of the borough and its customs ("beyond the memory of man"); the long connection between the borough and the "progenitors and ancestors" of the monarch making the grant; and the importance of such charters to good governance of the town, and by implication of the realm at large.[14] Most English borough charters state that the grant is made by the monarch at the petition of the local community; occasionally preambles include the name of a patron, through whose efforts a petition for incorporation was granted.[15] Preambles usually included language stating that the monarch granted the charter for the purpose of maintaining or enhancing the peace and good order of the locality. Northampton's charter of 1618 declares it is granted "for the amendment of the town and the keeping of the peace there," while Cambridge's 1605 charter states its purpose as "the better government and ruling of the same borough." King Charles granted Huntingdon's charter with the intention that the town would "remain a borough of peace and quietness, to the fear and terror of bad men and offenders, and to the reward of good men." Southampton's 1640 charter was granted "for the public good and common benefit of the said town."[16] While not novel to early Stuart charters, this language reinforced the strong sense of order typical of the period.

Preambles also emphasized the need for certainty and clarity in form of government and understanding of privileges. The 1605 Cambridge charter declares that "forever continually there should be one certain and undoubted method in the same borough of and in the ruling and government of the

---

[13] P.A.S. Pool, *The History of the Town and Borough of Penzance* (Penzance, 1974), p. 214. Mishra, *A Business of State*, pp. 23–5, points out the significance of charter language regarding governance of trading companies, as well.

[14] Bond and Evans state that the officers of the crown likely drafted preambles, but the particularity of some of them suggests local input. Shelagh Bond and Norman Evans, "The Process of Granting Charters to English Boroughs, 1547–1649," *English Historical Review* 91 (1976), 108.

[15] For example, *RBL*, vol. 4, p. 79; H.W. Gidden (ed.), *The Charters of the Borough of Southampton*, vol. 2 (Southampton, 1910), p. 77; F.W. Maitland and M. Bateson (eds), *The Charters of the Borough of Cambridge* (Cambridge, 1901), p. 119; Robert Carruthers, *The History of Huntingdon, from the Earliest to the Present Times* (Huntingdon, 1824), Appendix [unpaginated]. Northampton's 1618 charter states it is granted at the instance of Sir Henry Yelverton, attorney general and recorder of Northampton. C.A. Markham (ed.), *The Records of the Borough of Northampton*, vol. 1 (Northampton, 1898), p. 127.

[16] Markham (ed.), *Records of the Borough of Northampton*, vol. 1, p. 127; Maitland and Bateson (eds), *Charters of the Borough of Cambridge*, p. 117; Carruthers, *History of Huntingdon*, Appendix; Gidden (ed.), *Charters of the Borough of Southampton*, p. 77.

URBAN GOVERNMENT AND THE EARLY STUART STATE

same borough and of the people dwelling." The purpose is not simply to have a certain method of government, but "also that our peace and other deeds of justice and good ruling there may be able to be and should be better kept and done."[17] For Portsmouth, which as a port and garrison town had a sensitive strategic purpose, the 1627 charter was even more specific about the nature of the need for good government. The king granted the charter considering:

> that the aforesaid borough of Portsmouth is a port and frontier town on the maritime confines of our county of Southampton aforesaid situate and lying near the High Sea – the strength and security of which it is therefore the more necessary we should earnestly study and provide for – and willing that hereafter forever in the same borough there be continually had one certain and undoubted manner of and for the keeping of the peace and good rule and government of our people there and of others thither resorting.[18]

The language set the tone for shared ideals of good government between sovereign and community.

In addition to these statements about good order and prosperity, charters could include clauses acknowledging the reciprocal aspect of governance: the crown granted charters to towns because it would make them more loyal. King Charles bestowed Portsmouth's charter "hoping that if the Mayor and Burgesses ... [by] our more ample grant shall enjoy liberties and privileges, that they will then feel themselves more especially and strongly bound to perform and manifest their services in their power to us our heirs and successors...." James's charter to Cambridge likewise stated the hope that "royal concession [of] greater and ampler dignities" would cause the townsmen to "feel themselves more specially and strongly bound to discharge and fulfill the services which pertain to us." Similar language can be found in other boroughs' charters.[19] The connotation is clear: the monarch grants privileges and liberties to towns in order to create obligations of loyalty, duty, and service. While most elements of early modern government operated on this principle of mutual obligation, the text of corporate charters made this explicit.

---

[17] Maitland and Bateson (eds), *Charters of the Borough of Cambridge*, p. 117.
[18] R. East (ed.), *Extracts from the Records in the Possession of the Municipal Corporation of the Borough of Portsmouth* (Portsmouth, 1891), pp. 585–6. Colchester's 1635 charter contains similar language. Colchester Borough, *The Charters and Letters Patent Granted to the Borough by Richard I and Succeeding Sovereigns* (Colchester, 1904), p. 82.
[19] East (ed.), *Extracts from Portsmouth*, p. 579; Maitland and Bateson (eds), *Charters of the Borough of Cambridge*, p. 117; Cornelius Brown, *The Annals of Newark-upon-Trent* (London, 1879), p. 100; W. Birch (ed.), *The Royal Charters of the City of Lincoln, Henry II to William III* (Cambridge, 1911), p. 202. This language was not present in all charters of the period; Leicester's for instance, has no such clause. *RBL*, vol. 4, p. 79. It is perhaps suggestive that Portsmouth's Elizabethan charter used the phrase "bestow and offer" the services of the borough to the crown, while the Caroline charter used the stronger and more concrete phrase of "perform and manifest."

Charter language tended to reinforce commonplaces regarding good government and firm connection between crown and town, but some went beyond the standard boilerplate to make more political statements. The most notable and novel of these is the 1638 charter of the borough of Reading. William Laud, a Reading native, took a personal interest in the borough and offered his patronage in obtaining its reincorporation.[20] His high sense of the king's authority shines through in the language of the charter's preamble:

> Whereas in every Monarchy the safety of the people depends upon the Crown and all authority is derived from the Prince and Kings for that purpose are placed on the high throne of Majesty that as Fathers of the Country they should protect the people committed to them by the King of Kings refresh with the Dew of their benignity their faithful Subjects either employed in Arts or in any other manner howsoever uniting for the good of the commonwealth and should ordain Officers who for the purposes of administering Justice and keeping of the peace should govern Cities and other places of their Dominions and the people inhabiting the same ...[21]

It goes on to say that the king hopes that, by confirming the borough's ancient privileges and conferring new ones, "these Burgesses being invested with our authority and animated with our favor will, as is meet, cause the Arts to be encouraged, our peace within the same Borough to be kept, the depravity of morals to be corrected by the more severe sword of Justice, and suitable reward be given to the well deserving."[22] Most charter preambles, if they had unique elements, said something specific about the town being incorporated, as in the charter of Lincoln that highlighted the city's importance as a market for wool, its towers and walls, and its position on the river Witham.[23] Reading's, in contrast, offers a didactic or prescriptive statement about the nature of royal government and the relationship between the sovereign and subjects on whom he bestows authority. This charter does not simply offer royal confirmation of rights and privileges that existed "since time out of mind of man," but instead states explicitly that all authority derives from the king. The personal connection of Archbishop Laud to Reading's charter suggests that this unusual preamble was his brainchild. It is certainly indicative of his views and in keeping with a more vigorous stance of the crown toward charters that developed in the 1630s. Charters were often read aloud in towns to remind inhabitants of their liberties, but they also reminded townsmen of the sovereign authority of the king and the corporation's role in keeping the king's peace and prosperity.[24]

---

[20] J. Bruce (ed.), *Original Letters, and Other Documents, Relating to the Benefactions of William Laud, Archbishop of Canterbury, to the County of Berks* (London, 1841), p. 19.
[21] C.F. Pritchard (ed.), *Reading Charters, Acts, and Orders 1253–1911* (Reading and London, 1913), p. 54.
[22] Pritchard (ed.), *Reading Charters*, p. 55.
[23] Birch (ed.), *Royal Charters of the City of Lincoln*, p. 200.
[24] For instance, in Boston, Great Yarmouth and Lincoln (J.F. Bailey (ed.), *Transcription of the*

URBAN GOVERNMENT AND THE EARLY STUART STATE

The process of incorporation, 1603–40

Much of the attention historians have given to corporate charters focuses on the mid- to late Tudor period, when towns began to appeal in large numbers for legal incorporation, in many cases to secure lands and liberties made available in the wake of the Reformation. Robert Tittler's seminal work makes a strong case for the critical nature of incorporation during that era and into the seventeenth century.[25] The concentration on Tudor charters tends to disguise the fact that the early Stuarts granted more borough charters, if one counts both incorporations and reincorporations, to towns in the thirty-eight years between 1603 and 1641 than Edward, Mary, and Elizabeth combined did in the fifty-six years between 1547 and 1603.[26] James I's reign was a highly active period. While Elizabeth granted seventy charters (of which seventeen were reincorporations) during her nearly forty-five years of rule, James granted seventy-three to English and Welsh boroughs (forty-two incorporations and thirty-one reincorporations) during his twenty-two years on the throne (see Map 1.1). This is in addition to the at least thirty-two less-extensive confirmations of charters that passed during his reign, as well as numerous incorporations and reincorporations of Irish boroughs. Much of this can be accounted for by the fact that towns eagerly took the opportunity to have the new king confirm and extend privileges to avoid any possible questioning of vague or disputed liberties, or simply wanted to strike while the iron was hot and secure the king's endorsement of their privileges while he was newly on the throne. This in turn offered the king an opportunity to forge bonds with towns and cities as he established his rule. King Charles's reign saw a slow-down in incorporations relative to that of his father. Charles granted thirty-five charters – more than two-thirds of them reincorporations – between 1625 and 1641, in addition to numerous confirmations (see Map 1.2). Only modestly sized towns such as Taunton, Liverpool, and Leeds obtained completely new incorporation during the first sixteen years of his reign, while a handful towns like Colchester, Derby, Dorchester, and Shrewsbury obtained reincorporations that significantly altered their corporate structure.[27] One should not conclude too much from such simple counting, but it is clear that James's reign saw the most active period of incorporation and reincorporation, cementing connections between borough governments and the new dynasty.

For the most part, the charters granted by the early Stuart kings are not dramatically different from those granted by the Tudors. They spelled out key

---

Minutes of the Corporation of Boston, vol. 2 (Boston, 1981), p. 340; NRO, Y/C19/5, fol. 66, Y/C19/6, fol. 155; LA, L1/1/1/4, fol. 231).

[25] Tittler, *The Reformation and the Towns*, pp. 149–209.

[26] Calculations are based on the list of charters of incorporation in Tittler, *Reformation and the Towns*, Table I, pp. 345–7 and Martin Weinbaum, *British Borough Charters, 1307–1660* (Cambridge, 1943), *passim*.

[27] Weinbaum, *British Borough Charters*, pp. xlii, xxxiv, xxxvi; C.H. Mayo and A.W. Gould (eds), *The Municipal Records of the Borough of Dorchester, Dorset* (Exeter, 1908), p. 56.

20

SHAPING THE BODY POLITIC

points of borough constitutions; granted rights to markets, tolls, and the like; and gave legal and administrative oversight of the locality to the corporate body, excluding county justices and other authorities from the borough's jurisdiction. Incorporation generally granted a town the right to hold its own courts and control its own property, two things that had historically been the purview of landed gentry and nobles. Many early Stuart charters named mayors as escheators and clerks of the market, placing financial oversight in the hands of borough officials. James I and Charles I largely continued trends begun by their predecessors in the great wave of incorporation in the sixteenth century, though emphasizing even greater corporate narrowness.[28]

Through the process of obtaining letters patent, boroughs, central authorities, and often other interested parties negotiated the outlines of borough government and the extent – physical, administrative, and financial – of corporate liberties. Shelagh Bond and Norman Evans have detailed the process of incorporation and the key elements that most towns sought to gain from them.[29] Each of the many steps involved – from initial petition, to reference to legal officials, through the drawing up of the bill, to the final preparation and sealing of the charter – offered a critical point of contact between town and crown and an opportunity to work out the relationship between them. The many petitions to be found in the State Papers and in borough records show that in most cases, the initiative for charters and the privileges they granted came from the boroughs. Their petitions to the crown laid out the privileges they wished to have confirmed and the new liberties they hoped to secure.[30] Central authorities reviewed such requests carefully before granting any particular privileges, but typically accepted most of what the boroughs requested. It was usually up to the attorney general to "certifie how farr it is expedient for his Majestie to condescend" to a borough's suit for new liberties, and documents detailing proposed privileges frequently show the attorney generals' marks indicating what items they found "convenient" or "inconvenient."[31] These interactions involved give and take, weighing the advantages or disadvantages to the king, the borough, and, often, others who might have interests. In most cases, ancient prescriptive liberties were confirmed, but any new privileges received rigorous scrutiny. A borough could almost invariably expect approval of a request to

---

[28] Tittler, *Reformation and the Towns*, pp. 87–96, 161–6, 188.

[29] Bond and Evans, "The Process of Granting Charters," pp. 102–20; Robert Tittler, "The Incorporation of Boroughs, 1540–1558," *History* 62 (1977), 24–42; Tittler, *Reformation and the Towns*, especially Part III, "Politics and Authority."

[30] See, for example, TNA, SP14/13, fol. 163 (Newbury), SP14/104, fol. 137 (Northampton), SP16/14, fol. 54 (Exeter), SP16/142, fol. 104 (Grantham).

[31] R.W. Hoyle and D. Tankard (eds), *Heard Before the King: Registers of Petitions to James I, 1603–16*, List and Index Society Special Series, vol. 38 (London, 2006), p. 47; WAAS, Coventry Docquets, MS 705:73/BA14450/380/24; Bodl. Lib., MS Bankes 12, fol. 98; TNA, SP16/27, fol. 63, SP16/142, fol. 104.

Map 1.1. Incorporations and Reincorporations of Provincial Towns and Cities in England and Wales, Reign of James I (1603–25).

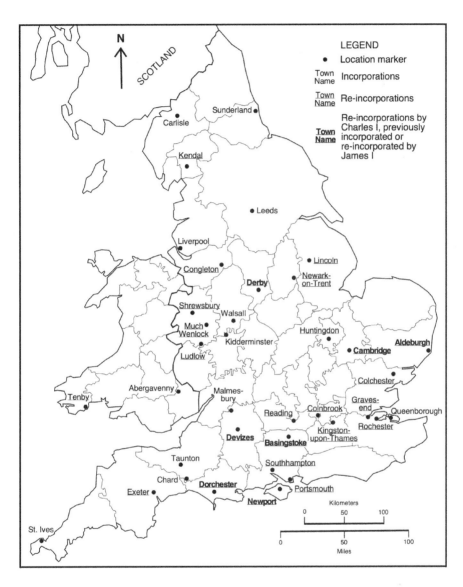

Map 1.2. Incorporations and Reincorporations of Provincial Towns and Cities in England and Wales, Reign of Charles I (1625–41).

URBAN GOVERNMENT AND THE EARLY STUART STATE

confirm or reformulate its governing body, as the crown supported the trend toward more concentrated authority in the hands of borough governors. The negotiation of interests was apparent when the small town of Congleton in Cheshire sought reincorporation early in 1625. Through the process of give and take, the townsmen gained most of what they requested, but the attorney general, Sir Thomas Coventry, reviewed their petition carefully and adjusted the final charter to reflect what he considered legally appropriate and most convenient for town and crown. Coventry limited or omitted some items the borough petitioned for, indicating that they would impinge on the Duchy of Lancaster's liberties. But other changes put more authority into the hands of the mayor and aldermen than they requested. To the request that Sir Thomas Savage (a patron who helped procure the charter) and his heirs be granted the office of steward of the borough, Attorney General Coventry assented, but limited it only to the lives of Savage and his son. The town's petition also proposed that the steward, the mayor, and one alderman serve as JPs for the borough; Coventry altered this (with Savage's consent) to omit the steward from the borough commission. Instead, the mayor and two aldermen would be the town's JPs, the aldermen "being readier for the occasions" of the town than the steward.[32] The attorney general's actions indicate he saw the crown's best interest in validating the townsmen's ability to govern themselves, though sensitive to other considerations.

Requests involving changes that might impact the king's revenues or authority received special scrutiny and were more likely to be curtailed or disapproved. King James authorized the incorporation of Lancaster once informed that the privileges requested were "not entented to the dyminicion of his Majesties revenuewes nor prejudiciall to the crowne," but not all boroughs saw the same success. Newark-upon-Trent hoped in 1626 to gain rights to leets, courts, tolls, felons' goods, and other perquisites from the king in fee farm, but the attorney general rejected that item, as potentially prejudicial to the crown. When Grantham lobbied to gain the escheatorship of the town *absque computo* (without audit), Attorney General Sir Robert Heath declared it to be "inconvenient and of ill precedent," and the king omitted it from the charter.[33] Heath also carefully reviewed Leicester's petition for new privileges in 1629. He saw little harm in granting the corporation's request for extended jurisdiction over the suburban enclave of the Bishop's Fee, but other items he rejected. Expanding the borough's control over its militia, making the mayor escheator, and obtaining the profits of the courts Heath shot down as unacceptable novelties. Given the political moment of 1629, it is perhaps not surprising that the attorney general focused on elements that might touch on the king's revenues and military control.[34] Rochester's 1629 charter petition

---

[32] TNA, SO3/8 [unpaginated, January 1624/5].
[33] Hoyle and Tankard (eds), *Heard before the King*, p. 62; TNA, SP16/27, fol. 63, SP16/142, fol. 104v.
[34] ROLLR, BRI/2/45 ("Remembrances in Renewing the Charter" 1629); *RBL*, vol. 4, p. 250; TNA, SP16/146, fols 29–31. It was also the case that the lord lieutenant of Leicestershire,

SHAPING THE BODY POLITIC

apparently made it through an initial review by the attorney general, but Sir Thomas Walsingham, a Kent JP as well as a bridge warden of the borough, warned Edward Nicholas that the requested privileges would impinge on the king's Admiralty jurisdiction. He begged Nicholas to alert the Privy Council to the problem. Despite incurring "a great deal of displeasure of the city for this business," he felt it was his "duty" to protect the king's interests.[35] While early Stuart monarchs generally supported the aspirations of borough corporations to strengthen their hold on local government and promote order, this did not extend to privileges that might work to the detriment of the crown.

Petitions for new charters sometimes failed completely, often due to other interested parties. Episcopal objections scuttled the city of Salisbury's efforts to obtain a royal charter numerous times between 1590 and 1610 before James finally granted one in 1612. The town of Cambridge's attempt at reincorporation in 1616 fell victim to the university's strenuous opposition. Westbury, a market town with the parliamentary franchise but no charter, attempted to obtain royal incorporation from James in 1609. The effort failed, most likely because Chief Justice Fleming and Sir James Ley, to whom the petition was referred, did not approve it. The borough had hoped to expand its jurisdiction into its "suburbs" and gain other liberties, which Ley, an important local landowner, may have opposed.[36] Richard Hoyle has argued that Sheffield never achieved full royal incorporation because the earls of Shrewsbury, lords of the manor, thwarted it.[37] Leicester's 1629 charter attempt, though initially supported (with some modification) by Attorney General Heath, stalled due to opposition by local landowners who contested the town's claim for extended jurisdiction in the Bishop's Fee. The proposed charter actually made it all the way to the Great Seal, where it was stopped by Lord Keeper Coventry in 1630.[38] While the crown often promoted corporate liberties, jurisdictional wrangling with other local players could prevent a borough from gaining its ends.

---

the earl of Huntingdon, was well-known to be jealous of his military authority. See Thomas Cogswell, *Home Divisions: Aristocracy, the State, and Provincial Conflict* (Stanford, CA, 1998), pp. 30, 149, 191.

[35] TNA, SP16/138, fol. 123.

[36] Catherine Patterson, "Whose City? Civic Government and Episcopal Power in Early Modern Salisbury, c. 1590-1640," *Historical Research* 90 (2017), 493-9; C.H. Cooper (ed.), *Annals of Cambridge*, vol. 3 (Cambridge, 1845), pp. 106-14; Hoyle and Tankard (eds), *Heard before the King*, p. 99; Westbury Constituency Report, *HoP 1604-29*, www.historyofparliament online.org/volume/1604-1629/constituencies/westbury.

[37] R.W. Hoyle, "The Sheffield Cutlers and the Earls of Shrewsbury: A New Interpretation," in R.W. Hoyle (ed.), *Histories of People and Landscape: Essays on the Sheffield Region in Memory of David Hey* (Hatfield, 2021), pp. 25-45. Hoyle stresses the suspicions with which some perceived corporations in this period.

[38] TNA, SP16/146, fol. 30; *CSPD 1629-31*, p. 379; TNA, PC2/42, fol. 15. In 1632, the Privy Council would hear the jurisdictional dispute over the Bishop's Fee once more, making a final determination that Leicester's corporation had no jurisdiction there and must not try to exercise it in the future, much to the corporation's chagrin. TNA, PC2/42, pp. 14-16.

The process of granting a charter, with its opportunities for connection between locality and crown, lay largely the hands of the attorney general and the lord keeper (or lord chancellor). While almost invariably towns brought petitions for incorporation or reincorporation to the government for action, it was the attorney general who determined the legitimacy of requests, the appropriateness of items in the petition, and the recommendation to the lord keeper to seal the charter (or not). We can say with assurance that the men serving in these offices under the early Stuarts understood how corporate charters worked and how important they were to those who sought them. With the exception of Bishop John Williams (lord keeper 1621-25) and Sir John Bankes (attorney general 1634-41), all of the men who held these offices under James and Charles had served as recorder or chief legal officer of one or more towns prior to ascending to their positions of state.[39] While examining charters according to the law, an attorney general or lord keeper had a good deal of latitude in determining the best interests of the state in approving or striking particular privileges requested by towns. Typically (though not invariably) lord keepers approved what attorney generals determined, and the king gave his imprimatur to what the lord keeper approved.

The views of a particular attorney general had an impact on how a charter proceeded. The fingerprints of Sir Robert Heath, appointed by Charles in 1625, have already been seen above; he played a critical role in applying the king's views of corporate order in charters, as we will see. In Sir Edward Coke's years as attorney general (1594-1606), he presided over more borough incorporations and reincorporations than any other attorney general between 1540 and 1640. A significant majority of these (twenty-five of forty-one) obtained the Great Seal in the first three years of James's reign. As attorney general, Coke seems to have supported granting corporate liberties and expanding the control of civic governments over their people. Coke had long familiarity with town governance and borough constitutions, having been recorder of at least four provincial towns, as well as London, by the time that James came to the throne.[40] His

---

[39] The attorney generals in the early Stuart period were Sir Edward Coke (1594-1606); Sir Henry Hobart (1606-13); Sir Francis Bacon (1613-17); Sir Henry Yelverton (1617-21); Sir Thomas Coventry (1621-25); Sir Robert Heath (1625-31); William Noy (1631-34); and Sir John Bankes (1634-41). Lord keepers were Sir Thomas Egerton, Lord Ellesmere (1596-1617); Sir Francis Bacon, Lord Verulam (1617-21); John Williams, Bishop of Lincoln (1621-5); Sir Thomas Coventry, Lord Coventry (1625-40). See biographies in the *ODNB* (www.oxforddnb.com) and *HoP 1604-29* (www.historyofparliamentonline.org/research/members). Paul Halliday has also noted the connection between recorders of urban corporations and high legal office for the later seventeenth century, with a particular partisan thrust. Halliday, *Dismembering the Body Politic*, pp. 138-9.
[40] "Coke, Sir Edward," *HoP 1604-29*, www.historyofparliamentonline.org/volume/1604-1629/member/coke-sir-edward-1552-1634. On Coke and his career and legal thinking more generally, see David Chan Smith, *Sir Edward Coke and the Reformation of the Laws* (Cambridge, 2014).

strong advocacy for custom and common law may have encouraged his sympathies for towns seeking to strengthen their liberties through charters.

Coke's promotion of corporate liberties can be seen in his support of the borough of Leicester's attempts to gain a new charter in 1604–05. The borough had been incorporated by Elizabeth in 1589 and reincorporated with additional privileges in 1599.[41] These charters bolstered but did not clinch the corporation's authority over suburban areas adjacent to the town, the Bishop's Fee and the Newark, and to the bailiwick of the borough, part of the Duchy of Lancaster. Eager to settle all uncertainties and expand corporate authority, the townsmen lobbied for a new charter that would grant them unequivocal jurisdiction, a privilege contested by Sir Henry Harrington and the young earl of Huntingdon, among others.[42] According to Mayor Thomas Chettle, who, with two of the town's aldermen, pursued the charter in London, Attorney General Coke firmly supported the borough's jurisdictional claims. Coke told Chettle that "for the Bishop's Fee it was most fit for us to have it and that it was no prejudice to Sir Henry, and that the matters alleged against us were but trifles." The attorney general promised to certify this view to Lord Chancellor Ellesmere, saying he did so "not for any private respect, but for Conscience sake he must stand close to us ... for that so many great men did oppose themselves against us."[43] Chettle reported that the chancellor and attorney of the Duchy both thought the proposed charter contained "nothing but that which was fit" for the corporation and "no way prejudicial either to his Majesty or to any subject."[44] Unfortunately for Leicester, Coke's advocacy did not win the day, due to strenuous opposition from the earl of Huntingdon. Lord Keeper Ellesmere ultimately refused to affix the Great Seal to the charter despite Coke's approval. Four years of maneuvering and negotiation of patronage relations by the town eventually led to a charter confirmation in 1609, but Leicester's corporation never fully established its jurisdiction over the areas in question.[45] Nevertheless, Coke's words to Mayor Chettle suggest the attorney general's willingness to advocate for the expansion of borough jurisdiction.

The pivotal role of Lord Keeper Ellesmere in Leicester's failure to gain final authority over the Bishop's Fee is notable, since in other cases he seems to have supported borough governments in consolidating their authority and

---

[41] M. Bateson (ed.), *Records of the Borough of Leicester*, vol. 3 (Cambridge, 1905), pp. 247, 359.

[42] *RBL*, vol. 4, pp. 12–16.

[43] *RBL*, vol. 4, p. 34 (Thomas Chettle *et al.* to deputy mayor and aldermen of Leicester, 3 May 1605).

[44] *RBL*, vol. 4, p. 35.

[45] *RBL*, vol. 4, p. 91; TNA, PC2/42, p. 15. See also Catherine F. Patterson, *Urban Patronage in Early Modern England: Corporate Boroughs, the Landed Elite, and the Crown, 1580–1640* (Stanford, CA, 1999), pp. 203–9, and Patterson, "Leicester and Lord Huntingdon: Urban Patronage in Early Modern England," *Midland History* 16 (1991), 45–62 on the charter. Ellesmere had married Alice Spencer Stanley, mother of the earl of Huntingdon's wife, so his intervention likely stemmed from this personal connection.

URBAN GOVERNMENT AND THE EARLY STUART STATE

their ability to maintain control within their boundaries. In the pursuit of security and order, Ellesmere (lord chancellor 1596-1617) tended to place more authority in the hands of mayors and aldermen, and in cases of conflict between churchmen and townsmen in cathedral cities he often supported civic officials. For instance, he supported Chester's right to hold up the civic sword in the cathedral precincts.[46] He supported granting a royal charter of incorporation in 1612 to the city of Salisbury, which had tried for decades to obtain privileges that would release the city from the control of the bishops of Salisbury. He stated that though he was careful to preserve the rights of the church, "so have I a respect for the good of the church and city both, that both may be well and justly governed," which for him meant incorporation for the city.[47] Under Ellesmere's watch, the town of Cambridge and city of Oxford both received royal incorporation in the face of pushback from their respective powerful universities. Louis Knafla has characterized Ellesmere as "a champion of local interests" and has emphasized his willingness to support the legal rights of borough corporations.[48]

The monarch's personal interest also helped shape the limits of borough authority as negotiated through charters. Charters embodied the king's will, and both James and Charles seem in at least some instances to have taken interest in specific details of borough petitions regarding their privileges. Hoyle has noted that James had some commitment to hearing petitions personally, and this holds true for petitions for incorporation.[49] When Newark-upon-Trent sought a confirmation in 1604, James stated that he was "not inclined to give from himself the benifitt of forfeited recognizances as herin is desired." Banbury's 1607 petition for new privileges met with the king's general approval, but he would not approve their request for an additional burgess for Parliament in their single-member constituency. Charles likewise directly intervened in the specific details of corporate charters, as in Plymouth and Kingston-upon-Thames in 1628 and Great Yarmouth in 1629-31.[50] While the attorney general and the lord keeper were responsible for vetting petitions for borough charters, it was in the king's name that they were issued, and the personal mark of both James and Charles can be seen in the process. As will be shown at greater length below,

---

[46] BL, Harl. MS 1944, fol. 92.

[47] WSHC, G23/1/223 (copy letter, Ellesmere to Sir Henry Hobart, attorney general, 15 February 1610/11, copy letter, Ellesmere to [Bishop of Salisbury], undated). See Patterson, "Whose City?," p. 498.

[48] L. Knafla (ed.), *Law and Politics in Jacobean England: The Tracts of Lord Chancellor Ellesmere* (Cambridge, 1977), pp. 145, 149-50.

[49] R.W. Hoyle, "The Masters of Requests and the Small Change of Jacobean Patronage," *English Historical Review* 126 (2011), 553, 563. Hoyle notes that James's "usual attitude" was to refer petitions having to do with incorporation to the attorney general. James does, however, appear to have weighed in personally on some.

[50] Hoyle and Tankard (eds), *Heard before the King*, pp. 47, 92; J. Broadway, R. Cust, and S. Roberts (eds), *A Calendar to the Doquets of Lord Keeper Coventry 1625-1640*, Part 1, List and Index Society Special Series, vol. 34 (London, 2004), p. xii; TNA, SP16/121, fol. 113.

King Charles took special interest in corporate charters and at times used them in promoting his policies.

The early Stuart monarchy saw the importance of borough corporations in England in securing order in the state. Charters of incorporation provided a strong link between local and national governance, giving royal sanction to customary liberties and new privileges for which borough governors negotiated. The impetus for incorporation and the particular contents of charters generally came from the towns, though local opinion on the privileges therein could differ, as will be seen. Central authorities – and kings themselves – paid attention to the details of charters as a means of promoting the security and prosperity of the realm and the crown. Both James and Charles used incorporation and the advancement of borough privileges to cement the relationship and bolster the safety of royal government.

Corporate liberties and narrowing authority

Through the chartering process, borough governors laid out what they hoped to gain and royal officials determined what the limits of corporate governance would be. The charters of the early seventeenth century were frequently, although not exclusively, reincorporations, where an already incorporated town or city asked for further liberties and privileges or new forms of constitutional structure. It is often in the reincorporations that we can see another group being defined out of civic governance, and that is the common burgesses or freemen of a town. Tittler has argued convincingly that the early Stuart period saw a rise in oligarchy, the intentional concentration of power, perhaps even a corrupt concentration of power, in the hands of a small elite.[51] There is little question that across the late sixteenth and early seventeenth century, the freemen in England's corporate towns came to have less direct voice in the decision-making of government. Charters increasingly constituted governments that were filled by co-optation, and even mayoral elections were not always open to all freemen. There are a number of examples of attempts by the freemen to challenge the narrowing of authority onto the close corporation – for instance, in Ludlow in the 1590s, which Phil Withington has detailed in his work – indicating that this concentration of local power could spark contention. Most of these attempts came to naught, however, as borough leaders requested and the early Stuart kings granted charters that rebuffed "popularity."[52] In most boroughs, power rested in the hands of a narrow band of better off, "more discreet" townsmen.

---

[51] Tittler, *Reformation and the Towns*, pp. 139–47, 182–209.

[52] Withington, *Politics of Commonwealth*, pp. 69, 73, 94–5. Given the lack of sources revealing popular attitudes toward proposed charters (most extant material coming from official sources), it is difficult to know how frequently unhappiness over constitutional change occurred, but it was not uncommon.

URBAN GOVERNMENT AND THE EARLY STUART STATE

Both borough leaders and central government had motivations to concentrate authority as a means of suppressing popularity and the disorder it was presumed to bring. Towns, with their higher population density and lack of connection to traditional land-based social structures, epitomized the potential dangers.[53] By keeping a firm grasp on borough government, through a purposely narrow body of men who ran the towns, king and Privy Council hoped to contain the threat.[54] Town leaders had the same goal in mind – to maintain order and authority in the locality – with the added incentive of increasing their personal power and honor. In requesting charters that narrowed borough constitutions, petitioners used language sure to appeal to the crown's concerns. Gravesend's corporation requested a new charter in 1631 "for their better government in regard ... they are grown populous, and the people increasing, they are grown refractory for want of power to order them according to his majesty's laws."[55] Malmesbury's 1635 petition noted their town had lately grown more populous, especially by the "meaner sort" of people; the aldermen and burgesses requested new privileges so they would have sufficient authority over them to do the king's service. Likewise, the 1637 petition from Carlisle's mayor, bailiffs, and citizens averred that "some defects of power and authority in point of government and some irregularities committed there by the popular and tumultuous elections of the principal Magistrate and other Officers" caused them to be humble suitors to the king for a new charter. The king's grant would "prevent many inconveniences to which your petitioners are now liable, and will much tend to the Weale and quiet and orderly government of the said city." The king granted the charter, omitting the old practice of popular election of the mayor and restricting the franchise to the close corporation.[56] The needs and interests of authorities in center and locality meshed in the granting of the corporate charter, often with the erosion of older, more participatory customs.

An analysis of the changes made to the constitutional structure of borough corporations in the early Stuart period confirms that corporations generally became more closed and powers more concentrated in mayors and aldermen.

[53] See Alan Dyer, "Warwickshire Towns under the Tudors and Stuarts," *Warwickshire History* 3 (1976-77), 131-2, for a discussion of this problem in the towns of that county.

[54] Historians have debated the extent to which true oligarchy existed in England's towns, but unquestionably borough governments trended toward concentration of authority in the close corporation. See Tittler, *Reformation and the Towns*, pp. 182-209; J.T Evans, "The Decline of Oligarchy in Seventeenth Century Norwich," *Journal of British Studies* 14 (1974), 46-77; Rosemary O'Day, "The Triumph of Civic Oligarchy in Seventeenth Century England," in R. O'Day *et al.* (eds), *The Traditional Community under Stress* (Milton Keynes, 1977), pp. 103-36. Withington, *Politics of Commonwealth*, pp. 66-84, argues for a conflict between "democratic" and "aristocratic" forces in towns, with aristocrats gaining the upper hand. Whether most townsmen saw themselves in these civic republican terms is an open question.

[55] WAAS, Coventry Docquets, MS 705:73/BA14450/380/19.

[56] Bodl. Lib., MS Bankes 12, fols 5-8; TNA, C233/4 (Great Seal Docket Book 1631-1638), fol. 165. The town's petition included a schedule of eight specific privileges they sought, including a narrowing of the franchise.

At the same time, these trends were not borne out in every case, and it would be difficult to argue that early Stuart government engaged in a strict campaign to ensure that all corporations precisely followed the same formula. Most of the charters granted from 1603 to 1641 explicitly included co-optation as the method for choosing members of the common council, while the mayoralty was usually restricted to a narrow band of aldermen and frequently chosen by the governing council only.[57] But the crown did not use the opportunity of a town's request for new privileges to enforce a consistent or uniform policy in that regard. When the city of Chester petitioned for a confirmation of its charter in 1605, the crown did not seek to alter the pattern set in Chester's 1506 charter, which gave an important role in the mayoral and shrieval elections to the "community" and contained more popularity than most others of the time.[58] Most incorporations reduced or even omitted participation by the burgesses in decision-making, though in a number of reincorporations the governing body itself grew to include more members. For example, Bideford gained two aldermen and three capital burgesses in 1609; the 1632 charter of St. Albans added a whole new group of twenty-four assistants to the previous governing body of a mayor and ten capital burgesses; and Reading gained three more aldermen in its 1638 charter.[59] Both Great Yarmouth and Shrewsbury were able to retain larger governing bodies even when central authorities tried to reduce them during the reign of Charles.[60] Enlarged corporate bodies provided a means of doing the work of government, perhaps even as county benches grew throughout this period. Local interest drove the particulars of these grants, and the crown supported those changes that corresponded with its interests. Exclusion of freemen and narrowing of governing bodies predominated in early Stuart charters, but some variation still persisted as local customs and practices could move central authorities.

One form of narrowing is the change in constitutions regarding the top office of borough government. In the sixteenth century and before, town governments not uncommonly had two bailiffs rather than a single mayor. Few major towns or cities had this arrangement, but some important county towns like Ipswich, Shrewsbury, and Derby, as well as more modest places like Bridport

---

[57] Weinbaum, *British Borough Charters*, passim.

[58] Weinbaum, *British Borough Charters*, p. 11. The community nominated the men who would stand for mayor, from whom the aldermen chose the one who would serve; the community also chose one of the two civic sheriffs. This is in partial contrast to Norwich, the "popular" electoral process of which the king and Privy Council actively tried to regulate; yet even in Norwich, no attempt was made to alter Norwich's constitution to create a fully closed corporation. TNA, SP14/108, fol. 117; *APC 1627–28*, p. 141. See also Evans, *Seventeenth-Century Norwich*, pp. 69–70, 75–7; Fiona Williamson, "When 'Commoners Were Made Slaves by the Magistrates': The 1627 Election and Political Culture in Norwich," *Journal of Urban History* 43 (2017), 6–8.

[59] Weinbaum, *British Borough Charters*, pp. 6, 22–3, 55; Pritchard (ed.), *Reading Charters*, pp. 19, 56.

[60] See below for Shrewsbury and Chapter 2 for Great Yarmouth.

URBAN GOVERNMENT AND THE EARLY STUART STATE

and Basingstoke, did.[61] Tudor incorporations changed a number of "bailiff" boroughs to mayoral ones, and the early Stuarts continued that movement. Twenty towns having two bailiffs received charters of incorporation or reincorporation between 1603 and 1641.[62] In eight cases - Basingstoke, Colchester, Derby, Dorchester, Huntingdon, Shrewsbury, Stafford, and Worcester - the borough constitution changed from the two-bailiff model to the one-mayor model.[63] The reigns of James I and Charles I show quite different trends in this regard, with the reduction of two bailiffs to one mayor becoming more pronounced under Charles. During James's reign, twelve boroughs having a two-bailiff constitution requested incorporation or reincorporation. Of these, ten retained their two-bailiff form and two were reconstituted with a mayor. In contrast, during Charles's reign, nine boroughs sought new charters (reincorporations in every case), and of these, six were reconstitutions into the mayoral model and only three retained the two-bailiff form. Three towns with bailiffs - Aldeburgh, Basingstoke, and Dorchester - petitioned for new charters under James and once again under Charles; in two of these three cases, the Jacobean charter retained the two-bailiff structure while the Caroline charter changed to the mayoral form. In addition, Great Yarmouth experienced a serious attempt in 1629-31 to reconstitute the corporation with a mayor instead of two bailiffs, though in the end, the change did not materialize.[64] Sir Robert Heath, Charles's attorney general from 1625 to 1631, declared corporate bodies with two bailiffs "monstrous" and hazardous to proper government, a view shared by his royal master.[65] The model of the family and the monarchy, accepted as the norm by most in this period, made the mayoral structure appealing.

The impetus for constitutional change to borough leadership seems largely to have come from the towns themselves, as leading townsmen concentrated their authority and in doing so played to the interests of the crown. Petitions from towns requesting new charters show that the changes originated within

[61] Weinbaum, British Borough Charters, pp. 100, 21, 28, 45.
[62] Aldeburgh, Basingstoke, Bridport, Chipping Norton, Colchester, Derby, Dorchester, Droitwich, East Retford, Godmanchester, Great Yarmouth, Huntingdon, Kingston-upon-Thames, Langport, Lichfield, Ludlow, Shrewsbury, Stafford, Tewkesbury, Worcester. The discussion of corporate forms and dates that follows is based on analysis of Weinbaum, British Borough Charters, and Tittler, Reformation and the Towns, Table I (pp. 346-7).
[63] Weinbaum, British Borough Charters, pp. 45, 36, 21, 29-30, 56, 100, 107, 124-5. All except Basingstoke were county towns.
[64] Weinbaum, British Borough Charters, pp. 108, 45, 29-30. Only Aldeburgh retained its dual-bailiff constitution through both reincorporations. See Chapter 2 for more extensive discussion of the attempted change to Great Yarmouth's charter.
[65] TNA, SP16/143, fol. 2 (Sir Robert Heath and Sir Humphrey Davenport to the Privy Council, 22 May 1629). On Charles's views on popularity, see Richard Cust, "Charles I and Popularity," in T. Cogswell, R. Cust, and P. Lake (eds), Politics, Religion, and Popularity in Early Stuart Britain: Essays in Honour of Conrad Russell (Cambridge, 2002), pp. 235-58; Alistair Bellany, "'The Brightness of the Noble Lieutenants Action': An Intellectual Ponders Buckingham's Assassination," English Historical Review 118 (2003), 1261-2.

32

SHAPING THE BODY POLITIC

the borough and were not simply imposed by the crown through the reincorporation process.[66] Huntingdon's 1630 charter states that the king granted the new charter, with its single mayor, "at the humble petition of the Bailiffs and Burgesses" of the borough, though as will be shown below, not all burgesses supported it. The specific purpose was "to prevent and remove all occasions of popular tumult and to reduce the elections and other things of public business of the said Borough into certainty and constant order."[67] Derby's reincorporation in 1638 transformed the traditional dual bailiwick into a single mayoralty. It also reduced the size and reconfigured the shape of the corporate body from twenty-four brethren and twenty-four chief burgesses to eleven aldermen (of which the mayor was to be one), fourteen brethren and fourteen chief burgesses. The bailiffs and burgesses requested the changes to the constitution in their petition to the king "for the more decent and better government of the town," aligning their request with the known preferences of Caroline government.[68] Lack of corporate records for this period prevents us from knowing whether the petition from Derby reflected broad sentiment or only that of the borough's elite; no evidence of controversy has survived in central records.[69] Such alterations of corporate structure confirmed the long alliance between the leaders of provincial towns and the king, with their mutual goal of strengthening authority and preserving order.

As evidenced by Attorney General Heath's negative comments on dual bailiffs, Charles's government had a pronounced bias toward the mayoral model. Yet it did not institute an unbending policy in this regard. Longstanding tradition could succeed in preserving a two-bailiff structure, even in the face of views like Heath's. The king granted three charters – those of Ludlow in 1627, Kingston-upon-Thames in 1628, and Aldeburgh in 1637 – that retained the dual-headed constitution.[70] Great Yarmouth, during a period of bitter controversy over governance and religion, managed to keep its two-bailiff structure despite efforts on the part of a local faction, the attorney general, and even King Charles himself to replace it with a mayoral model.[71] The argument of ancient practice could still trump the seeming unnaturalness of a body with two heads.

While many borough leaders promoted views of hierarchical order in town governance they shared with other authorities in the state, local opinions often diverged. The potential change ignited controversy in a number of boroughs.

---

[66] See, e.g., TNA, SP16/146, fol. 96 (Dorchester), SP16/160, fol. 101 (Huntingdon).
[67] Carruthers, *History of Huntingdon*, Appendix.
[68] TNA, SP16/378, fol. 172, C233/4, fol. 192v, PC2/48, p. 512.
[69] There was apparently controversy concerning the two bailiffs in 1616–17, in the wake of the town's charter granted by James in 1614, but no evidence has survived regarding the 1637 charter. Robert Simpson, *A Collection of Fragments Illustrative of the History and Antiquities of Derby* (Derby, 1826), pp. 92, 94.
[70] Weinbaum, *British Borough Charters*, pp. 111, 97, 113, 108.
[71] Patterson, *Urban Patronage*, pp. 114–17. See also Richard Cust, "Anti-Puritanism and Urban Politics: Charles I and Great Yarmouth," *Historical Journal* 35 (1992), 1–26.

URBAN GOVERNMENT AND THE EARLY STUART STATE

The text of Dorchester's 1629 charter states that its constitutional transformation occurred at the humble petition of the bailiffs and burgesses, but the freemen in general may have had little to say in it. By 1631, conflict arose that partly involved constitutional changes brought in by the 1629 charter.[72] Several boroughs that obtained charters transforming corporate leadership from two bailiffs to one mayor experienced tensions or even significant dysfunction. When Worcester's corporation voted in 1621 on whether to petition for a new charter that would make the city a county and have a mayor rather than two bailiffs, the town clerk recorded the civic assembly's vote in the corporation minutes, a rare occurrence for that city. The result showed a near-even split in the corporate body: twenty-five in favor and twenty-four against. The prospect of change sparked disagreement, but unfortunately no evidence survives of the points of debate or the heat they generated. Stafford's 1614 charter establishing a mayor-led constitution and generally narrowing participation resulted in a good deal of acrimony, including a petition signed by eighty unhappy townsmen.[73] As will be seen, Huntingdon, Colchester, Shrewsbury, and Great Yarmouth all experienced discord related to the constitution of corporate government, as groups within those communities either supported or protested change in the chief office. Altering the shape of corporate governance sparked controversy, even if movements toward a single executive generally succeeded.

Huntingdon's drive for a new charter in 1630 reveals the friction that could arise when a portion of a corporation's leadership promoted a narrower constitution that conformed to the crown's favored pattern, while others supported a more participatory tradition. This passage from Huntingdon's history is well known because it involved the early career of one of the town's most famous sons, Oliver Cromwell. Cromwell had been elected as parliamentary burgess for the town in 1628 and participated in the discussions over obtaining a new charter, which would replace the two bailiffs with a single mayor and reduce the freemen's role. Much of the senior leadership, including the mayor and the town's legal counsel, favored the more restrictive charter. In this, the town's elite saw common interest with central government, which routinely pressed for greater order and less popularity. Cromwell himself seems initially to have

---

[72] Mayo and Gould (eds), *Municipal Records of Dorchester*, pp. 56, 60; William Whiteway, *William Whiteway of Dorchester His Diary 1618 to 1635*, ed. S. Bridges, trans. B. Bates, Dorset Record Society, vol. 12 (Dorchester, 1991), pp. 106, 118. Whiteway noted the new charter with its revised constitution in his diary in 1629 without comment, but related in 1631 that "discontented persons" complained that the charter did not give the common council the right to choose their own members, among other things. See also David Underdown, *Fire from Heaven: Life in an English Town in the Seventeenth Century* (New Haven, CT and London, 1992), pp. 151-2.
[73] WAAS, A.14 Box I (Worcester Chamber Order Book 2, 1602-1650), fol. 71v; A. Kettle (ed.), "Matthew Cradocke's Book of Remembrance 1614-15," in *Collections for a History of Staffordshire*, Staffordshire Records Society, 4th Ser., vol. 16 (Stafford, 1994), pp. 68-9; Tittler, *Reformation and the Towns*, p. 189-90.

34

SHAPING THE BODY POLITIC

supported the new constitutional structure as being for the good and quiet of the town. The new charter, granted in July 1630, included Cromwell by name amongst the handful of men who would be the town's JPs.[74] Despite his inclusion among the magistracy, Cromwell did not quietly accept the charter. He allegedly made "disgraceful and unseemly speeches" against the new mayor and others. Those contesting the charter suggested it would give the town's governing elite free rein to benefit themselves at the expense of more lowly burgesses.[75] For this, Cromwell landed before the Privy Council, as the borough's aggrieved leaders invoked the Board's aid to resolve the local controversy. The Council heard the parties on both sides, finding "much contrariety and differences" in the allegations. They referred the matter to the earl of Manchester, lord privy seal, to settle.[76]

Unsurprisingly, the crown firmly backed the corporation's senior leaders in this conflict. Manchester notified the Board that the fears raised over the altering of the borough constitution were "causeless and ill grounded," and that the change was "fair and orderly done, being authorized by common consent of the Town." Manchester eventually reconciled the parties and "found Mr. Cromwell very willing to hold friendship" with those he had maligned.[77] Cromwell's motivations in the matter are obscure. John Morrill suggested a religious dimension to these divisions, leading to a personal dispute between Cromwell and his rivals; Phil Withington, in contrast, has argued that Cromwell held democratic leanings and opposed oligarchy.[78] Cromwell's initial support for the new constitution and his later desire to be forgiven for words said "in heat and passion" would seem to suggest that the more narrow form of governing body in itself was untroubling to him, even if he feared that some of the men holding positions of authority might use them to further private interests rather than the public good of the town. Regardless, discord over the charter exposed fault lines in the corporation, as at least some members feared the consequences to borough liberties of these innovations. Gaining a charter of incorporation strengthened the legal position and authority of the town by linking it firmly to the crown, but it also bound the corporation to a vision of order favored by royal government.

Narrowing corporate bodies and reshaped corporate constitutions testify to the early Stuarts' growing concern about popularity in government, particularly

---

[74] TNA, C233/3, fol. 251v; Carruthers, *History of Huntingdon*, Appendix; John Morrill, "The Making of Oliver Cromwell," in J.S. Morrill (ed.), *Oliver Cromwell and the English Revolution* (London and New York, 1990), pp. 31–3. See also Withington, *Politics of Commonwealth*, p. 74.

[75] TNA, SP16/176, fol. 58 (Earl of Manchester to Privy Council, 6 December 1630); *APC 1630–31*, p. 140.

[76] *APC 1630–31*, p. 140.

[77] TNA, SP16/176, fol. 58–58v.

[78] Morrill, "The Making of Oliver Cromwell," p. 33; Withington, *Politics of Commonwealth*, p. 74.

URBAN GOVERNMENT AND THE EARLY STUART STATE

in the 1630s. Magistrates in many towns shared this concern, pressing for changes in corporate charters that concentrated their authority. That such changes sparked controversy in some towns speaks to the endurance of older participatory patterns in borough governance. The response of royal government was to reinforce borough magistrates through the process of reincorporation.

Irish boroughs: enforcing order through incorporation

If the early Stuart crown saw incorporation of English towns as a useful means of strengthening royal government, it appreciated the value of towns and incorporation as a tool of state-building even more in Ireland. While the full story of early Stuart urban policy in Ireland cannot be told here, a brief foray into the subject offers an instructive comparison.[79] Elizabeth's government had initially encouraged Ireland's major towns, granting fulsome privileges in charters that the regime later came to regret. Under James, and continued by Charles, incorporation and urbanization came to be significant tools in the government's kit to bring Ireland under the firm control of Protestant, English-style governance.[80] Whereas England's process of incorporation developed somewhat organically, as boroughs with ancient customs and prescriptions sought formalization through royal charters, in Ireland the crown actively set about to create and manage new and renewed incorporations. Establishing new boroughs in plantations, mostly in Ulster, and strictly controlling chartered privileges in established towns like Dublin and Waterford became key elements in English plans for economic and politico-religious development and dominance in Ireland.

From the very beginning of James's reign in England and Ireland, his government focused attention on Irish towns and their charters in its plans for control of that kingdom. Upon James's accession, a number of Irish towns resisted by setting up the mass and closing their gates to the new king's forces

[79] Ireland's place in the early Stuarts' multiple kingdoms and the relationship of the English crown to Irish government is much larger than can be addressed here. The broader context of this problem is discussed in M. Perceval-Maxwell, "Ireland and the Monarchy in the Early Stuart Multiple Kingdom," *Historical Journal* 34 (1991), 279–95, though the author focuses little on incorporated boroughs. See also T.W. Moody, F.X. Martin, and F.J. Byrne (eds), *A New History of Ireland*, vol. 3, *Early Modern Ireland* (Oxford, 1978), pp. 187–292; Jane Ohlmeyer, "'Civilizinge of Those Rude Partes': Colonization within Britain and Ireland, 1580s–1640s," in N. Canny (ed.), *The Origins of Empire: British Overseas Enterprise to the Close of the Seventeenth Century* (Oxford, 1998), pp. 124–47. The present author is undertaking a study of early Stuart policy toward Irish corporate towns, particularly Waterford.
[80] Anthony Sheehan, "Irish Towns in a Period of Change, 1558–1625," in C. Brady and R. Gillespie (eds), *Natives and Newcomers: Essays on the Making of Irish Colonial Society 1534–1641* (Newbridge, 1986), pp. 105–18; Micheal O'Siochru, "Civil Autonomy and Military Power in Early Modern Ireland," *Journal of Early Modern History* 15 (2011), 34–7; Matthew Potter, "The Greatest Gerrymander in Irish History? James I's 40 Boroughs of 1612–13," *History Ireland* 21 (2013), 14–17.

36

under Lord Deputy Mountjoy. This perceived sedition and revolt of Waterford, Limerick, Cork, and Kilkenny prompted Mountjoy to target the strongly Catholic corporate towns in the south, marching his forces there to demand capitulation.[81] Some, like Kilkenny, dropped their resistance quickly, but Waterford remained fractious.[82] With the lord deputy and his forces encamped just outside the city, officials from the town went out to Mountjoy and appealed for public toleration of the mass and for limiting the number of Mountjoy's men entering the city to a number the corporation would allow. They did so by claiming their liberties granted in the city's original charter from King John. Not surprisingly, Mountjoy dismissed their arguments, saying that "he would oppose King James's patent made unto him [as lord deputy] against King John's charter granted to them."[83] He forced the city fathers to open the gates and garrisoned 150 soldiers there to keep order.[84] These early difficult interactions signaled to James's government the importance of managing Ireland's corporate towns to its rule in that realm.

Granting and revising of charters became a frequent tool of statecraft in Ireland. In the decade following James's accession, the crown renewed the charters of several Irish corporate towns, offering them an opportunity to request new privileges, but also giving James's government reason to examine charters and curtail liberties as warranted.[85] Sir Arthur Chichester, lord deputy 1605-16, wished to keep a tight rein on corporations. When Dublin lobbied the Privy Council for a renewed charter, Chichester requested that he and his council in Ireland would retain oversight of the particulars, so that the citizens would have a greater regard for the state "of which they have not of late been so respective as they ought."[86] Sir John Davies, attorney general of Ireland, likewise pointed out the "absurd and unreasonable" clauses in some of the old charters of Irish cities that must be omitted.[87] Revised Irish charters, as with those in England, generally reduced participation of the inhabitants and focused authority on a small number of trusted men who controlled nearly all governance. Of course, the matter of "trusted men" was a delicate one in a largely Catholic realm. More than Mountjoy, Lord Deputy Chichester promoted an aggressively Protestant policy, strictly enforcing the oath of supremacy as well as the oath of allegiance.

---

[81] A.J. Sheehan, "The Recusancy Revolt of 1603: A Reinterpretation," *Archivium Hibernicum* 38 (1983), 3-13; Nicholas Canny, *Making Ireland British, 1580-1650* (Oxford, 2001), pp. 170-1.

[82] *CSP Ireland, 1603-1606*, p. 32 (Lord Deputy Mountjoy to Privy Council, 4 May 1603).

[83] *CSP Ireland, 1603-1606*, p. 39 (Humphrey May to [Robert Cecil], 5 May 1603).

[84] *CSP Ireland, 1603-1606*, pp. 32, 39.

[85] *CSP Ireland, 1603-1606*, pp. 141, 228, 440, *1606-1608*, pp. 223, 248, 416, 521, 576, *1608-1610*, pp. 54, 132, 214, 222, 523, *1611-1614*, p. 20.

[86] *CSP Ireland, 1603-1606*, p. 440.

[87] *CSP Ireland, 1608-1610*, p. 214. For an extended discussion of Davies's role in Jacobean policy in Ireland, see Hans Pawlisch, *Sir John Davies and the Conquest of Ireland: A Study in Legal Imperialism* (Cambridge, 2002).

URBAN GOVERNMENT AND THE EARLY STUART STATE

This meant that corporations could have difficulty filling offices of magistracy, whose holders had to swear these oaths.[88] The charters also frequently revised the collection of customs and other duties, as the crown pushed forward on a policy of enhancing revenues and putting the customs of Ireland on the same footing as the king's other realms.[89] Ensuring and increasing representation of towns in the Irish Parliament – with the intent of increasing Protestant power there – also played a role in incorporation and charter renewal.[90] Some charters were seized and only reissued when central government relented.[91] For reasons that intertwined religious, political, and economic considerations, early Stuart government in Ireland paid close attention to the kingdom's main cities and regularly manipulated charters and incorporation in pursuit of conformity and control.

The plantation endeavor in Ulster likewise involved a clear urban policy on the part of the English crown. From late in Elizabeth's reign, government officials and other commentators promoted the value of incorporated towns as a means to control and develop Ulster politically, economically, and religiously. After James's accession, the earliest plans to establish a plantation in Ulster included the creation and incorporation of towns.[92] In his original "Notes of Remembrance" regarding Ulster in 1608, Sir Arthur Chichester stated his wish that the Irish towns of Cavan and Lifford be incorporated and given land, and that Derry (first incorporated in 1604) be further fortified and walled. He expressed sympathy for Derry, which he said was greatly decayed and likely to come to ruin "if it be not supported by more comforts from the king and better government from the chief officer there."[93] A year later, the "Project for Ulster Plantation," in its plan for dividing the land, included two to five "corporate towns or boroughs" in each of the counties in Ulster. A number of these already existed as towns, monastic sites, or fortified places; others were to be created from scratch. Derry was reincorporated in 1613 with a patent to the city of London to develop both the town and county (renamed Londonderry).[94] In contrast, the plan in Fermanagh called for three corporate towns to be

---

[88] Canny, *Making Ireland British*, pp. 170–3; William Lynch, *The Law of Election in the Ancient Cities and Towns of Ireland as Traced from Original Records* (London, 1831), p. 54.

[89] *CSP Ireland, 1603–1606*, p. 228, *1606–1608*, pp. 248, 252, *1608–1610*, p. 132. See also Victor Treadwell, "The Establishment of the Farm of the Irish Customs 1603–13," *English Historical Review* 93 (1978), 580–602.

[90] *CSP Ireland, 1611–1614*, pp. 165, 179, 267; Potter, "The Greatest Gerrymander," pp. 14–15.

[91] *CSP Ireland, 1615–25*, pp. 187–8, 190, 543; *APC 1625–26*, p. 397.

[92] R.J. Hunter, "Towns in the Ulster Plantation," *Studia Hibernica* 11 (1971), 40–79 provides a succinct account of the origins of Ulster towns during the establishment of the plantation. See also Raymond Gillespie, *Colonial Ulster: The Settlement of East Ulster 1600–1641* (Cork, 1985).

[93] W.T. Moody (ed.), "Ulster Plantation Papers," *Analecta Hibernica* No. 8 (1938), p. 284.

[94] Moody *et al.* (eds), *New History of Ireland*, vol. 3, pp. 160, 204, 265–6; Canny, *Making Ireland British*, pp. 202, 214–15. While efforts to improve Derry as a fortified town were

"erected," at Lisgoole, Castlekeagh, "and the third in the middle way between Lisgoole and Ballyshannon (the place or seat of the Town to be chosen by the Commissioners)."[95] Towns were to be granted property and to have corporations consisting of a chief officer called a portreeve or sovereign, a bailiff or two, and typically ten or twelve chief burgesses.[96] In the end not all twenty-five of the intended towns were incorporated, and the fundamental problem of organizing and peopling the towns was never resolved. Most remained small and largely dominated by undertakers rather than merchants and artisans.[97] But there can be no doubt of Jacobean government's intention to promote towns and corporate-ness as critical components of its policy for planting and controlling Ulster.

Jacobean and Caroline governments had few compunctions about making changes to Irish boroughs, both in Ulster and in the established towns and cities of the south. The incorporation of new boroughs – sometimes from whole cloth – and the restriction, manipulation, and in some cases seizure of liberties in already-incorporated towns and cities offered the crown a means of control and a mechanism through which to impose English ideals of governance, order, and religion. In 1619, the Privy Council even conceived a plan for an incorporation *de novo* of Waterford (which had been notably uncooperative with English Protestant government) that would include a mixture of English and Irish in the governing corporation. They endeavored to recruit men from Bristol, who would act as agents of both economic enterprise and stable Protestant government, to become part of the magistracy of the city. Only those who were "persons of good temper and condition, not violent or turbulent" need apply. Despite the centuries-old trade ties between Waterford and Bristol, no Bristolians felt compelled to transplant themselves to Ireland, and the effort faded.[98] The abortive plan is another indicator of early Stuart government's active management of towns and incorporation in Ireland, which served as critical tools for order and state-building there.

The changing use of incorporation

This brief look at the Irish experience illustrates the significance of incorporation and urban policy to governance in that realm. The early Stuart crown intervened regularly in Ireland's towns to promote political, religious, and

---

relatively successful, London ultimately lost its patent in 1635, ostensibly for failing to bring in sufficient British settlers to develop the plantation in the county as a whole.

95 Moody (ed.), "Ulster Plantation Papers," p. 293.
96 Moody (ed.), "Ulster Plantation Papers," p. 243.
97 Hunter, "Towns in the Ulster Plantation," pp. 51-6, 79.
98 *APC 1619–21*, p. 99 (Privy Council to mayor and aldermen of Bristol, 29 December 1619); TNA, SP63/235, fol. 135 (Mayor and aldermen of Bristol to Privy Council, 31 January 1620); Brendan Smith, "Late Medieval Ireland and the English Connection: Waterford and Bristol, ca. 1360-1460," *Journal of British Studies* 50 (2011), 546-65.

URBAN GOVERNMENT AND THE EARLY STUART STATE

economic ends. It begs the question of whether any similar patterns can be seen in England. Neither James nor Charles engaged as actively in manipulating charters in English boroughs as they did in Irish ones, but both valued the importance of borough charters in promoting orderly government and enhancing royal authority in the provinces. At the same time, the regimes of the first two Stuarts displayed different attitudes toward charters and the extent to which the crown would intervene in them.[99]

There is some evidence to suggest that James and his advisors favored incorporation as a strategy for governance in England. The large number of charters sealed during his reign indicates his government did not hesitate to approve them. In 1604, James expressed his "good liking for corporations, especially for government" in reference to a petition for incorporation.[100] Though careful not to allow clauses that might reduce his revenues, the king regularly supported petitions for incorporation and expansion of privileges on the grounds of good government. The small town of Tiverton in Devon obtained incorporation in 1615 "in consideration that it hath been twice of late almost utterly consumed with fire"; the formalization and extension of liberties would strengthen government and aid in recovery.[101] James favored additional privileges by charter to places like Stratford-upon-Avon, Stafford, and Westbury, "with such increase of liberties and aucthoritie for government" that would help secure peace and good order in those towns. He granted the city of Salisbury its first royal charter of incorporation "with adicion of these liberties desired to the petitcioners tending especiallie to government."[102] Strengthened authority for borough corporations was expected to bring orderly government in potentially unruly towns. Phil Withington has suggested that James "distrusted" civic authority, which may have been true in some contexts.[103] This was not, however, reflected in an unwillingness to grant new privileges to England's towns or to support borough corporations as agents of royal government.

A different pattern emerges when examining Charles's approach to charters of incorporation. More than his father, Charles seemed to doubt the reliability of urban magistrates to maintain order and conformity. Throughout Charles's reign, but especially after 1630, the crown clamped down on perceived threats of popularity and made examples of erring corporations. The king also expanded authority of entities that competed with corporations for local jurisdiction, like universities and cathedrals. For instance, Charles granted a new charter to

---

[99] W.A.H. Schilling briefly touched on this distinction, noting a contrast in the evidence available on central oversight of municipal corporations under James to that in the 1630s in particular. Schilling, "The Central Government and the Municipal Corporations in England, 1642-1663" (PhD dissertation, Vanderbilt University, 1970), pp. 9-11.
[100] Hoyle and Tankard (eds), *Heard Before the King*, p. 47.
[101] TNA, SO3/6 [unpaginated, July 1615].
[102] Hoyle and Tankard (eds), *Heard Before the King*, pp. 47, 59, 62, 88, 97, 99, 105; Patterson, "Whose City?," pp. 498-9.
[103] Withington, *Politics of Commonwealth*, p. 152.

40

Oxford University in 1636 which enhanced the university's authority relative to the civic corporation, giving more power over bylaws and markets and fairs to the university.[104] Though not consistently applied, novel actions targeting borough charters emerged in the environment of vigorous administration during the Personal Rule. Caroline government at times actively used its power over charters to push an agenda emphasizing hierarchical order and, in some cases, changing or limiting long-held corporate liberties.

Perpetuation of the long-term trend toward concentration of authority in narrow corporate bodies characterized Caroline government, but some charters of the 1630s manifested this trend in new ways as the crown used them to constrain what it saw as particularly disorderly government. Among other towns, Colchester found itself under the judgmental gaze of royal authority several times in the 1630s, as differing factions in the corporation engaged in infighting over the distribution of power. James Davis's work on Colchester indicates that the town experienced serious economic dislocation, religious strife, and political tension between the free burgesses and the corporate hierarchy in the early Stuart period. John Walter likewise highlighted "conflicts between the Corporation (or at least a section of it) and the freeburgesses" in the 1630s.[105] These various tensions likely contributed to the push for reform of the charter and the desire of some elements in the corporation to strengthen the hands of the borough's chief magistrates, a plan fully supported by the Privy Council and the king.

Disputes within the town's government resulted in quo warranto proceedings in the early 1630s, which eventually led to an overhaul of the borough's charter of incorporation. While likely not a unanimous decision, the corporation petitioned the king in 1633, hoping to avoid the hazards of this legal action. The townsmen agreed to surrender their charter back into the hands of the king, and the Privy Council ordered the attorney general to draft a new one that "may best stand with the good government of the town, and the maintenance of such fitting and ancient privileges as are not inconvenient to his majesty's service."[106] The charter that Attorney General Bankes drew up changed the borough's constitution from two bailiffs to one mayor and altered the number and pattern of aldermen, assistants, and common councilmen. This set off divisions in the corporation between those for and against this new structure, which brought down more regulation by the Privy Council.

---

[104] Alan Crossley, "City and University," in *The History of the University of Oxford*, vol. 4, *Seventeenth Century Oxford*, ed. N. Tyacke (Oxford, 1997), pp. 114–15.

[105] James R. Davis, "Colchester, 1600–1662: Politics, Religion, and Officeholding in an English Provincial Town" (PhD dissertation, Brandeis University, 1980), pp. 170–208; VCH *Essex*, vol. 9, *The Borough of Colchester*, eds. Janet Cooper and C.R. Elrington (London, 1994), p. 115; John Walter, *Understanding Popular Violence in the English Revolution: The Colchester Plunderers* (Cambridge, 1999), p. 82.

[106] TNA, PC2/43, p. 365; VCH *Essex*, vol. 9, p. 115; Davis, "Colchester," pp. 205–7.

In November 1634, the Board again considered Colchester and its charter, hearing spokesmen on both sides of the controversy. The Council came down firmly for the more hierarchical pattern, with a single mayor at the head and restrictions on voting and participation.[107] In addition to changing the corporate structure, the charter also included some unusually specific passages that spoke to maintaining good order and dignity in the town. The charter explicitly excluded certain occupations and categories of people from participating in elections and nominations, "so that faction and division among the voters, as far as can be done, may be removed, and lest an unworthy and unfitting person be preferred as an officer or minister within the Borough aforesaid by favor, without merit." Brewers and alehouse keepers could not be nominated as aldermen, and

> no Free Burgess of the Borough aforesaid who at the time of such nomination or election made, should use the trade of baker, alehousekeeper, brewer, [or] butcher, or hold and keep a common inn, tavern or alehouse, or serve as chamberlain, drawer in a common inn, tavern, or alehouse, or in any other manner, or shall serve another in any trade for wages, or be not a householder ["*paterfamilias*"] within the borough aforesaid, and pay not scot and lot there, or be lawfully convicted of felony, adultery, fornication, drunkenness, or profanation of the most Holy Name of God by frequent oaths or of other crime whereof by the laws and statutes of this our kingdom of England there is constituted a punishment for the guilty, or doth live by alms, shall henceforth have a vote in any such nomination or election in any way.[108]

This language, unusual for charters of the period, probably found favor with at least some townsmen in godly Colchester. But it also indicates the crown's endeavor to clamp down on the potential for disorder it believed was present in the town.[109] With its focus on strong drink, sexual sin, and other disorders, the charter also exemplified the desire to control popular behavior that characterized Caroline governance (ironically, exhibiting common interest between the king and the puritans he generally disliked and distrusted). Despite the divisions it created in the town, the charter finally received the Great Seal in July 1635.[110] The alliance between the crown and leading elements of borough government, which together pressed for narrower participation and greater hierarchy in the corporation, enforced its will.

In addition to using charters as a means of containing disordered corporations like Colchester, Caroline government also manipulated charters to forward

---

[107] TNA, PC2/44, p. 220; Colchester, *Charters and Letters Patent*, pp. 84, 86.
[108] Colchester, *Charters and Letters Patent*, p. 92.
[109] On Colchester's religious outlook, see Davis, "Colchester," pp. 174-98. Chichester's charter of 15 James also prohibited innkeepers, vintners, ale-sellers, and bakers from being elected mayor, but the town's new charter of 21 James explicitly withdrew that prohibition, at the request of the townsmen. TNA, C233/1, fol. 114.
[110] TNA, PC2/45, p. 4, C233/4, fol. 102. Caroline government's focus on alehouses and other aspects of social control will be discussed further in Chapter 4.

SHAPING THE BODY POLITIC

policies that promoted the Church and its jurisdiction.[111] On 3 June 1638, King Charles declared in the Privy Council that all charters of incorporation granted or confirmed from that point forward must include the bishop of the particular diocese or his chancellor as one of the members of the corporate bench.[112] The charters of Derby and Shrewsbury, both of which cleared the Great Seal just days after the king's pronouncement, included the bishop of Coventry and Lichfield and his chancellor as JPs of those corporations. Reading's 1638 charter and Southampton's of 1640 likewise included their respective bishops as justices.[113] The city of Salisbury, after working for decades to obtain a charter that excluded the bishop and ecclesiastical officials from its jurisdiction, saw its 1612 charter overturned when King Charles imposed the bishop, dean and other cathedral officials as justices of the peace for the city.[114]

The presence of such figures could be controversial. While county commissions of peace routinely included (if only *ex officio*) ecclesiastical officials as well as members of the Privy Council and noble lord lieutenants, borough commissions generally did not. The Henrician statute (27 Henry VIII, c. 24) that codified the monarch's exclusive right to name justices explicitly exempted cities, boroughs, and towns, which the statute confirmed had authority to choose their own JPs according to their charters. Michael Dalton, in his 1635 *The Countrey Justice*, declared that "if the King granteth to a Mayor, or other head Officer of a Citie, or Corporate Towne, and to their successors, to be Justices of Peace in their Citie or Towne, and after maketh out a Commission of Peace to others there, yet the authority and jurisdiction of the Mayor, etc., remaineth good, for that it was granted to them and their successors, and is not revocable at the Kings pleasure, as a Commission of the Peace is."[115] In most cases, town benches included only members of the corporation's governing body - the serving mayor and a few senior aldermen, and often the recorder - as defined by charter. Including diocesan officials in borough magistracy was new for most corporations and frequently unwelcome. It also, as in the case of Salisbury, might alter chartered privileges, imposed by central authority and not solicited by the corporation.

King Charles's concern to protect the Church also led him to exert his prerogative to demand the surrender of charters by borough corporations without

---

[111] This point will be discussed more fully in Chapter 7.

[112] TNA, PC2/49, p. 250.

[113] TNA, C233/5, fol. 192–192v; TNA, SO3/12 [unpaginated, December 1638]; Bruce (ed.), *Benefactions of William Laud*, p. 19–20; Pritchard (ed.), *Reading Charters*, p. 71; Gidden (ed.), *Charters of the Borough of Southampton*, p. 107. Shrewsbury's charter also expressly stipulated that the civic sword was not to be borne erect in any church or chapel. Llewellyn Jewitt, *The Corporation Plate and Insigniae of Office of the Cities and Towns of England and Wales*, vol. 1 (London, 1895), p. lxxi.

[114] TNA, PC2/47, p. 404; Patterson, "Whose City?," p. 503.

[115] *Statutes of the Realm*, vol. 3, p. 556; Michael Dalton, *The Countrey Justice* (London, 1635), p. 10.

43

URBAN GOVERNMENT AND THE EARLY STUART STATE

benefit of legal process. Chichester experienced a lengthy conflict between the city and the cathedral there – touched off by differences over Ship Money – over jurisdictional boundaries and authority; the city's corporation had, by previous charters granted by James, obtained jurisdiction in the cathedral close, which the churchmen resented. King Charles chose to hear the matter himself at the Council Table on 6 June 1636. After reading the attorney general's report and hearing the mayor and recorder speak on the city's behalf, Charles determined "that the Mayor and Citizens should forthwith surrender their said Charter, and upon the surrender thereof, his Majesty declareth that he will be pleased to grant a new Charter to the said city," which would exclude the church and close of Chichester from the city's jurisdiction.[116] The same day, the king heard a similar matter from York, as both the cathedral clergy and residents of various suburban parishes, recently annexed to the city by its 1632 charter, protested against the authority of the lord mayor and corporation over them. King Charles heard arguments from the learned counsel of the city, the bishop and dean, and the suburban petitioners, after which he determined "it was no part of his Royal intention that any the liberties or privileges of that Church should be infringed, or that any other persons his tenants should sustain any wrong by his Majesty's said new Charter granted to that City." As with Chichester, "his Majesty was pleased to order that the said Lord Mayor and Citizens of York surrender and submit the said Charter, and that thereupon another should be passed unto them whereby what shall be fit may be granted to the said city."[117] Even if the city gained back all of its ancient rights and privileges, except for the jurisdiction in the cathedral close and suburban areas, this was a significant blow to their liberties, effected through the king's prerogative power over their body politic.

Caroline government also intervened in corporate liberties by dictating the personnel of corporations. There is no evidence of the wholesale remaking of corporations that occurred under the later Stuarts, but there are hints of experimentation. Charters excluding or requiring various categories of people appeared, as with Colchester's 1633 charter that excluded all brewers, bakers, and innkeepers from the corporation. This exclusion may have been promoted and cheerfully accepted by at least part of the town's leadership, but it marked a significant shift from previous charters and aligned strongly with crown policy. There are also anecdotes, if not systematic evidence, of the crown during Charles's reign requiring particular individuals to be accepted into borough offices, with a promise (which could be interpreted as a veiled threat) to remake corporate liberties in order to accommodate the change. Charles wrote twice to the corporation of Doncaster requiring them to choose his cousin, Viscount Ayr, as their high steward in 1628, saying that if they stood on their chartered liberties in not choosing Ayr, then as king he would simply redraw their charter.

[116] TNA, PC2/46, p. 245; Catherine Patterson "Corporations, Cathedrals, and the Crown: Local Dispute and Royal Interest in Early Stuart England," *History* 85 (2000), 567–8.
[117] TNA, PC2/46, p. 247; Patterson "Corporations, Cathedrals, and the Crown," pp. 568–9.

SHAPING THE BODY POLITIC

"[I]f you shall make any scruple herein, for want of power to make choice of such a High Steward ..., you must know that we shall not take that for an answer, because we are able, both to supply that defect and to dispense with any error formerly committed in that kind."[118] A request by the monarch to a town to accept a nominee into borough office was not unusual; King James, for example, asked the corporation of Chester to accept Hugh Mainwaring to the office of recorder in their city in 1606. The outcome of that exchange, however, differed strikingly from Doncaster's with Charles. The mayor and assembly of Chester met to consider the king's letter but determined that accepting Mainwaring, a non-freeman and a "mere stranger to us," would contravene their charter, which they had sworn to uphold. The king responded not by forcing Mainwaring on the city, but by celebrating and supporting its privileges. "We being therefore moved by a Princelike and tender care of the Weal and well government of that our city, we are well-pleased to grant unto you your free election herein, according to your Charters and liberties, which we wish not to be infringed."[119] In contrast to the sentiment expressed by King James, Caroline government willingly manipulated or ignored chartered privileges to press forward favored individuals or points of view.

The 1630s in particular saw the king and Privy Council actively managing charters to manifest aspects of royal policy. Yet this was not always a simple matter of royal prerogative constraining borough liberties. Local actors often invoked intervention by the crown to achieve their own ends, and at the same time central authorities were not entirely insensitive to local customs and concerns. These complexities are on display in the battles over Shrewsbury's charter in the late 1630s. A city with a history of bitter factional strife, Shrewsbury's government was far from the orderly ideal envisioned by King Charles. According to one of the bailiffs, Thomas Nicholls, the town was "very much embroiled and contentious, and divisions in all businesses." Disagreements, often tinged with religious overtones, brought the corporation to the attention of central government on more than one occasion.[120] Matters reached a high pitch in 1637, however, when Shrewsbury's corporation was hit

---

[118] TNA, SO1/1, fols 123, 177. Charles also asked Cambridge to accept his nominee for town clerk in 1629, but in that case, the corporation readily complied, although another had the reversion to the office. CambA, City/PB vol. 7 (Common Day Book 1610-1647), fol. 177v.

[119] BL, Harl. MS 2082, fols 149, 157.

[120] Bodl. Lib., MS Bankes 13, fol. 64, MS Bankes 64, fol. 8; TNA, SP16/323, pp. 115-16. For Shrewsbury, see Barbara Coulton, "Rivalry and Religion: The Borough of Shrewsbury in the Early Stuart Period," *Midland History* 28 (2003), 28-50; and W.A. Champion, "Shrewsbury 1540-1640," in *VCH Shropshire*, vol. 6, pt. 1, *Shrewsbury General History and Topography*, eds. W.A. Champion and A.T. Thacker (London, 2014), pp. 136-79. Coulton describes the divisive politics of Shrewsbury throughout the early Stuart period and details the religious affiliations of many of the participants. See also Schilling, "Central Government and the Municipal Corporations," pp. 19-21.

URBAN GOVERNMENT AND THE EARLY STUART STATE

with a quo warranto.[121] This legal action and its origins will be discussed below in Chapter 2. The significance for the purpose here is that the quo warranto led to the surrender of the town's charter and a redrawing of its constitution, as various parties within the borough negotiated with each other and with the Privy Council to reshape the corporate body.

Concerns over disorder emerged both from figures of central authority like Archbishop Laud and from townsmen. Some elements in the corporation eagerly sought intervention from the Privy Council to restore unity and bring in a more hierarchical constitution. Bailiff Nicholls petitioned the Council "on behalf and by the direction of divers of the Aldermen and Common Councilors and other inhabitants," requesting a stop to the quo warranto proceedings; the corporation would surrender its charter and obtain a new one from the king, more "conduceable to the peace and welfare" of Shrewsbury. Nicholls, appealing to the king's interests, criticized the popularity of his town's government. He complained that all burgesses of the town, "of what rank soever," give their voices at all elections. The town's two bailiffs, he said, seldom agree with each other but side with opposing factions. Such disorder brought obloquy upon the town, and he begged the Privy Council to devise a plan "for the establishing of a better government in the said town."[122] Nicholls decried the tactics of Thomas Owen, the town clerk, who in Nicholls's view promoted popular disorder to support his own faction.[123] Religious differences as well as political ones played a role in the factional rivalries, but in an interesting twist, it was godly magistrates like Nicholls who protested against popular government, while the Arminian-leaning town clerk, Owen, supported broader participation in borough government.[124] We should not jump to conclusions that puritan religious views invariably meant support for more participatory urban governance. Shrewsbury's experience highlights the many facets of these issues. A variety of concerns - religious, political, administrative, and most likely personal - contributed to the disorder that surrounded charters and borough government in the 1630s. The crown sought to clamp down on disorder in all its forms, and could find local allies of various viewpoints to support its policies.

The king responded positively to Nicholls's petition, referring the matter to Archbishop Laud, Lord Keeper Coventry, and Secretary Windebank in June 1637. Charles tasked them with examining the town's charters and liberties,

---

[121] SSRC, SSR3365/581 (Shrewsbury accounts, 1636-7); TNA, SP16/323, p. 115 (Petition of T. Nicholls, bailiff of Shrewsbury, [6 June 1637]).

[122] TNA, SP16/323, pp. 115-17.

[123] TNA, SP16/366, fols 89-90.

[124] Coulton, "Rivalry and Religion," p. 44; VCH Shropshire, vol. 6, pt. 1, pp. 153-4. A Norwich electoral dispute in 1627 likewise saw a puritan group supporting a strict seniority principle and a moderate and anti-puritan group pushing for "free" elections. This contrasts with Great Yarmouth, where, as Richard Cust has shown, the godly supported broader participation and those favoring Arminian views favored narrower. Williamson, "When 'Commoners Were Made Slaves,'" p. 9; Cust, "Anti-Puritanism and Urban Politics," pp. 13-17.

SHAPING THE BODY POLITIC

rooting out all of the abuses and miscarriages of the officers of the town, and devising a way to establish better and more quiet government in Shrewsbury.[125] The matter ultimately came before the full Privy Council, which heard the parties multiple times in November 1637. While it is impossible to know how many townsmen opposed the idea of having one mayor rather than two bailiffs, at least a handful ("divers inhabitants," possibly including the town clerk) appeared at the Board to state their case for preserving the traditional constitution. A "long debate" ensued before the Privy Council. The townsmen appeared to have some discretion in the matter, but there was also a dangling threat: the king's intention was that the townsmen would enjoy all of their other liberties and privileges *if* they agreed to changes in their government that the Council advised. The parties ultimately agreed, with the "good liking" of the Board, to the idea of altering the borough constitution and replacing the two bailiffs with a single mayor.[126]

This major hurdle having been overcome, it remained to work out the details of the new charter. The Privy Council, while keeping a firm hand on the business, also showed itself to be flexible on some points of local concern. Identifying the corporation of Worcester as a model for Shrewsbury, the parties negotiated a revision along those lines, including an expansion of the number of aldermen from twelve to twenty-four and a method for choosing them. The group that originally opposed any change in the constitution went along with these alterations, but chafed against certain elements that would narrow the corporation. The initial plan recommended that there be forty-eight total members of the governing body, of whom twenty-four would be aldermen. The opposing party wished instead to retain a common council of forty-eight members in addition to the bench of aldermen, as in the old charter. The Council advised against this, presumably fearing the potential for popularity that such a large corporate body might foster, but did not force the issue. Admitting that the opposing party had "showed themselves conformable in all matters, they [the Privy Council] would not refuse them in this desire if they shall persist therein."[127] The Board approved a corporation with one mayor, twenty-four aldermen, and forty-eight common councilors.

The Council may have regretted this leniency. Some townsmen continued to press for participation, requesting that all burgesses in the corporation have a hand in selecting the first common councilors under the new charter. The Board's response suggests their desire to enforce order on Shrewsbury's elections and their fear of the potential for turmoil. The Council allowed that the burgesses could participate in the selection of common councilors, but only with strict limitations. The present bailiffs were to make a list of the fifty

---

[125] TNA, SP16/323, p. 117.
[126] TNA, PC2/48, pp. 369, 390. Some of the many points argued in the matter are articulated in TNA, SP16/366, fols 85–92.
[127] TNA, PC2/48, p. 390.

URBAN GOVERNMENT AND THE EARLY STUART STATE

most ancient burgesses of the corporation and submit it to the town's recorder, Sir John Bridgeman. Bridgeman was to peruse the list, strike off any names he thought unfit for service, and rank order the remaining names. The bailiffs would then propound this ranked list to the burgesses, who would select the requisite number for the common council. The Board's ambivalence with this arrangement is indicated by the threats they attached to the provisions. If disorder arose over the selection of common councilors, the Privy Council would reduce the size of the common council, reinstitute the quo warranto, and punish those responsible.[128]

The Privy Council's handling of Shrewsbury's charter reflects the complicated relationship between crown and towns in the 1630s. Concerned about political disorder and religious debate, Caroline government intervened in Shrewsbury, chastening the corporation and promoting a more hierarchical constitution. It acted firmly to suppress disorder in an important provincial town. Yet in doing this, the crown was not simply enforcing its will on a resistant borough. Instead, it found common ground with a portion of the town's governors and did not impose the new constitution entirely by prerogative power. The Council's acquiescence to the townsmen's desire for a larger common council suggests that while the Board prioritized order in corporations, it did not have a clear-cut pattern for borough government to which all must conform. The new charter served as a frame for negotiating the outlines of Shrewsbury's body politic, shaped both by royal policy and local interests.

Shrewsbury's unusually divisive case reflected particular political and religious divisions of the time and place. Nevertheless, it embodies some of the broader patterns that characterized corporate charters and their importance within early Stuart government. Towns valued charters as a means to secure their legal standing, their local privileges, and their connection to the crown. Borough governors, in particular, sought the reinforcement of their own authority that often came with new charters in the early seventeenth century, and frequently the interests of the crown and of town officials meshed. Through the process of petitioning for charters, borough governors negotiated the outlines of local privileges, intending both to enhance borough liberties and reinforce their commitment to preserving the order and stability expected by the crown. Central authorities tended to support local liberties, but also scrutinized them closely to ensure their "convenience" to the larger needs of royal government. At times central authorities intervened actively to create or modify charters when boroughs were seen to be disordered, if loyalties were suspect or in order to promote specific policies. While W.A.H. Schilling's view that the early Stuart period saw "no widespread effort ... to regulate or otherwise undermine [corporations'] chartered liberties" is largely correct, this should not be taken as a lack of interest in corporations on the part of the first James and Charles.[129] In both

---

[128] TNA, PC2/48, p. 407.
[129] Schilling, "Central Government and the Municipal Corporations," p. 26.

their English and Irish realms, the early Stuart monarchs saw the importance of incorporated boroughs and charters of incorporation in advancing their rule and securing the state. That Charles took a stronger personal interest in corporate liberties also seems clear.

2

Challenging Charters: Borough Corporations and Quo Warranto

Charters of incorporation formed a critical connection between the crown and the towns in the early Stuart period. Through charters, both local actors and central authorities expressed ideas about governance, established the bounds of local jurisdiction, and clearly identified and reinforced corporate leaders as the king's direct deputies in urban communities. The corporate charter gave borough governors both a sense of autonomy through legally defined privileges and self-government and a clear and direct tie to the monarch and the powers of the monarchical state. No county or hundred or parish had quite the same relationship with central government and royal authority as did incorporated boroughs. Yet, while charters created strong bonds between corporate boroughs and royal authority, the corporate form also made town governments vulnerable. With liberties and privileges laid out in written "constitutions," borough governors knew that deviation from their charters in any way could be tested in court or questioned by the royal authority that granted them. Such a challenge to corporate liberties had the potential to reshape borough government – even threaten its very existence – and to realign the relationship between town and crown.

This chapter explores the connection between urban governments and royal authority through an investigation of the legal process of quo warranto. In the context of early modern towns, the term "quo warranto" usually evokes ideas of absolutism and arbitrary authority, an instrument of high prerogative that the later Stuart kings wielded against England's towns and cities. In a drive to control borough governments and the politics of the men who constituted them, both Charles II and James II used quo warranto to reshape corporations, forcing them to surrender their charters. Charles II's government notoriously initiated quo warranto against the charter of the city of London, resulting in a 1683 judgment for the king declaring the seizure of the city's liberties. Paul Halliday has shown that local initiative played a key role in the later Stuarts' use of quo warranto, but for all of its complexities, it became an important tool of Stuart policy in the later seventeenth century.[1] Historians of the early

---

[1] J.H. Sacret, "The Restoration Government and Municipal Corporations," *English Historical Review* 45 (1930), 232-59; Jennifer Levin, *The Charter Controversy in the City of London, 1660-1688, and Its Consequences* (London, 1960); John Miller, "The Crown and the Borough Charters in the Reign of Charles II," *English Historical Review* 100 (1985), 53-84; Paul Halliday, *Dismembering the Body Politic: Partisan Politics in England's Towns, 1650-1730*

50

CHALLENGING CHARTERS

seventeenth century have paid less attention to quo warranto. Robert Tittler addressed this legal action in *The Reformation and the Towns*, interpreting it as "a useful weapon in the battle for and against the encroachment of oligarchy."[2] That was certainly a key element of quo warranto's use, but it can be framed more broadly than the context of debates over oligarchy. An exploration of quo warranto and the challenges to chartered liberties of provincial towns it presented in this period reveals how borough corporations related to the crown and perceived its actions, how they negotiated challenges to their privileges through the central courts, and how individuals or entities other than the king could manipulate prerogative processes to gain their own ends. It also illuminates the use of royal prerogative vis-à-vis corporate charters and how this changed over the early Stuart period, as the crown's motivations for using quo warranto's power evolved.

The story of quo warranto and challenges to charters under the early Stuarts is not a simple one of central application of coercion and arbitrary power on corporate boroughs nor of local resistance to central authority. Instead, a subtler, more complex pattern can be traced, one that displays the vital role of local concerns in the origins of central policy.[3] As will be shown, local people regularly promoted the initiation of quo warranto proceedings, using the central courts to solve differences in borough government or simply to get back at neighbors. At the same time, the crown challenged the charters of corporate towns for its own purposes, which might be financial, administrative, or political, as it sought to shape or influence urban governments. The ways in which the crown used quo warranto also fluctuated over time, as government under James I and Charles I adopted different strategies to fulfill changing objectives. Though not systematically, it could serve as a tool for exerting the power of royal authority over corporations thought to be straying from the patterns of orderly government ordained by the crown. Instances of purposeful use of quo warranto to achieve royal policy regarding religion and government became more prominent under Charles, especially in the 1630s, causing some anxiety among England's chartered corporations. Quo warranto always served as a signal to corporations that they existed at the will of the monarch, but it also demonstrated the dynamic tension between crown and towns, with both local actors and central officials finding ways to use it toward their ends.

(Cambridge, 1998), pp. 189–236. Halliday's thorough reinterpretation of the extensive use of quo warranto in the later seventeenth century is an important corrective to an older view that simplistically tied quo warranto to "Stuart Absolutism."

[2] Robert Tittler, *The Reformation and the Towns in England: Politics and Political Culture, c. 1540–1640* (Oxford, 1998), pp. 193–5. For a legal history perspective, see W.S. Holdsworth, "English Corporation Law in the 16th and 17th Centuries," *The Yale Law Journal* 31 (1922), 401–3.

[3] See Michael J. Braddick, *State Formation in Early Modern England* (Cambridge, 2000) and Steve Hindle, *The State and Social Change in Early Modern England* (New York, 2000) for broader discussions of relations between central and local elements in the English state.

51

URBAN GOVERNMENT AND THE EARLY STUART STATE

Boroughs and quo warranto, 1603–40

While challenges to charters could take a number of shapes, the one most commonly experienced by town governments was quo warranto. With quo warranto, the monarch questioned "by what warrant" any individual or group exercised rights, privileges or franchises of any sort. Originating in the thirteenth century, the writ was a general order for the recipient to come into court and prove privileges. Its use can be found as early as the reign of Henry III, but Edward I used it extensively and systematically to boost his power by recovering jurisdictional and fiscal rights allegedly usurped by his subjects.[4] Edward's successors did not press quo warranto rigorously, but it saw a resurgence under the early Tudors. Henry VIII in particular used it to extend the reach of his authority.[5] By the sixteenth century, proceedings using the actual prerogative writ had largely been replaced by the use of the "information in the nature of a quo warranto." The information was more specific, defining particular franchises and misuses and requiring an equally specific response. In addition, judgment on a writ resulted in immediate dissolution of franchises, while a judgment on an information could be interpreted more flexibly.[6] The quo warranto, whether writ or information, provided a useful mechanism for questioning the many liberties and privileges claimed by the monarch's subjects and forcing them to prove or relinquish them.

The great raft of royal incorporations by charter of towns across England and Wales in the wake of the Reformation created many new and expanded franchises and liberties. It also made incorporated boroughs susceptible to quo warranto proceedings.[7] The monarch's ultimate authority to rescind a charter and (at least theoretically) dissolve the legal existence of a corporation gave town governors an incentive to obey and to follow their charters to the letter. In the Tudor period, the crown did, on occasion, use quo warranto to punish an errant town. Queen Mary's government, for instance, used it to revoke the charter of Maidstone after the implication of members of the corporation in Wyatt's rebellion. The town remained unincorporated until 1559, by which time Queen Elizabeth's accession had changed the political climate.[8] Quo warranto's broad powers had the potential to punish misbehavior or strictly to enforce central

---

[4] Donald Sutherland, *Quo Warranto Proceedings in the Reign of Edward I, 1278–1294* (Oxford, 1963). The Statute of Quo Warranto dates to 1290.

[5] Harold Garrett-Goodyear, "The Tudor Revival of Quo Warranto and Local Contributions to State-Building," in Morris Arnold *et al.* (eds), *On the Laws and Customs of England: Essays in Honor of Samuel E. Thorne* (Chapel Hill, NC, 1981), pp. 231–95.

[6] William Blackstone, *Commentaries on the Laws of England*, vol. 2 (Philadelphia, PA, 1893), pp. 262–3; J.H. Baker, *An Introduction to English Legal History*, 3rd edn (London, 1990), pp. 167, 578; Holdsworth, "English Corporation Law," p. 402.

[7] See Tittler, *The Reformation and the Towns*, esp. pp. 177–8, 192–5, for a discussion of borough incorporation as the Reformation unfolded.

[8] Peter Clark and Lyn Murfin, *A History of Maidstone: The Making of a County Town* (Stroud, 1995), p. 57.

52

CHALLENGING CHARTERS

policy. At the same time, some Tudor scholars have suggested that it was not simply a hammer that the crown used against over-mighty individuals or communities. Harold Garrett-Goodyear, in his thorough study of the early Tudor revival of quo warranto, showed that it could be a tool used by people in the localities to achieve their own ends. Tittler noted quo warranto's relatively regular use from the mid-sixteenth century onward, identifying it with a drive toward oligarchy in borough government and not simply a policy of control by the center.[9] With widespread incorporation of boroughs, the control and maintenance of liberties and privileges vitally interested crown and localities alike.

In the first four decades of the seventeenth century, many if not most of England's incorporated boroughs faced quo warranto proceedings at least once. Just as the reign of King James saw a surge of incorporations and reincorporations, so it also saw a high mark in the questioning of liberties through quo warranto. Quo warranto might come out of a number of courts, but corporate towns most consistently had to prove their privileges in King's Bench and Exchequer. A systematic analysis of quo warranto in the records of King's Bench speaks to the ubiquity of the process.[10] A large proportion of the realm's incorporated boroughs confronted quo warranto at least once between 1603 and 1640. For that period, references to at least 165 separate quo warranto suits regarding borough corporations appear in the Controlment Rolls and/or Crown Side Order Books of King's Bench, with a handful of additional references to King's Bench suits appearing in records such as State Papers, Privy Council Registers, or local archives. Of the approximately 175 corporate towns in England and Wales in this period, at least 121 faced quo warranto in King's Bench, and numerous of these encountered it more than once. These numbers count only those initiated in King's Bench from the start of James's reign in 1603 forward; the total including Exchequer and other courts would be significantly higher.[11] Looking across the whole period, on average a handful of cases

[9] Garrett-Goodyear, "The Tudor Revival of Quo Warranto," pp. 231–95; Tittler, *Reformation and the Towns*, pp. 177–8, 192–5. I wish to thank Professor Tittler for generously sharing with me some of his unpublished findings on quo warranto under the middle Tudors.
[10] Information in this section is based on systematic searches through the King's Bench Controlment Rolls (KB29) and the Crown Side Order Books of King's Bench (KB21) at The National Archives for the period under study. The Controlment Rolls exist in a full run from Elizabeth's reign through Charles's; the Order Books begin in 32 Elizabeth (1589–90) and contain a significant lacuna from Trinity, 14 James (summer 1616) to Easter, 17 James (spring 1619).
[11] For the purposes of counting here, cases begun in Elizabeth's reign and continued past 1603 are not counted; those begun in 1640 or before but continuing past 1640 are counted. Due to the difficult nature of the King's Bench sources, which seem not always to have been completely reliable in recording suits, these numbers are almost certainly conservative. John Guy makes some reference to these records in "The Origins of the Petition of Right Reconsidered," *Historical Journal* 25 (1982), 289–312. I wish to acknowledge the assistance of my colleague Robert Palmer at the University of Houston, who generously offered his skills as a Latinist and legal historian in working through some of the difficulties of these materials.

URBAN GOVERNMENT AND THE EARLY STUART STATE

occurred in each year, but the distribution varied widely over time.[12] The first years of James I's reign continued a pattern set during Elizabeth's: from 1590 until about 1615, the court of King's Bench saw about one to two new cases per year. Things began to change fairly dramatically after 1615, however, and the next five years saw rapidly increasing numbers. The all-time high for quo warranto came in 1618–19 (16 James). The King's Bench Controlment Rolls contain notices for sixty separate instances of quo warranto process regarding incorporated boroughs. After 1620, the numbers dropped, but could vary considerably between three in 1624–25 and fourteen in 1628–29. After 1630, the numbers dropped again, moving toward their pre-1615 levels, ranging from nil to four new cases found in each year from 1630–40 (6 Charles–15 Charles).

Just as the frequency of quo warranto could be quite variable, so could the course that a case took. Suits began with a court's issuance of a *venire facias*, requiring members of the corporation (usually the mayor or bailiffs and burgesses) to come to the court to answer the quo warranto by a particular date. Failure to appear according to the *venire facias* was to result in seizure of the franchises. While it is not always possible to tell when or why a quo warranto proceeding stopped, it seems clear that in most instances the process went no further than this first stage. Many entries indicated that suits ended in non-prosecution by order of the attorney general before any pleading occurred, often within a term or two of the issuance of the *venire facias*. Presumably, in most cases borough officials or their counsel appeared in court with their charters and satisfied the court of their validity. About one-third of the cases went on to the pleading stage. Of these, some ended in non-prosecution, again determined by the attorney general. Some seem to have disappeared without a recorded resolution, with many imparlances, continuances, and delays noted along the way. Other cases ceased when the corporation formally proved legal privileges upon pleading in court and the judges dismissed the defendants *sine die*. Still others resulted in the corporation disclaiming certain privileges while retaining the bulk of them. A small number of cases went through the full legal process and reached their conclusion by a judgment being entered, either for the defendant (the corporation) or for the crown. Cases could last as little as one legal term and as long as many years. A quo warranto involving the corporation of Ludlow began in 1628–29 and ended in a non-prosecution in Easter term of 1652.[13]

Borough records from across the realm reflect the anxieties that these suits generated. A number of towns experienced more than one legal challenge to their charters in this period. Not only did corporations fear the loss of privileges, they also despaired of the significant financial burden that the legal defense of quo warranto typically entailed, as cases ground their way through the courts in London. Even if a suit went no farther than a summons to King's Bench or

---

[12] The mean number per year was 5.2.
[13] TNA, KB29/277, m. lxxii; KB29/278, mm. lxi, cli.

54

CHALLENGING CHARTERS

Exchequer to prove the liberties, town officials had to bear the cost of travel to London for themselves and their attorneys, as well as any court fees incurred. Maidstone's corporation expected to "disburse much moneys" for the defense of a suit of quo warranto in 1626; the town council agreed to borrow £60 from some leading members of the corporation as a start. Great Yarmouth's corporation minutes record a discussion in the assembly in 1637 over what legal strategy to follow in answering a quo warranto, one of which would cost £60 or £80 more than the other; the assembly agreed to go with the less expensive option. Shrewsbury's accounts show that the corporation spent over £45 just in their first answer to a quo warranto against their liberties in 1636–37. Ipswich granted £17 16s 4d to one of their town's solicitors for his disbursements in obtaining the discharge of a quo warranto against that corporation in 1637.[14] It could be a considerable expense, on top of the potential legal jeopardy to the corporation.

Not surprisingly, given the money, time, and anxiety involved, many corporations did everything they could to waylay the process. A number of corporations included language about protection against quo warranto proceedings explicitly in the charters they procured from the crown.[15] Most used their recorders and men-of-business in London to keep a weather eye out for possible danger and had "friends" they hoped would assist them. The dual corporation of Weymouth and Melcombe Regis received advance notice in 1632 that a quo warranto might be brewing against its franchises. In response, the town's assembly agreed to pay the fees for Francis Gape, their town clerk, to ride to London "and to make what friends he can procure by Sir Robert Napier & others to prevent Mr Attorney generall from bringing a Quo warranto against this town for the privileges thereof." Their attempt failed, since a year later the assembly was sending one of its bailiffs, again at the charge of the corporation, to consult with the town's recorder about the "Quo Warranto brought by Mr. Attorney Generall against this Towne, whereby their liberties are questioned, and to advise with him what Course is fittest to be taken therein." One strategy they contemplated was "whether it be not the safest way to petition his Majesty therein, and to get a reference thereof (if it may be) from his Majesty to some Lords of the Council or others."[16] The corporators of Weymouth–Melcombe Regis, like those of many

---

[14] KHLC, Md/ACm1/2, fol. 198; NRO, Y/C19/6, fol. 383v; SRRC, Shrewsbury Records, SSR3365/581; Nathaniel Bacon, *The Annalls of Ipsw'che*, ed. W. Richardson (Ipswich, 1884), p. 516.

[15] Martin Weinbaum, *British Borough Charters, 1307–1660* (Cambridge, 1943), pp. 23, 133; TNA, C233/1, fol. 114v, C233/4, fol. 16v; Ernest J. Homeshaw, *The Corporation of the Borough and Foreign of Walsall* (Walsall, 1960), p. 26; William Dickinson, *The History and Antiquities of the Town of Newark* (London, 1819), p. 374; G.H. Martin (ed.), *The Royal Charters of Grantham* (Leicester, 1963), p. 127.

[16] M. Weinstock (ed.), *Weymouth and Melcombe Regis Minute Book 1625–1660*, Dorset Record Society, vol. 1 (Dorchester, 1964), pp. 23, 25, 26. The town's liberties were eventually proved in court, and the corporation sought confirmation of its charter, succeeding in 1638.

URBAN GOVERNMENT AND THE EARLY STUART STATE

towns, feared the consequences of quo warranto, but they were also resourceful enough to believe there were ways to avoid or deflect the legal process by working through other channels of central and regional government.

Central policy and corporate liberties

How are we to understand the frequent use of quo warranto against the liberties of corporate boroughs in this period? At first glance, looking only at the records of King's Bench, the large numbers, particularly in the 1610s, might give the impression that early Stuart government conducted an aggressive campaign to strengthen its hand over incorporated boroughs. Close examination, however, suggests a more nuanced reality. While not every instance can be traced in local records, those cases that have local documentation show that often the initiative for the quo warranto came from local actors. The central court records also show that very few reached the stage of final judgement, and those few were as likely to result in a judgment for the corporation as a judgment for the king. Out of all the quo warranto proceedings for corporate towns in England and Wales found in King's Bench between the last decade of Elizabeth's reign and 1640, only five seem to have ended in a judgment for the crown and an order to seize the liberties of a town.[17] This would seem to be a particularly ineffective means of prerogative enforcement, if the intent of quo warranto were to dismantle corporate government. Instead, the patterns of quo warranto show that the full legal weight of the prerogative rarely jeopardized corporate liberties as a whole. The crown seemed largely, though (as we shall see) not entirely, content to allow the governing bodies of corporations to maintain or even expand their authority over the urban populace and boundaries.[18]

Even when the legal finding in a quo warranto suit ostensibly resulted in the revocation of corporate liberties, the crown and the courts did not always move to do so. Canterbury faced a quo warranto suit beginning in 1622 that ultimately resulted in a judgment for the king.[19] The city seems to have been plagued with poor legal counsel; the lawyers continued to change their pleas, provoking the judges to order them to make a response "*sine alteracione*" [without alteration] or the liberties would be seized. The court then ordered the corporation to

---

[17] Denbigh, 1595 (TNA, KB29/232, m. xx); Canterbury, 1623 (KB21/8, fol. 34v); Maidstone, 1623 (KB21/8, fol. 55); Salisbury, 1626 (KB29/275, mm. xxxxvii, xxxxviii); Trellick (Monmouth), 1627 (KB29/275, m. cvi).

[18] See Sybil Jack, *Towns in Tudor and Stuart Britain* (New York, 1996), p. 74.

[19] TNA, KB21/7, fol. 46. It is difficult to know the precise origins and context of this case, as the corporation's minute book and most correspondence is no longer extant for the 1610s and 1620s. Canterbury in this period experienced infighting among members of the corporation over matters of governance and religion, as well as tensions with the cathedral and its clergy. See Thomas Cogswell, "The Canterbury Election of 1626 and *Parliamentary Selection* Revisited," *Historical Journal* 63 (2020), 291-315.

56

CHALLENGING CHARTERS

demur – in other words, to let the case be decided on points of law rather than points of fact.[20] Again, the city's lawyers dragged their feet, and the judges threatened Canterbury's corporation with peremptory seizure of liberties if they did not cooperate. Finally, in the autumn of 1624, the court issued a judgment that contained the seizure of the liberties of Canterbury's corporation.[21] One might assume that when the king took Canterbury's charter into his own hands, the corporation dissolved and consequently lost its governing authority, as well as its status and honor. But the meaning and effect of such a judgment seems to have been very much open to question. Could a corporation's liberties actually be seized? Did the seizure dissolve the corporation or cause the corporate "individual" to die? These questions were not settled in the law at this time.[22] In Canterbury's case, within days of issuing the judgment, the justices of King's Bench ordered that counsel for the corporation be given a copy of the judgment for their perusal, and if they had any objections to it, they and the counsel for the king were to appear before justices William Jones and James Whitelocke, who would resolve the differences between the parties if they were able.[23] That apparently failed, as the suit surfaced again when the court ordered that it be tried at the bar and then ordered the sheriff of Kent to summon a sufficient jury. After being required to plead "*de novo*" in 1626, the city disclaimed specific liberties, and the case ended in non-prosecution in 1627.[24] The corporation of Canterbury clearly suffered by the judgment against its liberties, but the court's own ambiguity over what such a judgment meant suggests that, in addition to any unclarity in the law, the crown had little interest in disbanding the corporate body. Though the king had the power to seize the charter, it was still in the royal interest to maintain the corporation to ensure strong government in this important city.

Breaking English borough corporations by use of quo warranto was not a goal of the early Stuart crown, but the renegotiation of liberties and privileges sometimes was.[25] Between 1603 and 1640, Shrewsbury, Weymouth–Melcolme Regis, Colchester, Ipswich, York, Chichester, Abingdon, Maidstone, Coventry, Worcester, Lichfield, Newark-upon-Trent, Huntingdon, Salisbury,

[20] TNA, KB21/7, fol. 48, KB21/8, fol. 7.
[21] TNA, KB21/8, fol. 34v.
[22] Holdsworth, "English Corporation Law," p. 403.
[23] TNA, KB21/8, fol. 35v.
[24] TNA, KB21/8, fols 70v, 72v, KB29/272, m. lxxiii, KB29/274, m. xxx; KB29/275, mm. cxi, cxii. The fact that no jurors were to be tenants of the archbishop suggests that the root of the problem was likely a jurisdictional dispute with the cathedral.
[25] Other corporations were more susceptible to corporate "death" under the early Stuarts. Waterford, Ireland, lost its charter by quo warranto and was disincorporated in 1618, part of the push to control Irish towns. The charter of the Virginia Company was revoked on quo warranto, by Privy Council order, to put the colony directly under royal authority rather than the trading corporation's. APC 1623–25, pp. 103, 119; Mary Sarah Bilder, "English Settlement and Local Government," in M. Grossberg and C. Tomlins (eds), *The Cambridge History of Law in America*, vol. 1, *Early America (1580–1815)* (Cambridge, 2008), p. 71.

57

URBAN GOVERNMENT AND THE EARLY STUART STATE

and Grantham all endeavored to have their charters renewed or confirmed shortly after facing quo warranto proceedings, though none of their cases reached a final judgment in court.[26] As noted in Chapter 1, quo warranto and charter renewal or confirmation could be related. Ipswich's corporation in 1632 issued letters of attorney to two of its members, directing them to answer the quo warranto against the town and to attempt to obtain a confirmation of the charter. While obtaining a new charter "shall amount to a greater sum than the town and inhabitants may well spare," better that "than hazard the loss of the liberties and privileges of this town." Great Yarmouth's corporation ordered its attorneys to seek a confirmation of the town's charter as a means of "clearing" a quo warranto in 1635; likewise, the 1638 confirmation of Weymouth-Melcombe Regis's charter came in response to quo warranto.[27] Corporate boroughs worried more about their liberties in the 1630s as quo warranto threats proliferated.

Quo warranto proceedings thus prompted some corporations to fend off the danger by appealing for inspection, confirmation, or revision of their charters. It does not appear that corporations invariably lost ground in the process, and in most cases, privileges previously granted were confirmed and ambiguities clarified, though some required tweaking of specific liberties. Weymouth-Melcombe Regis's 1638 charter seems to have confirmed all of its previous liberties, which had also been upheld in the pleadings on the quo warranto.[28] In Great Yarmouth's 1635 quo warranto, the king's attorney advised the corporation that if they wished to clear the quo warranto by confirmation of their charter, they would have to resign a certain clause regarding Admiralty rights and "then resume the same again by a grant from his Majesty in such sort as the City of Bristol hath done in the very like case." The town's assembly eventually agreed to attempt renewal of the charter, hoping to obtain additional privileges for the good of the town.[29] The process involved both give and take. Southampton's 1640 charter reveals that liberties and franchises had been "taken and seized" into the king's hands and "entirely extinguished and amoved" on a quo warranto in Exchequer. Yet in the same breath the charter offers a full pardon and release to the corporation from any seizures or penalties, restoring the liberties entirely back to their previous state,

---

[26] TNA, KB29/265, mm. cxxv, cciv, xcviii, KB29/266, m. cxid, KB29/269, m. xxxxii, KB29/272, m. xxid, KB29/278, m. xxxvi, KB29/277, m. cxxxi. Numbers are conservative, reflecting only cases that could be clearly documented; other corporations may have attempted to renew or confirm charters in the wake of quo warranto, but failed. Cf. Tittler, who emphasized the rarity of new charters coming out of quo warranto proceedings.

[27] SA/I, C6/1/5, fol. 108v; Bacon, *Annalls of Ipsw'che*, pp. 498-9; NRO, Y/C19/6, fols 328, 336v; George Alfred Ellis, *The History and Antiquities of the Borough and Town of Weymouth and Melcombe Regis* (Weymouth and London, 1829), p. 48.

[28] Ellis, *Weymouth and Melcombe Regis*, p. 48; TNA, KB29/284, m. clxxviid.

[29] NRO, Y/C19/6, fols 411v, 420.

58

CHALLENGING CHARTERS

a few small alterations excepted.[30] The corporations of Chichester and Maidstone actually gained more privileges in new charters that came on the heels of quo warranto proceedings.[31] The use and frequency of quo warranto in this period suggests its importance as a means of shaping relations between borough corporations and the crown, but not as an unambiguous tool for overthrowing corporate liberties.

Quo warranto and the negotiation of authority

The significance of quo warranto in the early Stuart period comes into clearer focus if we think about it not simply as an expression of central power, but as part of a network of institutions and mechanisms in the state that local actors, as well as central authorities, could invoke.[32] It proved to be a powerful and quite flexible legal device, employed for varying purposes. While the process had to be legally initiated in Westminster, many of these challenges to charters grew out of local conflicts brought to the attention of the crown by local actors. The central courts might serve as venues for negotiation between parties to differences that originated in the provinces, as well as negotiation between center and locality; through the courts, local debates over jurisdiction, participation, and power could be adjudicated.[33] Particularly when matters could be tied to the interests of the crown or the concerns of a particular monarch, quo warranto might offer an effective means of gaining one's ends.

Some suits bear out Tittler's view that quo warranto emerged from disputes over participation between burgesses and borough magistrates. In a case from just before the start of James's reign, Queen's Bench called the corporation of Totnes (Devon) in on quo warranto in 1600 to prove the charter they had received only four years before. The 1596 charter, motivated by the corporate elite, excluded the majority of burgesses from elections and other important civic business; it restricted membership on the corporate assembly and made the body self-selecting.[34] The town's leaders had obtained the new charter

---

[30] H.W. Gidden (ed.), *The Charters of the Borough of Southampton* (Southampton, 1910), pp. 155-7.
[31] L.F. Salzman (ed.), *VCH Sussex*, vol. 3 (London, 1935), p. 96; TNA, KB29/265, mm. clxii, cciv, KB29/266, m. xlii; Maidstone, *Records of Maidstone* (Maidstone, 1926), pp. 10, 74; William James (ed.), *The Charters and Other Documents Relating to the King's Town and Parish of Maidstone* (London, 1825), pp. 66-7, 91, 97; Clark and Murfin, *History of Maidstone*, pp. 58, 60. As will be seen more fully below, Maidstone's complicated domestic politics made this charter a point of contention in the borough.
[32] Braddick, *State Formation*, p. 92.
[33] See also Hindle, *State and Social Change*, chap. 3, for a discussion of Star Chamber as a court that "served the interests of both sovereign and subject" (p. 68).
[34] John Roberts, "Parliamentary Representation in Dorset and Devon 1559-1601" (MA thesis, University of London, 1958), pp. 224-5; Weinbaum, *British Borough Charters*, p. 30; *APC 1597-8*, pp. 168, 451, 507-8. See Phil Withington, *The Politics of Commonwealth: Citizens*

URBAN GOVERNMENT AND THE EARLY STUART STATE

without the consent of the majority of the burgesses, who disputed the charter from the time it was brought back from London to Totnes. The result was four years of strife, disputed elections, and general disturbance in the town. The burgess group's leaders managed to convince the Privy Council to order the assize judges to inquire into the matter.[35] It is likely that ongoing efforts by this group prompted the attorney general's decision to proceed by quo warranto against the corporation in 1600.[36] The crown's purpose in this was not, however, to undermine Totnes's corporate status. Instead, the main consideration was maintenance of stability and order in the locality, furthering the trend toward narrower, less open corporate governance.[37] The quo warranto proceedings in Totnes served to support this principle. After over a year in court, the suit resulted in a judgment in favor of the corporation.[38] Yet this legal judgment for the defendant against the crown was actually in royal favor in a more general sense. It upheld the new, restrictive charter of 1596, guaranteeing that the close corporation prevailed over the burgesses. The interests of the town's elite meshed with those of central authority, and the actions of the court on the quo warranto reinforced this bond.

This episode from Totnes shows that quo warranto proceedings in the central courts could provide a useful royal forum for townsmen to play out conflicts at home. Those conflicts were not invariably ones between burgesses and "oligarchs." Other internal tensions could precipitate quo warranto, as Salisbury's corporation found to their grief in 1626. The official minutes of the corporation state that Mr. Jole, one of the city's aldermen, "took upon himself the office of a Bailey arrant and served Mr. Coward then and now Mayor of the City with process to enforce the mayor and commonalty of this city to appear and answer a suit by Quo Warranto in the King's Bench."[39] At the center of the unhappiness stood the city's common brewhouse, newly built to support poor relief in Salisbury. While some members of the corporation favored the brewhouse and other innovative elements of the city's poor relief scheme, a number of important citizens, especially master brewers like Jole, disliked it intensely. Jole, likely supported by others, managed to convince officials in King's Bench that the corporation exceeded its liberties by erecting and maintaining the brewhouse. The corporation charged Jole personally

---

and *Freemen in Early Modern England* (Cambridge, 2005), pp. 69-74, for a similar case in Ludlow around the same time.

[35] Roberts, "Parliamentary Representation," pp. 226-9.

[36] TNA, KB21/2, fol. 59; Roberts, "Parliamentary Representation," pp. 228-9.

[37] The debate over oligarchy can be seen in Rosemary O'Day, "The Triumph of Oligarchy in Seventeenth Century England," in R. O'Day (ed.), *The Traditional Community under Stress* (Milton Keynes, 1977), pp. 103-36; J.T. Evans, "The Decline of Oligarchy in Seventeenth Century Norwich," *Journal of British Studies* 14 (1974), 46-77; Tittler, *The Reformation and the Towns*, pp. 192-5.

[38] TNA, KB21, fol. 59.

[39] WSHC, G23/1/3, fols 327v, 329v.

CHALLENGING CHARTERS

with procuring the quo warranto and thereby causing the mayor and citizens to be "charged with 16 and more false, slanderous things, to the dishonor of the mayor and commonalty."[40] The quo warranto was symptomatic of discord already present in the corporation, and disgruntled parties were able to gain the attorney general's ear.[41] The suit ended in a judgment for the king, yet the impact was ambiguous. The city continued to run its brewhouse for some years to come, and the corporation preserved most of its liberties.[42] Salisbury's experience with this challenge to its charter emerged from internal strife among leading corporators who co-opted central authority to push their own interests.

Complicated jurisdictional and personal differences in a locality regularly found their way to quo warranto proceedings in King's Bench, as demonstrated by a case from Maidstone. First appearing in King's Bench in Hilary term of King Charles's first year, the suit moved to pleading the following year.[43] While the case pended, the corporation was to desist from prosecuting taxations upon any in the town who were not "*antiqua membra corporationis*" - ancient members of the corporation.[44] Borough records tell us specifically that the suit came not out of the crown's interest in local business, but rather out of the unhappiness of certain residents who managed to make this an issue at King's Bench. In an entry dated 31 May 1626, the corporation's minutes refer to "the suit depending before the Court of King's Bench" which is "prosecuted by" Sir John Astley and Sir Humphrey Tufton.[45] These two gentlemen resided in suburban precincts within the town and disputed the corporation's jurisdiction over them.[46] The disagreement in 1626 was not new, but perpetuated arguments that had been in play for years. The seeds of conflict were sown in 1618, the last time the corporation had to prove its rights and privileges upon a quo warranto.[47] That experience had caused the corporation to seek a confirmation of its charter, which it obtained in July 1619. The charter expanded the liberties and privileges of the corporation, which Astley and other gentle inhabitants

---

[40] TNA, KB27/1547, m. xxi, KB29/274, m. lvi; WSHC, G23/1/3, fol. 329v. See P. Slack (ed.), *Poverty in Early-Stuart Salisbury*, Wiltshire Record Society, vol. 31 (Devizes, 1975) for more on the various poor relief schemes developed in Salisbury in this period. Religious tensions were also often interwoven in Salisbury's disputes.

[41] It is notable, though it cannot stand as evidence for the attorney general's political interests, that just prior to the suit's initiation, the corporation of Salisbury had rejected Attorney General Heath's nomination of Sir John Evelyn to be one of Salisbury's MPs. WSHC, G23/1/3, fol. 326v; G23/1/38 (draft letter from Salisbury corporation to Sir Robert Heath, 16 January 1625/6).

[42] TNA, KB29/275, mm. xlvii, xlviii, lxxxviid.

[43] TNA, KB29/274, m. l, KB21/8, fols 47v, 48.

[44] TNA, KB21/8, fols 47v, 48, 49v. The document leaves unclear whether "antiqua membra" refers to individuals or to the disputed territory of Maidstone's suburban enclaves.

[45] KHLC, Md/ACml/2, fol. 97v.

[46] *Records of Maidstone*, pp. 86-7, 99.

[47] TNA, KB29/265, m. xcviid; *Records of Maidstone*, p. 74.

61

URBAN GOVERNMENT AND THE EARLY STUART STATE

contested.[48] The particular issue that touched off the conflict near the start of King Charles's reign was the corporation's assessment of rates throughout its claimed jurisdiction. According to the borough records, the two knights alleged the corporation's liberties to be "much prejudicial" to themselves, a contention town leaders refuted.[49] The quo warranto stemmed directly from Tufton and Astley's self-interest; they hoped to gain their own ends by calling the corporation's liberties into question in King's Bench.

Not just the motivation for the suit, but also its resolution reflected the multi-layered nature of quo warranto proceedings. Even as the legal process ground its way through the court, other forces came to bear on the problem with the intention of sorting out the parties in a friendlier manner. The earl of Westmorland, head of the locally prominent Fane family and long connected to the town, offered to try to "mediate with the ... Attorney General and the before-mentioned knights touching a cessation of the said suit." The members of the corporation eyed this compromise warily. In the end they consented, saying that although it was of "very great consequence" to the town, they had faith in the earl's "great care and favour" for them.[50] The justices of King's Bench ordered the corporation's counsel to attend the earl of Westmorland and the attorney general (Sir Robert Heath), who would end the dispute if they could.[51] Even the court itself seemed to believe that a friendly resolution, avoiding a decision at law, was the best way forward. Westmorland's and Heath's imprint on the Maidstone case shows the interconnectedness of the local and central, the personal and the legal, in challenges to charters through quo warranto.

The earl's arbitration, brokered during the summer of 1626, brought the parties together but did not stop the legal proceedings. At the end of Trinity term, judgment was entered against the corporation of Maidstone. Upon this judgment, the court issued a writ to the sheriff of Kent to seize the liberties on behalf of the king.[52] While this has the ring of finality to it, in practice it provided a point for further negotiation. In September 1626, the court ordered that the *rotulus* on which the judgment against the corporation was entered not be filed, and the writ of seizure not be executed by the sheriff until the court wished it. In the meantime, the corporation could enjoy all of its liberties and franchises, so long as its members abided by the agreement made between the parties by the earl of Westmorland and the attorney general.[53] All of this suggests that the court had little interest in pressing the king's prerogative against the town's liberties. From the court's perspective, ending contention stood at the heart of quo warranto.

---

[48]   *Records of Maidstone*, pp. 10, 79.
[49]   KHLC, Md/ACml/2, fol. 97v; TNA, KB21/8, fol. 47v.
[50]   KHLC, Md/ACml/2, fol. 97v.
[51]   TNA, KB21/8, fol. 52v.
[52]   TNA, KB21/8, fols 52v, 55.
[53]   TNA, KB21/8, fol. 55.

CHALLENGING CHARTERS

The court's willingness to postpone filing judgment against Maidstone benefited the corporation but did not free it completely. The justices ordered Maidstone's lawyers to resubmit their plea on the quo warranto, amending it "according to the order before made ... by the most noble earl of Westmorland and the Attorney General of the Lord King."[54] A crucial point on which the outcome of the suit balanced was the extent to which the justices of peace of the county of Kent could intervene in the town. This issue held tremendous significance for any corporate borough, since one of the key advantages that corporate status gave to a borough was freedom from county jurisdiction. The court referred this jurisdictional matter "completely" to Attorney General Heath to resolve; the corporation was to "stay and be obliged" by his order.[55] Maidstone's corporators can only have feared that some of their privileges might be lost even if the judgment was never filed against them.

The specifics of Heath's determination on Maidstone's liberties are not clear, since no description of it appears in the Order Books or in Maidstone's records. In fact, the case disappears from King's Bench records for two years. When it reappears again in 1628 the justices and the parties still seem to be unsure of what the outcome of the case was. They were uncertain even as to the wording of the plea and the judgment, and the attorney general was ordered to bring in his own records on the case and certain words were to be revised and rewritten into the rolls.[56] The final entry on the case has more the tone of an arbitration or compromise than of a decision based on points of law. The court declared, with the agreement of Sir Humphrey Tufton and Sir John Astley and of the mayor and jurats of Maidstone, that if any "unequal taxations" for the relief of the poor of Maidstone were levied on the two gentlemen or other residents of the suburban enclaves, that the aggrieved parties were to inform the justices of assize, who would examine any alleged inequities and make a binding decision.[57] While this somewhat weakened the corporation's ability to levy taxes on its inhabitants, it did save the town from the incursion of the county JPs, which would have represented a very serious threat to corporate liberties. Despite losing the quo warranto suit, the corporation did not lose its charter and maintained most of its privileges.

These cases of quo warranto offer critical insights into how the process worked. First, they illustrate that challenges to charters could originate in local struggles. The crown may have had an interest in these matters, but local actors

54 TNA, KB21/8, fols 58v, 60v, 64v.
55 TNA, KB21/8, fol. 64v.
56 TNA, KB21/9, fols 43v, 68v. This lack of clarity in the official records and the court's decision to revise and rewrite them opens some interesting questions about the absolute nature of legal records. It is not clear whether a clerk simply made a mistake in transcribing or whether the attorney general had his own agenda in this case. See Mark Kishlansky, "Tyranny Denied: Charles I, Attorney General Heath, and the Five Knights' Case," *Historical Journal* 42 (1999), 53–83 for a discussion of Heath's role in dealing with the documents of King's Bench.
57 TNA, KB21/9, fol. 68v.

63

often spurred the proceedings. Secondly, they suggest that the main purpose behind prosecution of quo warranto was not to break corporate liberties, but rather to enforce order and ensure good government. With a judgment against the corporation and a seizure of the liberties, the king could have ended the corporate "life" of Salisbury or Maidstone, yet in practice the legal judgments did not have this result. Although there was ambiguity in the law as to whether seizure of the liberties and revocation of the charter actually dissolved a corporation, it is certainly the case that loss of a charter would seriously damage a town's authority.[58] Borough government might continue to function, but it would have no legal guarantees of its authority or jurisdiction. The crown had little incentive to dissolve English borough corporations, since it had a vested interest in maintaining strong governance over towns through "small knots of reliable men."[59] Thirdly, these cases show the flexibility of the court in dealing with the matters that brought about a quo warranto. In the case of Maidstone, arbitration of a local patron was intricately connected to the legal process in the court, something that the attorney general, the judges of King's Bench, and local parties appeared to have found entirely acceptable. The cases of Totnes, Salisbury, and Maidstone all bear witness to the fact that quo warranto was not simply a tool of royal prerogative, but could be invoked and used for various reasons by the king's subjects, as well.

Quo warranto and royal policy under James and Charles

To say that quo warranto challenges to corporate liberties often stemmed from local motivations is not, however, to say that the crown never used quo warranto for its own purposes. Early Stuart monarchs and their agents could and did use quo warranto proceedings to achieve particular royal ends or to send political messages. James's government did this overtly in regard to Irish cities that continued to elect Roman Catholics to civic office; the Privy Council ordered that "some lawful proceedings be now had to overthrow the charters of one or two principal cities or towns, by *Scire facias*, *Quo warranto*, or otherwise." The crown seized Waterford's charter and dissolved the corporation in 1618 as part of this policy.[60] In England, however, more subtle and complex efforts emerged. Questioning charters through quo warranto was one means through which the crown might regulate corporations or advance policies affecting towns, when the need arose. And in some cases, shrewd local actors, perceiving the crown's interests, hitched their own disputes to the crown's agenda. That agenda

[58] Holdsworth, "English Corporation Law," pp. 401–3. Maidstone would presumably have been particularly sensitive to the loss of a charter, having experienced it under Queen Mary.
[59] Peter Clark and Paul Slack (eds), *Crisis and Order in English Towns 1500–1700* (Toronto, 1972), p. 22.
[60] *APC 1615–16*, p. 689–90 (Privy Council to the lord deputy and council of Ireland, 21 July 1616); *CSP Ireland, 1615–25*, pp. 142–3, 174–5, 183, 187–8, 190.

CHALLENGING CHARTERS

changed over time, and corporations faced different – and sharper – challenges from quo warranto under Charles than under James.

The later 1610s saw a significant uptick in quo warranto cases in King's Bench, as James's government used the process for its own venal purposes. Thirteen writs of *venire facias* for quo warranto were issued to borough corporations in 1614–15. The following three years saw only two or three new quo warranto cases each year, but then in 1618–19 sixty were initiated, and another twenty-two in 1619–20. A Whiggish interpretation of this outbreak of quo warranto might suggest the crown's intention to crack down during this period of economic dislocation and international strife. This surge, however, was more grasping than authoritarian. Suffering from unrelenting financial woes in the later 1610s, King James's government sold monopolistic patents to generate ready money.[61] The patentees, in turn, figured out how to co-opt the king's prerogative through quo warranto as a means of forcing the recipients to answer them or compound. Hundreds of quo warranto proceedings issued forth against both corporations and individuals in these years. Most involved inn and alehouse licenses, concealed lands, and markets and fairs, all of which had special resonance in towns. Royal commissions targeted corporate towns specifically. In July 1618, the king issued a commission to Sir Lawrence Tanfield, chief baron of the Exchequer, and others to compound with cities and corporate towns for pardons and discharges for tolls and customs "usurped" by them, and for obtaining new charters to define those privileges.[62] Challenging towns' customs formed part of a larger royal policy, the main purpose of which appears to have been revenue generation rather than suppression of borough privileges.

Many corporations felt the sting of this quo warranto "campaign." The city of York, for instance, was hit with a quo warranto concerning markets and fairs in 1619. According to the town clerk, the men involved in the business admitted that the city's title to the market tolls was good, but that further litigation would come at great expense. They were willing to bargain; if the city would pay 20 marks, a non-prosecution would be entered into the record.[63] Pay-off, rather than any real legal difficulty with York's charter, seemed to be at the root of the matter. Many towns felt vulnerable to such demands. The Ludlow corporation minute book complains of the "great sums of money demanded of this corporation" through lawsuits, patents, recognizances for alehouses, and the like.[64] Corporate towns may have feared for their privileges, but they also resented the expense and mercenary origins of such proceedings.

---

[61] John Cramsie, *Kingship and Crown Finance under James VI and I, 1603–1625* (Woodbridge, 2002) discusses many of James's fiscal expedients. Evidence of patents can be found throughout the State Papers for this period; see *CSPD 1611–18*, pp. 439, 441, 449 on the king's grant of patents for inn and alehouse licensing. A local report on the phenomenon can be seen in YCA, B.34, fol. 217v.

[62] *CSPD, 1611–18*, p. 550.

[63] YCA, B.34, fols 167, 167v.

[64] SRRC, LB2/1/1 (Ludlow Minute Book), fol. 121.

65

URBAN GOVERNMENT AND THE EARLY STUART STATE

The patents that fomented this quo warranto glut became a serious grievance and a key topic of discussion in the 1621 Parliament. Mps vilified Sir Giles Mompesson, a client of the duke of Buckingham and the lightning rod for unhappiness over patents and quo warranto. Mompesson held patents for inn and alehouse licensing, among other things, and he allegedly brought over 3,000 quo warranto proceedings involving inn-keeping between 1617 and 1619.[65] In the House of Commons, members excoriated Mompesson and other patentees for the novelty of their use of quo warranto, for their extortion of local people, and for their defrauding of the king. According to Thomas Crew, MP for Northampton, "In times past a quo warranto for keeping of an inn was never known" and those that were brought almost never came to legal issue. Patentees simply demanded composition and then, according to one witness, charged a significantly higher composition fine than they reported to the king.[66] Mompesson himself eventually fled the country to avoid prosecution and parliament's wrath.[67]

The proceedings of the 1621 Parliament did not completely stop this sort of use of quo warranto, however. Local records from the corporation of St. Albans show evidence of the practice in the early 1620s in Exchequer as well as King's Bench. Attorney General Sir Thomas Coventry issued an information against the corporation at the instance of Mr. Charles Walker, the deputy clerk of the market of the king's household. In it, the crown complained about abuse of privileges concerning their market measures. The townsmen believed that their case was good in law, but they wanted to avoid the expense and trouble of further legal proceedings. They decided to admit themselves delinquent and promise to maintain conformity in all market requirements in the future.[68] This was not an isolated instance. A 1623 letter from a St. Albans town attorney working in London to his cohorts in the town states, "There are at least a hundred [quo warrantos] to that purpose directed to the mayors, bailiffs, etc., of other corporations as well as St. Albans, but the Barons seem to distaste of these printed warrants. Therefore I hope they shall not have any great favor at their hands."[69] The clerks of the king's household initiated these proceedings to strengthen their own position; they presumably hoped that most corporations

[65] W. Notestein, F. Relf, and H. Simpson (eds), *Commons Debates 1621*, vol. 2 (New Haven, CT, 1935), p. 182; *CSPD 1619–1623*, p. 225.
[66] *Commons Debates 1621*, vol. 2, pp. 182–3. See also *Commons Debates 1621*, vol. 5, pp. 52, 475–6, 488, and vol. 4, pp. 40–1, 83, 252, 378.
[67] Robert Zaller, *The Parliament of 1621* (Berkeley and Los Angeles, CA, 1971), p. 62; S. Lee, "Mompesson, Sir Giles (1583/4–1651x63), projector," *ODNB*, accessed 6 Dec. 2018 www.oxforddnb.com/view/10.1093/ref:odnb/9780198614128.001.0001/odnb-9780198614 128-e-18932; J. Larkin and P. Hughes (eds), *Stuart Royal Proclamations*, vol. 1, *Royal Proclamations of King James I 1603–1625* (Oxford, 1973), pp. 502–3; TNA, SP14/120, fol. 6.
[68] HALS, St. Albans Borough Records, Off Acc 1162, Miscellaneous Papers Box 178, nos 103, 104.
[69] HALS, St. Albans Borough Records, Off Acc 1162, Miscellaneous Papers Box 178, no. 106.

would do as St. Albans did and give up the struggle as not worth the expense of ongoing legal fees. Regulation of markets and businesses played into Jacobean government's interest in increased order and tightened administration. But it was the crown's dire need for ready money, as much as any real concern for the size of market measures or other corporate privileges, that drove the government to issue myriad patents. The patentees made active use of King's Bench and Exchequer as venues to maximize their profits by bringing royal authority to bear. Borough corporations, while frustrated, generally complied in hopes of reducing expense and avoiding further questioning of their privileges.

During James's reign the crown and its patentees most fully exploited quo warranto for financial purposes, but Charles's reign demonstrates a shift. Some trends continued, such as using quo warranto to challenge borough corporations' privileges for holding markets and fairs, tolls, and the like. The first five years of Charles's reign saw quo warranto initiated regularly (on average about six per year) in King's Bench against corporations, and many were of this type.[70] But new patterns also emerged. There were pointed moves to inquire into alleged encroachment of Admiralty jurisdiction by corporate towns through use of quo warranto in Exchequer.[71] Caroline government also proved readier to question the corporate privileges of towns to specifically political ends. The story of quo warranto during Charles's reign is more complex than a simple exercise of prerogative power over England's corporate towns. Yet it indicates increased suspicions on the crown's part regarding corporate governance and a greater willingness to try to manipulate corporate liberties.

Caroline government's increased interest in shaping borough corporations through legal means can be seen in the case of Great Yarmouth in the late 1620s. In that town, riven by factional strife over governance and religion, local actors exploited royal interest in order and conformity to perpetuate internal debates. A challenge to the charter through quo warranto proceedings in King's Bench became a centerpiece of conflict, highlighting differing views of governance and proper order. Over the course of two years, Attorney General Robert Heath repeatedly called into question the legal basis for Great Yarmouth's liberties and attempted to bring the divided corporation into firmer government under the king. The incident clearly reveals an attempt by the crown to exert pressure on the town's liberties. At the same time, the story is not simply one of heavy-handed royal power but rather an interchange between local actors, the royal law courts, the Privy Council, and the king himself.

The conflict in Great Yarmouth had both religious and political origins. As Richard Cust showed in his detailed study of urban politics in Yarmouth, the struggles emerged from various quarters but were rooted in differences among members of the corporation and community over religious practices and the

---

[70] See TNA, KB27/1547, mm. xxv, xxvii, xxix; SRRC, LB2/1/1, fol. 161.
[71] *CSPD 1633–34*, pp. 50, 63, 70, 80, 109, 286, 290.

URBAN GOVERNMENT AND THE EARLY STUART STATE

constitution of town government.[72] One group, seemingly the minority of the corporation, had strong connections to key figures in King Charles's government, both ecclesiastical and legal. Led by Alderman Benjamin Cooper, they generally sympathized with Arminian views and sought to invite intervention by bishop, Privy Council, and king, so as to enforce the appropriate beliefs and atmosphere in the town. Cooper and his allies attempted to procure an alteration of the town's charter that would consolidate the leadership of the corporation from two bailiffs into a single mayor at the head and reduce the numbers of aldermen and common councilors.[73] A majority in the corporation, led by Alderman William Buttolphe, opposed this plan and sought to preserve the town's original charter and protect its Calvinist religious tradition. This group believed that the quo warranto stemmed solely from the malice of some few in their body who wished to overturn the traditional government for their private interests.[74] No doubt the conflicts involved personal in-fighting and power struggles, as well; Cooper and Buttolphe, who served as dual bailiffs in 1629, submitted dueling petitions against each other's behavior to the Privy Council.[75]

Cooper and his confederates, in their attempt to change the borough's constitution, made two-fold use of the central courts: to convince the attorney general to bring quo warranto proceedings against the corporation's existing charter in King's Bench, and simultaneously to procure a new charter through Chancery.[76] Despite opposition in the governing body, Cooper's plan saw initial success. First, Cooper and his compatriots had the advantage of surprise in their assault on Yarmouth's traditional constitution. They managed to procure the initiation of quo warranto in King's Bench and the drafting of a new charter, all without the knowledge of fellow townsmen. Secondly, Cooper had excellent connections in the metropolis. Personal relationships with Viscount Dorchester, the king's principal secretary, and – importantly – with Attorney General Heath helped him push his agenda in London, despite having no official authority from the corporation in Great Yarmouth. Cooper meanwhile convinced court officials that his rival William Buttolphe, the town's authorized agent, was using fraudulent credentials.[77] Likely knowing his views might receive a sympathetic hearing at court, Cooper pressed his advantage in promoting his side of the conflict and in encouraging the legal challenge to the corporation.

The crown's position on Great Yarmouth was far from neutral. The king himself viewed the town as factious and religiously unorthodox, having already

---

[72] Cust, "Anti-Puritanism and Urban Politics," 1–26. See also Catherine Patterson, "Conflict Resolution and Patronage in Provincial Towns, 1590–1640," *Journal of British Studies* 37 (1998), 21–5.

[73] TNA, SP16/147, fol. 83, SP16/148, fol. 52, SP16/154, fol. 1.

[74] NRO, Y/C19/6, fols 122v–123v; TNA, SP16/147, fol. 84.

[75] TNA, SP16/147, fols 83, 84, 85.

[76] NRO, Y/C19/6, fols 122v–123v, 126; TNA, KB21/10, fols 11, 12v, SP16/143, fol. 2.

[77] NRO, Y/C19/6, fols 127, 161v; APC *1629–31*, pp. 112–13.

CHALLENGING CHARTERS

been acquainted with "unorderly" dealings there as early as 1627.[78] From Charles's perspective, the corporation failed to operate within the bounds of good government and order delimited under royal authority, and an example had to be made. As the dean of Norwich opined, "Something exemplary done upon this place, may prove of great consequence with all great towns Corporate ... perhaps the instance of Yarmouth reduced may prove very medicinal."[79] Early in 1629, the Privy Council directed Attorney General Heath and Humfrey Davenport, serjeant at law, to determine the "fittest" course to fulfill the king's wishes regarding the town. According to a letter from Heath and Davenport to the Council, they "resolved to bring a quo warranto against the corporation, and so by a legal way to bring them into his Majesty's power, that then his Majesty might better mould them."[80] For Heath and his royal master, the apparent turmoil in Great Yarmouth signaled a disordered relationship between the king's authority and borough government. Challenging the liberties and privileges of the corporation by quo warranto was the means by which to restore the correct power relationship and to shape the town's government into the pattern he thought best. The king's "gracious purpose" in pursuing the quo warranto, according to Heath and Davenport, was "not to destroy them, but to rectify them."[81]

The shape that Heath, and presumably King Charles as well as Alderman Benjamin Cooper, thought best was not the corporation's longstanding constitution headed by two bailiffs. Heath proposed to change the corporate structure to have a single mayor at its head. The two-bailiff model, in his view, could never bring peace; "as it is monstrous in nature so it is very dangerous and inconvenient in government."[82] Reconstituting the corporation in order to reduce the number of officers was one way of maintaining a stricter hold on Great Yarmouth, in keeping with the crown's preference for narrow governing bodies. Heath took vigorous steps to bring about the desired end. He took steps to encourage the king to order that the corporation's warrants of attorney in King's Bench be strictly examined. He also urged that the townsmen be given only limited time to plead their case. Such strictness was necessary, in Heath's view, to "stand with the King's justice and honor," and it also would lead to the king's goal of rectifying and reshaping the corporation. Indeed, King Charles did issue a warrant to Heath to prepare a bill for his signature, reincorporating the town with a mayor rather than bailiffs.[83]

---

[78] TNA, SO1/1, fols 49, 236v; APC 1627–28, p. 133.
[79] TNA, SP16/148, fol. 52 (John Hassall, dean of Norwich, to Dudley Carleton, 11 August 1629).
[80] TNA, SP16/143, fol. 2 (Robert Heath and Humfrey Davenport to Privy Council, 22 May 1629).
[81] TNA, SP16/143, fol. 2.
[82] TNA, SP16/143, fol. 2.
[83] TNA, SP16/143, fol. 2, SP16/154, fol. 3.

The justices of King's Bench seem to have deferred to Attorney General Heath in adjudicating the quo warranto in their court. In Trinity term of 1629, they ordered the defendants to attend the attorney general during the vacation, at which time Heath would "reconcile all the parties." But reconciliation did not mean neutral arbitration. The court directed Heath to propose to the parties that they accept new letters patent for the corporation that created the narrower, mayor-led governing body. The defendants were to submit themselves to the attorney general's orders, considered to be "more convenient and profitable for the public good of the same town." The townsmen who wished to preserve the old charter did have some recourse. The justices declared that if the defendants "departed" in anything from the attorney general's plan, the court might then proceed to justice. The intention of the whole process, according to the court, was that "the aforesaid town shall be led back into such firm governance" and "good government" as the king desired.[84]

Back in Great Yarmouth, this plan did not sit well. The majority in the corporation indeed "departed" from the attorney general on the matter. William Buttolphe, deputed by the corporation to follow the business in London, reported in late May 1629 that the attorney general demanded they give up their charter, to which Buttolphe replied that it "would not be yielded unto, but day given by the Court to bring in our Answer."[85] In early July, Yarmouth's corporate assembly heard another report from Buttolphe containing the attorney general's orders. These were examined by the town attorney and vetted by the assembly, who found "much and many differences" with them. They decided on the spot to put it to a ballot whether they wished to have a single mayor or the customary dual bailiffs at the head of the corporation. A significant majority voted to preserve the old ways. They then put it to another ballot whether the town should pay the costs of continuing to defend the charter in London. In a majority vote, all but three aldermen and ten common councilors then present agreed to absorb the cost.[86] The strong, if divided, feelings among the town's leaders guaranteed that the attorney general's attempted settlement would not go uncontested.

Fortunately for the traditionalists in the corporation, the attorney general's orders were not a final mandate. The quo warranto suit continued to move its way through the court of King's Bench, with further pleadings and appearances before the attorney general.[87] It must have been clear to Heath by this time that most members of Great Yarmouth's corporation disagreed with his orders. He may have been misled by Benjamin Cooper as to the town's support for the

---

[84] TNA, KB21/10, fol. 28. The king's desire to bring Great Yarmouth back into order manifested itself at the Privy Council as well as in King's Bench. The Board heard testimony regarding the town multiple times in this period while the King's Bench suit went forward. NRO, Y/C19/6, fols 155, 161v, 198; APC 1629–30, p. 112, 148.

[85] NRO, Y/C19/6, fol. 127.

[86] NRO, Y/C19/6, fols 129–129v.

[87] TNA, KB21/10, fols 39, 63v.

CHALLENGING CHARTERS

plan for a single mayor. Early in 1630, the court declared that the counsel for the defense and the attorney general, if they still had differences between them, should both appear before the chief justice of King's Bench, Sir Nicholas Hyde, in order that he might reconcile the parties. The Great Yarmouth assembly arranged for their recorder and three of their members, along with Sir John Wentworth (their MP in 1628), to travel to London to meet with the chief justice in his quarters in Serjeants' Inn on 13 April 1630.[88] If the chief justice made a reconciliation, the record of it has not survived; certainly, no immediate changes ensued. Some additional controversies concerning the charter rose again in 1631, but no further pleadings or judgments emerged on the quo warranto in King's Bench.[89] A non-prosecution was finally entered in the court record in 1639.[90] The historic charter of Great Yarmouth survived.

In the end, the king's wish "not to destroy" the corporation turned out to have been fulfilled, though his "gracious purpose ... to rectify them" was not achieved in the way that he wanted. The quo warranto never resulted in forfeiture of the town's liberties or a legal finding against the corporation. Likewise, a new charter with a reformulated constitution never received the Great Seal, despite a draft warrant from the king to his attorney general approving it.[91] Since the old charter was not officially surrendered or seized, a new one could not be put in its place. The quo warranto opened the corporation to intense scrutiny, and Great Yarmouth experienced an unusually high level of direct intervention by king and privy councilors into its business, yet the corporation managed to preserve its traditional shape and size. Attorney General Heath's machinations and the strong support of King Charles did not force a particular outcome to the legal case. Even when extremely unhappy with a corporation's doings, early Stuart monarchs found it difficult to - or perhaps chose not to - revoke legitimate privileges.

As the crown's priorities regarding religion and governance became clearer in the late 1620s and into the 1630s, it became easier for those interested in chipping away at corporate liberties to do so. As Peter Lake has suggested, local actors became adept at phrasing their petitions to the crown in terms likely to meet with sympathy in London.[92] For instance, between 1632 and 1635, Ipswich's corporation became involved in a heated dispute with Lady Blount, a local noblewoman who wished to claim greater authority in the town. As a quo warranto involving the corporation worked its way through King's Bench, Lady Blount repeatedly petitioned the crown, alleging "manifold misuses, usurpations, and offences under colour of a pretended corporation" by the

---

[88] TNA, KB21/10, fol. 66; NRO, Y/C19/6, fol. 153; "Wentworth, Sir John," *HoP 1604–1629*, www. historyofparliamentonline.org/volume/1604–1629/member/wentworth-sir-john-1578-1651.
[89] NRO, Y/C19/6, fol. 197.
[90] TNA, KB29/278, m. xxvii; NRO, Y/C19, fol. 442v.
[91] TNA, SO3/9, June 1630 (copy warrant of grant of incorporation for Great Yarmouth).
[92] Peter Lake, "Puritanism, Arminianism, and a Shropshire Axe-Murder," *Midland History* 15 (1990), 50.

URBAN GOVERNMENT AND THE EARLY STUART STATE

townsmen. She also claimed the town presumed to enlarge their corporation through "inventions" that were against law and "derogating from his Majesty's prerogative royal."[93] Directed to a king known to be especially attuned to his prerogative, such accusations against the corporation might be expected to be greeted favorably. The quo warranto initiated in 1632 ended in a non-prosecution, but Lady Blount's allegations opened the corporation up to close scrutiny by central authorities, which became particularly troublesome after 1636, when certain members of borough government ran afoul of the Laudian Bishop Wren of Norwich.[94] The corporation spent most of the later 1630s expending significant resources defending their privileges in legal proceedings against their charter.[95] Likewise, Salisbury's corporation was plagued with lawsuits from the bishop of Salisbury, who framed his legal assaults on the corporation in the 1630s in terms of the "disinheritance of the Church" that he alleged the townsmen intended. This, too, fell on sympathetic ears at Court.[96] In 1638-39, York, Salisbury, and Lincoln corporations, all of which had been involved in disputes with bishops or cathedral clergy, appeared in King's Bench on quo warranto.[97] Local actors - whether cathedral clergy, powerful neighbors, or disgruntled corporation members - brought the supposed "usurpations" of corporate liberties to the attention of the crown in the first instance, but their appeals fed into a set of policies that the king was known to favor and for which quo warranto could serve as a useful tool.

While the early Stuarts did not *systematically* use the prerogative authority of quo warranto to punish or constrain corporations, reorder their personnel, or create new models for governance as their later Stuart descendants did,[98] it did become more politicized in the 1630s. Not only did quo warranto become entangled in disputes involving Caroline policies like Ship Money and the expansion of ecclesiastical jurisdiction, but the crown at times experimented with quo warranto as a deliberate threat to corporations judged to have been factious or disobedient to royal authority. Local actors with axes to grind against corporations also took advantage of quo warranto, using legal proceedings already in motion as cover for their own skirmishes or inciting actions in King's Bench directly. King Charles, as his own priorities developed, saw the possibilities of quo warranto as a useful tool for making corporations conform to desired standards of order and obedience. Even as the actual number of quo

---

[93] TNA, KB29/280, mm. xxi, cv; SA/I, C5/14/1, fol. 353v, C5/14/3, fols 262v, 274v.

[94] See Chapter 7 for more on this incident and on Caroline religious policy.

[95] Bacon, *Annalls of Ipsw'che*, pp. 516, 519, 522, 523.

[96] WSHC, G23/1/3, fols 364v-365. For a fuller discussion of Salisbury corporation's experiences with the bishop in the 1630s, see Catherine Patterson, "Whose City? Civic Government and Episcopal Power in Early Modern Salisbury, c. 1590-1640," *Historical Research* 90 (2017), 486-505.

[97] TNA, KB29/287, mm. lxiii, cc, ccxi, ccxii.

[98] See Halliday, *Dismembering the Body Politic*, esp. pp. 147-262 for a detailed investigation of later Stuart policy toward corporations and quo warranto.

72

CHALLENGING CHARTERS

warranto proceedings in King's Bench dropped to pre-1615 levels, the threat of quo warranto saw increased use as a warning to the errant. Privy Council Registers for the 1630s reveal regular orders regarding quo warranto proceedings against corporations, something uncommon in the first two decades of the seventeenth century. In December 1633, the Board heard a petition from the bailiffs and commonalty of Colchester complaining that their charter was being called into question by the attorney general on a quo warranto. As noted in Chapter 1, the townsmen agreed to surrender their old charter in order to put an end to the looming court case.[99] In 1635, when two aldermen of Norwich refused to appear for military service, claiming civic exemption from the lieutenancy, King Charles took personal umbrage, stating unequivocally that all corporations were subject to the lord lieutenants and through them to the king. He declared:

> ... we do take the maintaining of this our power so much to heart, being of such consequence to the government and safety of our people, as that we hold any endeavor to resist or dispute our power in that kind to be tending to faction and sedition. And therefore do command that if hereafter any city being a county or any other corporation, or any particular person therein whatsoever shall presume to resist or dispute our said power of lieutenancy given by us, from which no corporation have exemption, That our Attorney General for the time being shall not only proceed against them by a quo warranto or otherwise to call in their charter, but by Information into our Court of Star Chamber or otherwise bring the corporation or party or parties so offending to such exemplary punishment as shall be fit.[100]

The king saw the threat of quo warranto as a political tool for securing obedience and proper behavior from corporations and their members.

Charles and his government continued to use this strategy in other ways, deploying quo warranto to promote ecclesiastical authority in this period. The evidence bears out Andrew Foster's suggestion of a "mini quo warranto campaign" in the later 1630s.[101] In several cases the king supported initiating proceedings against the charters of cathedral cities where disputes over Ship Money arose between cathedral and city officials. A rating dispute in Lichfield between cathedral and civic authorities resulted not only in victory for the cathedral in the dispute, but also in a quo warranto against the corporation.[102] Other cathedral cities experienced similar threats to their charters, as wrangling over Ship Money and jurisdiction brought corporations to the attention of the king, which in a number of cases resulted in revision or constraint of corporate liberties. This pattern will be explored more fully in Chapter 7, but suffice it to say here that Charles took a personal interest in these cases and attended the

---

[99] TNA, PC2/43, p. 365.
[100] TNA, PC2/45, p. 101. See pp. 192–3 below for more on the precipitating incident.
[101] Andrew Foster, "Church Policies of the 1630s," in R. Cust and A. Hughes (eds), *Conflict in Early Stuart England* (London, 1989), p. 208.
[102] TNA, PC2/45, p. 201.

URBAN GOVERNMENT AND THE EARLY STUART STATE

Privy Council specifically to oversee them. Through the course of these quo warranto suits, the king made clear his support of the church and his willingness to curb the corporate authority of cities and boroughs.[103] Corporations that appeared to touch on the king's authority or to cross his policies made their charters vulnerable to quo warranto.

Two cases, that of Shrewsbury and that of Coventry, where the crown used quo warranto to challenge the liberties of corporations deemed to be factious, were notorious enough to end up as evidence of arbitrary power and overreach in the 1644 trial of Archbishop William Laud. In both cases, the twin concerns of disorderly "popular" government and religious irregularity loomed large in the circumstances that led to quo warranto suits. The suit involving Shrewsbury, as shown in Chapter 1, came in response to a period of conflict in the corporation that both local actors and central authorities like Laud wanted to suppress.[104] Petitions to the Privy Council and king reveal serious divisions within the ruling corporation, with the two bailiffs who headed the body often at odds. Charges of laboring the voices of the commons, perverting local election rules, stirring up the multitude, and threats of physical violence were levelled against various members of the corporation. During elections, while the aldermen and common council deliberated in an inner room, the town clerk allegedly stayed outside in the Guildhall, permitting "all the Rascality of the town to come into him, and there is ... singing of scurrilous and obscene songs in the audience of all present."[105] The bugbears of popularity and faction were likely to capture central attention, but religious irregularity intensified the problem. When the curate's position at St. Chad's, Shrewsbury, came vacant, controversy arose over who might fill it. The corporation claimed control over the curacy, and rival groups backed different candidates. Both factions appealed to Archbishop Laud at various times. Laud, who as early as 1634 had expressed concern to Attorney General John Bankes over Shrewsbury's religious leanings, gave the case close scrutiny due to the town's reputation for puritanism.[106] The result for Shrewsbury's corporation was a quo warranto in King's Bench, lengthy appearances before the Privy Council, and a new charter that substantially changed the size and organization of the corporation.

Who was responsible for initiating the quo warranto was a point of contention at Laud's trial. The prosecution accused him of having personally

---

[103] TNA, PC2/46, pp. 245-7, 432-3. See Catherine Patterson, "Corporations, Cathedrals, and the Crown: Local Dispute and Royal Interest in Early Stuart England," *History* 85 (2000), 546-71.

[104] On Shrewsbury's religious outlook, see Barbara Coulton, "Rivalry and Religion: The Borough of Shrewsbury in the Early Stuart Period," *Midland History* 28 (2003), 28-50. See also W.A. Champion, "Shrewsbury 1540-1640," in *VCH Shropshire*, vol. 6, pt. 1, *Shrewsbury General History and Topography*, eds. W.A. Champion and A.T. Thacker (London, 2014), pp. 136-79.

[105] TNA, SP16/366, fol. 84v.

[106] TNA, SP16/366, fol. 92v; Coulton, "Rivalry and Religion," p. 39.

CHALLENGING CHARTERS

instigated it in order to subvert the town's liberties; Laud denied the charge. The fact that Laud knew many of the particulars in the case of Shrewsbury lends credence to his involvement in its origins, though he seems to have had local contacts who brought matters to his attention.[107] The crown, through key officials like Laud, had an interest in suppressing faction and used the tools at its command to do so. In this case, the threat of quo warranto had the desired effect. Rather than pursuing a legal judgment in King's Bench, the corporation moved to surrender its charter and accept a new, significantly revised one.[108] The Privy Council agreed to stop prosecuting the quo warranto while a new charter went forward, but left the legal threat dangling before the town. The Board warned that "if there is any disturbance by faction ... the Lords reserve to themselves the power to ... stay the proceedings of this charter and to have the quo warranto proceed, as they shall find fit, and the fomenters of the disturbances to be severely proceeded against."[109] Local actors played a role in bringing Shrewsbury's conflicts to the attention of king and Council, and at least some townsmen seem to have welcomed the scrutiny of central authorities. Once the crown perceived the extent of disorder in Shrewsbury's government, the Council and the courts cracked down on the corporation, using quo warranto and other means to enforce the royal will on the locality.

The second case, that of Coventry, provides a clear instance wherein King Charles used a threat of quo warranto directly to punish a corporation for a specific action he viewed as disobedient and factious. On 27 July 1637, the king sitting in Council, ordered that "for certain reasons unto his Majesty and the Board well known, Mr. Attorney General should in Michaelmas term next proceed by a Quo Warranto, to question the Mayor and other the Magistrates and Burgesses of the City of Coventry as touching the Charters, privileges and immunities of the said city in such of his Majesty's courts of Justice where it appertains." It became clear to all what the "certain reasons" were in November, when the Privy Council called four aldermen of the corporation to appear before them and to answer "whether they or any of the other Magistrates of the said city, did by any Act either in public or private, give any countenance, or unfit respect, or applause, or gift, or entertainment to Burton and Prynne, passing by

---

[107] TNA, SP16/500, fol. 42 (Deposition of Humphrey Mackworth, January 1644); William Laud, *The History of the Troubles and Tryal of the Most Reverend Father in God and Blessed Martyr William Laud, Archbishop of Canterbury, wrote by Himself during his Imprisonment in the Tower* (London, 1695), pp. 288-9; see also Coulton, "Rivalry and Religion," p. 29. Mackworth, who had been the town's counsel during the charter controversy, deposed in 1644 that Laud's interference with the charter stemmed from a dispute between the town and St. John's College, Cambridge, regarding the mastership of the Shrewsbury Free School, though there may have been other reasons, as well.
[108] TNA, SP16/323, p. 115 (Petition of Bailiff Thomas Nicholls on behalf of the aldermen and common councilors of Shrewsbury, [6 June 1637]).
[109] TNA, PC2/48, pp. 369, 390, 407.

URBAN GOVERNMENT AND THE EARLY STUART STATE

that city to their confinement."[110] Giving succor to William Prynne and Henry Burton on their way to prison after conviction in Star Chamber was dangerous business, particularly if the crown believed that the town's magistrates, not just its private citizens, participated. The members of the corporation, in an attempt to redeem themselves and escape potential penalties, petitioned the Privy Council to relieve them from prosecution of the quo warranto, claiming that the offense was committed only by "some few indiscreet persons, especially women."[111] The Board ultimately did request the attorney general to stop the proceedings in King's Bench, at least until they had examined the incident more fully.[112] In the case of Coventry, the king made a clear political statement with quo warranto. The process served as a sharp reminder to Coventry's magistrates and citizens that all liberties and privileges came from the monarch and could return to him if they flouted the will of their sovereign.

The cases from the 1630s suggest the crown's (and likely the king's own) identification of quo warranto as one means of imposing particular notions of order on corporate boroughs. Earlier in the century, the process was used to enforce good government or raise revenue, but by the mid-1630s, it was being used to make corporations conform to particular standards required by King Charles. In doing this, the king acted within his prerogative rights, exercising authority that had lain in the crown's hand for centuries. Charles's actions toward Coventry are in the same vein as Queen Mary's quo warranto against Maidstone's charter in 1554, when leaders of that town engaged in Wyatt's Rebellion.[113] In the 1630s, it was the threat of quo warranto, more than the practical ability of the crown to prosecute it to its fullest extent in court, that gave it potency. Although it appears that no quo warranto went as far as a judgment in King's Bench in the 1630s, a number of corporations, as Chapter 1 showed, submitted their old charters in return for ones newly issued by Charles in order to avoid conflict with the crown.

William Laud's accusers in 1644 alleged that the archbishop (if not his royal master) used quo warranto to threaten good government in English towns and subvert the common law in the process. Close study of quo warranto across the early Stuart period paints a more complicated picture, but one that reveals why quo warranto came to be a touchpoint of conflict. The legal process of quo warranto had for centuries provided the crown with a prerogative tool for enforcing its will on subjects. The members of England's corporate boroughs fully understood that their charters emanated from the crown, and the king could question the privileges granted in those charters or seize their liberties. That is why quo warranto held such a potent threat and why corporations often

---

[110] TNA, PC2/48, pp. 185, 359.

[111] CovA, BA/F/A/17/1.

[112] TNA, PC2/48, pp. 373, 374. The quo warranto appears not to have proceeded any further in King's Bench.

[113] It should be noted, however, that Coventry's magistrates did not participate in outright rebellion, which Maidstone's did.

took the opportunity of quo warranto proceedings to reconfirm or revise their chartered liberties. At the same time, records from King's Bench and other central courts indicate that quo warranto was not a particularly efficient tool if the goal was to curb local franchises. First, quo warranto may have been an instrument of royal power, but in practice local players used and manipulated it regularly to gain their own ends. The central courts often served as venues for local initiatives of one sort or another. Second, it appears that quo warranto proceedings did not regularly cause significant loss of privileges in English corporate towns in this period, though it did in at least one important town in Ireland, where the crown used a heavier hand. Final legal judgments against charters were rare, they might as easily go against the crown as for it, and they could be modified so that liberties were not seized. The challenges to corporate charters by quo warranto manifest the complicated network of connections, combining local initiative and central enforcement, that characterized relations between crown and towns in the early Stuart state. Yet they also show the crown's increasing readiness, particularly in the 1630s, to use prerogative power, or the threat of it, to instill a particular version of order on corporate towns.

3

Managing Division: Borough Government, Central Authority, and Municipal Elections

The early Stuart crown took a keen, if not always systematic, interest in borough governments and the charters of incorporation that ruled them. A charter provided a specific instrument through which the crown delegated authority and (it was expected) received the benefit of peace and stability in provincial towns. Both local actors and central authorities had a significant stake in the orderly patterns that were meant to distinguish successful borough government, under the authority of the monarch. The corporate form and the charters that shaped borough liberties provided a specific blueprint for proper governance, in addition to the broad ideals of hierarchical order, obedience, and peace common to this society. Central authorities, urban magistrates, and regular townsmen alike could look to the charter to evaluate whether government functioned in the manner intended – though they might differ in its interpretation.

Despite the admonitions for order laid out in corporate charters, towns could also be sites of discord and disorder in their governance. While a corporation was a single (ideally unified) entity – a legal body acting as a fictive individual – it was also a group of real individuals who had their own interests and ideas. Divided elections, magistrates behaving badly, ejections from office or franchise, and conflicts between magistrates and common burgesses punctuated civic politics. The regular pattern of voting that characterized urban government was a prized liberty as well as a potential stimulus for disagreement and disorder.[1] Such disruptions caused consternation among both borough governors and central authorities, as concern over "popularity" grew and bonds between borough magistrates and the state strengthened across the period. The crown expected borough elites to maintain control over their towns and unity among themselves; discord within governing bodies set a poor example to the urban populace. As the Privy Council, reproving a mayoral election gone wrong in Newcastle upon Tyne, declared "... division between the head and principal members of that politic body should, if not speedily be reconciled, may [sic] breed many other inconveniences, and finally disturb the peace and good government of the said town."[2] Towns experienced a persistent tension between

---

[1] See Catherine Patterson, "Consensus, Division and Voting in Early Stuart Towns," in P. Halliday, E. Hubbard, and S. Sowerby (eds), *Revolutionising Politics: Culture and Conflict in England, 1620-60* (Manchester, 2021), pp. 145-63.
[2] APC 1613-14, p. 103 (Privy Council to Lord Sheffield, 26 June 1613).

78

MANAGING DIVISION

the perceived necessity of order and the messier realities of urban government and community.

Given the "constant and at times almost obsessive concern for order" that pervaded government in this period,[3] it should be unsurprising that central authorities took an interest in the orderliness with which boroughs ran their corporations. Robert Tittler has argued that Tudor and early Stuart monarchs empowered urban elites to carry out policy and maintain order in towns, which were "so distinct from the administrative apparatus of the countryside." This led to a strengthening of civic self-government, in oligarchical form. The desired order did not always result, as differences over narrow participation arose in a number of towns, even among magistrates themselves, as Phil Withington has shown.[4] The crown delegated authority to borough oligarchs who were expected to maintain order; in turn, they did their best to avoid closer scrutiny from the center by striving for good order in their corporations.

In light of these arguments, it is worth taking a closer look at the ways that borough governments intersected with central authorities on questions of their internal order. How often did the crown become involved in the regular workings of borough politics? And to what extent was this involvement a sign of an increasing interest in control by Stuart government over urban governance and political order? Investigating the ways that central institutions intersected with municipal politics under the early Stuarts opens questions about order and disorder, hierarchy and "popularity," and control over corporate membership. It also reveals how townsmen – both borough magistrates and freeman commoners – saw themselves as part of the larger state.

Considering questions of division and order in corporate bodies and the state's response, this chapter looks at some key spaces in which divisions might be played out and through which they were resolved or suppressed. Closely examining municipal elections and corporations' control over their own membership, it assesses the crown's interest in the everyday electoral politics of England's towns and the response of townsmen to it. In municipal elections, borough corporations exercised control over their own membership and leadership, with a goal of maintaining unity and exerting civic authority. We see an increasing interest on the part of royal authority in enforcing order and insisting that borough governors follow particular patterns to achieve it. Yet this was not a one-way street of centralizing power over local government. Local actors co-opted central institutions to resolve conflicts and control corporate membership. While a shared interest in order bound provincial towns to the wider network of authority of the monarchical state, episodes of disorder reveal

---

[3] Robert Tittler, *The Reformation and the Towns in England: Politics and Political Culture, c. 154–1640* (Oxford, 1998), p. 185.
[4] Tittler, *Reformation and the Towns*, pp. 184-5, 191; Phil Withington, *The Politics of Commonwealth: Citizens and Freemen in Early Modern England* (Cambridge, 2005), pp. 69-75.

both the tensions that could exist within corporate boroughs over elections and participation, and how they negotiated the crown's priority to curb "popularity."

Managing municipal elections

Municipal elections happened every year in every corporate town. They were both routine enactments of local governance for towns and cities and somewhat unusual and idiosyncratic exercises within a monarchical state. Charters of incorporation spelled out liberties to elect men to office and to dismiss them for cause, but even those towns without charters engaged in these rituals of self-government. Parliamentary elections have garnered the most attention when investigating borough politics in the early Stuart period, and the publication of the *History of Parliament* volumes for the House of Commons 1604–29 has done much to expand our knowledge and understanding of these important political moments under the early Stuarts.[5] Yet for seventeenth-century townsmen, municipal elections, especially the annual mayoral election, were more familiar and formative experiences, wherein men of the borough annually gave their voices to choose those who would govern in the king's name. They were both an affirmation of the borough's orderly self-government and a symbolic link between the monarch's sovereign power and the town.

For townsmen and crown alike, peaceful order served as the prescriptive goal for elections. The selection of mayors by seniority from among the aldermen, the use of a *cursus honorum* for movement through civic government and the selection of common councilors and aldermen by co-optation all promoted the ideals of consensus and order in borough government.[6] Rules both local and central increasingly entrusted governance to the better sort. They mitigated the possibility of disorder by reinforcing hierarchy and, in most towns, limited the participation of the broader body of freemen or burgesses.[7] Directions for orderly elections regularly appeared as borough bylaws, and the customs around

---

[5] A. Thrush and J.P. Ferris (eds), *The History of Parliament: House of Commons 1604–1629* (Cambridge, 2010). See also Thomas Cogswell, "The Canterbury Election of 1626 and Parliamentary Selection Revisited," *Historical Journal* 63 (2020), 291-315; Mark Kishlansky, *Parliamentary Selection: Social and Political Choice in Early Modern England* (Cambridge, 1986); John Gruenfelder, *Influence in Early Stuart Elections* (Columbus, OH, 1981); Derek Hirst, *The Representative of the People? Voters and Voting in England under the Early Stuarts* (Cambridge, 1975). Hirst does make connections between municipal and parliamentary electoral patterns and divisions; see esp. pp. 197-212.

[6] On the *cursus honorum*, see Robert Tittler, *Townspeople and Nation: English Urban Experience 1540–1640* (Stanford, CA, 2001), pp. 24-5; Tittler, *Reformation and the Towns*, pp. 196-7; Peter Clark and Paul Slack, *English Towns in Transition 1500–1700* (Oxford, 1976), pp. 128-9.

[7] E.g., C.H. Cooper (ed.), *Annals of Cambridge*, vol. 3 (Cambridge, 1845) pp. 218-19 ("Orders for the better government and quiet of the town," 14 August 1629); BL, Add. MS 33,512, fols 18, 19; KHLC, Sa/Ac7, fols 1, 21; J.T. Evans, *Seventeenth-Century Norwich: Politics, Religion, and Government 1620-1690* (Oxford, 1979), p. 69. In the case of Sandwich,

election days involved pomp and circumstance displaying civic honor and order. The freemen of Sandwich, for instance, annually assembled themselves "at the sound of the Common Horn" on the Monday after the Feast of St. Andrew at the church of St. Clements, "as hath been accustomed for the election of the Mayor of the Town." They followed rules in the election set down for them by the Privy Council and Lord Wardens, which elaborated and revised practices enshrined in the borough's ancient liberties.[8] These sorts of orderly, ritualized gatherings to select the following year's corporate officers reinforced the expectations of consensus and order that characterized corporate ideals.

Yet even if local elections were often ringed around with customs promoting the "good and tranquility of this little commonweal," as the corporation of Sandwich put it, and placing government in the hands of the reliable few valued by the crown, division was in some ways a natural byproduct of the electoral process, and the idealized orderly selection of a pre-ordained choice did not invariably occur.[9] Factions among corporators could develop along religious, political, or purely personal lines; tensions could flare between urban oligarchs and commoners who wanted their voices heard. This sometimes made municipal elections rather different from the pacific and orderly affairs desired by authorities. Thomas Cogswell has shown for Canterbury that significant internal disagreements among members of that corporation lay under any surface calm they may have attempted to project, affecting local governance as well as parliamentary elections.[10] While most municipal elections came off with little strife, divisions did arise, whether among magistrates themselves or between magistrates and commons.[11] When conflict, misunderstanding, or maladministration gave rise to disrupted elections or dismissals from office, it raised questions over borough government's ability to carry out the public duty to maintain order for which the crown granted charters.

Many such moments of discord never came to the attention of external authorities, but they made borough corporations vulnerable to intervention. The republican sensibilities at the root of elections sat in delicate balance with the ideals of order in the early modern state. On one side, the crown did not contest the liberty of corporate boroughs to elect their own leaders and

---

this narrowing of participation in elections occurred despite a charter that allowed broader participation.

8 B. Challenor (ed.), *Selections from the Municipal Chronicles of the Borough of Abingdon from A.D. 1555 to A.D. 1897* (Abingdon, 1898), Appendix, pp. x–xi; Cooper (ed.), *Annals of Cambridge*, vol. 3, pp. 167–8; Maidstone, *Records of Maidstone* (Maidstone, 1926), p. 10; KHLC, Sa/Ac7, fol. 121v; BL, Add. MS 33,512, fols 18–19v.

9 KHLC, Sa/Ac7, fol. 132. For more on the tension between consensus and division in borough elections, see Patterson, "Consensus, Division and Voting," *passim*.

10 Cogswell, "Canterbury Election of 1626," *passim*. See also Canterbury Constituency Report, *HoP 1604–29*, www.historyofparliamentonline.org/volume/1604-1629/constitu encies/canterbury and Hirst, *Representative of the People?*, pp. 197–212.

11 See Withington, *Politics of Commonwealth*, pp. 69–75, on different ideas about participation in towns like Ludlow and Huntingdon.

URBAN GOVERNMENT AND THE EARLY STUART STATE

continued to grant charters containing that privilege, as their predecessors had for generations. On the other, James I and Charles I continued and extended earlier patterns that sought to constrain elections, often curbing participation and reinforcing hierarchical ideas of order through the charters and letters patent they issued. As will be shown, the Privy Council became involved, increasingly over the period, in the adjudication of differences over election and dismissal of borough officials. The Board took seriously its authority and duty toward corporate towns in particular, "being careful to maintain and protect the peaceable and orderly government of cities and corporations."[12] While this was in keeping with the generally more activist stance of the Privy Council in the Caroline regime, we should not necessarily read this as a sign of a simple increase of enforcement on the part of centralizing authority. Local actors – sometimes magistrates and sometimes less lofty freemen – often brought matters to the attention of the Board as a means of bringing the state's power to bear on their local problems. Townsmen valued their liberty of elections and upheld their right to elect and dismiss their own officials, but they also saw the utility of involving central authorities to achieve their own ends. This tension between local control and an impulse for connection shaped the way that borough corporations interacted with the crown around matters of municipal elections and order.

The Privy Council served as the main venue for hearing and resolving disputes that either could not be resolved informally or were significant and divisive enough to attract Conciliar attention.[13] It offered borough officials a means to legitimate their decisions, brought the authority of the Board to bear on those who would not bend to corporate pronouncements, and helped forge a shared image of good governance between town and crown. The mayor of Chester and fellow civic officers emphasized the importance and freedom of their corporation when they claimed that Chester had always enjoyed the privilege of having differences they could not settle themselves "heard and determined" by the Privy Council alone, and no "other persons whatsoever have at any time intermeddled with the affairs or controversies of the said city."[14] When the town of Portsmouth, wracked by plague in 1625, faced the constitutional crisis of not being able to hold the annual mayoral election and thus endangering their charter, they turned to the Privy Council for guidance and relief.

---

[12] *APC 1627*, p. 157 (Privy Council to mayor and aldermen of Chester, 24 March 1627). Chester, with its relatively large electorate, had some notorious disorders in municipal elections. CCRO, CR60 (Mayors and historical events in Chester [n.d., early seventeenth century]).

[13] A few suits that include allegations of improper borough elections can be found in Star Chamber, e.g., TNA, STAC8/20/14 (Carmarthen), STAC8/93/5 (Doncaster), STAC8/121/12, STAC8/98/9 (Lincoln). See also Tittler, *Reformation and the Towns*, pp. 198–201.

[14] BL, Harl. MS 2105, fol. 191 (Petition of Nicholas Ince, mayor of Chester, *et al.*, to the Privy Council).

MANAGING DIVISION

The Board authorized the sitting mayor to continue in office for another year, "if it may stand with the charters of the town," or otherwise to serve as the king's bailiff there until it was safe to assemble again. When the plague did finally clear, the Council legitimated a diversion from the borough's charter, authorizing an election on a different day "without any impeachment or prejudice to their corporation, regardless of the time limited by their charter."[15]

The Council could also be called upon to order uncooperative members to take up offices to which they had been elected. Thomas Walker's refusal to serve as mayor of Exeter in 1625, during an outbreak of plague, prompted the corporation to appeal to the Board to force Walker to assume the mayoralty. While expressing some sympathy for Walker, the Councilors were most concerned with securing government in the hard-pressed city; they ordered him to fulfill the office to which the corporation had elected him.[16] Likewise, when Mr. Richard Duke refused to take his oath to serve as jurat of Maidstone, the corporation, after failed attempts at persuasion, agreed to proceed against him "either by suit at the Council Table or otherwise as the counsel of the Town shall think fittest."[17] The corporation brought the matter to the Board, which condemned Duke's example as prejudicial to the king's service and "to the disrepute and the overthrow of the good government of the said town." They ordered Duke to take up his post.[18] All of these cases acknowledge the Privy Council's role as arbiter of disputes over borough elections and corporate belonging.

The unfortunate loss by fire of the Privy Council Registers from 1603 to 1614 means that we cannot know precisely how often the Board took notice of electoral disputes under the early Stuarts. But the records that we do have reveal that at least twenty-one such cases appeared before the Privy Council for determination or further action between 1604 and 1640[19] (see Table 3.1 at the end of this chapter). In addition, the Board took notice of a wide variety of other matters related to corporate office or membership: disagreements or questions over the selection or dismissal of borough officials such as recorders, stewards, and town clerks, or of other corporate officers, such as aldermen, sheriffs, or jurats; contested disfranchisements from borough corporations; and

---

[15] APC 1625–26, pp. 184, 244.

[16] APC 1625–26, p. 21; Wallace MacCaffrey, Exeter, 1540–1640: The Growth of an English County Town (Cambridge, MA, 1958), p. 234. Walker was not the only magistrate accused of abandoning the city during the plague crisis.

[17] KHLC, Md/ACm1/2, pp. 150, 152, 153.

[18] KHLC, Md/ACm1/2, p. 156; APC 1623–25, pp. 210, 233. Duke would later appeal this decision, and while the Board upheld their original decision, they also admonished the corporation not to intentionally choose men obviously above the quality for that service to be jurats.

[19] These numbers are largely gleaned from the published Acts of the Privy Council and Calendar of State Papers Domestic along with the manuscript Privy Council Registers (PC2), and State Papers (SP14 and SP16). In two instances, local records describe matters that were apparently referred to the Privy Council, but no central record exists, due to the lacuna in the Privy Council registers for the first decade of James's reign.

URBAN GOVERNMENT AND THE EARLY STUART STATE

complaints against corporate officers who refused to take their oaths or assume office.[20] Both nervous magistrates hoping to co-opt the power of the Privy Council to tamp down local disorder and frustrated freemen looking for justice against allegedly corrupt borough officials invoked the Board's intervention. Solicitation of Privy Council involvement in borough divisions happened regularly; the Board was seen as the proper place for settling urban government and its corporate membership.

The Privy Council generally responded to these disruptions to the peace of borough governance according to the perceived level of danger to authority. Allegations of "popularity" in important provincial towns as well as the metropolis occasioned firm action. When it came to the Board's "certaine knowledge" that innovations had been introduced into the election of the lord mayor of London in 1628, the Council wrote a strongly worded letter to the lord mayor, recorder, and aldermen of the city demanding that they seek out the ringleaders and bring their names to the Board. The "popular and turbulent spiritts" who had "misled" the commons into these innovations required prompt punishment. The lord mayor drew particular ire for his "relaxation of government" and failure to report the disorder to the Board himself. After taking examinations, the Council ultimately handed the matter off to the attorney and solicitor general for further proceedings.[21] With similar vigor, the Board, on two different occasions (1619 and 1627), heard testimony on allegedly popular and factious municipal elections in Norwich, resulting in new orders intended to limit popular participation there.[22] At the other end of the spectrum, the Board tended to hand off less critical matters, in obscurer places, to assize judges or local gentlemen. Alerted by local petitioners to a disputed mayoral election in the small borough of Hartlepool (County Durham), the Board immediately commissioned Sir David Fowles, Sir Henry Anderson, and other county gentlemen to investigate the allegations. Upon their certificate, the Council ordered the gentlemen to call the parties before them and make peace,

---

[20] The court of King's Bench began to challenge the Privy Council's primacy on the matter of contested removals from office and disfranchisements during the early Stuart period, as the writ of restitution became increasingly common as a remedy for dismissed burgesses or borough office-holders to seek restoration. See Edith Henderson, *Foundations of English Administrative Law: Certiorari and Mandamus in the Seventeenth Century* (Cambridge, MA, 1963), pp. 46–82. The present author is engaged in a study of the growth of writs of restitution in the early Stuart period.

[21] APC 1628–29, pp. 187, 205. This occurred in a period of some tension between magistrates and citizens over financial and other matters. Valerie Pearl, *London and the Outbreak of the Puritan Revolution* (London, 1960), pp. 73–7.

[22] APC 1617–19, p. 484, 1627–28, pp. 75, 140–1; Evans, *Seventeenth-Century Norwich*, pp. 69, 71, 75–6; Fiona Williamson, *Social Relations and Urban Space: Norwich, 1600–1700* (Woodbridge, 2014), pp. 171–3; Fiona Williamson, "When 'Commoners Were Made Slaves by Magistrates': The 1627 Election and Political Culture in Norwich," *Journal of Urban History* 43 (2017), 6, 8.

so that the Board would not be "further troubled therewithal."[23] A complaint regarding the undue election of a bailiff in the small town of Chipping Norton (Oxon.) similarly resulted in the Board assigning the matter to a county JP for "arbitrament" and settling, so the Council would be no more troubled by it.[24] Electoral disturbances large and small drew the interest of the Privy Councilors; those perceived as more dangerous to the commonwealth qualified for final resolution by the Board itself.

While the pattern of seeking Privy Council intervention to resolve disputes over municipal elections and offices is clear, it was not without controversy. Concern that corporate integrity and chartered liberties might be damaged through such intervention also resonated in some cases, where corporators criticized their fellows who brought debates over local office-holding to Conciliar attention. In a lengthy and bitter dispute in Chester over the office of clerk of the pentice, Alderman William Gamull accused the mayor, Nicholas Ince, of having broken his oath to the corporation by bringing the business before the Privy Council.[25] Likewise, when Maidstone's corporation appealed to the Board for assistance in requiring those elected to take up their offices, John Taylor and Edward Michell viewed this as an "overthrow of our Charter in the late business before the Council Table." They allegedly published rumors to this effect, for which they were called to account before the town council.[26] Some of this pushback may well be ascribed simply to personal infighting, with parties using any means available to undermine their rivals. Yet this undercurrent of disquiet over dangers to corporate integrity and the sanctity of the charter cannot simply be dismissed. As Phil Withington has argued, multiple discourses regarding civic identity and chartered liberties existed.[27] Even those within the narrower body of influential men governing the towns might differ in attitude on such matters.

The tensions that provoked disputed elections could reveal quite different views within a corporation about the relationship of borough and state. In 1633, the former mayor of Berwick-upon-Tweed, William Grigson, and fifty or so of his fellows complained to the Privy Council of a disputed mayoral election that autumn.[28] In Grigson's telling, Edward Moore, an alderman of somewhat

---

[23] TNA, SP16/36, fol. 24; APC 1627–28, p. 329.
[24] TNA, PC2/44, p. 246.
[25] TNA, SP16/84, fol. 7a. Gamull was an active partisan in this fight, so his argument in support of civic "independence" may have been as much about protecting his own interests as those of the corporation. See also BL, Harl. MS 2105, fols 183, 191–1v, 197.
[26] KHLC, Md/ACm1/2, pp. 153, 155.
[27] Withington, Politics of Commonwealth, pp. 69–75. Withington sees discourses of this sort in Aristotelian terms, "democrats" and "aristocrats," which do not seem entirely appropriate here; more relevant to these cases seems to be the particular focus of the parties, either inward on corporate privileges or outward on order in the state.
[28] TNA, SP16/248, fols 201–4 ("A True Relation of Edward Moore his Proceedings & his abettors on Sunday the 29th of September last within the Tolbooth or Guildhall of Berwick in usurping the office of Mayoralty there").

URBAN GOVERNMENT AND THE EARLY STUART STATE

junior standing but with important family connections, determined to become mayor by any means necessary. By lobbying for voices ahead of the election, he gained support from a large portion of the freemen as well as part of the corporation's ruling body, including some of his relatives. Grigson, who as outgoing mayor presided over the election, found Moore to be entirely inappropriate as a candidate. In addition to his relative youth (not yet thirty-five) and documented hot-headedness, Moore had been reported the previous year to the Privy Council for an alleged riot and seditious words to the derogation of the king's government.[29] Moore viewed these accusations as trifles hurled against him by unhappy rivals, but Grigson feared that electing someone under investigation and possible censure by the Privy Council could seriously damage the town. Grigson therefore did everything he could, short of canceling the election, to avert this outcome.

The details of this tumultuous election, as alleged by the mayor and worthies of the town, reveal divergent priorities between Mayor Grigson's associates and those who supported Moore. Unsurprisingly, as a senior official in the corporation, Grigson sought to preserve order and authority, and his concerns went well beyond the boundaries of the town. He focused his rhetoric on the dangers of bringing down the king's ire upon Berwick, emphasizing the "exceptions in all likelihood to be taken by his Royal Majesty & the State" to the election.[30] He did his best to dissuade the burgesses from choosing Moore on these grounds. Once it became clear that his persuasions fell on deaf ears, he announced to all that if the burgesses continued in their choice, he would not hand his staff of mayoral authority over to Moore. Unable to stop the torrent against him, Grigson eventually stepped aside fearing bloodshed and further disorder.[31] For him and his compatriots, the disorderly election of an unfit candidate would provoke the king, endangering the "general estate of our town and commonwealth" and potentially undermining their chartered privileges.[32] Moore and his supporters, on the other hand, seemed to care little about what anyone outside the town might think. Moore himself was reported to have said that he wanted the mayoralty only to "become equal with mine adversaries who seek to overthrow me and mine."[33] The majority of burgesses who supported him (the "heady multitude," according to Grigson) were dead set on choosing Moore, even holding the doors closed and making threats to prevent the departure of their opponents until they achieved their end. When Mayor Grigson attempted to show them the bishop of Durham's letter warning them against Moore's candidacy, they reportedly said "that they had nothing to

---

[29] TNA, SP16/248, fols 203–203v ("Reasons of exception against the Election of Edward Moore to the Mayoralty of Berwick upon Tweed for the present year 1633 made by most of the Justices and well-nigh half of the Commons of that corporation").
[30] TNA, SP16/248, fol. 201.
[31] TNA, SP16/248, fol. 202.
[32] TNA, SP16/248, fol. 201v.
[33] TNA, SP16/248, fol. 202v.

do with the Lord Bishop's letter, nor he with the choice of their mayor; their Charter gave them liberty to choose whom they best list, and they would do so, whosoever would withstand."[34] By the end of election day, they got their way, as Moore prevailed by "9 or ten voices odd" and, after more tumultuous events, was sworn into office contrary to normal procedures.[35] The "multitude," with their inward-looking focus on their rights under the town's charter, prevailed over the "better sort" who looked outward to the relationship between the borough and the state.

Moore's victory did not last long. Grigson and his party (which included many local worthies like alderman Sir Robert Jackson, who served as the town's burgess in all the parliaments of the 1620s[36]) immediately reported the events of the election to the Privy Council, emphasizing the dangerous popularity, verging on sedition, of Moore and his associates. According to Grigson's complaint, their most important consideration in protesting the election was that Moore was under investigation by the Board for his previous alleged misbehavior, and until that was cleared, in their view he could not legitimately hold the office. Had the election merely been divided and disorderly, but with candidates not fundamentally unfit, they would have accepted the outcome, "though very ill procured." The Privy Council took swift action in the face of such disorder. Moore was called to London to appear before the Board, with a large bond of £200. The Lords heard both Bishop Morton's report on Moore's earlier "lewd speeches" as well as the lengthy complaint of Grigson and his associates regarding the 1633 election. They found that his behavior in "pretending himself to be chosen mayor" in Berwick, as well as in his appearance before them in the hearing, "was such as gave all their Lo[rdshi]ps just cause to think him an unfit person to be mayor of any Town, much less in a place of such importance as the Town of Berwick." The Board committed him to the Fleet and determined to solicit the king for a "writ of discharge" to annul Moore's election, with a further order to Berwick's corporation to proceed to a new and orderly election for mayor.[37]

Berwick's position as a border town made it particularly vulnerable to disorder, and the Council had reason to take strong action there. But crucial to their ability to do so was the fact that William Grigson, Sir Robert Jackson, and a significant portion of the town's aldermen and burgesses identified the town's

---

[34] TNA, SP16/248, fol. 201v. The bishop was Thomas Morton, a moderate churchman of Calvinist views. Brian Quintrell, "Morton, Thomas (bap. 1564, d. 1659), bishop of Durham," *ODNB*, accessed 19 Dec. 2019, https://doi-org.ezproxy.lib.uh.edu/10.1093/ref:odnb/19373.

[35] TNA, SP16/248, fols 202, 202v.

[36] Berwick-upon-Tweed Constituency Report, *HoP 1604–29*, www.historyofparliament online.org/volume/1604-1629/constituencies/berwick-upon-tweed.

[37] TNA, PC2/43, pp. 292, 310, 329. It is notable that the Board did not (or could not) simply throw out a borough election, but obtained a legal writ from the king to follow prescribed procedure.

URBAN GOVERNMENT AND THE EARLY STUART STATE

safety with its relationship to the state and to the king. While it seems that personal animus, concerns over popular participation, and perhaps other factors played a role in the divisions that wracked Berwick in this election, Grigson and his associates expressed most concern about Moore's bad standing with the bishop of Durham and the Privy Council. With its military garrison gone following the accession of King James, a precarious position in the far north, and a less-than-robust economy, Berwick relied heavily on the crown's favor.[38] Moore and his supporters appeared to have taken a localist view, trumpeting their chartered liberties to choose whom they wanted, without the bishop's intervention. In contrast, Grigson and other key members of the corporation linked the town's destiny to the authorities of the broader state, bolstering their own power by seeking the intervention of the crown.

While there is no question that the Privy Council took a firm hand in regulating disordered elections like that in Berwick, the strength of their response often came at the behest of local actors. With some regularity, mayors and aldermen recruited the aid of the Board to enforce order at moments when they could not guarantee it themselves. This is demonstrated clearly in the events surrounding a disputed election in Norwich in 1632. In the face of divisions in an aldermanic election, the mayor and sheriffs of the city wrote directly to the Council for advice and assistance. According to their story, upon the death of Alderman Blosse, they called an election following the procedures laid out in their charter, and nearly 160 men gathered to give their voices, some of whom were "foreigners not qualified according to the Charter." The vote was divided, and upon scrutiny Mr. Gostling, "an able sufficient and discreet Citizen," lost by five voices to Mr. Carver, who had garnered the votes of foreigners. The citizens and inhabitants who voted for Gostling complained to the mayor that they were "wronged in the election" by the foreigners. The mayor, "being desirous to avoid all disputes and controversies and to maintain peace and quietness," asked Carver to accept a new election, but he "utterly refused."[39] The mayor and his brethren, fearing the danger to the charter raised by this tumultuous election and the divisions it represented, cannily appealed to the Council for reinforcement of their authority and to affirm their own proper behavior.

Presented with this information, as well as a petition from Carver justifying his actions, the Board reinforced the mayor and his allies. The Council's concern was to prevent future disorders and bolster the authority of those in government. They stated that "it is expedient that the Governors of the City should receive countenance" in the face of such dissension, ordering that Mr. Gostling should be admitted and sworn alderman. In addition, to prevent future disorders, all elections were to be made by freemen and qualified citizens only,

---

[38] For a detailed examination of Berwick as a border town under James I, see Janine van Vliet, "From a 'Strong Town of War' to the 'Very Heart of the Country': The English Border Town of Berwick-upon-Tweed, 1558–1625" (PhD dissertation, University of Pennsylvania, 2017).

[39] TNA, SP16/225, fol. 102.

with a scrutiny taken by poll.[40] Regardless of the underlying cause of the dispute, in this case the interests of the mayor and civic hierarchy meshed perfectly with the interests of the crown to maintain peace in an important provincial city. The mayor calculatedly couched his communication in the way most likely to arouse the sympathy of the Board. Involving the Council may have been some risk to local control, but, as John Evans has pointed out, it "freed the corporation from assuming complete responsibility for compelling submission" to its orders.[41] With the Council already predisposed to find on the side of established authority, bringing the issue to the attention of the crown put the mayor in a strong position to conclude the matter to his own advantage.

But it was not only mayors and magistrates who solicited the Privy Council to bolster their authority; those on the outs also might attempt to bring local electoral disputes to central attention, in hopes of gaining justice. This was a riskier strategy, since in general the Council carefully avoided anything that encouraged the populace to dispute with their governors. Nevertheless, when pushed to frustration, townsmen appealed to the Council for redress against magistrates. In 1633, a large group of burgesses and commons of Newcastle upon Tyne petitioned King Charles about the manner of municipal elections and other business in the corporation. Unhappiness simmering among the commons against the town's oligarchs resulted in a "riot" over the town's lime kilns, a proxy for frustration over the lack of participation in electoral choice and civic business.[42] The commons' petition complained to the Board of self-dealing on the part of the mayor and aldermen, irregularities in the charter-mandated audit of town finances, and the narrowness of all decision-making in municipal business and elections; they claimed they presented their grievances to borough governors in 1625 and again in 1629, to no avail.[43] In the first instance the king referred the petition to the president and council of the North, but the matter eventually came before the Privy Council, which firmly rebuffed the unhappy commoners. The Council determined that the corporation conducted elections in accordance with the charter granted by King James and ordered the complainants to yield their obedience to the charter. While the Board did caution the mayor and aldermen to provision the commons fairly, they aimed most of their ire at the complaining burgesses. "[T]his Board doth dislike and condemn the manner of the said complainants' proceedings, as not admitting that Complaints of Multitudes against their Governors should receive any countenance here, being in effect no other than popular mutinies

---

[40] TNA, PC2/42, p. 292. See also Evans, *Seventeenth-Century Norwich*, pp. 78–9.
[41] Evans, *Seventeenth-Century Norwich*, p. 65.
[42] TNA, SP16/240, fol. 122, SP16/233, fols 99, 109, 124, SP16/234, fols 76, 96 140. For more on this incident of the riot and the nature of local politics in Newcastle, see Roger Howell, *Newcastle upon Tyne and the Puritan Revolution: A Study of the Civil War in North England* (Oxford, 1967), pp. 53–9.
[43] TNA, SP16/240, fols 123–4; Richard Welford, *History of Newcastle and Gateshead*, vol. 3 (London, 1887), pp. 313–15.

URBAN GOVERNMENT AND THE EARLY STUART STATE

and oppositions against Government itself."[44] The Board nevertheless wished to retain the image of fairness; they informed the burgesses that "in case there shall arise any just cause for complaint against any of the Magistrates of the said town, exhibited by any particular persons of the said corporation and prosecuted in an orderly way, This Board will be ready to hear the same and to afford all just favor and redress therein."[45] The Privy Council's stated goal in handling disputes of this sort was good government and proper order, which generally meant suppression of popularity and reinforcement of hierarchical authority.

A similar pattern can be seen in Abingdon in 1634, when a group of inhabitants petitioned the Privy Council alleging that Benjamin Tisdale had caused himself to be elected mayor unduly. The process, they said, was executed as required by the secondary burgesses and assistants of the corporation, and resulted in an equality of voices (twenty-eight on either side) between Tisdale and a rival nominee, Mr. Mayott. According to the borough's charter, this equality of votes should result in a new election, but Tisdale claimed victory.[46] In invoking the charter, the burgesses sought to legitimize their position, undermine the actions of the "factious" Tisdale, and prevent Tisdale from being sworn in. But the Board was already attuned to Abingdon's fractious municipal politics. Disorder intermittently reigned in mayoral elections, despite attempts to tamp it down through the establishment of a strict rotation pattern. Tensions over participation and openness intermittently disturbed the corporation through the first three decades of the seventeenth century; the Privy Council adjudicated a disordered election for recorder in 1628 and heard the complaint of an unhappy former mayor about disordered mayoral elections in 1630.[47] In studying the electoral problem in 1634, the Lords sought to re-establish peace. They ordered that the oath not be tendered to Tisdale, but that the current mayor should be continued in office until the matter was concluded. Their goal, they said, was the "good and quiet of the town," that "all disorders and inconveniences be prevented."[48]

In the event, the petitioners' attempt to gain the Board's favor backfired. The Privy Council reinforced the decisions of borough authorities, who had informed the Board that in fact there was not an equality of voices if one counted the voice of the recorder. The inhabitants had argued that their recorder (Bulstrode Whitelocke[49]) should not have a voice in the election because he was not resident in Abingdon. The Board rejected this argument, noting that recorders in many towns and cities, though non-resident, functioned

---

44 TNA, SP16/240, fol. 122, PC2/43, p. 295.
45 TNA, PC2/43, p. 295.
46 TNA, SP16/274, fol. 107.
47 Challenor (ed.), *Municipal Chronicles of Abingdon*, p. 140, Appendix, pp. x–xii, xvi–xix; TNA, SP16/120, fol. 38 (Petition of Charles Halloway, 1628); APC 1628–29, pp. 227, 230–1, 1629–30, p. 358.
48 TNA, PC2/44, p. 129.
49 Challenor (ed.), *Municipal Chronicles of Abingdon*, p. 140.

MANAGING DIVISION

as full members of borough government. The Council confirmed the election of Tisdale. The petitioners, attempting to discredit Tisdale, then presented articles against him concerning his religion, alleging his nonconformity. They strategically couched their concerns in terms that they expected would resonate with the center.[50] Abingdon had a long reputation as a resort for the godly; Whitelocke himself, as recorder, found himself called before the Privy Council in 1634 for failing to punish so-called puritans in the town who would not conform to the Church.[51] Perhaps surprisingly, the Board chose not to take up the *ad hominem* attack against Tisdale, instead saying that there was insufficient evidence of his nonconformity. They left open to the townsmen the option of resorting to the attorney general if they felt they had just cause to complain further.[52] Tisdale remained in office, despite his detractors' efforts.

Abingdon's troubles demonstrate how townsmen actively sought out the direct intervention of central institutions as a potentially important means to a local end. A portion of Abingdon's residents distrusted the borough's leadership, hoped to influence the outcome of the election, and believed they would never gain what they saw as a just result unless they could incite the strong arm of the state to force the borough's governors to it. But it also shows that the Council typically responded by suppressing popular sentiments, reinforcing borough governors rather than common burgesses.

While the Council most frequently supported borough magistrates in disputed matters, they did exercise discretion if circumstances warranted it. When some leading inhabitants of Hartlepool petitioned the Board in 1626 alleging a disorderly election wherein recusants had been allowed to vote for mayor, the Council appointed local gentlemen as referees to investigate the veracity of the claims. The referees found the facts in the townsmen's petition to be true. Not only did the outgoing mayor, Robert Ridlington, allow three recusants to vote, but the votes being equal between the "popish faction" and the "best affected burgesses," he gave his "casting vote" for the popish faction's candidate, William Wright. When newly elected Mayor Wright called the chief burgesses to swear their oaths for the coming year, it put those who had objected to the initial vote in a difficult position. They attempted to resolve it by submitting to take an oath from Wright, but only if it contained the exception that it might "not be derogating or disagreeable to the laws of the kingdom." Wright's opponents demonstrated their belief in local liberties and also their connection of those liberties to a broader view of government and law. Mayor Wright rejected their gambit, dismissing the men from their places for refusing

---

[50] Peter Lake identified this strategy used regularly by local actors in the 1630s in his article "Puritanism, Arminianism, and a Shropshire Axe-Murder," *Midland History* 15 (1990), 37-64. See also Lake, "The Collection of Ship Money in Cheshire during the 1630s: A Case Study of Relations between Central and Local Government," *Northern History* 17 (1981), 44-71.
[51] R. Spalding (ed.), *The Diary of Bulstrode Whitelocke 1605-1675* (Oxford, 1990), p. 92-3.
[52] TNA, PC2/44, p. 151.

91

to swear the standard oath.[53] Given the facts, the Board could not defend the actions of either the outgoing or the incoming mayor.

In this case, we can see evidence for the Council's concern to reinforce stable government generally in corporate boroughs rather than simply to buttress a mayor's authority. The Board, "being very sensible of the present distraction and ill effects and consequences thereby happening to the said towne, and being carefull to mayntaine and preserve the peaceable and orderly government of cittyes and corporacions," ordered that the five chief burgesses who had been dismissed by the new mayor be restored immediately. The Council also required the gentry referees to "accommodate and determine" the differences among the parties.[54] Notably, the Board did not prescribe any particular resolution to the referees, nor were the offending mayor and other borough officers called to London to answer for their actions. It seems unlikely that this stemmed from indifference about recusants being allowed to participate in local government, but rather that the Privy Council had more important business to attend to in late 1626 and early 1627 – the war with Spain, the Forced Loan – than this small-town drama. Stating they wished to be "no further troubled" by the parties, the Council put the resolution of the matter into the hands of local gentlemen who understood the religious and political dynamics in this northern backwater.[55] While we do not know the final outcome of the resolution, the aggrieved petitioners of Hartlepool got what they wanted. They appealed to central authorities as a way to play out their local differences and obtain the state's sanction for their actions, calling attention to religious and political irregularities and regaining their positions in the corporation. The Privy Council, in turn, promoted peace during a troubled time and sent a clear message to an erring mayor.

The combination of concern to suppress popularity and disorder along with some respect for a borough's liberties and good government characterized the Board's actions in many cases. This principle can be seen in a significant disagreement over the form of municipal elections in Cambridge that came before the Board in 1624. In their resolution, the Council curbed popularity and emphasized a narrow electorate – the "commoners" were not to have a role in the choosing of aldermen – but also took matters of fairness and custom into consideration. They recommended that the mayor and aldermen officially select the two men as aldermen that the commons wanted, and they squelched the practice of allowing the "four ancient aldermen" to have a veto in the process. Aldermanic elections should, they said, "go by the major part of the mayor and

---

[53] TNA, SP16/36, fol. 24 (Sir David Fowles and Sir Henry Anderson to Privy Council, 19 September 1626).

[54] *APC 1627–28*, pp. 329–30 (Privy Council to Sir D. Fowles, *et al.*, 26 February 1626).

[55] *APC 1627–28*, pp. 330. It should be noted that Caroline government chose to soften its stance toward Catholic town governments in Ireland at this same time. Micheal O'Siochru, "Civil Autonomy and Military Power in Early Modern Ireland," *Journal of Early Modern History* 15 (2011), 36–7.

MANAGING DIVISION

aldermen then present as in other corporations is accustomed."[56] Cambridge experienced repeated upsets in its municipal elections; in addition to the 1624 incident that came before the Privy Council, Lord Coventry in 1629 intervened to establish orders for peaceful elections on a strict seniority principle. Coventry's orders required reiteration in 1632 and 1633, even as magistrates successfully petitioned for a new charter that more specifically articulated the powers of the mayor and aldermen.[57] These judgments of the Board and its members show their appreciation for the nuances of local circumstances within a particular borough, but also reflect the prioritization of order and seniority in borough governance generally.

Corporate liberties and hierarchical order

Corporations' strong sense of their own right to choose and dismiss whom they would, according to their charters, at times clashed with the Privy Council's focus on deference and hierarchy, revealing differing understandings of order. When, for instance, boroughs fell afoul of their own elected officials, the Board showed a pronounced bias toward supporting men of higher social status, despite a borough's privileges of election and dismissal. John Finch, a gentleman and attorney elected as Canterbury's recorder in 1617, complained to the Privy Council in 1619 that he had been displaced without cause and another elected by the corporation into his place. The Board referred the matter to George Abbott, archbishop of Canterbury, and Edward Lord Zouche, who sympathized with Finch. Upon their report, the Council, out of concern both to establish civic government "in good peace and concord" and also to preserve the credit of Finch, a gentleman of whom the Board held a "good opinion," required that the corporation re-admit Finch as their recorder. With little apparent concern for the corporation's liberties, the Board instead focused on what it saw as the dangerous precedent of removing persons of Finch's "place and quality, that are the only eyes of light and direction to cities and corporations." This would be of "ill consequence ... to the prejudice of government in other cities and towns corporate" in the realm. Canterbury's corporation initially tried to avoid the order to readmit Finch, writing to Abbot and Zouche that to take Finch back would contravene both their charter and their consciences, greatly disquieting the city. But the danger of opposing the Privy Council's wishes eventually impressed itself on the corporation, and they wrote to the Board of

---

[56] APC 1623–25, pp. 319–20; Cooper (ed.), Annals of Cambridge, vol. 3, p. 167.
[57] CambA, City/PB vol. 7 (Common Day Book 1610–1647), fols 183v–184v, 198v, 210v–211, 218–19; Cooper (ed.), Annals of Cambridge, vol. 3, pp. 218–19; F.W. Maitland and M. Bateson (eds), The Charters of the Borough of Cambridge (Cambridge, 1901), pp. 137–8, 143. The corporation would later repeal Coventry's 1629 orders in the changed atmosphere of 1641. CambA, City/PB vol. 7, fol. 341.

93

URBAN GOVERNMENT AND THE EARLY STUART STATE

their willingness to re-elect Finch, craving pardon for "discontenting" them.[58] Canterbury's concern for its chartered liberties had to give way to the crown's broader sense of hierarchical order and stability.

This same tension between a borough corporation's exercise of its liberties and the Council's ideals of hierarchical order played out a few years later in Chichester. There, Thomas Whatman, the city's recorder, complained to the Privy Council in 1626 that the corporation displaced him without cause. The Board, "having seldom heard of a complaint of that nature that a person of his place and quality having continued so long should be lightly or upon humor or haply for executing justice ... removed and put out of his place without cause showed," called Mayor George Greene and Alderman Henry Chitty to answer for the corporation's proceedings. Despite a number of depositions and written explanations of Whatman's alleged malfeasance, the Board demanded that Chichester restore Whatman to his office. Hierarchical order – the "place and quality" of the recorder – held greater weight for the Privy Council than the corporation's privilege of election and dismissal, the exercise of which bred discord. In Chichester as in Canterbury, the Board found the corporation's reasons specious and gave the benefit of the doubt to Whatman, he being "so well known to us for his integrity and sufficiency."[59] Perhaps in recognition that the recorder's behavior had not been perfect, the Board ordered Whatman as well as the corporation "expressly to lay aside all thought of former dissensions and to live together hereafter in such peaceable and quiet manner and with so good correspondence in all things that may concern both the benefit of the city and the advancement of his Majesty's service."[60] The Privy Council prioritized stability and hierarchical order over the borough's liberties and expected the mayor and aldermen to do so, as well.

The response by borough governors to such interventions was not always enthusiastic. In Chichester, Alderman Henry Chitty allegedly scoffed when the mayor read the Council's letter to the assembled town council: "Tush, this is an ordinary matter, I will get such a letter any day as this is," for "if a man get

---

[58] APC 1619–21, pp. 31, 61, 65; BL, Egerton MS 2584, fol. 100–100v; TNA, SP14/111, fol. 193 (Petition of John Finch to Privy Council, [December 1619], SP14/115, fols 32 (Archbishop Abbott and Lord Zouche to mayor of Canterbury, 12 May 1620), 57 (Mayor et al. of Canterbury to Abbot and Zouche, 19 May 1620), 81 (Mayor et al. of Canterbury to Privy Council, 28 May 1620). Finch's dismissal may have been related to religious frictions in the town; Finch was firmly Calvinist in his views (as was Archbishop Abbott), while Mayor Sabin, whose factious dealings Finch blamed for his dismissal, tended to support the more high-church position of the cathedral clergy. See "Finch, John II (1584–1660)," HoP 1604–29, www.historyofparliamentonline.org/volume/1604-1629/member/finch-john-ii-1584-1660; and Cogswell, "Canterbury Election of 1626," p. 8.

[59] APC 1626, p. 223; TNA, SP16/34, fol. 112 (Petition of Thomas Whatman to Privy Council, August 1626). Whatman was also recorder of Portsmouth. R. East (ed.), Extracts from the Records in Possession of the Municipal Corporation of the Borough of Portsmouth (Portsmouth, 1891), p. 154.

[60] APC 1626, pp. 222–3, 246, 253, 254, 264.

MANAGING DIVISION

the Lord Keeper's hand and one more of the Council, all the rest of them will sign of course."[61] Chitty viewed the Council's communication as simply a form letter. "He did know where was such a letter sent to the Mayor of Canterbury word for word." (This was no idle boast – the Council's letter to the Canterbury corporation regarding their recorder, John Finch, had indeed used identical language.) Chitty also allegedly counseled the mayor and aldermen that they need not rush to answer the Board's letter.[62] Thomas Whatman, the aggrieved recorder, was quick to alert the Privy Council to Chitty's insolence, forcing the mayor and Chitty to appear before the Board (where they denied all charges) and provide an indemnity.[63] While the Privy Council may have promoted hierarchical order, local actors like Henry Chitty did not always simply submit to that order.

To promote their ideals of order and to root out faction and popularity, king and Council occasionally intervened directly in the composition of a corporation, requiring a particular borough officer to be dismissed or restored after dismissal. The Board sent the mayor of Harwich a letter in 1632 ordering the removal of Thomas Webb, the town clerk, from his office. The town, the Board chided, had been plagued with vexatious suits, brought on largely by the "turbulent and factious spirit" of their town clerk, to the scandal of peaceable government.[64] Stamford was likewise required by the Privy Council to dismiss its town clerk for his disorderly words.[65] The corporation of Lincoln, which had experienced considerable disruption in its government in the first ten years of the seventeenth century, received a letter from the Privy Council in October 1610, demanding that they show cause why Mr. Beck and Mr. Wharton had been "disaldered." A year later, a writ from the Crown Office arrived, demanding the restoration of these two men and the dismissal of those who had been chosen into their places. Unfortunately, evidence of the Privy Council's deliberations and findings on the matter are lost, but other records indicate that both electoral malfeasance and religious controversy lay at the heart of Lincoln's troubles.[66] Great Yarmouth's corporation received a Signet Office letter from King Charles in 1627 demanding that they restore Jeffrey Neve, a royal servant, to his place as an alderman of the town. The crown alleged that

---

[61] TNA, SP16/34, fol. 113 (Statement of Peter Cox, August 1626).
[62] TNA, SP16/35, fol. 106 (Statement of John Pannett, [12 September] 1626). Chitty's exchange offers an intriguing glimpse into news networks among urban magistrates.
[63] APC 1626, pp. 246, 253; TNA, SP16/34, fol. 112, SP16/35, fol. 105 (Answer of George Greene and Henry Chitty, [12 September] 1626; CSPD 1625–26, p. 468.
[64] TNA, PC2/41, p. 417.
[65] TNA, PC2/43, pp. 481-2.
[66] LA, L1/1/1/4, fols 68, 74v, 87, 88-88v, 89v, 96, 97v; R.W. Hoyle and D. Tankard (eds), Heard Before the King: Registers of Petitions to James I, 1603–16, List and Index Society Special Series, vol. 38 (London, 2006), p. 12; TNA, STAC8/121/12 (Dennys and Gosse v. Beck, Hollingworth, et al.), STAC8/98/9 (Callis v. Ellis). See also Tittler, Reformation and the Towns, pp. 200-1.

URBAN GOVERNMENT AND THE EARLY STUART STATE

Neve had been dismissed only because of his absence on the king's business, and that the dismissal was a plot by factious men. The corporation of Yarmouth saw things quite differently. They viewed Neve as a non-resident who had engaged in nefarious practices in Yarmouth; the corporation had dismissed him for cause. The borough governors protested the readmission of Neve, claiming that the liberties of the town prevented them from bringing Neve back and either dismissing the man already chosen to fill his place or to exceed the number of aldermen dictated in their charter. Yarmouth, already under close scrutiny for allegations of religious nonconformity and popularity in government, had to exert an extraordinary effort to make its case without jeopardizing its privileges.[67]

The Board did have some care for local liberties and made decisions based on more than just status. In Great Yarmouth's case to dismiss the king's servant Jeffrey Neve, the corporation managed to show proof of Neve's wrongdoing and convince the Privy Council to uphold the dismissal. The Board eventually left the matter in the hands of the corporation, "to bee ordered by them according to the orders and constitution of the place."[68] The Council likewise showed flexibility and a willingness to listen to all parties in the 1628 dispute over the election of the recorder of Abingdon. Charles Halloway complained to the Privy Council in 1628 that, despite being duly elected as recorder, he had been unjustly dismissed from office, and Thomas Teisdall "super-elected" in his place. The Board, inclined initially to sympathize with Halloway, declared that this "kind of proceeding, if it be so, is so merely factious [it] must needs tend to the disturbance of the quiet government of the said Town and may in no sort be tolerated." They called Halloway, Teisdall, and the mayor and several burgesses, along with the town's vicar, to appear before them in person. Upon hearing all sides, the Board found the town "troubled with faction, by means whereof things were not carried in so direct and fair a manner as were fit." The corporation was certainly divided. The body's minutes explicitly state that the "mayor and the major part of the company" had been against Holloway's election to office as surreptitiously done without due warning, and that the "major part of the principal burgesses" voted for Halloway's dismissal. Faced with this contentious situation, the Board did not simply reinstate Halloway and deny the concerns of the majority. Rather, they voided both the election of Halloway and that of Teisdall, declaring that a new and "free" election must be made, with proper warning to be given to the electors and no soliciting or indirect practices on any side.[69] The Council prioritized peace, stability, and hierarchy, but ideas of fairness also played some role their adjudications.

---

[67] TNA, SO1/1, fol. 4v, SP16/90, fol. 64 (Certificate of T. Woodhouse, *et al.*, 10 January 1628); NRO, Y/C18/6, fols 239–241, Y/C19/6, fols 67v, 71v, 72.

[68] NRO, Y/C19/6, fols 82v, 85, 87; TNA, SP16/90, fol. 64; APC *1627–28*, pp. 133, 258. Richard Cust notes that Neve's failure to pay the Forced Loan played an important role in the Council's change of heart. Cust, "Anti-Puritanism and Urban Politics: Charles I and Great Yarmouth," *Historical Journal* 35 (1992), 11.

[69] APC *1628–29*, pp. 226–7, 230–1; TNA, SP16/120, fol. 38; Challenor (ed.), *Municipal*

In most cases, electoral processes in early Stuart boroughs, weighted toward hierarchy and stability as they were, maintained the order that both urban governors and central authorities expected. Choosing their own officials was a deeply treasured privilege of borough governments, and townsmen prized their right to participate in municipal elections and defended the electoral rights laid out in their royal charters. At the same time, the charters that granted privileges of self-government and control over election and dismissal also defined a close connection between local governance and royal authority. Borough governors called on that connection in circumstances where orderly patterns of election came under threat of disruption. Rather than invariably avoiding or resisting Privy Council intervention, some towns solicited it in order to achieve their own ends of imposing order or suppressing popularity. Other local actors, like freemen unhappy with their leaders' improper actions or recorders dismissed allegedly without cause, also felt free to draw Privy Council scrutiny into local electoral matters. The "independence" of municipal elections was not entirely sacrosanct, and townsmen saw the utility of engaging with central government to achieve local purposes. Attitudes varied from town to town – Norwich's leaders reached out for assistance with elections more than once, while Chester's were more ambivalent – but some saw the utility of such engagement. For its part, the Privy Council responded to these solicitations by focusing on order and the suppression of popularity, in keeping with the longstanding pattern of supporting oligarchical rule and narrower franchises in towns. There was no systematic policy of intervention in local affairs, but the Board clearly viewed adjudication of discord over borough elections as a regular and important part of its business, to preserve order in the state.

Borough elections and the Privy Council during the Personal Rule

Whether mediated through internal mechanisms or the Privy Council, differences over corporate belonging, office-holding, and elections posed regular challenges to governance for corporate boroughs. Some level of disorder was endemic among most towns, as the form of government presented potential for division through regular votes, stated (if not always realized) majority principles, and participatory traditions.[70] Both borough governors and central authorities attempted to control those more disorderly impulses of civic life, but they could not be entirely squelched. Tensions over participation of the commons, fairness and propriety in election and dismissal, and in some cases religious differences strained the peace in a number of towns. Throughout the early Stuart period, the crown pressed policies intended to reinforce hierarchy and promote

---

Chronicles of Abingdon, pp. 140, 141. Teisdall gained the office in the end.
[70] See Patterson, "Consensus, Division and Voting," pp. 149-52, 155-8; Tittler, *Reformation and the Towns*, pp. 199-201; Withington, *Politics of Commonwealth*, pp. 69-75.

URBAN GOVERNMENT AND THE EARLY STUART STATE

narrowness in governing bodies as the best means of containing the more disorderly tendencies of borough governments.

King Charles himself had a keen awareness of and concern for order, in a number of cases personally intervening in municipal elections to suppress alleged faction or to put in place a preferred candidate. His intervention in Doncaster, requiring the townsmen to choose Viscount Ayr as their high steward, was noted in Chapter 1, while his personal interest in Great Yarmouth's elections will be discussed further below. He likewise intervened directly in the election of the chamberlain of Bristol in 1639, quashing the election in the belief that the man the corporation chose to the office, William Chetwyn, was ineligible and the process done toward private ends, "to the prejudice of common libertie." He named Ralph Farmer (a client of the earl of Berkshire) to be chosen instead. As David Harris Sacks has shown, the corporation obeyed the king's directive, but they also petitioned him both to affirm that they had acted without any hint of faction – reinforcing the critical concern for order – and reminding the king of their chartered privileges of election. They asked to be allowed to hold a new election. Charles assented, and the common council of Bristol promptly chose Chetwyn again, by a modest majority.[71] Charles's personal interest in borough governance is clear, as is his willingness to take direct action in ways that were not entirely comfortable to the corporations in question. Obeying the king's command for order while praying for the defense of liberties that had been granted by royal power in the first place was a common response.

Despite the shared desire for stability on the part of both central authority and borough governors, disorderly municipal elections appeared with increasing frequency before the Privy Council over time, particularly during the 1630s. The lacuna in the records from 1603 to 1613 prevents any certain calculation, but even accounting for this, the uptick in numbers under King Charles is marked (see Table 3.1). In the twelve years from 1613 (when Privy Council records resume) through 1624, the Board took notice of five incidents of mayoral or aldermanic elections that were disputed or divisive in one way or another. These included "indirect courses" by a mayor in an aldermanic election in Newcastle, confused and popular proceedings in Norwich in 1619, and a "disorderly tumult" in Oxford in 1621.[72] Irish boroughs also provoked the interest of the Privy Council in the 1610s; the Council directed orders to the lord deputy in

[71] TNA, SO1/3, fol. 150 (King to mayor, et al., of Bristol, 1 November 1639); David Harris Sacks, The Widening Gate: Bristol and the Atlantic, 1450–1700 (Berkeley and Los Angeles, CA, 1991), pp. 222–3. Sacks surmises that Farmer, with his court connections, likely managed to draw the king's attention and portray the first election as illegitimate and troubled. As a candidate in the first election, Farmer received no votes.

[72] The other two disputes were in Winchelsea and Cambridge. APC 1613–14, pp. 103–4, 1617–19, p. 484, 1619–21, p. 245; TNA, SP14/121, fols 73, 74, 111; APC 1623–25, p. 443. A dispute in Lincoln in the late 1610s came before the court of Star Chamber, so the Lords of the Council would have been part of the adjudication, though it did not come before the Privy Council per se. TNA, STAC8/98/9 (Callis v. Ellis).

98

MANAGING DIVISION

1616 for regulating Irish corporations that elected recusants to borough offices. In particular, Waterford had its royal charter revoked in 1618 for what the government defined as a disorderly election, wherein the corporation chose a Catholic as mayor.[73] In the succeeding thirteen years from 1625 through 1637, the Council took notice of thirteen controversies over mayoral or aldermanic elections in England, some of which, like those in Great Yarmouth, Colchester, and Shrewsbury, were deeply entangled in the challenging of their charters, as discussed in previous chapters.[74] Of these thirteen incidents, ten took place between 1630 and 1637. In addition, we know of some orders for borough elections made not by the full Privy Council but rather by individual members of the Board. Lord Keeper Coventry's orders for Cambridge in 1629-30 have already been noted. In 1628, Theophilus Howard, earl of Suffolk, lord warden of the Cinque Ports, at the Board's request heard a complaint by the commons of Sandwich over participation in municipal elections. He ultimately determined that the commons did have the right to vote for mayor, an unusual case of broadening rather than restricting a mayoral franchise in this period.[75] Acknowledging that we cannot know for certain what occurred between 1603 and 1613, it still appears that the period of Personal Rule marked a high point for Council intervention in municipal electoral matters under the early Stuarts.

An obvious question is whether this represents a more proactive policy on the part of the crown regarding disorder in England's towns in the 1630s or an increase in conflict within corporations over elections and corporate office – or perhaps both. The question regarding levels of local conflict is difficult to answer with certainty. Complaints before the Privy Council or the royal courts about disorder in municipal elections or the participation or exclusion of the commons in them cropped up occasionally throughout the sixteenth century (with the 1590s a seeming high point) as well as the early seventeenth. While

---

[73] APC 1616-17, p. 91; CSP Ireland, 1615-1625, pp. 142-3 (Lord Deputy St. John to Sir R. Winwood, 31 December 1616), 197 (Report of Commissioners at Waterford), 1615-25, pp. 174-5 (Sir Henry Docwra to Sir Thomas Lake, 23 December 1617), 183 (Lord Deputy St. John to Sir Thomas Lake, 22 January 1618), 184 (Lord Deputy St. John to Sir Thomas Lake, 3 February 1618, 187-8 (Sir Henry Docwra to [?], 3 March 1618); APC 1618-19, pp. 64-5 (Privy Council to Lord Deputy, 23 March 1618).

[74] Hartlepool, Norwich (twice), London, Abingdon (twice), Great Yarmouth, Newcastle-upon-Tyne, Berwick, Colchester, Chipping Norton, Bodmin, and Shrewsbury. TNA, SP16/36, fol. 24; APC 1626-27, p. 329, 1627-28, pp. 75, 140-1, 1628-29, pp. 187, 205; TNA, SP16/146, fol. 77; APC 1629-30, p. 368; TNA, PC2/43, p. 292, SP16/225, fol. 102, PC2/43, p. 295, SP16/234, fol. 140, SP16/248, fols 201ff, PC2/43, pp. 292, 310, 329, PC2/44, pp. 129, 151, PC2/44, p. 220, PC2/44, p. 246, PC2/47, p. 87, 458, PC2/48, pp. 369, 407. In addition, the Board reviewed a recurrence of electoral disruptions in Winchelsea that had begun in the 1610s, and in 1640 Lord Newburgh took note of a popular and divisive election in Higham Ferrers, which he intended to refer to the Lords, though no notice of a hearing could be found. APC 1629-30, p. 168; BL, Egerton MS 2584, fols 364, 366; TNA, SP16/470, fol. 70.

[75] KHLC, Sa/Ac7, fols 156v-157v.

99

local records tell us of some divisions, they do not always report discord that was present; it may be impossible to learn whether the appearance of peace masked a more disordered reality in many towns, whether in the 1610s or the 1630s.[76] Extant evidence rarely reveals all the factors causing these divisions, preventing a definitive answer as to whether or how often substantive disagreements over religion or local liberties or national issues like Ship Money directly affected municipal elections, making them more divisive in the 1630s.[77] In the handful of notable cases for which we have more evidence (like Shrewsbury, Great Yarmouth, and Colchester) religious divisions among the magistrates played a role.

If we cannot conclusively discern whether municipal divisions worsened during the Personal Rule, we can see an increased eagerness among borough governors to seek out Privy Council assistance in suppressing disorders that arose around municipal elections and office-holding, and a readiness to intervene on the part of the Council. Concern with disordered popularity and its suppression accelerated in Caroline government as well as among many borough magistrates. While James had no love for popular government, Charles was particularly attuned to its dangers, and the Privy Council intensified its focus on the issue. The Caroline Council widened its purview and took a more activist stance toward local order in all sorts of ways.[78] It had particular concerns regarding urban government, as upcoming chapters will show. Yet this was not simply a matter of the crown cracking down on local disorder, but also a reflection of the close alliance forged between borough governors and central authority. Alarm over popularity and a desire to contain potential disorder in borough elections were increasingly emphasized by both central and local authorities in the 1630s.

The bond that had been formed between the leaders of corporate boroughs and the crown, aiming to maintain control over urban populations, manifested itself in the late 1620s and 1630s in the management of disputed municipal elections. Borough magistrates actively solicited the assistance of king and Privy Council to reinforce their authority in the face of challenges coming from the broader body of freemen. As noted above, civic magistrates alerted the Privy Council to Norwich's electoral difficulties in 1632, which resulted in strict orders from the Board to suppress popularity. The disorder in Berwick's 1633 mayoral election displayed divided views on participation of the commons and

---

[76] Cogswell's work on Canterbury emphasizes the point that surface calm could mask underlying discord. Cogswell, "The Canterbury Election of 1626."

[77] See Chapters 6 and 7, for extended discussions on how issues like these were negotiated between boroughs and the crown across the early Stuart period.

[78] Sabrina Alcorn Baron, "'The Board Did Think Fit and Order': The Structure and Function of the Privy Council of Charles I, c. 1625-41, With Special Reference to the Personal Rule" (PhD dissertation, University of Chicago, 1995), p. 275. On Charles's views of popularity, see Richard Cust, "Charles I and Popularity," in T. Cogswell, R. Cust, and P. Lake (eds), *Politics, Religion, and Popularity in Early Stuart Britain: Essays in Honour of Conrad Russell* (Cambridge, 2002), pp. 235-58.

resulted in a stern clampdown by the Privy Council, at the behest of borough magistrates. The northern city of Carlisle, like Berwick, experienced the social and economic difficulties that attended the dissolution of the royal garrison there under James, and magistrates blamed the city's straits at least in part on "popular and tumultuous elections." They petitioned the crown for a new charter limiting participation in the mayoral election to the Twelve and Twenty-four only, which the crown granted in 1637.[79] As shown in previous chapters, allegedly disorderly proceedings in elections in Colchester and Shrewsbury were at least partly responsible for the quo warranto cases that challenged their liberties and ultimately led to a surrender of their charters to the crown and the issuance of new ones that carefully defined who might participate. In a number of these disputes, religious tensions contributed to local divisions, as groups formed around common beliefs or rallied for or against local clergymen. These were by no means new problems in the 1630s, but borough magistrates and central authorities alike strove to suppress the sources of division that threatened to undermine the order deemed necessary for stable rule.

The Caroline Council's keenness to intervene in local elections intensified when concerns for the king's service were particularly acute. The Board's desire to suppress disorder and reinforce a borough's magistrates while maintaining its focus on Ship Money collection is readily apparent in their intervention in a tumultuous election in Bodmin, Cornwall. In January 1637, Otho Stapp, the mayor or Bodmin, complained to the Board of "divers foul misdemeanors and insolent practices" of John Perryman, town clerk, in subverting the town's proper government. Stapp claimed Perryman refused to take the required oath from him, leading to Perryman's dismissal by the mayor, burgesses, and common council and the choosing of a new one, Thomas Hoblyn. In response, Perryman allegedly gathered a tumultuous and unlawful assembly in the town hall and declared Stapp to be "amoved and outed" from the office of mayor. A second unlawful assembly then elected William Stone as "pretended" mayor, and John Perryman as town clerk. While the source of this division remains obscure, Stapp blamed Perryman's personal disdain of proper government for the fracas, and he also cleverly linked his complaints with concerns he knew would resonate with king and Council. Stapp stressed to the Lords the "inconvenience" of the disordered state of things and particularly the risk to the levy of Ship Money.[80] The Board accepted Stapp's logic, focusing attention on resolving the disorder for the sake of the king's service. To avoid the distractions that would hinder the collection, the Council ordered Stapp to be restored as mayor and Hoblyn as town clerk, until the Board determined a further course of action. In the meantime, the corporation was to proceed with all diligence toward assessing

79 Bodl. Lib., MS Bankes 12, fols 5, 7–8.
80 TNA, SP16/344, fol. 189 (Petition of Otho Stapp, [25 January] 1637).

URBAN GOVERNMENT AND THE EARLY STUART STATE

and collecting Ship Money.[81] Both local actors and Privy Councilors made the connection between borough discord and the larger concerns of the state.

The convergence of national political concerns with borough divisions can also be seen in the bitter controversies in Great Yarmouth in 1629–31. There, local politics and religion entered into municipal elections, resulting in intense responses from both Caroline government and local actors. Borough governors diverged widely in their views on the Privy Council's intervention into their elections. As discussed in Chapter 2, Great Yarmouth's troubles involved differences over both religion and the corporate constitution. While one faction courted close ties with Privy Councilors and the Arminian bishop of Norwich, attempting to affect local elections through court connections, the other faction emphasized the traditional patterns of municipal elections and corporate governance, and chafed at the incursions of higher authority that their rivals brought about. The political disorder – and the religious tension that underlay much of it – was significant enough that it drew an unusually direct and firm response from the crown over elections and dismissals.

As the debate over the charter unfolded in 1629, King Charles himself wrote to the corporation prohibiting the municipal election that year, due to the faction and distraction in the town. The corporation was to send him a list of eligible aldermen, from whom he would declare two to be bailiffs for the year. Charles later relented (upon a petition from the corporation that Secretary Dorchester apparently supported) and allowed the election to go forward, but the corporation was to choose two men recommended to them by the king.[82] The Privy Council also demanded the restoration of men dismissed by the corporation for their roles in bringing about the challenge to the borough's charter, something that the corporation initially resisted.[83] According to Attorney General Heath, the town's disobedient disorder was so great that "unless His Majesty hold his strict hand of power over them," there would be no settlement. Heath suspected the influence of "a great party ... of sectaries, averse to all government but their own popular way," who must be reformed for the protection of the entire realm. "The government of the whole stands but upon the well ordering of the parts which make up the whole."[84] These central interventions were couched in the language of peace and order, yet they largely favored the views of one faction – the minority group favoring Arminian religion and less popular participation in borough government. Angered by strife and disorder, the king, Council, and attorney general invoked prerogative authority to control elections and the composition of borough government in Great Yarmouth.

---

[81] TNA, PC2/47, fol. 87.
[82] TNA, SP16/146, fol. 57, SP16/148, fol. 46; NRO, Y/C19/6, fol. 132.
[83] APC 1629–30, pp. 112–13, 148, 1630–31, pp. 140, 384; TNA, SP16/148, fols 99 (B. Cooper to Privy Council, 14 August 1629), 122 (R. Heath to Viscount Dorchester, 16 August 1629).
[84] TNA, SP16/148, fol. 122.

MANAGING DIVISION

While Great Yarmouth's case shows that Caroline government could take a firm hand in borough elections, it would be difficult to say that the crown systematically regulated local business from the center. The majority of Yarmouth's corporation, with help from men like Dorchester and the earl of Dorset, managed to convince the king to walk back from his original order to stop the election and choose the new bailiffs himself. The ground for their request seems rather weak – they petitioned that the legal trial regarding the charter was still pending – yet the king granted it. And though Charles and his Council seem to have been heavily swayed by the arguments made by the minority group within the corporation, at least some semblance of objectivity was maintained. Benjamin Cooper and other leaders of the minority faction wrote to Viscount Dorchester soliciting him to convince the king to nominate two men from their own faction to be bailiffs of the town, but their ploy failed. Charles nominated one man from Cooper's list, but for the second he chose a more neutral alderman not allied with Cooper. As Cust has suggested, it is likely that Dorchester, the king's delegate for handling the matter, wished to restore a level of peace and not just stir partisan passions.[85] The charter alteration that set off the controversy never passed the Great Seal, suggesting that king and Council chose to promote stability in the locality over pressing prerogative authority.

The great conflict in the corporation of 1629–31 eventually died down, but responses by the corporation's members to central interventions indicate the tensions engendered by the king and Council's actions. The corporation deeply respected the king's majesty. At the reading of the king's letter expressing his desire to restore peaceful government to the town, the corporators all stood silent, uncovered their heads, and "with a general acclamation or rejoicing" they cried out, "God Save the King!" Yet the majority of the corporation also felt deep connection to their traditional chartered liberties, endeavoring to protect them by reaching out to the king. They petitioned Charles to allow them to conduct their mayoral election as it had been done "anciently." At the same time, they initially refused, despite the king's direct order, to "redintegrate" Mr. Hardware, a Cooper ally who had been dismissed from his aldermanship, claiming that there was no "void" place in the body for him to fill.[86] They obediently elected the royal nominees, Mr. Norgatt and Mr. Medowes, as bailiffs "in all humble manner" at their election in late August 1629, but even as they did so, they reaffirmed the liberties of the borough. In recording the election, the corporation's minutes state that by "ancient order" no man should be elected bailiff more than once in every eight years, yet on this occasion only, because

[85] Cust, "Anti-Puritanism and Urban Politics," p. 13.
[86] NRO, Y/C19/6, fols 134, 132, 131, 133. They had dismissed Hardware and elected Thomas Crane in his place. After two weeks of wrangling, they eventually dismissed Crane, sending him back to the common council (which had an opening due to a death) and thus created a space among the aldermen to which they could elect Hardware. The king was obeyed and their ancient liberties preserved.

URBAN GOVERNMENT AND THE EARLY STUART STATE

the king requested it, they would forego that rule.[87] Corporate liberties did not necessarily conflict with royal authority, but the borough's magistrates strove to preserve the former in the face of the latter.

Great Yarmouth's experience demonstrates both the intensity of feeling townsmen had regarding control of their corporate government and the willingness of the Caroline state to intervene in what it saw as disorderly local politics. The attachment of many of the leading men of Great Yarmouth to traditional liberties and rights over their own elections was especially strong. The internal divisions among the magistrates reflected substantive questions over the corporate constitution and the borough's autonomy relative to royal authority. In response, the borough faced unusually sharp criticism and interventions by attorney general, Privy Council, and king. While other cases of disorderly elections that came before the Privy Council in this period may not have been as politicized as that in Great Yarmouth, they are indicative of the tensions that existed both within corporations and between corporations and the crown in this period.

The powers of election and dismissal were fundamental to the liberties of corporate boroughs. Townsmen valued the choice of their own officers as essential to the peaceful governance of their particular type of locality. Nevertheless, the nature of this government held at least a potential for division, at variance with the powerful prescriptions for unity and stable order that dominated this period. The early Stuart monarchs were attuned to corporate boroughs and the charters that defined their self-government, as previous chapters have shown. Both James and Charles took personal interest in the peace of borough governments, took steps to curb "popularity," and reinforced hierarchy and rule by the trusted few. This focused engagement was not simply part of a top-down policy, but rather was often invited by townsmen themselves. Local actors were keen to protect borough liberties as well as their own interests, but sometimes the best way to achieve that was by invoking the power of the state to enter into local conflicts. Such connections were, however, complicated. Borough governors, while accepting their subordination and obedience to royal commands, chafed at orders that challenged their liberties to elect and dismiss. Some of these cases, especially during the Personal Rule, became charged with political meaning, and the crown took strong steps to constrain municipal elections and dictate borough officers. Problems of order in borough government created opportunities for collaboration between local actors and central authorities, but they also opened questions of participation and governance that the early Stuart state could find difficult to manage.

[87] NRO, Y/C19/6, fol. 132v.

Table 3.1. Municipal Election Disputes Heard by the Privy Council, 1604–40

Year	Town	Nature of dispute	Result	Reference
1604	Nottingham	participation by "commoners" in elections and town business	Privy Council (PC) refers to earl of Shrewsbury; no PC records of dispute or determination	Lambeth Palace Library, MS 702, fol. 45; *RBNott*, vol. 4, pp. 269–70
1613	Newcastle upon Tyne	mayor used "indirect courses" to hinder mayoral election	PC refers to Council of the North for reconciliation	*APC 1613–14*, p. 103
1616	Irish towns	recusants elected as magistrates	Crown proceeds by quo warranto	*APC 1616–17*, p. 91
1619	Norwich	confused and factious forms of mayoral election	King James orders election procedure by seniority	*APC* 1617–19, p. 484
1621	Oxford	disorderly tumult in mayoral election	PC refers to assize judges for strict order	*APC 1619–21*, p. 245
1621	Winchelsea	disorderly election of jurats, faction, dispute eligibility	Lord Warden orders new election, but disputes continue	*CSPD* 1619–23, pp. 222, 255, 258
1624	Cambridge	participation of commoners in aldermanic election, number of aldermen	PC sets new orders for participation; election by commoners disallowed, further trouble to be quieted	*APC 1623–25*, p. 319–20
1626	Hartlepool	recusants voted in mayoral election; faction	PC refers to local gentlemen; dismissed burgesses to be restored	*APC 1627–28*, p. 329; TNA, SP16/36, fol. 24
1627	Norwich	disorderly and "factious carriage" in sheriff election	PC reaffirms actions of the mayor and aldermen; orders new bylaw for orderly election of sheriffs	*APC 1627–28*, pp. 75, 140–1
1627	Chester	faction in dismissal and election of clerk of the pentice; laboring of voices	PC wants matter "ordered in love"; referred to Lord Savage	*APC 1627–28*, pp. 164–5, 177–9

URBAN GOVERNMENT AND THE EARLY STUART STATE

Year	Town	Nature of dispute	Result	Reference
1628	London	disorderly and factious mayoral election	PC rebukes lord mayor to investigate and punish the principal actors, certify names	*APC 1628–29*, pp. 187, 205
1628	Sandwich	right of the commons to participate in town elections	PC refers to Lord Warden Suffolk; he determines commons have right of voices in elections	KHLC, Sa/Ac7, fols 156v–57v
1629	Cambridge	disorderly elections; rules for elections	Lord Coventry makes new orders; strict seniority principle	CambA, City/PB vol. 7, fols 183v–184v
1629	Winchelsea	disordered mayoral elections, dismissal from corporation	PC orders offending party before the Board and upholds disfranchisement	*APC 1629–30*, p. 168; BL, Egerton MS 2584, fols 364, 366
1629	Great Yarmouth	King Charles intervenes in election of bailiffs due to faction and distraction in the town	Corporation must elect bailiffs nominated by the king; part of charter controversy	TNA, SP16/146, fol. 57, SP16/148, fol. 46
1630	Abingdon	disordered mayoral election; commons overturned previous order for orderly succession	PC refers to assize judges to settle for best concord of the town	*APC 1629–30*, p. 368
1632	Norwich	disorderly election of alderman; non-freemen participated	PC confirms mayor's view that election was disorderly; in future, scrutiny to be taken by poll	TNA, PC2/43, p. 292; TNA, SP16/225, fol. 102
1633	Newcastle upon Tyne	form and participation in elections	PC in Star Chamber requires complainants to conform to charter and yield obedience	TNA, PC2/43, p. 295; TNA, SP16/234, fol. 140
1633	Berwick upon Tweed	disorderly and factious mayoral election	PC orders election voided and offender sent to Board; town ordered to proceed to new election in orderly way	TNA, SP16/248, fol. 201ff; SP16/254, fol. 28; PC2/43, fols 292, 310, 329.

MANAGING DIVISION

Year	Town	Nature of dispute	Result	Reference
1634	Abingdon	disorderly and divided mayoral election	PC stays election for further consideration; determines that recorder's voice must be counted and results confirmed	TNA, PC2/44, pp. 129, 151
1634	Colchester	participation in mayoral and alderman elections	PC orders attorney general to prepare draft charter strictly regulating elections; requires dismissed aldermen to be restored	TNA, PC2/44, p. 220
1634	Chipping Norton	"undue" election of bailiff	PC refers to "arbitrament" of Sir Francis Waynman	TNA, PC2/44, p. 246
1637	Bodmin	tumultuous mayoral election; misbehavior of town clerk	PC orders mayor to be restored, town clerk to step down and another elected	TNA, PC2/47, pp. 87, 458
1637	Shrewsbury	form and participation in mayoral and other elections	PC orders new charter, elections to be orderly like London's	TNA, PC2/48, pp. 369, 407
1640	Hastings	eligibility for mayoral election; faction	No final PC order; mayoral factions related to disputes over parliamentary election	TNA, SP16 /450, fol. 193, /451, fol. 14
1640	Higham Ferrers	tumultuous mayoral election; participation by "popular" group	Attorney general to consider and bring certificate to Star Chamber for Lords' consideration	TNA, SP16/470, fol. 70

Part 2

Corporate Towns and the Business of Government

4

Governing Poverty and Disorder: Corporate Towns and Social Policy

Political order and governance within a corporation formed only one type of order that borough magistrates were expected to keep. Maintaining socio-economic and moral order over a town and its inhabitants also ranked high among the duties of mayors and their fellow officers. In a time of great demographic pressure and economic stress, towns were crucibles of change. Many provincial towns (as well as London) experienced significant in-migration as the rural poor increasingly left their homes seeking employment or economic betterment.[1] Large-scale shifts in the economy across the late sixteenth and early seventeenth centuries due to war in Europe, trade stagnation, and inflation deeply affected urban economies, tied as they were to commerce and wage-labor. Taxed with concentrated populations of poor and un- or underemployed inhabitants, England's towns had the potential to be flashpoints for unrest. This incentivized local authorities and central government alike to enforce social and economic regulations designed to maintain order, promote appropriate behavior, and relieve those deserving help.[2]

This chapter examines some of the main points of connection and contention between borough governors and the early Stuart state on matters of social and moral control. Local and national policies on the poor, plague orders, alehouse regulation and brewing, and controlling the associated potential for disorder that went with them were vital concerns of governance in this period. Town governments had long experience in dealing with these matters; the social and economic trends tending toward increased poverty and mobility had been in play since at least the 1550s. Indeed, some of the policies adopted on a national scale regarding the poor originated first in England's towns as they experimented in the sixteenth century with programs to address poverty. As early as 1549, Norwich instituted a compulsory poor rate, followed by provision of grain

---

[1] Peter Clark and Paul Slack, *English Towns in Transition, 1500–1700* (Oxford, 1976), pp. 82–125.
[2] On the ideals and policies of social welfare and control in the early modern period, see Paul Slack, *From Reformation to Improvement: Public Welfare in Early Modern England* (Oxford, 1999) and Anthony Fletcher, *Reform in the Provinces: The Government of Stuart England* (New Haven, CT and London, 1986), esp. pp. 183–281; Steve Hindle, *The State and Social Change in Early Modern England, c. 1550–1640* (Basingstoke, 2000). Marjorie K. McIntosh, *Controlling Misbehavior in England, 1370–1600* (Cambridge, 1998), takes a longer view.

111

URBAN GOVERNMENT AND THE EARLY STUART STATE

for the poor and regulation of vagrants. Ipswich developed similar programs.[3] Balancing an impulse for charity and an imperative to maintain order, both local and central authorities attempted to knit up the unraveling social and moral fabric they saw as a particular problem in England's towns and cities.

As the king's deputies in their localities, the magistrates of provincial towns carried out parliamentary statutes and Privy Council orders, sharing common interest with the state at large to preserve order and protect the well-being of the commonwealth. At the same time, borough officials had local needs to meet and liberties and privileges to maintain. These interests were not inherently opposed, but were multidimensional. Addressing social problems like poverty, disease, grain shortages, and the proliferation of alehouses provided a common cause between urban magistrates and central authorities. It also could reveal fault lines of misunderstanding and frustration. Borough officials both invoked the magisterial authority of the state to mitigate the problems in their midst and attempted to protect their own liberties and authority over local business. Poor relief and related social issues drove the expansion of governance in the early Stuart state and became an increasingly important point of contact between borough governments and the crown in this period. As Steve Hindle has said, the execution and enforcement of social policy required negotiation at every level.[4] A more generalized anxiety about poverty relief and social control on the part of the crown in the first two decades of the seventeenth century gave way to stricter and more specific policies in the 1630s, particularly the Book of Orders of 1630-31.[5] The crown's assertion of prerogative authority through proclamations and orders throughout the period had a significant impact on corporate towns, but shared concern over social order largely fostered integration between corporate towns and the crown.

Poverty, poor relief, and governance

Economic challenges and intractable poverty were facts of life in early Stuart towns. Borough governors routinely referred to the poverty of their towns; a petition from Carlisle's corporation for a new charter called their city the poorest in the realm, while the corporation of Aldeburgh described their maritime

---

[3] John Pound, "Government to 1660," in C. Rawcliffe and R. Wilson (eds), *Norwich since 1550* (London and New York, 2004), pp. 49–50; Nathaniel Bacon, *The Annalls of Ipsw'che*, ed. W. Richardson (Ipswich, 1884), pp. 235, 245, 249; J. Webb (ed.), *Poor Relief in Elizabethan Ipswich*, Suffolk Records Society, vol. 9 (Ipswich, 1966).

[4] Hindle, *The State and Social Change*, p. 175.

[5] Paul Slack, "Books of Orders: The Making of English Social Policy, 1577-1631," *Transactions of the Royal Historical Society* 30 (1980), 1–22. As Slack has shown, the Caroline orders came in multiple parts and by rights should be termed "Books of Orders." For efficiency, "Book of Orders" will be used in this chapter.

112

GOVERNING POVERTY AND DISORDER

town as "very populous and much surcharged with poor people."[6] Managing the impact of poverty increasingly occupied urban magistrates' time.[7] While the overall English economy likely grew in the early seventeenth century, many towns experienced extraordinary economic hardship, some more than others.[8] The period saw years of economic crisis – the collapse of the cloth industry in the 1620s, the dearth of 1629–30 – that caused widespread distress.[9] The mayor of Wells wrote to the Privy Council in 1622 that the decay of clothing so increased misery among the poorer sort that they were "ready to fall into riotous and rebellious attempts," a concern shared by many borough magistrates.[10] The extent and depth of urban poverty has been open to discussion among historians; some perceive a real crisis with over 50 percent of the population of some towns living in poverty, while others have taken a somewhat less gloomy view.[11] Even the most optimistic accounts, however, admit that as much as 30 percent of the population in England's towns in the period may have been impoverished. Historians have sometimes characterized the towns as in "crisis" and "decline" in the early seventeenth century, and while this was not universally

---

[6] Bodl. Lib., MS Bankes 12, fol. 5; SA/I, EE1/E1/1, fol. 14v. Similar references to poor towns or cities can be found in RBL, vol. 4, p. 19 (The "poore of Leicesters humble peticion" to King James [n.d., but ca. 1604); Shakespeare Birthplace Trust, Stratford-upon-Avon archives, BRU15/13 (Petition of Stratford corporation to Privy Council, 1614); GA, GBR B3/1, fol. 210 (Petition of corporation of Gloucester to King James, August 1605); TNA, SP16/100, fol. 60 (Petition of town of Dunwich to duke of Buckingham, April 1628).

[7] The extensive literature on poverty and poor relief includes Marjorie K. McIntosh, Poor Relief in England 1350–1600 (Cambridge, 2011); Steve Hindle, On the Parish? The Micro-Politics of Poor Relief in Rural England c. 1550–1750 (Oxford, 2004); Paul Slack, Poverty and Policy in Tudor and Early Stuart England (London, 1988).

[8] Keith Wrightson, Earthly Necessities: Economic Lives in Early Modern England (New Haven, CT, 2002), pp. 159–60, 181; Paul Slack, "Poverty and Politics in Salisbury, 1597–1666," in P. Clark and P. Slack (eds), Crisis and Order in English Towns, 1500–1700 (Toronto, 1972), p. 171. A.L. Beier identifies 1590–1660 as the period of the worst economic conditions and 1620–60 as the period of strongest Poor Law implementation, though he recognizes that many towns instituted programs long before this. "Poverty and Progress in Early Modern England," in A.L. Beier, D. Canadine, and J. Rosenheim (eds), The First Modern Society: Essays in English History in Honour of Lawrence Stone (Cambridge and New York, 1989), pp. 202–3, 226, 235–6.

[9] See B.E. Supple, Commercial Crisis and Change in England 1600–1642: A Study in the Instability of a Mercantile Economy (Cambridge, 1959) for analysis of the fluctuating economy in the early Stuart period.

[10] TNA, SP14/130, fol. 142 (Mayor of Wells to Privy Council, 23 May 1622). One account estimated that 8,000 people were unemployed due to the clothing slump alone in 1622. Sybil Jack, Trade and Industry in Tudor and Stuart England (London, 1977), p. 104. On plague, see Paul Slack, The Impact of Plague in Tudor and Stuart England (London, 1985), and below, pp. 120–4.

[11] Wallace MacCaffrey, Exeter, 1540–1640: The Growth of an English County Town (Cambridge, MA, 1958), p. 249; John Pound, "The Social and Trade Structure of Norwich, 1525–1575," Past & Present No. 34 (1966), 50–1; Beier, "Poverty and Progress," pp. 226, 234–5; Thorold Tronrud, "Dispelling the Gloom: The Extent of Poverty in Tudor and Early Stuart Towns, Some Kentish Evidence," Canadian Journal of History/Annales Canadiennes d'Histoire 20 (1985), 1–21.

URBAN GOVERNMENT AND THE EARLY STUART STATE

true, economic distress and the problems of poor inhabitants strained most provincial towns.[12] Contemporary authorities decried the perceived rise in poverty, vagrancy, and social and economic disruption, believing that a large and growing population of the poor had to be both controlled and relieved. By both modern and contemporary accounts, towns faced serious economic challenges during the reigns of the early Stuarts.

Much of borough governance revolved around addressing the perceived causes of urban poverty, relieving and employing the deserving poor, and punishing the disorderly and wandering. While obviously not an urban problem *per se*, poverty affected urban communities disproportionately. They were particularly vulnerable to economic downturns and had multitudes of impoverished residents as well as newcomers from rural areas. Provincial towns found common cause in their distress, at times attempting group action. In 1610, Coventry allocated £40 toward an effort to pass a bill in parliament for the better relief of cities and corporations, while in 1614, the mayor and aldermen of Leicester wrote to their parliamentary burgesses to take notice of the "presente miserie and futer danger both of ours and other Corporacions," and promote "the good of our and other poore Corporacions."[13] The difficult economic circumstances besetting the realm in the early seventeenth century created a mutual concern for the problems of poverty among borough corporations and a consequent increase in interactions between them and central authorities.

Longstanding intractable problems stimulated multiple strategies for managing the poor, combining coercion and charity. In the wake of the Reformation, the sixteenth century saw the development of new structures for financing poor relief, through both private giving and public taxation. Parliamentary statutes under the Tudors, culminating in the comprehensive Poor Law of 1601, made parish-based rates for poor relief mandatory throughout England, but many towns already had local rates in place prior to the Elizabethan Poor Law. National orders regarding grain supplies for the poor also had local precedents.[14] Corporate charters empowered town governments to make bylaws and to charge rates on their inhabitants, and these liberties allowed many towns to develop systems of relief well before national legislation or royal proclamation caught up. Most borough corporations used these powers to establish schemes for "setting the poor on work," building houses of correction, providing grain

---

[12] Clark and Slack (eds), *Crisis and Order in English Towns*.
[13] CovA, BA/H/C/17/1, fol. 176; *RBL*, vol. 4, p. 140 (Mayor of Leicester, *et al.*, to Sir Henry Rich and Sir Francis Leigh, [9 May 1614)]. There was apparently an effort in the 1607 session of parliament regarding relief for "the decayed towns," but there is no evidence a bill came before the Commons. Boston Constituency Report, *HoP 1604–29*, www.historyofparliamentonline.org/volume/1604-1629/constituencies/boston.
[14] MacCaffrey, *Exeter*, p. 85; Pound, "Government to 1660," pp. 50, 55; Paul Slack, "Dearth and Social Policy in Early Modern England," *Social History of Medicine* 5 (1992), 1–17; Muriel McClendon, *The Quiet Reformation: Magistrates and the Emergence of Protestantism in Tudor Norwich* (Stanford, CA, 1999), pp. 229–31.

GOVERNING POVERTY AND DISORDER

in times of dearth, and collecting rates for poor relief. Leading residents also supported charitable works through private benefactions. These elements were firmly in place on a local level by the beginning of the seventeenth century in corporate boroughs and many market towns, as well.[15] National measures often lagged behind local ones, and borough officials exercised discretion, fitting their response to local circumstances. Paul Slack has argued that county JPs frequently instituted relief and correction schemes only in response to central directives – and then sometimes with resentment at the intrusion.[16] The evidence from towns, in contrast, indicates that borough authorities often took a more proactive approach.

Some of this enthusiasm can likely be ascribed to godly, or strongly reforming and Calvinist, religion. While it is not the purpose here to detail puritan or godly views regarding poverty, it is worth addressing briefly given the prevalence of godly religion in many towns.[17] In places like Ipswich, Gloucester, Dorchester, Salisbury, Great Yarmouth, Exeter, and Leicester (among others), godly ideas regarding poor relief, the suppression of drunkenness, and the control of disorder energized many magistrates. Historians have differed as to whether godly religion itself triggered the social and moral reform campaigns that characterized towns like these. Margaret Spufford argued that the reformation of manners of the early seventeenth century was less a function of puritan religious beliefs than a result of the economic and demographic disruptions of the period. In her view, moral reform does not require religious motivation. Many towns suffered intense economic troubles in the period that dramatically increased the numbers of the poor, requiring a response from local governors. Others, like Paul Slack, believe that view underestimates the social impulse of godly Protestantism in the late sixteenth and early seventeenth centuries. Bursts of civic reform did not always coincide chronologically with the moments of greatest demographic and economic pressure or disruption.[18] Divines like John White in Dorchester and Samuel Ward in Ipswich clearly spurred inhabitants and magistracy alike to address matters of poverty, drink, and disorder with vigor and persistence. That said, both the vigorously godly and the less enthusiastic established measures for managing the poor, often ahead of national requirements.[19] Godliness played a part in the responses to poverty and its attendant

---

[15] See McIntosh, *Poor Relief in England*, esp. pts II and IV; Marjorie K. McIntosh, *Poor Relief and Community in Hadleigh, Suffolk, 1547–1600* (Hatfield, 2013); Webb (ed.), *Poor Relief in Elizabethan Ipswich*; McClendon, *Quiet Reformation*, pp. 230–1.

[16] Slack, "Books of Orders," pp. 20–1.

[17] Borough government and religion will be discussed in greater detail below in Chapter 7.

[18] Margaret Spufford, "Puritanism and Social Control?" in A. Fletcher and J. Stevenson (eds), *Order and Disorder in Early Modern England* (Cambridge, 1985), pp. 47, 57; Slack, *Reformation to Improvement*, pp. 34–5. See also Keith Wrightson and David Levine, *Poverty and Piety in an English Village: Terling, 1525–1700*, rev. edn (Oxford, 1995).

[19] Slack, *Reformation to Improvement*, pp. 36–43.

115

problems in many English towns, but the severity of their economic difficulties drove them to find solutions with or without incitement by godly clergy.

While the early Stuart kings had no love for puritanism, they generally approved of the programs for reform and social control in so-called "godly towns," even if not the beliefs behind them. A clear example of this can be seen in Dorchester. As David Underdown's engaging study of that town reveals, the energetic preaching of conformist puritan Rev. John White placed the charitable impulse to relieve the poor, as well as the magisterial impulse to control and reform their behavior, at the center of borough life and government. While not all inhabitants shared the zeal for White's message, a majority of the town's governing council did. Dorchester's corporation instituted social programs, like the creation of a common brewhouse and a workhouse-hospital, that went beyond parliamentary statute or Privy Council orders. The town became a model of charity and order from the mid-1610s through (and past) 1640.[20] This did not go unnoticed in London. When the corporation petitioned for a new charter in 1629, Attorney General Robert Heath supported the town's request and praised its orderly governance. In a letter stating his official opinion on the town's petition, he pointed out that the corporation requested additional authority to regulate tradesmen and craftsmen, "the better to set their poor on work." Heath said that the men of Dorchester had already "given good Testimony of their care, for they suffer not a Beggar there." Indeed, if other towns would follow Dorchester's example, it would be to "much advantage" through the whole kingdom.[21] Slack has argued that the "early Stuarts were perfectly capable of borrowing the clothes of the godly if it looked as if they might be tailored to fit."[22] Dorchester, with its godly but generally conformist minister and magistracy, wore those clothes.

Regardless of the theological bent of a borough's clergy and corporate leaders, urban circumstances required attentive governance to maintain order and relieve destitution. Concerned with both stability and charity, most provincial borough corporations put extensive programs in place to manage poverty and control the poor. Nigel Goose, in his close study of poor relief in Colchester, states that from the late sixteenth century onward, that town's corporation

> launched a veritable assault on poverty, instigating voluntary collections, formal poor rates and extraordinary levies, distraining goods, reviving hospital foundations, establishing a workhouse, providing materials to employ the poor at home, administering loan funds, apprenticing poor children, dedicating an ever-widening array of fines and levies to the use of the poor, siphoning off some of the profits of the expanding textile industry, ensuring the corn supply and subsidizing its price, licensing beggars,

---

[20] David Underdown, *Fire from Heaven: Life in an English Town in the Seventeenth Century* (New Haven, CT, 1992), pp. 98, 114–18, 109–13, 232.
[21] TNA, SP16/149, fol. 43–43v.
[22] Slack, *Reformation to Improvement*, p. 43.

GOVERNING POVERTY AND DISORDER

regulating abuses amongst clothiers, regulating alehouses, removing vagrants, and punishing the idle in its house of corrections.[23]

This laundry list of schemes captures the breadth of activities that many corporate towns established to combat the problems of poverty in their midst. Few corporations matched Colchester's exhaustive efforts, but all instituted at least some of these programs as part of corporate governance. Addressing poverty and its consequences increased the bureaucratic and fiscal burden of borough corporations, strengthened and expanded their administrative capacity and sophistication, and provided a significant connection between them and the state more broadly.

While national legislation dictated some elements, many others stemmed from local initiatives. The Elizabethan Poor Law of 1601, rather than creating an entirely new system, gave statutory weight to a variety of efforts already underway in a number of towns. The key elements of the Poor Law included requiring local officials to provide support (in almshouses or through "outdoor relief") for the poor who could not work; to give work to the able-bodied poor; to bind poor children out as apprentices; and to punish idle vagrants in a house of correction or otherwise. Importantly, it authorized local officials to raise rates to support these efforts.[24] The Poor Law mandated action at the parish level, but in many towns the corporation managed poor relief in league with parish-based overseers of the poor.[25] In her study of Exeter's poor relief in the late sixteenth and early seventeenth centuries, Connie Evans assessed the corporation's administrative and financial activities, which included city-wide poor rates, subsidized grain prices, special contributions at Christmas, and other public relief. She found that in 1625, the corporation administered and expended approximately £300 on "public" poor relief, benefitting as many as 394 of that city's poor, in addition to assisting with the management and distribution of numerous philanthropic endowments made by better-off Exeter citizens.[26] Early Stuart Ipswich likewise had a sophisticated network, dating back at least to the reign of Elizabeth, of public aid based on poor rates and private philanthropy by individuals who were often themselves borough governors.

---

[23] Nigel Goose, "The Rise and Decline of Philanthropy in Early Modern Colchester: The Unacceptable Face of Mercantilism?," *Social History* 31 (2006), 484.

[24] 43 Eliz., c. 2.

[25] Hull's magistrates assisted the overseers of the poor to direct resources for the poor during the crisis period of the early 1620s. York's corporation merely oversaw the work of the overseers, supplementing parish alms, but not assuming poor relief as a civic matter. HHC, BRB3 (Hull Bench Book 5), fol. 119; "The Seventeenth Century: Economy and Poor Relief," in *VCH Yorkshire, The City of York*, ed. P.M. Tillott (London, 1961), pp. 166–173, *British History Online*, www.british-history.ac.uk/vch/yorks/city-of-york/pp166-173.

[26] Connie S. Evans, "'An Echo of the Multitude': The Intersection of Governmental and Private Poverty Initiatives in Early Modern Exeter," *Albion* 32 (2000), 414, 416, 425, 427.

URBAN GOVERNMENT AND THE EARLY STUART STATE

Corporate government developed deeply intertwined institutions, mechanisms, and revenue sources to oversee this web of relief.[27]

Relieving deserving residents was balanced by measures to control undeserving and non-resident poor. With dense populations and high proportions of the landless, most towns struggled to prevent, or at least constrain, the impoverished from inhabiting a town in the first place. Places like Salisbury whipped hundreds of vagrants out of town.[28] Borough governors established and maintained houses of correction, strictly enforced vagrancy statutes, and made local bylaws regarding residency, all of which aimed at making poor "strangers" unwelcome. The town of Newbury asked for greater power over "idle vagrant persons" in their charter of incorporation.[29] Local efforts received strong backing from the king's prerogative authority. Royal proclamations for preventing and punishing rogues and vagabonds issued forth in 1603, 1617, 1618, 1628, 1629, and 1630 (twice).[30] These proclamations reinforced the power of magistrates to control the bodies of the poor and avert danger to the realm.

Many corporations identified the proliferation of poor cottages as a problematic source of poverty, though it may have been more symptom than cause.[31] Borough officials across England, alarmed that large numbers of poor people crowded into subdivided tenements, tried to prevent it. Unlike vagrancy, which the crown, through its proclamations, avidly sought to suppress throughout the realm, "poor inmates" seem to have been viewed by the national government as a problem of London, where it had direct impact on the Court. Both James and Charles issued proclamations against inmates and subdivision of buildings in the metropolis, attempting to curb in-migration by limiting housing, though to small avail.[32] But this London focus ignored the provincial dimension of the problem. In the absence of statute or proclamation, corporations targeted local ordinances against poor "incomers" and the landlords offering them lodging. Aldeburgh's corporation criticized owners who impoverished the town by letting rooms to families who could not maintain themselves; they required a bailiff's assent for rentals to any newcomers. The corporations of Great Yarmouth and Worcester passed orders requiring landlords to hold the towns harmless for alms or other costs incurred in renting cottages to poor "foreigners." Tewkesbury banned renting to any who had not been resident for

[27] See Webb (ed.), *Poor Relief in Elizabethan Ipswich*; Bacon, *Annalls of Ipsw'che.*
[28] Slack, "Poverty and Politics in Salisbury," p. 166.
[29] TNA, SP14/13, fol. 163.
[30] J. Larkin and P. Hughes (eds), *Stuart Royal Proclamations*, vol. 1, *Royal Proclamations of King James I 1603–1625* (Oxford, 1973), pp. 51, 360, 480; J. Larkin (ed.), *Stuart Royal Proclamations*, vol. 2, *Royal Proclamations of King Charles I 1625–1646* (Oxford, 1983), pp. 185, 233, 261, 296.
[31] Oxford called the multitude of cottages the "principal cause" of the heavy charge of poor in the city. *APC 1625–26*, p. 304.
[32] Larkin and Hughes (eds), *Stuart Royal Proclamations*, vol. 1, pp. 47, 141; Larkin (ed.), *Stuart Royal Proclamations*, vol. 2, p. 280. See also Joseph P. Ward, *Metropolitan Communities: Trade Guilds, Identity, and Change in Early Modern London* (Stanford, CA, 1997), pp. 17–21.

GOVERNING POVERTY AND DISORDER

at least one year.[33] Some townsmen, even magistrates, profited from the influx of the poor, making full enforcement difficult. Nottingham's orders had to be reiterated multiple times, in part because a leading townsman, alderman and former mayor Leonard Nixe, "doth absolutely refuse" to obey the orders regarding inmates and foreign tenants.[34] The ubiquity of such orders indicates both the antipathy that "incomers" and poor cottages generated and the lack of success at stopping them.[35]

The difficulty of confronting this problem prompted some towns to solicit Privy Council backing to constrain their own inhabitants to abide by borough regulations.[36] The city of Oxford, along with the university, petitioned the Council early in 1626 against those who built cottages and tenements on the fringes of the city "only for their private gain and advantage." According to the petitioners, they had little power to control such behavior "through the want of such a statute law in towns corporate and cities." The Council authorized the mayor and vice-chancellor to prohibit the practice.[37] Petitions from Cambridge and Stratford-upon-Avon likewise appealed to the Board for support in suppressing cottages; while emphasizing the fire danger of thatched cottages, they tied their concern to the poverty that such cottages allegedly encouraged and the greed of the men who built and subdivided them.[38] Borough governors saw the value of inviting the Board's attention in order to solve a stubborn local problem.

At least one town looked to mitigate the intractable problem of poor inmates and the landlords who fostered them by seeking to co-opt the king's authority through its charter of incorporation. The corporation of Reading, beset by fears of increasing numbers of the poor as well as concerns about the strength of their jurisdiction in the mid-1630s, began to plan a renewal of their charter in 1635. An unusual item appeared among the fairly standard requests for adjustments to the mortmain license and the shape of corporate governance; the mayor and his brethren proposed a clause requiring landlords who rented to poor people to direct a portion of their rents to support their poor tenants who became sick

---

[33] SA/I, EE1/E1/1, fols 14v–15; NRO, Y/C19/5, fols 241, 266; WAAS, A.14 Box I (Worcester Chamber Order Book 2), fol. 21; GA, Tewkesbury Borough Records A1/2, p. 25.
[34] RBNott, vol. 4, pp. 364, 381, 382.
[35] RBNott, vol. 4, pp. 305–7; Nottinghamshire Archives, Newark Hall Book, DC/NW 3/1/1, fol. 194; LA, GRANTHAM BOROUGH/5/1, fols 19v–20v; HHC, BRB3, p. 42; J.F. Bailey (ed.), Transcription of the Minutes of the Corporation of Boston, vol. 2, 1608–1638 (Boston, 1981), p. 647; YCA, B.32, fol. 342, B.33, fols 173–4, 237–8, B.34, fol. 9; J.W.F. Hill, Tudor and Stuart Lincoln (Cambridge, 1956), p. 137.
[36] S. Bond (ed.), The Chamber Order Book of Worcester, 1602–1650, Worcestershire Historical Society, NS, vol. 8 (Worcester, 1974), p. 316.
[37] APC 1625–26, p. 303.
[38] APC 1618–19, pp. 462–3; Shakespeare Birthplace Trust, Stratford-upon-Avon Records, BRU15/16/17 (draft petition of bailiff and burgesses to Privy Council, n.d.). The Cambridge petition emanated from the university, and it is not clear if university officials implicated borough governors in the problematic practices.

URBAN GOVERNMENT AND THE EARLY STUART STATE

and required alms. Town officials complained that landlords converted good houses and rented them to poor people simply to increase their own profits, leaving the town responsible for relief.[39] The new charter, finally approved in 1638, included a stricture against poor cottagers.[40] By putting this power into the corporate charter, the mayor and aldermen strengthened their grip on governance over the problems of poverty with the king's imprimatur.

Borough governors and central authorities alike promoted poor relief and control throughout the early seventeenth century. In many ways, the towns were innovators in developing such programs, since the problems of poverty affected them so acutely. National efforts - whether parliamentary statutes or royal proclamations - often incited corporate boroughs to do things they were already doing in some fashion. Collections for public relief, exclusion of vagabonds, schemes for work, and houses of correction all were common elements of urban governance of the poor, regardless of laws or proclamations. Central government bolstered local initiatives, encouraged strict enforcement of statutes, and maintained a firm hand on poor relief, particularly during times of serious difficulty. Responding to the implosion of the cloth industry in the early 1620s, King James declared he was "very apprehensive of his people's wants and the great prejudice the public weal of this kingdom doth suffer."[41] No doubt, attention to the issue rose and fell with the economy, and enthusiasm varied between towns. Colchester, Ipswich, and Dorchester acted with zeal, while others lagged. One study found that York's corporation attended most assiduously to poor relief in periods of greatest central compulsion.[42] Nevertheless, nearly all towns faced with the stubborn problem of poverty shared the state's concern to reduce the potential for disorder that the impoverished posed and engaged actively to address it.

Plague and policy

Regular visitations of the plague made the problems of poverty and disorder all the worse. While outbreaks occurred intermittently across the period, more widespread infections raged in 1604-06, 1625-26, 1630-31, and 1636-38. Plague posed a powerful danger to towns and affected every aspect of urban life, business, and government. As Paul Slack showed in his seminal book on the impact of plague in the early modern period, this pandemic disease, while never

---

[39] J.M. Guilding (ed.), *Reading Records: Diary of the Corporation*, vol. 3 (London and Oxford, 1896), p. 302.

[40] C.F. Pritchard (ed.), *Reading Charters, Acts and Orders 1253-1911* (Reading and London, 1913), p. 68.

[41] Beier, "Poverty and Progress," p. 234; APC 1621-23, pp. 214-15.

[42] *VCH City of York*, pp. 166-73. The Privy Council hounded the erstwhile mayor of York in 1623 for failure to continue the "verie good worke" begun by his predecessor for setting to work the city's poor. APC 1621-23, p. 438.

GOVERNING POVERTY AND DISORDER

a strictly urban phenomenon, hit towns and cities far harder than it did rural areas. With large, densely packed populations, weak sanitation, and frequent traffic of people and trade goods in and out, urban settings made perfect breeding grounds for plague. Slack estimates that at least half of the roughly 660,000 people who succumbed to plague in England between 1570 and 1670 died in towns and cities – this at a time when less than 20 percent of England's population lived in them.[43]

Along with the deep personal and communal trauma attending mass mortality and morbidity, plague also brought economic devastation and problems of order. Outbreaks resulted in closed markets, canceled or postponed fairs, curtailed movement within or between towns, and interruption of imports and exports. Some accounts speak of grass growing in the streets, perhaps with only a modicum of hyperbole.[44] Those not sickened or quarantined lost livelihoods for extended periods during outbreaks, exacerbating the problems of poverty and unemployment that troubled most towns. Economic life's sudden halt led to destitution and near-starvation of the urban poor, while many of the best-off inhabitants simply left town. Plague affected the operation of borough government, as official meetings were reduced and elections relocated or postponed. Some magistrates abandoned their duties entirely. Exeter's mayor-elect refused to take up his office during the plague of 1625; he and other officials deserted the city, which managed to avoid collapse largely due to the heroic efforts of Alderman Ignatius Jurdain, who stayed. Salisbury in 1627 likewise saw many of its magistrates flee, leaving John Ivie, the mayor, to manage the crisis with little help.[45] It was a recipe for disorder, if not disaster.

While not all magistrates lived up to their duties, urban governments generally carried out the active management and communication with the Privy Council that plague orders demanded. In contrast to poor-relief policies, those for plague emerged in the sixteenth century as largely a top-down phenomenon; key orders developed in Elizabeth's reign were enforced from the center.[46] By

---

[43] Slack, *Impact of the Plague*, pp. 16, 133; E.A. Wrigley, "Urban Growth and Agricultural Change: England and the Continent in the Early Modern Period," *Journal of Interdisciplinary History* 15 (1985), 688.

[44] Larkin and Hughes (eds), *Stuart Royal Proclamations*, vol. 1, pp. 151, 175; Larkin (ed.), *Stuart Royal Proclamations*, vol. 2, pp. 45, 64, 287, 485, 509. One (rather bad) poem inspired by plague in Worcester elegized: "Thy naked streetes poore towne! And hatefull rest / Seeme for thy parted Ghost a solemne feast. / Thy pebbles polisht with much peoples feete, / O'er grown with grass, seeme Churchyard more than street." J.T., *Worcester's Elegie and Eulogie* (London, 1638), p. 9.

[45] Slack, *Impact of the Plague*, pp. 190, 258; *APC 1625–26*, p. 184; R.N. Worth (ed.), *Calendar of the Plymouth Municipal Records* (Plymouth, 1893), p. 155; NRO, Y/C19/5, fol. 332; Ferdinando Nicolls, *The Life and Death of Mr. Ignatius Jurdain* (London, 1654), pp. 14–15; Paul Slack (ed.), *Poverty in Early-Stuart Salisbury*, Wiltshire Record Society, vol. 31 (Devizes, 1975), pp. 117–23. It is likely no coincidence that both Jurdain and Ivie had reputations as godly magistrates.

[46] Slack, *Impact of the Plague*, pp. 200, 212.

URBAN GOVERNMENT AND THE EARLY STUART STATE

James's reign, however, these had been largely integrated into urban governance. Magistrates imposed stern measures to curb the spread, included "shutting up" infected households (the well and the sick together), building pest houses, stopping or limiting commerce, and restricting movement. Most set up strict watches, closed alehouses, and hired viewers and carers (mostly women) for the infected. Dorchester procured a barn as an isolation house for inhabitants suspected of plague, the town paying the cost of their diet and medicine, while in Newcastle, the sick were quarantined in their own homes or sent to a "lodge" outside the town's walls.[47] Local actions, managed by borough magistrates, complemented national ones from the Privy Council, which stopped goods from infected foreign countries from entering English ports, halted mustering and training in infected areas, prevented travelers from infected areas from coming to London or the Court, closed down regional events like Sturbridge and Bartholomew Fairs, and canceled some religious services.[48] These local and national measures were understood as necessary to limit plague's spread, but they also deeply affected urban life and government.

Only suppression of plague and relief of its attendant miseries and disorders would allow normal activity to return, leading most urban magistrates to perform plague orders diligently; heavy-handed central intervention rarely occurred. The Board did, however, reprove local officials who failed to be sufficiently vigilant. London and Westminster (not surprisingly) attracted most of the Council's attention, but provincial towns did not escape its gaze.[49] When plague came to England from the Low Countries early in 1625, the Council wrote to the "mayor and magistrates" of Great Yarmouth (which had extensive trade with the Netherlands) expressing confidence that town officials would act prudently against the threat, yet wishing to "quicken" their actions. Other towns received scolding, rather than encouraging, letters.[50]

The Council's sharpest focus on plague came during 1629–31. While this outbreak was, according to Slack, far from the worst, it coincided with Caroline government's broader push for reform associated with the Book of Orders (discussed below), leading to strict attention on the Council's part.[51] With

---

[47] GA, GBR G3/SO/2 (Gloucester sessions orders, 1633–70), fols 10–12; J.M. Guilding (ed.), *Reading Records: Diary of the Corporation*, vol. 2 (London, 1895), pp. 241, 244, 247; *RBL*, vol. 4, p. 108; *RBNott*, vol. 5, p. 151, 183–4; C.H. Mayo and A. Gould (eds), *The Municipal Records of the Borough of Dorchester, Dorset* (Exeter, 1908), p. 533; Keith Wrightson, *Ralph Tailor's Summer: A Scrivener, His City, and the Plague* (New Haven, CT, 2011), pp. 48–51.

[48] *APC 1616–17*, p. 352, *1623–25*, pp. 77, 302, *1625–26*, pp. 124, 134, 135, *1629–30*, p. 160; Larkin and Hughes (eds), *Stuart Royal Proclamations*, vol. 1, p. 151; Larkin (ed.), *Stuart Royal Proclamations*, vol. 2, pp. 45, 51, 485, 509; *CSPD 1635–36*, p. 524.

[49] *APC 1616–17*, pp. 339, 343, 352, *1625–26*, pp. 15, 128, *1629–30*, pp. 306, 313, 352, *1630–31*, pp. 91–2, 257.

[50] *APC 1623–25*, p. 457, *1625–26*, pp. 191, 199, *1629–30*, pp. 386, 402; TNA, PC2/50, p. 165. The Board was apparently unaware of Great Yarmouth's two-bailiff corporate constitution, something that would soon gain the crown's negative attention.

[51] Slack, *Impact of Plague*, p. 218.

GOVERNING POVERTY AND DISORDER

the king's personal interest, the Board wrote to over twenty port towns in October 1629 charging them to stop any goods from infected countries from entering the realm. This precaution proved unsuccessful, and infection spread. Cambridge suffered especially badly in 1630. The Board rebuked the mayor for not managing the "great Calamitie" properly, adjured the county JPs to help the town, and intervened to resolve serious food shortages and other problems there.[52] Magistrates in Rochester and Norwich received letters spurring them to stricter care. The Board accused Norwich's magistrates of not effectively shutting up infected houses or forbidding "assemblies unnecessarie on Sundayes and hollydayes in drawing people together by musick in publique places, wasterplaies and such like." They also ordered a stop to the annual Mayor's Feast, though Norwich's corporation convinced the Board to lift the prohibition.[53] Central authorities largely trusted town officials to manage plague, but the Council's interventions reinforce the point that local and national interests intertwined in epidemic disease and its management.

If borough magistrates might not always have appreciated scrutiny from on high regarding plague orders, they nevertheless regularly solicited the Privy Council's aid, marshaling central authority to solve local problems. Raising the funds necessary to support the poor and sick proved one of the most difficult aspects of plague management. Borough corporations had the privilege of raising local rates, which they did in times of plague, but the need outstripped the means of the inhabitants.[54] With trade depressed or stopped, even those who previously might have been capable of paying could not; some simply refused. Meanwhile, most of the "better sort" of inhabitants decamped to the country, making circumstances in town even more tenuous. In one ward of Plymouth in 1627, out of the sixty-seven persons to be assessed, twenty-seven were "not in town," of which several stated they "will not" contribute; of those in town, fifteen "refused to pay," six were dead, one "in Virginia," and others "not able." Plymouth was far from alone in its dilemma of having many of its leading inhabitants flee, and the fiscal – and magisterial – deficit that left. Mayors in Bury St. Edmunds and Grantham solicited Privy Council intervention in attempts to force inhabitants to return home, or at the least to pay their required rates.[55] Townsmen also appealed to the Board to solicit aid from beyond a borough's jurisdiction. By statute, those within five miles of an infected town could be required to pay rates for plague relief. Without any authority beyond their own boundaries, mayors sometimes had to call on the Council to require county

---

[52] *CSPD 1629–31*, p. 80; *APC 1629–30*, pp. 383–4, 386, *1630–31*, pp. 14–15, 26–7.

[53] *APC 1629–30*, pp. 398–9, 402, *1630–31*, p. 8; *CSPD 1629–31*, p. 275.

[54] Guilding (ed.), *Reading Records*, vol. 2, pp. 16, 32, 36, 40, 251, 271; *RBL*, vol. 4, pp. 110, 234–5; *RBNott*, vol. 4, p. 276; Thomas Kempe (ed.), *The Black Book of Warwick* (Warwick, 1898), p. 404.

[55] *APC 1625–26*, p. 217, *1626*, p. 83; TNA, SP16/71, fol. 57 (Mayor of Dartmouth to Privy Council, 19 July 1627), PC2/48, pp. 72, 97.

URBAN GOVERNMENT AND THE EARLY STUART STATE

JPs to fulfill their duty in this regard.[56] Hull, especially hard hit in 1637–38, complained to the Board that the JPs of Yorkshire had failed to collect the required contribution to relieve the town, giving either little or nothing at all. With 2,500 "necessitous persons," the town needed immediate help from the county or, according to the mayor, Hull would be ruined and the poor led into "outrageous courses" to feed themselves.[57] Borough magistrates, like those of Hull and Plymouth, cultivated connection with the center to bring the state's resources to bear on their local calamity.

Plague's deadly nature exacerbated every urban ill and intersected in some way with nearly all parts of urban life. Limiting its damage required coordination between the many layers of the early modern state and cooperation between town governments and the Privy Council. Central authorities depended heavily on urban magistrates to mitigate the spread and impact of disease; towns turned to the Privy Council to share the cost and obtain aid. Yet the early Stuart Council's assistance only went so far. While sympathetic to the misery caused in towns by plague, central authorities could be deaf to their cries for relief. Some of the worst outbreaks of plague – 1625–27 and 1636–38 – occurred just as the crown imposed new and heavy burdens, including billeting, the Forced Loan, and Ship Money. As will be seen in succeeding chapters, provincial corporate towns petitioned king and Privy Council exhaustively for remission from these levies based in part on their heavy expenses of supporting the infected and poor. These appeals often brought only temporary or partial relief, and sometimes proved fruitless.[58] The many public health and economic measures necessitated by plague encouraged connection between urban magistrates and the resources of the state to address shared concerns around disease and disorder. At the same time, the towns bore an especially heavy burden both from the disease itself and from the inefficiencies in the early Stuart state.

Regulating drink

Relief and control of the poor and sick formed a shared interest on the part of central and local government, as borough corporations carried out their own programs as well as national statutes and royal proclamations to reduce the potential for disorder that came with poverty. Other regulatory schemes, especially those for drink, brought towns into even more frequent and complex

---

[56] 1 Jac. I, c.31, *Statutes of the Realm*, vol. 4, p. 1060; TNA, PC2/48, p. 98, PC2/49, p. 183, SP16/330, fol. 173 (Petition of Hadleigh to Privy Council, [August] 1636), SP16/357, fol. 226 (Council to JPs of Suffolk, 30 May 1637), SP16/323, fol. 99v (Petition of Bury St. Edmunds to Council, 12 November 1637).
[57] TNA, SP16/381, fol. 22 (Mayor of Hull to Council, 2 February 1638), SP16/387, fol. 36 (JPs of East Riding to Council, 4 April 1638). The JPs of the East Riding, justifying their non-payment, claimed that the townsmen prevaricated about the numbers of sick and poor.
[58] See pp. 191, 201, 208–10, 215–16, below.

124

GOVERNING POVERTY AND DISORDER

interaction with the state. Beer and ale, and the institutions that served them, held a central place in the culture and economy of most localities; they also had associations with drunkenness and poverty. Alehouses in particular came under scrutiny, as they catered to the poorer sorts and hosted potentially disorderly conviviality. Because of the denser populations of towns relative to rural areas and their function as staging places for travelers, provincial towns had large numbers of alehouses and brewers of drink.[59] While alehouses formed a necessary part of the social and economic infrastructure of towns and cities, authorities believed they fostered disorder, troublesome on both political and moral grounds. Central and local authorities alike wished to control the misbehavior often associated with alehouses and with regulating the numbers of those licensed to keep one.[60] Enforcement and policy, however, ebbed and flowed with the changing priorities of the crown, and local officials could find themselves perplexed by inconsistent orders from the center. Magistrates at all levels shared an interest in maintaining order around alehouses and strong drink, but the process of regulation created both a bond and a source of friction between towns and the crown.

The licensing and ordering of inns and alehouses became an increasingly important aspect of governance under the early Stuarts. It required borough corporations both to maintain adequate control in their own localities and to follow orders and communicate frequently with central authorities - especially the Privy Council. As Mark Hailwood has shown, the early seventeenth century saw a novel attention to regulating alehouses and the disorderly conviviality they might harbor, as concerns about order and stability grew. In many places, local officials had been enforcing order on alehouses well before the nationwide regulatory system took hold.[61] Yet the focus on alehouses and recreational drinking intensified under the early Stuarts, and national statutes, proclamations, and orders proliferated. Multiple statutes and an extensive royal proclamation in 1619 ensured that alehouse regulation would be central to the work of government for borough magistrates in the period.[62]

National regulations for licensing and controlling alehouses were carried out by local officials, both rural and urban, but they had special resonance to borough authorities. Inns and alehouses (as well as other food and drink trades) played a vital role in urban life, and their regulation constituted a critical element of early modern governance. James Brown, writing about alehouses in the town

---

[59] The same is true of inns and taverns, but these were less regulated by central authority, in part due to their generally better-off clientele. Mark Hailwood, *Alehouses and Good Fellowship in Early Modern England* (Woodbridge, 2014), p. 57.
[60] Hailwood, *Alehouses and Good Fellowship*, pp. 24-6, 54, 59, 76. Hailwood points out that the regulations went beyond simply suppressing disorderly alehouses to restraining recreational drinking and conviviality in general among the poor.
[61] Hailwood, *Alehouses and Good Fellowship*, pp. 27-8.
[62] 1 Jac. I, c. 9; 4 Jac. I c. 4; 4 Jac. I, c. 5; 7 Jac. I, c. 10; 21 Jac. I, c. 7; 1 Car. I, c. 4; 3 Car. 1, c. 4; Larkin and Hughes (eds), *Stuart Royal Proclamations*, vol. 1, pp. 409-13.

URBAN GOVERNMENT AND THE EARLY STUART STATE

of Southampton, argues that alehouse regulation was, in fact, a key element of state formation in early modern England.[63] It connected in intricate ways with many aspects of social policy: concern for the well-being of the "impotent" poor and control and correction of the "sturdy" poor; provision of sufficient food and drink for all of the king's subjects; suppression of drunkenness and the sexual license that often accompanied it; and fear of disorder and tumult by common people. These problems affected alehouses whether rural or urban, but they presented particular challenges in the context of early modern towns.[64] Urban spaces contained multitudes of poor people who relied on alehouses. Not only did the poorer sort need a place to purchase affordable drink, but beer-brewing provided income to poor inhabitants to supplement meager livings.[65] Towns often had large numbers of alehouses within limited bounds. Leicester, a town of a few thousand souls, was reported "by credible information" to have "8 score alehouses in the Town," while Plymouth, a busy port town, listed 127 licensed tipplers and alehouse keepers.[66] Reading's mayor disciplined dozens of unlicensed alehouse keepers in 1622-23. A Nottingham jury in 1619 found that "every nook of the back side suffered tipplers."[67] Alehouses presented an accepted danger, as sites of disorder as well as necessities of urban life.

Regulation and control of alehouses formed a significant part of governance for mayors and their deputies.[68] They were responsible to suppress disorderly alehouses and to ensure that only townspeople of good behavior received licenses to keep alehouses; from these, town officials took recognizances which they reported to the crown. Magistrates also enforced order on those who frequented alehouses, imposing discipline against drunkenness.[69] Complaints about excessive tippling and alehouse haunting in several towns reveal that unlicensed brewing and alehouse-keeping was endemic, despite regulation efforts. John Ivie, the godly mayor of Salisbury during the 1627 plague there, vigorously suppressed all of the town's alehouses ("fourscore, licensed and not") during this crisis by refusing to renew their licenses and threatening those who sold illicitly with gaol. Officials in the small town of Dunwich, "considering well" upon the "needless multitude of alehouses and tippling houses within this

---

[63] James Brown, "Alehouse Licensing and State Formation in Early Modern England," in J. Herring, et al. (eds), *Intoxication and Society: Problematic Pleasures of Drugs and Alcohol* (Basingstoke, 2013), pp. 110-11, 127.

[64] On alehouses, see Peter Clark, *The English Alehouse: A Social History, 1200-1830* (London, 1983); and Hailwood, *Alehouses and Good Fellowship*, esp. chapters 1 and 2 on regulation and authority.

[65] See, for instance, YCA, B.33, fol. 184.

[66] *RBL*, vol. 4, p. 196; TNA, SP16/300, fol. 74.

[67] Guilding (ed.), *Reading Records*, vol. 2, pp. 114-15, 105; *RBNott*, vol. 4, p. 361.

[68] W.J. Connor (ed.), *The Southampton Mayor's Book of 1606-1608*, Southampton Records Series, vol. 21 (Southampton, 1978), pp. 69, 74, 108, 113; *RBNott*, vol. 4, pp. 336, 373; *RBL*, vol. 4, pp. 160, 192-3; Bacon, *Annalls of Ipsw'che*, p. 557; HHC, BRB3, pp. 27, 177.

[69] Connor (ed.), *Southampton Mayor's Book*, p. 75; *RBNott*, vol. 4, pp. 367-8; Bacon, *Annalls of Ipsw'che*, p. 429; YCA, B.34, fol. 87.

GOVERNING POVERTY AND DISORDER

corporation" determined to suppress all but eight of them. The borough court in Nottingham heard multiple complaints and presentments for the "infinite number of alehouses" in town which, despite attention to them at both assizes and local sessions, remained unreformed.[70] Borough magistrates had discretion over the number of alehouses and the suppression of those deemed unnecessary, but in doing so they had to balance local needs, especially the dependence of poor townsmen on alehouse-keeping to make a living, against the requirements of regulation.

Beer itself served up another problem of order. Magistrates had authority over this second staff of life, from who could brew it to how strong it could be.[71] Brewing of overly strong beer, above the assize, was a perpetual complaint against both master brewers and the alehouse-keepers who brewed on their own, licensed or not. Strong beer had two strikes against it, in the eyes of authority. It led more quickly to drunkenness and disorder, and it also "wasted" barley and malt that might better be used to feed hungry townsmen. The latter caused particular concern during times of dearth. Brewing could also lead to conflict between licensed master brewers and others – often poor men and women – who brewed and served small amounts to make ends meet.[72] Though magistrates respected the privileges of freeman brewers, they also saw the value of small-scale brewing and alehouse-keeping, since it helped keep some inhabitants off the poor rates.[73] Maintaining control over brewing, as well as of alehouses and other purveyors, had important consequences for social and political order in England's towns.

Regulation of alehouses and brewing had special resonance for urban governance, since in many towns, brewers, as freemen of the corporation, frequently served in the governing body. Thus, magistrates had to enforce regulations around beer and ale upon themselves that may not always have been in a brewer's self-interest. Some members of the corporation of St. Albans in 1606 opposed local orders regarding tippling and alehouses because they suspected that Robert Woolley, a tavern owner and innkeeper as well as a former mayor and JP, had undue and self-serving influence over their creation and execution.[74] Members of Canterbury's corporation petitioned the Privy Council against one of their own JPs, Joseph Colfe, a brewer who allegedly, "for his own private gain," delivered beer and ale to victualers and alehouses that the mayor had

---

[70] Slack (ed.), *Poverty in Early-Stuart Salisbury*, p. 122; SA/I, EE6/1144/11 (Dunwich Account and Order Book), fol. 39v; *RBNott*, vol. 4, pp. 326, 336, 361, 369.

[71] WAAS, A.14 Box I, fols 69v, 70v, 123v; GA, GBR B3/1 (Gloucester Common Council Minutes, 1565–1632), fols 530v, 539; Guilding (ed.), *Reading Records*, vol. 2, p. 106.

[72] TNA, PC2/45, p. 402; Judith Bennett, *Ale, Beer, and Brewsters in England: Women's Work in a Changing World, 1300–1600* (Oxford, 1996), pp. 106–11.

[73] Hailwood, *Alehouses and Good Fellowship*, pp. 47, 52, 81; TNA, SP14/109, f. 140; YCA, B.33, fol. 184.

[74] HALS, St. Albans Borough Records, Off Acc 1162/312, fol. 90; Henry Chauncey, *The Historical Antiquities of Hertfordshire*, vol. 2 (London, 1826), p. 295.

URBAN GOVERNMENT AND THE EARLY STUART STATE

suppressed for disorder. The corporation removed Colfe from his aldermanship because of his behavior and his "violent and contemptuous" opposition to the rules.[75] Salisbury suffered serious conflict in the later 1620s as brewers in the corporation – particularly the powerful Mr. Robert Jole – opposed the town's management of brewing. Mayor John Ivie claimed that the brewers were "the first that began to rail" when he suppressed drink sellers during the 1627 plague.[76] The conflict in Salisbury, as in other towns, reflected religious division, as well; the more godly, like Ivie, condemned the intemperance associated with brewing and drink. In Lincoln's corporation, a 1619 Star Chamber case included accusations by "good honest and religious magistrates" that "papistical" magistrates brought "alehousekeepers, tipplers, Brownists, and other irreligious persons" into the civic government.[77] Ambivalence regarding brewers and magistracy became more pronounced over time, and as noted in Chapter 1, Colchester's charter of incorporation of 1635 explicitly excluded brewers from selection to the town council.[78]

Alehouse regulation also led to routine interaction with the crown. Central government's increasing focus on alehouses in the late sixteenth century, in response to the devastating dearth of the mid-1590s, continued into the early seventeenth for reasons both social and fiscal.[79] Rising numbers of poor people, combined with fears about the disorders of alehouses and the "waste" of barley that accompanied unregulated brewing, motivated regulation and control. Plans to clamp down on superfluous alehouses developed in both Westminster and Whitehall. In James's reign, parliament made or reaffirmed five statutes regulating the sale of beer and ale, the licensing of alehouses, and repressing the "Odious and Loathsome Sin of Drunkenness."[80] The pattern continued in Charles's reign, with two parliamentary statutes restraining tippling and alehouses.[81] Royal proclamations paralleled and reinforced statutes, promoting action on immediate problems, particularly in times of dearth. King James issued an extensive proclamation for alehouse regulation in January 1619, later echoed in King Charles's Book of Orders.[82] The Privy Council wrote directives

---

[75] APC 1617–19, p. 199.

[76] WSHC, Salisbury City Archive, G23/1/3 (Ledger Book, 1571–1640), fols 326v, 328, 328v, 329–330, 333; Slack, "Poverty and Politics in Salisbury," pp. 186–7; Slack, *Poverty in Early-Stuart Salisbury*, p. 122.

[77] TNA, STAC8/98/9 (Callis v. Ellis); Slack, "Poverty and Politics in Salisbury," pp. 183–6.

[78] Colchester Borough, *The Charters and Letters Patent Granted to the Borough by Richard I and Succeeding Sovereigns* (Colchester, [1904]), p. 92. See above, p. 42.

[79] See Fletcher, *Reform in the Provinces*, pp. 229–52, and Clark, *The English Alehouse*, for more on alehouse regulation throughout the realm.

[80] 1 Jac. I, c. 9; 4 Jac. I, c.4, c.5; 7 Jac. I, c.10; 21 Jac. I, c.7 (*Statutes of the Realm*, vol. 4, pt. 2, pp. 1026, 1141, 1142–3, 1167, 1216).

[81] 1 Car. I, c.4; 3 Car. I, c.4 (*Statutes of the Realm*, vol. 5, pp. 3, 26–7).

[82] S.K. Roberts, "Alehouses, Brewing, and Government under the Early Stuarts," *Southern History* 2 (1980), 46–7; Larkin and Hughes (eds), *Stuart Royal Proclamations*, vol. 1, pp. 409–13; *Orders and Directions together with a Commission for the better Administration of Justice and More*

GOVERNING POVERTY AND DISORDER

and encouraged local officials to enforce the rules, periodically sending letters to mayors urging more enthusiastic execution and prosecution. Most directives involved eliminating unnecessary alehouses and requiring licensure – backed by recognizance bonds with two sureties – of those that remained.[83] Urban magistrates found themselves increasingly responsible to carry out both parliamentary statutes and royal orders regarding alehouses in the early Stuart period.

The varying intensity of enforcement of alehouse regulation across James's reign and the changing nature of communication between towns and the crown on the issue demonstrates a complex mix of cooperation and strain. The first major wave of enforcement came in 1608–09, when James's government, concerned about dearth, issued new orders for grain and alehouses.[84] Local officials were to suppress unnecessary alehouses, ensure proper licensing of those authorized, and make returns to the crown of the license fees.[85] Many corporate towns complied readily with these new orders. A partial account from November 1609, detailing the "counties, cities, and borough towns" that had paid their fines for alehouses, lists thirty-eight towns in twenty counties that had paid their fines, ranging from 43s. for Hythe to £146 8s for London. Most towns paid something in between, with substantial county towns like Leicester, Lincoln, and Worcester paying from £23 to £29.[86] At the same time, central administrators bemoaned the lack of accountability in this service. They noted that some counties, including Shropshire, Gloucestershire, Westmorland, Lancashire, and Cheshire, "have nothing for this year, nor in the succeeding year, nor any city or corporation within any of them." The assize judges called Hereford's mayor and magistrates to account in 1609 for having done little or nothing regarding unlicensed alehouses in their town, while a group of clerks of the peace, solicited to advise the Council, averred that the licensing was properly done "in all counties more or less, except in the Towns."[87] Inconsistent enforcement by the Privy Council allowed some localities, particularly more distant ones in the north and west, to avoid making the required returns altogether.

Since cities and towns had large numbers of alehouses, the crown had a stake – in both financial and governance terms – to ensure that urban

---

Perfect Information of His Majestie (London, 1630). These were in addition to a 1608 proclamation regarding the use of malt and grain by brewers and alehouse keepers. Larkin and Hughes (eds), *Stuart Royal Proclamations*, vol. 1, p. 200-1.

[83] Fletcher, *Reform in the Provinces*, p. 231; Larkin and Hughes (eds), *Stuart Royal Proclamations*, vol. 1, p. 411; Roberts, "Alehouses," p. 50.

[84] The crown issued proclamations regarding dearth of grain in June 1608 and regarding maltsters, brewers and alehouse keepers in December 1608. Larkin and Hughes (eds), *Stuart Royal Proclamations*, vol. 1, pp. 186-8, 200-6.

[85] *CSPD 1603–1610*, pp. 411, 434, 560; BL, Lansdowne MS 166, fols 252, 254, 269; *RBL*, vol. 4, p. 74.

[86] BL, Lansdowne MS 166, fols 254-6.

[87] BL, Lansdowne MS 166, fol. 257; Herefordshire Archive and Records Centre, Miscellaneous Papers 1600-1644, O/U 123, #12; TNA, SP14/49, fol. 70.

URBAN GOVERNMENT AND THE EARLY STUART STATE

governments all across the realm complied with the orders, but patchy record-keeping undermined central intentions. A note to the Privy Council regarding alehouse licenses in 1609 asks that all sheriffs be required to make "a perfect certificate how many corporate towns and market towns there be within their several Shires, that we may be the better able to charge the accountants with such sums of money as they are of right to be charged withal."[88] Central government understood the importance of towns to alehouse policy and the revenue it generated, but also appears to have been hazy on some basic practical details.

That said, the Privy Council at times used strong tactics to ensure that borough officials heeded central directives, with both order and revenue for the crown at stake. The magistrates of York found themselves the unwilling target of the Board's ire in 1609. In November, the lord mayor received a "hasty and galloping letter" from Mr. Christopher Brook, York's deputy recorder then in London, bearing a message of the Council's unhappiness concerning a "great affront" done by the city. The urgency of the matter resonates in Brook's letter:

> ... Our city, as it is said, of all others both northward and southward hath done nothing about the alehouses, and whereas Hull and Newcastle and other towns have made some return of a revenue, we of York, a City of Note, that the king loves and favors have used contemptuous negligence in that business. These were the very words, as I remember.[89]

Brook warned York's magistrates of the Board's threat that, if they did not make a satisfactory response within sixteen days, pursuivants would be sent for the mayor and three or four aldermen to make personal appearance before the Board to answer for it. "The matter is so ill taken," Brook said, "especially by my Lord Treasurer, that something must be done in it, I know not what to counsel in particular."[90] The warning had the desired effect. After reading out the king's directions regarding alehouses, the lord mayor and his brethren quickly determined that, although they had taken some action earlier, they must do more to satisfy the king. The magistrates of York worried that this rigorous enforcement would harm some of the poorest inhabitants who lived only on alehouse keeping, but the Board's vehement orders could not be denied.[91] The force of central authority overwhelmed the subtleties of York's local situation.

In the later 1610s, the crown again focused attention on alehouse licensing with particular impact in corporate boroughs. The renewed interest came from the king himself. In his 1616 speech in Star Chamber, James singled out the abundance of alehouses as an evil requiring immediate reformation for the debauchery and crime they fostered.[92] Council members and assize judges

---

[88] BL, Lansdowne MS 166, fol. 269.
[89] YCA, B.33, fol. 182.
[90] YCA, B.33, fol. 182v. Lord Treasurer Salisbury was York's high steward.
[91] YCA, B.33, fols 183v-184.
[92] C. McIlwain (ed.), *The Political Works of James I* (Cambridge, MA, 1918), pp. 342-3. James also highlighted bridge repair and regulation of new building in London.

GOVERNING POVERTY AND DISORDER

busied themselves to ensure that town magistrates did their duties.[93] While many borough governors shared an interest in suppressing drunkenness, those not quick enough to carry out the orders found themselves called to account. Rowland Pusey, mayor of Leicester in 1618, wrote to the town's recorder that he had been "threatened hard by the Judge to have a fine on my head if I did not take a course against Alehouses." Saffron Walden's magistrates felt the wrath of the Privy Council for allowing "the most detestable vice of drunkenness" to grow, chiefly due to the town officers' neglect and connivance, "as the like is hardly to be founde in any other incorporate towne within this kingdome."[94] Mayors and bailiffs, as the king's officers in the towns, were expected to enforce alehouse regulations strictly and felt the force of higher authorities if they did not.

But the crown's regulations also had baser economic motivations. As fiscal pressures on James's government mounted, the crown experimented widely with schemes intended to enhance royal revenues. The licensing of alehouses and inns offered a ready revenue stream, and the crown increasingly turned toward projectors and patents for fee collection. This complicated alehouse regulation, making what was ostensibly a regulatory regime for keeping order and reducing drunkenness into a money-making scheme for the crown.[95] Patents went to various gentlemen for collecting fees for alehouse and inn licensing, for issuing of new licenses, and for farming forfeitures of sureties and bonds for alehouses.[96] The proclamation of January 1619 reinforced the role of patentees for preventing unlicensed alehouses and seizing forfeited recognizances.[97] No longer simply making certificates of alehouses in their jurisdiction to the sheriff or Privy Council, corporations now had to negotiate with a changing constellation of patentees who rarely understood (or cared about) the complexities of local situations. Patentees could muddle or work at cross purposes to the decisions of borough magistrates or even challenge corporate charters.

The stepped-up enforcement of alehouse regulation, especially when mediated through patentees, led to confusion and frustrations over governance, putting borough magistrates into an awkward position. The town of Leicester offers a telling case in point. Mayor Rowland Pusey, having being threatened with fines for insufficiently suppressing alehouses, had strong motivation to carry out the crown's orders. Yet he found himself stymied and overturned due to confusing orders from London and the interference of the crown's patentees for licensing. According to Pusey's "private letter" to the recorder of Leicester in May 1618,

[93] For instance, assize judge Sir Henry Hobart was asked to assist Leicester's magistrates with uncooperative alehouse keepers in that town. *RBL*, vol. 4, p. 177.
[94] *RBL*, vol. 4, p. 174; *APC 1615–16*, p. 179.
[95] For further discussion of the Jacobean move toward projects and patents in regard to social and economic policy, see Slack, *From Reformation to Improvement*, pp. 69–74; Joan Thirsk, *Economic Policy and Projects* (Oxford, 1978).
[96] E.g., *CSPD 1611–18*, pp. 248, 439, 441, 449; *APC 1619–21*, p. 166.
[97] Larkin and Hughes (eds), *Stuart Royal Proclamations*, vol. 1, pp. 409–12.

URBAN GOVERNMENT AND THE EARLY STUART STATE

he had begun to call alehouse-keepers into question and impose fines on them when someone from the Crown Office arrived in town with a "sassary" [*certiorari*] removing all recognizances that had been taken from alehouses in the last year and requiring new ones. While Pusey noted this had never been done before, he tried to execute the orders and swear out new recognizances, fulfilling his duty as chief magistrate and the king's deputy in the town. But the very day that he received the *certiorari* and new orders, a patentee came to Leicester armed with a warrant for inns and alehouses, summoning many of the poor alehouse keepers to appear in London to have their alehouses made into inns. Mayor Pusey complained that he had already suppressed some of the alehouse-keepers so summoned, due to their disorder. The actions of the patentee undermined the mayor's authority, "so now the case is so with me that I do not know well how to proceed any way." In the confusion, various inns and alehouses refused to have bonds taken, and "it maketh occasion of a general exclamation of the Town by reason of this new and hard proceeding with them."[98]

Pusey's concern was both for his own authority and the interests of his town. Annoyed by the mixed messages from London, he also feared the undoing of poor men, who were bound for more than they were worth and likely to forfeit their bonds. The recorder's response to this litany of trouble is unknown, but Pusey's mayoral successor, Nicholas Gillott, and the town's JPs wrote to assize judge Sir Henry Hobart a few months later, complaining that the patentee licensed alehouse keepers previously suppressed by Leicester's magistrates. They asked Hobart to help ensure that no alehouse or innkeeper receive a license without a certificate from the town's mayor and justices as to their good behavior and suitability.[99] For Pusey, Gillott, and their fellows in Leicester, the crown's outsourcing of alehouse regulation posed a threat to their authority as the king's deputies as well as the good order of the town.

Patentees may have been an efficient means of promoting royal policy and raising revenue for the crown, but their intermediary position caused frustration. As a commentator writing from Coventry remarked, the grant of recognizance forfeitures to patentees would incentivize offenses to line private pockets, a "marvelous great disorder in the commonwealth." Michael Purefoy, parliamentary burgess for Nottingham, raised the complaint in the 1621 Parliament that alehouse patentees "did extremely offend" and "took the upper hand of the mayor."[100] In Chester, the pressing of alehouse regulation caused serious tensions in 1619, provoking grumbling, even among members of the corporation. One common councilman, shoemaker Thomas Ince, made "outrageous intemperate and irreverend speeches" regarding regulation of alehouses, which

---

[98] *RBL*, vol. 4, pp. 174–5.
[99] *RBL*, vol. 4, pp. 175, 176.
[100] TNA, SP14/109, fol. 28 (Sir Clement Throckmorton to Thomas Wilson, 9 May 1619); W. Notestein, F. Relf, and H. Simpson (eds), *Commons Debates 1621* (New Haven, CT, 1935), vol. 3, p. 83.

GOVERNING POVERTY AND DISORDER

he believed was "too much urged" in the city; the corporation removed him from his place for his outburst.[101] Patentees raised resentment in many towns.

Beyond general frustration, the patents also called chartered privileges into question. Chester's mayor, Sir Randle Mainwaring, wrote to the Privy Council in June 1619, complaining of the untenable situation created by the recent royal proclamation regarding alehouse licensing. He reported that the alehouse-keepers of Chester refused to be bound according to the king's proclamation, an act of disobedience that the mayor could not fail to report to the Board. But the mayor clearly sympathized with the basis of the alehouse-keepers' refusal, grounded on the city's corporate charter. Chester's alehouse-keepers could not be bound, they claimed, because according to the charter, all forfeitures of recognizances must belong to the city.[102] The reversion of forfeitures to a patentee under the proclamation, if honored, would overthrow corporate privilege. This placed the mayor in a difficult position, pressed by his dual responsibility to uphold local liberties and central authority. He could scarcely allow alehouse-keepers to refuse royal commands, and he had a strong incentive, as well as a duty as the king's deputy, to ensure that he carried out the crown's wishes and maintained local order. At the same time, he was bound to uphold the city's charter against threats like those of the patentees. And unlike the patentees, a mayor had real knowledge of local problems and people. In Chester, Mayor Mainwaring knew – and informed the Board – that the suppression of alehouses would impact many poor men who lived only on their alehouse-keeping.[103] Suppression of alehouses would throw these men deeper into poverty, forcing the city to relieve them and exacerbating rather than abating Chester's social problems. Mainwaring asked for the Board's direction regarding suppression, but he made clear to the Privy Council the challenges to local order and liberties that the situation presented him. As in Leicester, Chester's experience illustrates how the crown's strategy for alehouse regulation in this period raised problems of governance for borough corporations.

These strains over alehouse licensing fit within a broader pattern that caused consternation in towns across England in the later 1610s. Royal policy in this period, linking reforming zeal with a quest for enhanced revenues through patents and monopolies, had a direct impact on England's corporate towns. As shown in Chapter 2, alehouse licenses represented one of several aspects of governance – along with victualing, market measures, and others – wherein royal patents crossed corporate liberties.[104] The king's financial troubles sparked entrepreneurial patentees to find novel ways to raise revenues, using patents and legal processes that undermined or challenged borough government.

---

[101] M. Groombridge (ed.), Chester City Council Minutes, 1603–1642, Lancashire and Cheshire Record Society, vol. 106 (Blackpool, 1956), p. 98.
[102] TNA, SP14/109, fol. 140 (Randle Mainwaring to Privy Council, 3 June 1619).
[103] TNA, SP14/109, fol. 140.
[104] Larkin and Hughes (eds), Stuart Royal Proclamations, vol. 1, pp. 409–13.

URBAN GOVERNMENT AND THE EARLY STUART STATE

Particularly pernicious was patentees' use of quo warranto to force corporations to compound for licensing fees. In just four years, between 1615 and 1619, over seventy quo warranto informations, largely involving inns and alehouses, issued from King's Bench against borough corporations.[105] In Michaelmas term 16 James (autumn 1618) alone, quo warranto was initiated against the mayors or bailiffs of York, Beverley, Doncaster, Hull, Leeds, and Scarborough in Yorkshire, as well as a dozen or more towns in other counties.[106] Borough officials struggled with the expense of lawsuits in London, the danger to corporate liberties associated with quo warranto, and the annoyance of patentees having a hand in governance that urban magistrates believed rightly belonged to them. Town authorities accepted the crown's aim of regulation, but the means of execution had negative consequences for corporate boroughs.[107]

The loud outcry in the 1621 Parliament against patents and monopolies in general, and the king's response to it, squashed the most egregious abuses of alehouse licensing of the late 1610s.[108] The crown's regulatory policy nevertheless continued, its focus shifting from licensing itself to the broader problem of the relationship between alehouses and brewing to the price and availability of grain.[109] Throughout the 1620s, the Privy Council paid episodic attention to alehouses, strong beer, and brewing, most sharply at the moments of greatest economic dislocation. The serious slump in the clothing trade brought unemployment, poverty, and misery to many English towns in the early 1620s.[110] In the depths of the crisis, the Council issued orders to all justices of peace throughout England and Wales in October 1622 aimed specifically at ensuring provision of markets with grain that the poor could afford. They identified the "waste" of barley in brewing of strong beer and the disorder of excessive alehouses as the key evils leading to high prices. Their goal to suppress alehouses and manage the strength of beer would relieve "the poorer sort of his Majesties subjectes (who are like to suffer the greatest want)."[111] The Board initially addressed their orders only to the "counties of England and Wales," with letters directed to county JPs, suggesting that the separate jurisdiction of towns was not at the top of their minds when considering the problem. By December, however, they had issued similar letters specifically to corporate towns, which

[105] These numbers are based on an analysis of TNA, KB29/259–265.
[106] TNA, KB29/265, mm. cxxiiii–cxxv.
[107] See also Slack, "Books of Orders," p. 15.
[108] TNA, SP14/121, fol. 229 ("The patents which his Majesty in his own judgment did condemn," June 1621). The patents for inns and alehouses topped this list.
[109] Notestein, Relf, and Simpson (eds), *Commons Debates 1621*, vol. 2, p. 182; Larkin and Hughes (eds), *Stuart Royal Proclamations*, vol. 1, pp. 502–5; APC *1619–21*, pp. 97, 112, *1621–23*, pp. 87–8, 154.
[110] Beier, "Poverty and Progress," p. 234.
[111] APC *1621–23*, p. 337.

134

GOVERNING POVERTY AND DISORDER

felt the effects of the economic slump most keenly and where poor people and alehouses abounded.[112]

Towns responded relatively robustly, if not always swiftly. Between January and May 1623, at least thirty-seven towns and cities, including London, certified their activities in suppressing alehouses, controlling the strength of beer, and providing grain for the poor.[113] Most certificates, though of varying specificity, reported that they had done as the Privy Council required: mayors reduced the number of alehouses and regulated the price and strength of ale and beer. Local records also indicate increased activity. Corporation minutes in towns like Reading, York, Hull, and Leicester report mayors summoning brewers, innholders, and alehouse-keepers to hear the Council's letters and acting to suppress disorders of various sorts.[114] At the same time, borough officials executed the Council's orders with discretion and sensitivity to local circumstances. Mayors' returns show a wide latitude as to how many alehouses should be suppressed and how to define "unnecessary." Liverpool's mayor certified that he had suppressed as many alehouses "as we thought fit" for a port town with many travelers; Exeter's mayor did the same.[115] The mayor of Wycombe reduced the number of alehouses in his town from twenty-one to nine; the mayor of Banbury reported closing one-third and the mayor of Ripon one-half of all alehouses in their respective towns. The mayor of Hull, in contrast, vaguely reported suppressing "such of them as we thought unmeet," focusing his certificate mostly on grain supply.[116] Given the intensity of this economic crisis in many of England's towns, borough magistrates shared the interest of central government in relieving and controlling their poorest inhabitants by carrying out this policy. They also kept local circumstances and authority in mind as they did so.

This tension between central priorities and local interests shaped the execution of alehouse, grain, and drink regulation in James's reign. Inconsistent policy and enforcement sometimes frustrated urban magistrates, who had to balance local concerns. The crown's use of patentees in the late 1610s proved particularly irksome and difficult to navigate. At the same time, borough

---

[112] *APC 1621–23*, p. 387.

[113] TNA, SP14/137, fols 41, 60, SP14/138, fols 18, 45, 68, 72, 75, 90, 91, 92, 96, 104, 116, 117, 119, 120, 121, 136, 142, 143, 144, 145, 166, 167, SP14/139, fols 3, 31, 47, 92, 104, 121, SP14/140, fols 11, 14, 23, SP14/142, fols 41, 76, SP14/143, fol. 51, SP14/144, fol. 41. While it is possible that not all of the certificates remain among the State Papers, several major cities and county towns, including York, Bristol, Lincoln, and Worcester, among others, do not appear to have made returns. Returns from some smaller towns may have been subsumed under those of the counties.

[114] Guilding (ed.), *Reading Records*, vol. 2, pp. 106, 117; HHC, BRB3, p. 177; YCA, B.34, fol. 253; *RBL*, vol. 4, pp. 200–1.

[115] TNA, SP14/138, fols 91, 104.

[116] TNA, SP14/139, fols 121, 3, SP14/138, fol. 136, SP14/138, fol. 96.

URBAN GOVERNMENT AND THE EARLY STUART STATE

governors largely shared the crown's goals, and they engaged actively with the state to suppress the disorder that alehouses could represent.

The Caroline Book of Orders and its impact

Central enforcement during James's reign, while inconsistent, laid a groundwork for the towns' experience when Charles's government redoubled efforts to resolve social ills and stem disorder in the realm.[117] By the time the Caroline Book of Orders came to be issued in 1630-31, town magistrates were well-practiced at both dealing with the interconnected problems of alehouses, grain, and disorder, and with responding to central directives while protecting local privileges. The impact of the Book of Orders has been debated, and historians differ on the extent to which the Orders represented an unwelcome intrusion. Some have seen the Book of Orders as a contributor to breakdown between local government and the crown in the 1630s.[118] Other scholars have contested this view, emphasizing both the shared concern over poverty, dearth, and alehouses at local and central levels and the Privy Council's moderate enforcement. Paul Slack has argued that the Book of Orders created no deep rifts on matters of principle among county JPs, though local authorities did at times chafe at the means of enforcement. Brian Quintrell likewise states that the Orders were not intended as an "instrument of oppression" on the localities nor were they pressed in such a way as to elicit serious resistance.[119] Most studies of the Book of Orders have focused on the counties and the gentry JPs' responses, but the problems addressed by the Orders had special resonance in cities and towns. As they had in earlier periods of central focus on poverty and dearth, town magistrates found ways to adapt the Book of Orders to the particulars of local situations even as the crown proceeded with novel rigor and persistence. Provincial town governors by and large appreciated the goals of central policy regarding poverty and order in the 1630s, as it helped them address problems of order that oppressed towns disproportionately, but they did not always welcome the stepped-up scrutiny.

Beginning in 1629, widespread fears of dearth throughout England led to concerns about the distribution of sufficient food, the increase in numbers

[117] For the origins and purposes of the Caroline Books of Orders, see Slack, "Books of Orders," and B.W. Quintrell, "The Making of Charles I's Book of Orders," *English Historical Review* 95 (1980), 553-72. On their enforcement, see Henrik Langelüddecke, "'Patchy and Spasmodic'? The Response of Justices of the Peace to Charles I's Book of Orders," *English Historical Review* 113 (1997), 1231-48.

[118] W.K. Jordan, *Philanthropy in England, 1480-1660: A Study in the Changing Pattern of English Social Aspirations* (New York, 1959), pp. 134-5; John Morrill, *The Revolt of the Provinces: Conservatives and Radicals in the English Civil War* (London, 1976), p. 22.

[119] Slack, "Books of Orders," p. 15; Quintrell, "The Making of Charles I's Book of Orders," pp. 571-2.

GOVERNING POVERTY AND DISORDER

of the poor, and the general disorder associated with poverty and drink. Shortages in 1629 led to localized disorder, including grain riots in the town of Maldon.[120] In the sixth year of his reign, Charles issued twenty-one proclamations addressing various ills; five of these specifically concerned poverty and food supply.[121] To confront this collection of social dangers, the crown issued a series of Books of Orders and proclamations requiring magistrates to attend to matters of poor relief, social control, and food and drink regulation. While not a uniquely urban problem, dearth had significant effects on urban dwellers, who had to purchase most or all of their food. The "Orders appointed by His Maiestie to be straitly obserued, for the preuenting and remedying of the dearth of graine and victual" (1630) tacitly acknowledged the particular role of towns and cities in these interrelated problems. The document first addressed the lord mayor of London and the mayors and chief officers of all towns corporate, before mentioning the justices of peace in the counties.[122] Likewise, the Privy Council simultaneously sent out two sets of letters for the execution of the orders, one to the "Citties and Townes Corporate" and another to the sheriffs of the counties of England and Wales. The former included a detailed list of the cities that stood in their own right and the towns within each county.[123] The orders show none of the confusion about corporate boroughs exhibited by the center twenty years earlier. Mayors received specific authority to carry out the orders in their own jurisdictions, making clear that they, and not the county JPs, were to search markets, regulate alehouses and victualling houses, prevent the export of grain, and ensure proper provision for the poor.

While the Privy Council entrusted mayors and corporate officials with executing the orders, the enforcement push also brought out tensions between elements of local government. At heart lay a jurisdictional struggle between corporations and county authorities. For instance, the mayor, jurats, and inhabitants of Rye complained to the Board that the Sussex justices restrained the town's regular grain buyers from purchasing corn in the countryside to bring into the town.[124] More often, county justices, resentful of town magistrates' independence from county oversight on these matters, reported mayors to the Privy Council and assize judges for laxity. The JPs of Staffordshire wrote to the Board in April 1631 that while the county took good measures, there were "great abuses" in Lichfield, Stafford, and Tamworth, corporate towns that county justices had no authority to enter.[125] Similarly, the assize judges in Suffolk wrote

---

[120] John Walter, "Grain Riots and Popular Attitudes to the Law: Maldon and the Crisis of 1629," in J. Brewer and J. Styles (eds), *An Ungovernable People: The English and Their Law in the Seventeenth and Eighteenth Centuries* (New Brunswick, NJ, 1980), pp. 47–84.

[121] Larkin (ed.), *Stuart Royal Proclamations*, vol. 2, pp. 256–313.

[122] *Orders appointed by His Maiestie to be straitly obserued, for the preuenting and remedying of the dearth of graine and victuall* (London, 1630).

[123] *APC 1630–31*, pp. 213–15.

[124] *APC 1630–31*, p. 309.

[125] TNA, SP16/189, fol. 2. They reported that some of the magistrates and "best sort" in the

URBAN GOVERNMENT AND THE EARLY STUART STATE

the county's corporate boroughs in March 1632, claiming they had received numerous complaints about the shortcomings of corporate towns. "[W]ithin the corporations there are many disorders by an over multitude of Alehouses and excess of drunkenness and impunity of rogues and vagabonds which happeneth the rather because within these corporations they have Justices of Peace of their own body, and the Justices of the county do not intermeddle within the limits of the corporations."[126] For Suffolk's assize judges and JPs, this was as much about jurisdiction as it was alehouse regulation. Borough corporations were inherently suspect, not fully integrated into the governance of the commonwealth. Other authorities saw the separateness of corporations as a weakness in the state.

Another challenge for borough corporations in carrying out the Book of Orders lay in the conflict of interest of magistrates who themselves were brewers, whose business clashed with the requirements of the service. Keith Wrightson has pointed out that county justices often had their own motives - such as local patronage networks - for carrying out the orders regarding brewing and alehouses with a light hand.[127] Yet in towns and cities, some magistrates had direct business interests in what was being regulated, resulting in ambivalence or backwardness. William Salter, a brewer and JP in Stamford, fell afoul of the corporation as well as the Privy Council in 1631 for just this reason. He opposed the execution of the Orders and also continued to sell beer and ale at prices beyond those set by the alderman (the chief officer) of Stamford, "to the great oppression of the poorer sort." For this he was convented before the Privy Council and imprisoned in the Fleet. The Lords first ordered him sequestered from his office as borough JP, eventually requiring the corporation of Stamford to remove him from office completely. The Board viewed Salter's miscarriage as a symbol of larger problems in the locality. Not just Salter, but many brewers in Stamford had offended against the Orders. The Council thus required the alderman of Stamford to take recognizances in the amount of £100 from all brewers to sell their beer at the approved price and to be "very careful" in the future execution of all of the orders.[128] Salter's behavior was particularly egregious; rarely did borough magistrates thwart central directives so overtly. The events in Stamford indicate the complicated motivations of local actors in responding to the Book of Orders.

Stamford's case also reveals that significant tension, while not common, could arise between local officials and central authorities over the regulatory regime of the Book of Orders. Stamford's town clerk, Richard Butcher, provoked the Privy Council for promoting borough liberties in the face of central regulation. Butcher, an innkeeper, protested the treatment of Salter in being summoned by

---

towns were themselves "engrossers of corn, maltsters, and alehouse keepers."
[126] SA/I, EE6/1144/11, fol. 39v.
[127] Keith Wrightson, "Alehouses, Order, and Reformation in Rural England, 1590-1660," in Eileen Yeo and Stephen Yeo (eds), *Popular Culture and Class Conflict 1590-1914: Explorations in the History of Labour and Leisure* (Brighton, 1981), p. 3.
[128] TNA, PC2/41, pp. 536-7; *CSPD 1631-33*, pp. 194, 321.

GOVERNING POVERTY AND DISORDER

messenger to the Board. He allegedly made a principled defense of the town's privileges and connected them to the broader liberties of the subject. According to witnesses, Butcher said "the town of Stamford and other towns were as well governed by the constitutions of the same as the body of the Parliament (of wise men that should be) ever governed the Common Weal." He touched the royal prerogative by saying, "the King by Magna Carta ought not to fetch up any man by a messenger, and that the king had promised the contrary."[129] Judging these words likely to "do much hurt and breed disorder in a populous Town, if the same were not severely punished," the Board committed Butcher to the Fleet and demanded that the corporation remove him from the office of town clerk.[130] The combined impact of these perceived misbehaviors prompted the Privy Council to reflect on the larger problem of having magistrates involved in the drink trades serving in public office. The Board declared it "to be full of inconveniency and also much prejudicial to the public service that any Innkeeper, Common Brewer, or other Victualer should be a town clerk, or Justice of Peace, in a town where he keepeth victualling or brewing."[131] Just months later a prohibition against brewers and innkeepers serving as aldermen appeared as a clause in the corporate charter of Colchester.[132] Central enforcement brought out concern for local liberties, which in turn gave rise to further regulation concerning the drink trades.

Though local agendas sometimes rubbed against such enforcement, borough magistrates also saw the benefit of central policy when it helped to reinforce their authority and address pressing problems during times of want. This tension comes through in the returns of certificates by town officials, which show responses ranging from vigorous to lukewarm. Between April and December 1631, certificates from borough officials reporting measures for poor relief, including alehouse suppression and grain provision, for nearly three dozen towns and cities found their way into the State Papers. While a reasonably robust response in the first months after the Orders' release, it was hardly an overwhelming one. Some certificates came from substantial places, counties in their own right like York and Hereford, but many came from more modest places like Bridgewater and Taunton.[133] Borough officers varied widely in their

---

[129] TNA, PC2/42, pp. 481–2, SP16/251, fol. 68 (Information of recorder of Stamford against Richard Butcher, 27 November 1633).

[130] TNA, PC2/42, p. 482. The corporation complied in removing Butcher. He was restored to the office in 1663, though he died within a year of regaining the position. John Drakard, *The History of Stamford in the County of Lincoln* (Stamford, 1822), p. 107.

[131] TNA, PC2/42, p. 482. Highlighting the sometimes-shared interests between the godly and Charles's government, Thomas Scott of Canterbury, a godly thorn in the side of the Caroline regime, would have fully agreed with the Board's position. Thomas Scott, "A Discourse of Polletique and Civell Honor," in G.D. Scull (ed.), *Dorothea Scott, otherwise Gotherson and Hogben of Egerton House, Kent, 1611–1680* (Oxford, 1883), pp. 183–4.

[132] *Colchester Charters*, p. 92. See Chapter 1 for more on this charter.

[133] TNA, SP16/188, fols 19, 23, 91, 123, 138, 190, SP16/189, fols 14, 23, 70, 96, 118, 119, 128, SP16/190, fols 32, 96, 130, SP16/191, fols 29, 46, 68, 86, 88, 111, SP16/192, fols 18,

URBAN GOVERNMENT AND THE EARLY STUART STATE

diligence and enthusiasm. As in earlier periods of enforcement, some towns apparently made no returns – or at least none that came back to the Council – while others reported back multiple times. The mayor of Taunton proved especially keen. He made six certificates to the sheriff of Somerset between May and November 1631.[134] As late as 1634, the Board received certificates from mayors or bailiffs in Bodmin, Monmouth, Great Yarmouth, Shrewsbury, Bridgenorth, and Taunton, who were busily relieving the poor, apprenticing children, and punishing vagrants.[135] The bailiffs of the Suffolk market town of Eye reported their diligent attempts to carry out the orders, though they noted some inhabitants' backwardness.[136] Overall, reporting by borough authorities remained inconsistent, despite Privy Council efforts to remind and chastise.

Local records provide a brighter picture, though again enthusiasm varied. While no certificate from the town of Reading appears in the State Papers, local records show that the corporation read out the king's proclamation and Book of Orders on 23 October 1630 and established a committee to inquire into measures for the poor. This may have been a ploy to postpone real action, but efforts toward poor relief and grain supply eventually ensued. Nottingham's corporation met in late November 1630 to appoint a committee of leading citizens to provision the market with corn for the poor, while the mayor of Leicester certified that barley for the poor was sold at below-market value. The corporation of Hull, having consistently made orders regarding reformation of alehouses and provision for the poor prior to the Book of Orders, took special pains to act when the Orders arrived. The town's justices met in March 1631 to agree on orders for the poor, including monthly meetings of the mayor and JPs, certifying the resident poor by the constables, punishing idle and vagrant persons, and putting "honest" people, especially children, to work.[137] Banbury's magistrates reported enthusiastic compliance with the Orders in May 1631: the markets well-furnished with grain, the rate for the poor doubled upon the wealthier sort, "drunkards, tipsters, and swearers" punished, charity contributed beyond statutory requirement, poor people set on work, and "as for rogues and vagabonds, we are little troubled with them, they like their entertainment so

---

19, 94, 108, SP16/193, fols 33, 135, 149, SP16/194, fols 15, 30, 41, 71, 73, 135, SP16/195, fols 11, 15, 119, 121, SP16/197, fol. 71, SP16/198, fol. 98, SP16/200, fol. 84, SP16/201, fols 18, 89.

[134] TNA, SP16/192, fol. 94, SP16/198, fol. 6, SP16/199, fol. 11, SP16/200, fol. 84, SP16/201, fol. 19, SP16/203, fol. 10. The mayor of Taunton's eagerness may have been spurred by the diligence of Sir Francis Dodington, sheriff of Somerset, who made frequent returns from all of the areas of his county.

[135] CSPD 1634–35, pp. 441, 442, 444, 445.

[136] TNA, SP16/259, fol. 36 (Bailiffs of Eye to Privy Council, 20 January 1634). Two principal burgesses refused to attend the sessions for carrying out the Orders, while one "gent." refused altogether to take an apprentice as required.

[137] Guilding (ed.), Reading Records, vol. 3, pp. 35, 37, 43, 45; RBNott, vol. 5, p. 147; RBL, vol. 4, p. 262; HHC, BRB3, pp. 124, 177, 214, 244, 247, 253.

140

GOVERNING POVERTY AND DISORDER

ill."[138] Borough magistrates attended to the requirements laid down in the Book of Orders, even if they did not always buy into the rigorous regime of reporting laid out by central authority.

Town governors also proved adept at using the apparatus of regional and central government when it suited their purposes, particularly regarding the rules for provisioning grain in markets at prices suitable for the poor. This aspect of national policy again enforced something that many borough corporations had been doing for some time, arranging to bring in grain for their poorest inhabitants. Dover's corporation laid up corn to be sold to the poor at below-market prices periodically from 1604 forward; Boston dedicated funds for ongoing grain purchase and storage for the poor in 1621; while Salisbury started a similar storehouse in 1628.[139] But in times of dearth, urban magistrates could not ensure the supply of grain for their towns, depending upon farmers in surrounding agricultural areas to sell in local markets. They also encountered the problem of grain being shipped elsewhere, including abroad. These were serious concerns for urban magistrates, since lack of corn in the market could lead to "riot" by the poor. As John Walter has shown in his work on Maldon, local authorities understood that their inaction could spur popular action which, though illegal, was not incomprehensible.[140] During such times, co-opting the power of central government for the benefit of the town proved a useful strategy.

This marshaling of central authority can be seen particularly well in the Cinque Ports, where correspondence between mayors and the lord warden and his deputies reveals the interconnection of central and local concerns. Port towns like Dover had complained of the lack of grain in the market since at least early in 1630. The mayor and jurats of Dover wrote to the lord warden, Theophilus Howard, earl of Suffolk, and his deputy Sir Edward Dering, in April and May 1630, complaining about the lack of wheat in the market and the effect on the town's poor.[141] To the townsmen's minds, the trouble stemmed from local farmers refusing to supply Dover's market, out of some "evil disposition" for their own "particular gain and benefit." The potential for dangerous unrest hovered: "If a timely care and course be not taken our poor will much clamor." The men of Dover asked Dering to act where they could not. They appealed to his authority to deal with the recalcitrant farmers, "whereby our inhabitants' complaint may be stopped and their neighbourly charitable

---

[138] J.S.W. Gibson and E.R.C. Brinkworth (eds), *Banbury Corporation Records, Tudor and Stuart*, Banbury Historical Society Publications, vol. 15 (Banbury, 1977), p. 152.

[139] BL, Egerton MS 2096, fols 23, 130v, Add. MS 28,036, fol. 122; Bailey (ed.), *Minutes of the Corporation of Boston*, vol. 2, pp. 353, 355, 361, 362; Slack (ed.), *Poverty in Early-Stuart Salisbury*, pp. 11–12, 110.

[140] Walter, "Grain Riots," pp. 53, 59, 60.

[141] TNA, SP16/164, fol. 68, SP16/166, fol. 49 (Petition of Dover to Lord Warden Suffolk, [May?] 1630); BL, Add. MS 24,113, fols 27–27v, 28v–29v.

URBAN GOVERNMENT AND THE EARLY STUART STATE

readiness be commended."[142] Dover's mayor and jurats carefully shaped their rhetoric to make their case. Their letters framed the farmers as uncharitable men potentially endangering the commonwealth, placing private gain ahead of public good. The townsmen, in contrast, portrayed themselves as exhibiting both charitable concern for the well-being of the poor and judicious attention to the security and order of town and state. In appealing to Suffolk and Dering, they looked to external authorities to help solve their problem, but also to shape their image as important elements of local government who had the best interest of the realm in mind.

Throughout the ports during this period of dearth, mayors and jurats called on the lord warden and his deputy for aid. The large ports of Dover and Sandwich, as well as smaller "limbs" like Tenterden and Faversham, contacted Sir Edward Dering regularly, enlisting him to ensure that farmers brought grain into their markets, to prevent uncertified transportation of grain out of their harbors, and to alleviate scarcity and high prices.[143] Dover's magistrates even went so far as to ask Dering to have the lord warden chastise one of their own jurats, who refused "sundry times" to bring his wheat into Dover market despite his plentiful supply.[144] Mayors did what they could for their towns, but the problems of dearth and grain provision connected the ports to a regional economy, while a mayor's authority ran only as far as the boundaries of his own town. The mayor and jurats of Tenterden expressed the dilemma in a letter to Dering in February 1631. "The number of poor people of our Town ... is so great and our store of provision of corn in this time of dearth so little, that we are much feared that many of them will famish unless some competent proportion of corn be speedily had and provided for their relief." They tried to carry out the king's orders as well as they could, but "notwithstanding all our care and diligence therein, we cannot find how a sufficient provision of corn can be raised for them out of our own store." Even neighboring parishes could not help them, since they, too, were short of grain. Only by invoking authority that transcended local boundaries could the plight of Tenterden's poor be redressed. Dering proved a good friend in this instance, as he willingly bent the rules to aid them. He gave orders for shipping wheat into the town, "although it be neither orderly bought nor have I (as I ought) the testimonies of two Justices of Peace to warrant my license."[145] Aligning town authority with the broader machinery of the state both carried out central policy and provided important local benefits.

At the same time, the complicated interactions involved in addressing dearth and responding to the crown also reveals some of the fault lines in governance, as town magistrates attempted to uphold their own authority in the face of orders that could contradict local interests. The port towns relied on Sir Edward

---

[142] BL, Add. MS 24,113, fols 29, 27v.
[143] BL, Add. MS 24,113, fols 27–27v, 28v–29v, 43–43v, 48, 63v–64, Add. MS 47,789, fols 6v, 8–8v, 16v.
[144] BL, Add. MS 47,788, fols 40–40v.
[145] BL, Add. MS 24,113, fols 63v–64, 64–64v, Add. MS 47,789, fol. 16v.

142

GOVERNING POVERTY AND DISORDER

Dering to aid them, but they did not always trust him. Dering's letters, though not an unbiased source, suggest that borough officials sometimes ignored his directives or slow-walked their responses when it suited them. He accused the mayor of Sandwich of allowing food to be shipped out of the port without warrant, reminding the mayor that the Book of Orders did not "enlarge any power unto the particular towns beyond their usual and regular bounds."[146] He reprimanded the mayor and jurats of Faversham for purposely misconstruing his orders and for failing to certify their enforcement of the Book of Orders, despite three letters from him.[147] The mayor and jurats of Winchelsea returned flawed and partial certificates, to which Dering responded that they must make "a more punctual answer, that thereby you may quit yourselves of that disregard, which yet you seem culpable of."[148] He especially distrusted the mayor of Dover in 1630, Stephan Monins, whom Dering labeled a puritan, for being insufficiently eager to enforce the Orders.[149] These accusations clearly reflect Dering's prejudices, but they reveal that borough officials attempted to exert their own authority and focus on town (or possibly their personal) interests even during a period of crisis and vigorous central enforcement.

The Cinque Ports' experience also illuminates how overlapping jurisdictions and confusions among elements in the state caused frustration for town governors and signaled a lack of understanding on the part of central government even when promoting a policy as far-reaching as the Book of Orders. Dering himself thought (incorrectly, as it turned out) that the Council had forgotten to include the Cinque Ports in the Orders altogether.[150] Mixed signals and confusions abounded. A consistent theme in borough correspondence is frustration at the transportation of grain out of the ports. Mayors had some ability to control export and transportation from their ports, but they had to contend with both the strictures laid down in the orders and exceptions licensed by king, Privy Council or lord warden. The mayor and jurats of Dover complained about the transportation of corn out of town on licenses granted by royal authority; with impoverished townspeople unprovided and "ready to mutiny," the magistrates could do nothing to prevent it. In Faversham, the mayor and jurats received a certificate from the king's baker to allow the shipment of 200 quarters of wheat to London, which they hesitated to fulfill, despite the seeming imprimatur of the king's household: "Our care is & must be in performance of the said proclamation and orders to provide for our own poor, which we daily endeavor to our uttermost." They eventually did ship wheat to bakers in London, obeying a letter from the lord warden.[151] Henry Forestall, mayor of Sandwich, had little option but to obey when presented with licenses granted by the lord warden to ship

[146] BL, Add. MS 47,789, fol. 10v.
[147] BL, Add. MS 47,789, fols 14–14v, 17.
[148] BL, Add. MS 47,789, fol. 19.
[149] BL, Add. MS 47,788, fols 10–10v.
[150] BL, Add. MS 47,788, fol. 10; *APC 1630–31*, pp. 18–19.
[151] BL, Add. MS 24,113, fols 28v–29v, 48, 53–53v; TNA, SP16/166, fol. 49.

URBAN GOVERNMENT AND THE EARLY STUART STATE

grain out of the port. Yet he groused that "our market is very ill served" as he watched the grain leaving Sandwich. When pressed by Dering's order to allow a Mr. Banks to ship out eighty quarters of barley, the mayor noted that "it were against some of the Jurats' will and with the much murmuring of many of our inhabitants."[152] While central authority and town governors seemingly shared a common goal in this period of dearth – security of the food supply and care for the poor – the execution of policy in the Book of Orders raised tensions when central officials either did not understand or chose not to honor local considerations.

The Book of Orders and the more concerted central efforts at management of poverty and control of disorder in the early 1630s met with mixed responses in borough corporations. On one hand, the demands made on towns in the enforcement of the orders raised some strains over jurisdiction and a certain amount of annoyance at (and avoidance of) the crown's reporting requirements. The more strenuous execution of policy gave borough corporations less leeway to prioritize local considerations. In some instances, it challenged corporate liberties. On the other hand, however, the problems that the Orders addressed plagued towns especially badly. Most corporations attended closely to the relief and control of the poor and the regulation of grain and alehouses as a regular part of borough governance. Many towns – particularly those with magistrates influenced by puritan zeal – already had programs in place to deal with the poor, and the Orders reinforced them. While sometimes flouting reporting requirements, most towns nevertheless continued to provide relief, build and support houses of correction, regulate alehouses, bind out poor children, and carry out many of the activities defined in the Orders, just as they had for many years prior. The Book of Orders occasionally vexed borough magistrates, but they were not a major grievance.

Poverty, plague, and the attendant problems of alehouses and drink, provision of grain, and control of the wandering or undeserving poor were of deep concern in the early Stuart period, to local magistrates and king and Privy Council alike. The ordering of these associated social problems constituted an important element of governance within borough corporations and in the state more broadly. Towns had since at least the reign of Elizabeth instituted a wide variety of measures to control and relieve their poor populations, and some of these local efforts found their way into national legislation. A shared interest in maintaining and reinforcing order, as well as to support the poor and weak as Christian duty required, bound borough magistrates to central authorities in regulating these matters. It served as a link between center and locality, as magistrates at all levels understood the obligation to address social problems in the name of order. That Sir Robert Heath, a key figure in Charles I's government and no friend to puritans, could hold up the godly town of Dorchester as an

---

[152] BL, Add. MS 24,113, fols 49, 49v–50.

GOVERNING POVERTY AND DISORDER

example to the realm of good government in relation to poor relief and control confirms the link between towns and crown on this issue.

While the concerns at the heart of these efforts were mutual, the crown's methods and central authorities' perceived ignorance of local considerations could breed frustration. Urban governors at times found central orders insufficiently sensitive to the deep fiscal and governance challenges facing them. Poverty was an especially intractable problem in urban communities, and (as will be shown more fully in Chapters 5 and 6) central policies on trade, piracy, and war often deepened the problems of poverty in the towns. In times of plague, the suppression of trade and restriction of movement, while necessary, imposed a heavy penalty on towns, where most inhabitants, many already poor, relied on commerce for their livelihoods. And some of the crown's heaviest financial levies occurred in periods of economic downturn, trade depression, and serious plague outbreaks, particularly in the 1620s and 1630s. Petitions from borough magistrates to the Council in this period stressed the poverty of their towns, which were being asked to contribute to national costs even as they were paying heavy local rates for their own impoverished and plague-ridden inhabitants.[153] On balance, social regulation of all sorts played an integrative role in connecting corporate towns into the broader state through expanded governance and concern for order. This integration was not, however, without tension.

[153] See, for instance, *CSPD 1619–23*, pp. 23, 27, 387, 391, *1625–26*, p. 418, *1627–28*, pp. 66, 156, 157, *1636–7*, pp. 287, 288.

5

Promoting Peace and Plenty: Corporate Towns and Trade

The essence of an urban place, whether a small market town or a commercial metropolis like London, was trade. Exchange and commerce defined a town, the reason for its separate existence from the county in which it sat. This had implications for demographic patterns, social organization, political structures, and local culture, but it also helped dictate the relationship between central government and borough communities. Towns and cities, though they did not fit comfortably within privileged hierarchies based on land ownership and agriculture, held a special place in the early modern state. Because of their significance to the economic health and growth of the realm, towns received significant attention from the crown, which recognized their importance to the kingdom's prosperity, as well as its orderly governance. The close link between order and profit was widely acknowledged and helped shape urban political culture. As Francis Parlett, recorder of King's Lynn, declared in 1630, "peace [produces] plenty, than which nothing is better and nothing more to be required. For peace is the ornament and plenty the complement of all blessings in a civil state."[1] King Charles echoed this sentiment in a royal proclamation concerning market measures, saying he desired "by all good meanes to further and advance the peace and plenty of our loving Subjects."[2] The dual motivators of prosperity and peace organized and energized the government of urban places, from the perspective of both local leaders and central government.

Governance of the commerce that constituted much of town life intertwined deeply with the liberties and privileges granted by the crown in a borough's charter. Borough corporations enjoyed rights to hold markets, regulate weights and measures, appoint market officials, hold courts of pie powder during market or fair time, and oversee companies that organized crafts and occupations within their liberties. The corporation determined who was (and who could become) a

---

[1] NRO, King's Lynn Borough Records, MF/RO Reel 396/13, "The Book of Francis Parlett," [unpaginated]. On urban political culture in this period, see Robert Tittler, *The Reformation and the Towns in England, c. 1640–1640* (Oxford, 1998), pt. 4. Phil Withington, *The Politics of Commonwealth: Citizens and Freemen in Early Modern England* (Cambridge, 2005), chap. 6, discusses economic aspects of urban political culture, though it focuses principally on the later seventeenth century.

[2] J. Larkin (ed.), *Stuart Royal Proclamations*, vol. 2, *Royal Proclamations of King Charles I 1625–1646* (Oxford, 1983), p. 523. King James had earlier used this language in a similar proclamation in 1619. J. Larkin and P. Hughes (eds), *Stuart Royal Proclamations*, vol. 1, *Royal Proclamations of King James I 1603–1625* (Oxford, 1973), p. 417.

member, with rights to trade freely in a town, and who was a stranger who could be excluded or required to pay tolls. The right to make bylaws that regulated trade and kept order was also a valued corporate liberty.[3] Through charters, the crown placed authority over economic regulation squarely in the hands of the merchants, tradesmen, and craftsmen who largely constituted borough corporations. Governors of the provincial towns used those corporate privileges to oversee internal trade within their liberties, but also to defend and support local commerce as it extended outward. Royal charters gave corporate boroughs the legal foundation to work toward the peace and plenty of their towns, which reverberated to the peace and plenty of the realm.

While charters offered towns certain protections, they did not result in an insular focus in borough governments. Corporations, enjoying privileges confirmed to them through the prerogative power of the crown, relied on the crown to protect their prosperity. Not just borough records, but State Papers and Privy Council Registers teem with references to cloths and kersies in Exeter and Barnstaple, Norwich and York; leather and hides in Chester and Bristol; coals in Newcastle; herring in Great Yarmouth. As economic lives became increasingly integrated into the expanding network of trade extending through the realm and beyond, urban governors had to remain ever vigilant of decisions being made at the Privy Council, as well as parliament, that affected their business. Many towns, even quite small ones, sent agents to London to treat on their behalf to transact town business, counter the lobbying of London merchants, inform the crown of local conditions, or influence trade policies more broadly. Provincial towns also depended on central authorities to help support local needs, like assistance in repairing havens or building bridges, that were critical to the success of their trade. International conditions and foreign policy decisions – the crown's determinations of war and peace, enemies and friends – had immediate impact on merchants who traded abroad, with ripple effects throughout England's economy. Borough officials, often merchants themselves with direct interest in the trades being affected, voiced their concerns and promoted local interests to authorities in London and Westminster, but they also served as agents of central authority, expected to enforce order and carry out policies that affected the state as a whole, locality and center. Borough corporations firmly defended their interests, but those interests were not merely local – they were constitutive of national conversations on matters of trade and economy.

This chapter examines how towns negotiated this connection across the changing landscape of economic conditions and policy under the early Stuarts. It does not attempt a comprehensive analysis of the urban, commercial economy in the early seventeenth century,[4] but rather considers key dimensions of

---

[3] Shelagh Bond and Norman Evans, "The Process of Granting Charters to English Boroughs, 1547–1649," *English Historical Review* 91 (1976), 104–5.
[4] For an economic analysis of commerce in the period, see B.E. Supple, *Commercial Crisis*

URBAN GOVERNMENT AND THE EARLY STUART STATE

trade through which borough governments and the crown negotiated their relationship. In charters of incorporation, the monarch confirmed and endowed corporate boroughs with privileges over their own trade, but also created a firm link between town and crown in economic matters. Provincial towns regularly reached outward to accomplish their business, whether protection from London merchants, maintaining the infrastructure for commerce, or navigation of threats to foreign trade by piracy and war. The crown, for its part, relied on borough governors as local experts and promoters of economic order; central authorities proved open to local concerns and willing to change direction at the request of local actors on trade matters. Nevertheless, particularly when faced with threats to their economic well-being, provincial towns found central government at times unable or unwilling to provide resources to protect local interests that they believed constituted the common good of the realm. Questions over competing metropolitan and provincial interests and over who bore responsibility for the protection and advancement of trade caused tension and misunderstanding, especially in times of economic downturn and war. The 1620s proved particularly difficult. Trade served as a critical connection between provincial towns and the crown, but it also could reveal the weaknesses of the early modern state.

Towns, corporations, and the governance of trade

Matters of trade pulled townsmen and borough corporations into relationships with central authority and the broader state by the very nature of their business. Merchants and tradesmen from towns and cities across the realm engaged in commerce, both domestic and foreign. Governing trade and regulating markets lay largely in the hands of various corporate institutions – guilds and merchant companies as well as borough or civic corporations.[5] At the same time, ultimately the governance of trade lay in the hands of the monarch, the arbiter of policy, politics, and international diplomacy. Every merchant who imported or exported goods to or from England engaged with the king's customs and port officials, followed (or evaded) rules for shipping and trade laid down by royal policy, and risked his capital in foreign ports or on the seas. Even local craftsmen and merchants plying entirely domestic markets intersected with the crown's weights and measures, regulations assuring the quality of goods, and the king's authority over local markets represented in the person of the mayor. Borough charters placed power to govern trade in the hands of a town's magistrates, who were deputies of the crown, and responsible to it. Corporations

---

and Change in England 1600–1642: A Study in the Instability of a Mercantile Economy (Cambridge, 1959).

[5] Philip J. Stern, "'Bundles of Hyphens': Corporations as Legal Communities in the Early Modern British Empire," in L. Benton and R. Ross (eds), Legal Pluralism and Empires, 1500–1850 (New York, 2013), pp. 23–4, 33.

PROMOTING PEACE AND PLENTY

(of boroughs and of trading companies) likewise interacted regularly with the broader state, exercising responsibility for commerce within their jurisdictions and advocating for it beyond local boundaries, both legal and geographical. At every turn, trade brought townsmen and corporations into contact with the state, putting borough officials at the forefront of governance and deeply engaging them in conversations touching commerce both domestic and foreign.

While entrusting borough magistrates with authority over trade, central government also displayed some ambivalence about townsmen's ability to govern trade adequately. Oversight was necessary to ensure that private profit did not supersede the king's good. Early Stuart government, perpetually concerned with royal finance, remained jealous of customs collection, Admiralty jurisdiction, and market regulation, making proclamations and enforcing rules that affected towns and cities disproportionately.[6] James's government made concerted efforts to reframe financial relations with Irish towns to regularize and enhance customs duties for the crown.[7] Both James (in 1619) and Charles (in 1636) tackled what they saw as urban ills, issuing extensive royal proclamations for stamping out "false and deceitfull Weights and Measures" and assuring good quality and fair prices in the market. "We are informed that the greatest deceipts and abuses are committed in Cities, Boroughs, and Townes Corporate, by the chiefe Officers there, who ought to reforme themselves and others within their several Jurisdictions."[8] While intermittent, such intervention meant that borough leaders could expect the watchful eye of central authority to fall upon them through proclamations, Privy Council letters and orders, and law.

Mayors and aldermen took the brunt of central ire when local behavior failed to meet expectations. Newcastle's magistrates received sharp letters from the Privy Council in 1616 for neglecting the Board's orders concerning duties to be paid by merchants in their port, among other infractions.[9] The Council chastised the mayor of Cardiff for allowing goods to be embezzled from a ship stayed in Cardiff harbor, allegedly with the complicity of an alderman. The Board acknowledged Cardiff's remoteness, yet emphasized that no borough government should become "a refuge and receptacle of such ill-disposed persons."[10] The Council charged the mayor of Reading in 1639 with

6 Michael Braddick, *State Formation in Early Modern England, c. 1550–1700* (Cambridge, 2000), pp. 246–7. Between 1603 and 1639, James made about fifty-six and Charles about sixty-six royal proclamations dealing with trade in one way or another, regulating everything from the price of poultry to the making of soap to the transportation of goods in foreign ships. Larkin and Hughes (eds), *Stuart Royal Proclamations*, vol. 1, and Larkin (ed.), *Stuart Royal Proclamations*, vol. 2, *passim*.
7 Aiden Clarke, "Pacification, Plantation, and the Catholic Question, 1603–23," in T.W. Moody, *et al*. (eds), *A New History of Ireland*, vol. 3, *Early Modern Ireland 1534–1691* (Oxford, 1976), pp. 230–1.
8 Larkin and Hughes (eds), *Stuart Royal Proclamations*, vol. 1, pp. 416, 417, 419; Larkin (ed.), *Stuart Royal Proclamations*, vol. 2, pp. 519, 522, 524.
9 APC 1616–17, pp. 38, 146, 147–8, 261.
10 APC 1615–16, p. 402.

149

URBAN GOVERNMENT AND THE EARLY STUART STATE

"connivance" in opening trade in his town despite his knowledge of plague there. They condemned him for putting private interest above public good, inviting infection through the "carelessness and negligence of yourself who are the chief magistrate there."[11] The crown expected magistrates of even small and distant towns to fulfill the state's purposes. Borough governments exercised significant local authority, but they did so as participants in a royal state that regularly reminded them of their duty to serve interests beyond their own.

Despite the crown's sometimes doubtful assessment of borough magistrates' honesty and competence, the early Stuart monarchs granted extensive privileges to borough corporations, linking royal authority to local liberties. Most of the towns that sought new incorporation or reincorporation in the early Stuart period did so both to gain enhanced economic privileges and to strengthen the governing body. Those advantages made paying the hefty sums required for a new charter a worthwhile bargain. While towns often claimed some privileges for fairs or markets by prescription, theirs since "time out of mind," they legally secured these privileges and gained new grants through the prerogative authority of the monarch, by charter.[12] Penzance achieved royal incorporation in 1614, as the crown recognized its ancient exercise of merchandise and confirmed to it two weekly markets and seven annual fairs. Northampton's reincorporation charter of 1618 made the mayor clerk of the market and prevented foreigners from selling by retail in town, except during fairs. Grantham requested an additional fair when renewing its charter in 1631; Derby did the same in 1638, along with more authority over the fairs.[13] Through its charter, a borough corporation gained critical economic liberties and also forged strong links to the crown for the governance of its economic life.

Corporations, both for borough government and for trade, engaged in economic governance at every level, putting the prerogative authority of the crown at the heart of trade everywhere from London to small provincial towns. Historians of London's trading companies, and especially the East India Company, have increasingly focused on the ideas of governance that shaped those agents of imperial expansion, noting the importance of their corporate nature and their deep connections to crown and state.[14] In many

---

[11] TNA, PC2/50, p. 165.

[12] See, e.g., TNA, SP14/190, fol. 22, a gloss of Boston's chartered privileges, indicating which privileges were held by prescription and which by charter. See also William Sheppard, *Of Corporations, Fraternities, and Guilds* (London, 1659), pp. 7–8, and Harold Laski, "The Early History of the Corporation in England," *Harvard Law Review* 30 (1917), 567–8 on prescriptive vs. chartered privileges.

[13] P.A.S. Pool, *The History of the Town and Borough of Penzance* (Penzance, 1974), pp. 214, 220; TNA, SP14/104, fol. 137, SP16/142, fol. 104, SP16/378, fol. 172; Martin Weinbaum, *British Borough Charters, 1307–1660* (Cambridge, 1943), pp. 87, 71, 21.

[14] Philip Stern, *The Company State: Corporate Sovereignty and the Early Modern Foundations of the British Empire in India* (Oxford, 2012); Rupali Mishra, *A Business of State: Commerce, Politics, and the Birth of the East India Company* (Cambridge, MA, 2018).

PROMOTING PEACE AND PLENTY

ways, their experience echoed those of the borough corporations that governed England's towns. As David Harris Sacks showed for Bristol, the concerns of the civic corporation linked that city with a state from which it required help to accomplish its goals.[15] Borough corporations interacted directly with agents of central authority, whether Privy Councilors or local customs officials. They also contended with other corporations, from London trading companies like the Merchants Adventurers to guilds and companies within their own jurisdictions. The livery companies of London, as well as the London-based great trading companies, had their own royal charters of incorporation; on the other end of the spectrum, a number of provincial towns had incorporations of particular occupations or trades, subordinate to the borough corporation and sometimes spelled out in the borough's royal charter. The merchants of Exeter, Bristol, and Hull each had their own charters, under the auspices of their respective cities.[16] The corporation of Dorchester obtained a sub-corporation for "the better ordering of trade and commerce" when they petitioned for a new charter of incorporation for the borough in 1629.[17] Incorporation played a fundamental role in the governance of trade in this period, imprinting royal authority into every level of interaction.

The interlocking network of corporate privileges was intended to bring order and control to the potentially unruly arena of exchange, where private gain and public good intermingled.[18] Yet ambiguity and conflict could arise. Powerful provincial trade companies might vie with the governing corporation of a borough as the voice of the locality. Bristol's Merchant Venturers' company had a complex relationship with that city's corporate body and wielded tremendous influence.[19] In Shrewsbury, the interests of the town's Drapers' Company and the interests of the town itself blended together; the Drapers had their own lobbying arm and used the borough's parliamentary burgesses to solicit legislation useful to company interests.[20] Likewise the Hostmen's guild of Newcastle dominated corporate government there, and municipal politics often centered on protecting the Hostmen's interests.[21] While incorporating local merchants and crafts ostensibly created better order in trade, the goal was often also

---

[15] David Harris Sacks, *The Widening Gate: Bristol and the Atlantic, 1450–1700* (Berkeley and Los Angeles, CA, 1991), p. 196.

[16] M.S. Guiseppi (ed.), *Calendar of the Manuscripts of the Most Honourable Marquess of Salisbury*, vol. 20 (London, 1968), p. 107 (George Smythe *et al.* to earl of Salisbury, 15 March 1608); Sacks, *Widening Gate*, pp. 96, 210–11; *APC 1618–19*, p. 482. On London's companies and guilds, see Joseph P. Ward, *Metropolitan Communities: Trade Guilds, Identity, and Change in Early Modern London* (Stanford, CA, 1997).

[17] TNA, SP16/146, fols 96, 97, 43.

[18] See Withington, *Politics of Commonwealth*, p. 92, for brief discussion on the complex interaction of various corporate bodies within what he calls city commonwealths.

[19] Sacks, *The Widening Gate*, pp. 87–9, 210–12, 219–21.

[20] Shrewsbury Constituency Report, *HoP 1604–29*, www.historyofparliamentonline.org/volume/1604-1629/constituencies/shrewsbury.

[21] Roger Howell, *Newcastle-upon-Tyne and the Puritan Revolution: A Study of the Civil War in*

URBAN GOVERNMENT AND THE EARLY STUART STATE

increased power and wealth for particular townsmen; such companies could become sources of disorder, not sufficiently subordinate to the governance of the town. Bristol's Merchant Venturers dominated the city's government, but other companies were less welcome. The civic corporation complained to the Privy Council in 1619 that Bristol's bakers procured a charter, "whereby they exempt themselves from the government of the city" and commit "many unsufferable abuses." The referees who investigated the case found that the bakers, "only for their own private gain," obtained the charter "contrary to all good policy" and directly in conflict with Bristol's charter of incorporation. The Board ordered the attorney general to proceed against the bakers' charter by quo warranto or *scire facias*.[22] The city and university of Oxford jointly complained to the Board about letters patent granted by the crown to the company of masons, slatterers, carpenters and joiners for the "insufferable inconvenience" it caused; the Board demanded the submission of this charter to the clerk of the Council.[23] Local actors at various levels sought out connection to the crown to endow them with privileges and authority, and it was to the crown they appealed to sort out the differences that so often arose both within and beyond borough boundaries.

This complex interplay of levels of governance and notions of economic order, public good, and corporate authority is demonstrated in the resolution of a dispute over the cloth trade in Ipswich. Early in 1620, in the midst of nationwide disruption in the cloth industry, the Privy Council heard a complaint of the bailiffs, common council, and chief burgesses of Ipswich regarding an incorporation of the tailors and clothworkers of the town. The dispute involved longstanding rivalries between those who sold the cloth, more heavily represented among the town's elite, and those who worked it. Having obtained their own charter of incorporation, the tailors and clothworkers allegedly abused their privileges, disrupting the good governance and prosperity of the town. Petitions from merchants, clothiers, and clothworkers contended that the incorporation of the tailors and clothworkers had led to disputes, law suits, unfair fines and fees on the members, and – to the detriment of the town's reputation – shoddy workmanship and poor quality of cloths.[24] They asked the Council to revoke the company's charter. Royal authority had incorporated the tailors and clothworkers initially, so the bailiffs and burgesses of Ipswich appealed to that same authority to redress the danger to peace and prosperity they believed the company posed.

The Privy Council proved supportive of the town's corporate liberties and critical of the tailors' charter. Praising the borough corporation for maintaining good government, "under which that towne hath ever florrished," they passed

---

North England (Oxford, 1967); J.R. Boyle and F.W. Dendy (eds), *Extracts from the Records of the Merchant Adventurers of Newcastle-upon-Tyne*, vol. 1 (Durham, 1895), pp. xxxii, xli.

22 *APC 1619–21*, pp. 49, 60–1.

23 *APC 1613–14*, pp. 295–6.

24 *APC 1619–21*, pp. 122–3; TNA, SP14/112, fols 62–4.

the matter to referees for further investigation.[25] The referees saw the larger scope of the dispute and made recommendations that both resolved local problems and established policy furthering the interests of the crown and the state at large. First, they opined that "these under-corporations in towns and inferior cities are seldom of good use, but do rather disturb the general government of such places." They recommended that the Council prevent other such incorporations in future. At the same time, since King James had granted the charter to the tailors and clothworkers, to revoke it would be of "ill consequence and example." Additionally, such a corporation had a public value: it recognized the importance of tailors and clothworkers, and not just the more powerful clothiers and merchants, to the clothing business of Ipswich that employed so many inhabitants, including the poor. Instead of voiding the charter, the referees proposed keeping the new corporation but revising the ordinances under which it operated, placing it securely under the governance of the borough corporation.[26] "We judge it reasonable that the magistrates of the town of Ipswich, who are so generally recommended for the orderly government of that town, should be the rather encouraged than receive discontentment under your Lordships' good favor."[27] Suffolk's assize judges, assigned to review the old ordinances, found that they "too muche abridge the lawfull libertie of the subjects in use of their trades," and at the same time impeach "some ancient liberties and usages of the towne."[28] Newly drafted ordinances received the "full consent" of the local parties as well as the Privy Council's approval.[29] The Board charged the bailiffs of Ipswich with executing these new orders, thus bringing the resolution and the oversight back to the local governors who first brought the problem to the Council's attention.

The case of the Ipswich tailors demonstrates the complex ways that governance of trade linked town and crown in this period. A problem of internal regulation of trade challenged the borough's good order, but it also implicated the monarch as author of both the borough's and the tailors and clothmakers' charters. Only the king could resolve this local problem. While borough governors wished simply to dismantle the tailors and clothworkers company, allowing the merchants and clothiers, as well as themselves, to regulate the clothing market in Ipswich, the Privy Council applied a broader perspective. The Board's decision addressed the quality of cloth and the good order of the trade while also maintaining the king's authority in the charter. The matter received lengthy and multilayered consideration by the Board, its referees, and the assize judges, who ultimately reinforced borough magistrates' authority to manage local business and maintain quiet government in the town. Questions

---

[25] APC 1619–21, pp. 122–3.
[26] APC 1619–21, p. 123; BL, Lansdowne MS 162, fol. 195; TNA, SP14/112, fol. 105.
[27] BL, Lansdowne MS 162, fol. 195.
[28] APC 1619–21, p. 208.
[29] APC 1619–21, p. 209.

URBAN GOVERNMENT AND THE EARLY STUART STATE

of public good, corporate authority, and royal power ran through this intricate network of governance.

For borough corporations like Ipswich, the competitive, transactive nature of commerce and its movement across boundaries both physical and jurisdictional required resort to central government to solve difficult problems. Parliament served as one venue for economic concerns, and certainly many parliamentary boroughs used their burgesses to pursue local agendas, such as Southampton defending its trade in sweet wines, as well as those of broad concern, like free trade or the decay of the cloth trade. Yet the relatively infrequent and unpredictable meeting of parliament, and its preoccupation (especially in the mid-1620s) with war, taxation, and other public business, meant that it could be difficult to achieve satisfaction there.[30] Many towns instructed their burgesses on matters that never grabbed the attention of the House.[31] The courts, too, offered a venue for trade disputes between individuals as well as corporations. The expense and unpredictability of the law could argue against its use, however. A dispute between Hull and York in 1622 over market privileges started as a suit in Common Pleas, but ended before the Privy Council, where Hull's governors thought they might have better success.[32] The Board's authority transcended the legal action. In this case, it did not work to Hull's benefit, as the Board found in York's favor. But the Council also considered the larger picture of orderly governance in this suit, seeing the "reason of State" involved in such questions of corporate liberties and trade. They prioritized reconciliation of the two cities, desiring "free intercourse to be continued" between "those two places being both of them great corporations and places of principal importance."[33] The crown's authority both calmed local contentions and determined broader matters of policy. As it did for many matters regarding town governance, the Privy Council served as a definitive venue to which borough governments brought matters for resolution.

Across the early Stuart period, the settlement of trade disputes constituted an important part of the Privy Council's activities. Indeed, Sir John Coke, secretary of the Council, identified the adjudication of trade matters, along with resolving issues involving towns and cities generally, as central components

---

[30] See Southampton Constituency Report, *HoP 1604-29*, www.historyofparliamentonline. org/volume/1604-1629/constituencies/southampton, for the borough's attempts to secure its trade against London through parliament.

[31] See the constituency reports for, e.g., Boston, Berwick-upon-Tweed, Shrewsbury, Hull, and York in *HoP 1604-29*.

[32] HHC, BRB3 (Hull Bench Book 5), pp. 110, 111-12, BRL (Hull Borough Letters) 190, BRL 191; YCA, B.34 (York House Book 1613-1625), fols 265v, 270, 291; TNA, SP14/138, fol. 183 (Petition of the mayor of York to the Privy Council, [February?] 1623). See also Kingston-upon-Hull Constituency Report, *HoP 1604-29*, www.historyofparliamentonline. org/volume/1604-1629/constituencies/kingston-upon-hull.

[33] *APC 1621-23*, pp. 405-6, 476.

154

of the public business of the Board.[34] If we take the first early Stuart volume of the published *Acts of the Privy Council* (May 1613–December 1614) as an example, we find the Board dealing with over twenty different matters of trade, commerce, or industry that involved communication between the Council and urban governors in London and the provinces. These ranged from orders from the Board regarding the control of trade in French wines and exportation of sheep, to hearings in a long and complex dispute of the drapers of Shrewsbury, Oswestry, and Whitchurch against London merchants over the production and trade in Welsh cloths, which the Board heard at least seven times.[35] While frequently engaged in trade regulation, the Board did not display a rigid attitude or clearly defined policy. As a number of scholars have suggested, the Council tended to be reactive, responding to what came to their attention.[36] As will be shown below, the Board reversed its own decisions on numerous occasions, as circumstances changed or lobbying from local interests persuaded them. What does come through clearly in the Privy Council's judgments is the extent to which they engaged with local concerns and attempted to address both peace and prosperity. They emphasized orderly governance of trade, as well as fairness and public interest, but the merchants and magistrates of England's towns regularly sought to bend the Council's decisions to achieve local ends.

The crown's interest in maximizing its revenues while ensuring the effectiveness of trade and the quality of products required borough magistrates to attend carefully to both local interests and central policy. With some regularity, they succeeded in swaying central decisions. Townsmen acknowledged the crown's authority over regulation, but they also contested actions they believed harmed them, attempting to educate central authorities on the realities of trade that local actors were best-placed to know. When King James issued letters patent for surveyors of coal at Newcastle, ostensibly to prevent fraud in the quality of the coal (but primarily to enhance the king's revenues), the mayors of Newcastle and King's Lynn acted to stop it. John Wallis, mayor of Lynn, wrote

[34] TNA, SP16/8, fol. 128 (Sir John Coke's notes on Privy Council procedure, October 1625).
[35] *APC 1613–14*, pp. 9–10, 10–11, 34–40, 51–3, 169, 187, 190–2, 198–9, 207, 226, 232, 236, 239, 247, 280, 295, 303–4, 310–11, 314, 320, 341–3, 351–5, 355–61, 367, 403, 445, 522–3, 538, 594, 591. The dispute involving the Shrewsbury Drapers and the market for Welsh cloths dragged on for years, coming before the Board again in 1619 and featuring in parliamentary debates over free trade in 1621. BL, Lansdowne MS 162, fol. 197 ("The True State of the Cause between the City of London and the Drapers of Shrewsbury," 6 February 1619); *CSPD 1619–23*, pp. 88–9, 116–17, 124, 135, 259, 329, 407, 404, 432, 447, 463. See also Thomas Mendenhall, *Shrewsbury Drapers and the Welsh Wool Trade in the XVI and XVII Centuries* (London, 1953); Shrewsbury Constituency Report, *HoP 1604–29*.
[36] Anthony Fletcher, *Reform in the Provinces: The Government of Stuart England* (New Haven, CT and London, 1986), pp. 44–5, 52. See also Brian Quintrell, "Government in Perspective: Lancashire and the Privy Council, 1570–1640," *Transactions of the Historical Society of Lancashire & Cheshire* 131 (1981), 40. According to Quintrell, the Privy Council was "always better suited to muddling through than to well ordered administration."

URBAN GOVERNMENT AND THE EARLY STUART STATE

to Sir Nathaniel Bacon asking for aid with a suit to the Privy Council, saying the patent for surveying coal was "injurious to all the country." Wallis entreated Sir Nathaniel to join in petitioning his brother, Sir Francis Bacon, as well as Lord Chancellor Ellesmere, "hoping that if we can obtain but friends of some of the Lords to lay down such reasons for the overthrow of this unnecessary office, as shall plainly appear to be both just and equal."[37] The mayors of Newcastle and Lynn also appealed directly to the Privy Council, saying that the Board had been misinformed by the patentee; there was no deceit in the quality of coals, making the surveyor's place unnecessary. The Council, after investigation, voided the patent.[38] King Charles's government likewise voided letters patent for measuring yarns in 1636 upon protest by provincial officials, while Great Yarmouth convinced the Privy Council in 1635 to revoke the patent of the new office of gauger of red herrings. The townsmen alleged it simply charged "a duty for nothing doing," as well as being "contrary to the laws" of England and "very prejudicial to the state and commonwealth."[39] Local business was vulnerable to the inroads of entrepreneurial patentees who could gain the ear of the king or Council, but borough magistrates could also be effective advocates of their own business, convincing central authorities to change policy based on local knowledge.

Provincial towns regularly brought their business before the Privy Council, but the Board also solicited the input of townsmen, experts on matters of both local and national conditions of trade. London merchants, being close to hand, claimed the attention of the Board more frequently, but those from provincial towns had expertise that could influence the Board, as well. In 1605, the earl of Dorset solicited the mayor of Hull to send merchants to confer on trade with the Levant.[40] In September 1621, at the height of concerns over decay of trade, the Privy Council determined to seek information from mayors of those places "most interested," calling on twenty important provincial towns to send representatives to testify before the Board on the problem and its local manifestations.[41] Borough records in Boston, Plymouth, King's Lynn, Great Yarmouth, Hull, Ipswich, and Chester confirm that those places, at least, sent representatives to London to confer.[42] Mr. Ramsden of Hull reported back to his brethren

---

[37] BL, Add. MS 41,140, fol. 104 (Mayor and aldermen of King's Lynn to Sir Nicholas Bacon, 29 January 1616).
[38] *APC 1615–16*, p. 520, *1616–17*, pp. 138–9, 165–7.
[39] Larkin (ed.), *Stuart Royal Proclamations*, vol. 2, pp. 520–1, 543; TNA, PC2/45, pp. 268, 283, 298, SP16/298, fol. 169, SP16/303, fol. 119.
[40] HHC, BRL 152 (Earl of Dorset to mayor of Hull *et al.*, 20 July 1605).
[41] *APC 1621–23*, p. 40. The towns were Sandwich, Chichester, Southampton, Poole, Exeter, Plymouth, Bridgewater, Bristol, Gloucester, Cardiff, Milford, Chester, Carlisle, Berwick, Newcastle, Hull, Boston, Lynn, Yarmouth, Ipswich.
[42] J.F. Bailey (ed.), *Transcription of the Minutes of the Corporation of Boston*, vol. 2 (Boston, 1981), p. 362; R.N. Worth (ed.), *Calendar of the Plymouth Municipal Records* (Plymouth, 1893), p. 153; KLTH, KL/C7/9, fol. 176v; NRO, Y/C19/5, fol. 244; HHC, BRB3, p. 91; SA/I, C6/1/5, fol. 27v; CCRO, ML/6/155, 156.

PROMOTING PEACE AND PLENTY

on the meeting and the provincial ports' recommendations to the Council, which not surprisingly, laid some of the fault on the London companies.[43] The Board eventually created a formal commission to enquire into the decay of trade and recommend solutions, though it reflected a strong metropolitan, rather than provincial, influence.[44] While the early Stuart crown had neither the resources, nor perhaps the will, to micromanage the regulation of commerce, it sought to connect with those who had the greatest stake in trade and the means to govern it, to provide for the peace and prosperity of the realm.

Provincial trade and the metropolis

For many provincial towns, their peace and prosperity seemed most jeopardized by London. Increasing numbers of royally incorporated joint-stock and regulated companies, mostly based in the metropolis, affected the privileges of many corporate boroughs, who complained bitterly to the Privy Council about their losses. Londoners expanded their reach along with the expanding economy, capturing trade and markets and throwing the weight of their wealth and their chartered privileges against their provincial brethren. Provincial townsmen detested Londoners' monopolistic aspirations. An especially egregious example of these was the failed Cockayne Project, in which London merchant William Cockayne (in exchange for a hefty sum to the crown) in 1614 gained a monopoly on cloth exports that brought grief to the cloth trade for years, especially in the early 1620s.[45] The cries of the outports over this project and others mingled with vigorous debates over free trade of the 1610s and 1620s. Provincial ports condemned the chartered companies' restrictive practices, seeing them as a plot against the provinces. The bailiffs of Great Yarmouth said of London merchants, "We may well perceive their purposes to engross all trades, by sea and land, both great and small, and their intents to impoverish all others, to

---

[43] HHC, BRL 176 (John Ramsden to mayor of Hull, 12 October 1621), BRB3, p. 91. Sir Robert Heath's notes confirm that the government perceived the provincial merchants' identification of heavy impositions, the restrictions and difficulties caused by the large merchant companies, and the "false making" of cloth as key contributors to problems with trade. TNA, SP14/130, fols 35-6.

[44] APC 1621-23, pp. 79-80, 208. Membership included London merchants like former mayor Sir Thomas Low and Alderman William Holiday, and gentlemen associated with the Merchant Adventurers, Virginia Company, or East India Company, like Sir Arthur Ingram and Sir Dudley Digges. "Lowe, Sir Thomas," "Ingram, Arthur," "Digges, Sir Dudley," HoP 1604-29, www.historyofparliamentonline.org/research/members/members-1604-1629; G.E. Cokayne, Some Account of the Lord Mayors and Sheriffs of the City of London during the First Quarter of the Seventeenth Century (London, 1897), pp. 20-1, 78.

[45] Astrid Friis, Alderman Cockayne's Project and the Cloth Trade (London, 1927); Supple, Commercial Crisis and Change, pp. 52-72.

URBAN GOVERNMENT AND THE EARLY STUART STATE

enrich themselves."[46] For most of the outports, they fought not for an abstract notion of free trade, but for their own economic survival.[47]

The pervasive influence of London pinched provincial trade across England. Shrewsbury's conflict with the French Merchants on the marches of Wales dragged on for years. Southampton kept up a nearly perpetual battle in parliament, the courts, and the Privy Council to defend its commercial interests and corporate liberties against London merchants. The corporation of York in 1621 hoped to obtain either an act of parliament or an order from the king to restrain Londoners from coming to fairs north of the Trent.[48] Trade rivalries between provincial towns and London showed up frequently before both Privy Council and parliament. In the 1621 Parliament, Sir Edward Coke spoke on behalf of provincial liberties, arguing that London's monopolization of trade endangered the public good of the whole realm. Coke professed his love for London and its prosperity, but declared he would "have other towns prosper also." London would fail and the whole commonwealth would suffer, he said, if the outports decayed away.[49] Provincial authorities agreed, and they invoked the powers of the state to fend off what they saw as the overweening ambitions of the metropolis.

The burgeoning number and power of London-based trading companies created an ongoing threat to provincial trade, and it often fell to borough corporations to challenge the Londoners' dominance. Mayors and bailiffs, particularly of port towns heavily involved in international trade, regularly resorted to the Privy Council, seeking intervention by the state to protect local economic interests. The corporations of the great trading companies lobbied hard for their exclusive rights laid out in their charters, while borough corporations resisted threats to their historic trades protected by their own corporate charters or even parliamentary statutes. The Cinque Ports, bound in an ancient alliance by corporate charter, repeatedly combined to appeal to both Privy Council and parliament for redress of their grievances against the Merchant Adventurers for restraint of trade and infringement of liberties.[50] The corporations of Newcastle,

---

[46] Henry Swinden, *The History and Antiquities of the Ancient Burgh of Great Yarmouth in the County of Norfolk* (Norwich, 1772), p. 467, n. (q). Mishra, *Business of State*, chap. 5, provides a useful analysis of key pamphlets in these debates.

[47] Robert Ashton, *The City and the Court 1603–1643* (Cambridge, 1979), pp. 106–8; R. Ashton, "The Parliamentary Agitation for Free Trade in the Opening Years of the Reign of James I," *Past & Present* No. 38 (1967), 41, 44.

[48] Southampton Constituency Report, *HoP 1604–29*; *CSPD Addenda, 1580–1625*, pp. 596, 598, 663–4; YCA, B.34, fol. 210v.

[49] ESRO, RYE 47/97 (Mayor and jurats of Sandwich to brethren and comburgesses, May 1621); W. Notestein, F. Relf, and H. Simpson (eds), *Commons Debates 1621* (New Haven, CT, 1935), vol. 2, p. 364, vol. 3, p. 246, vol. 4, pp. 338–9.

[50] TNA, SP14/108, fol. 98 (Petition of Cinque Ports to Privy Council, 21 April 1619); SP14/120, fol. 193 (Petition of Cinque Ports to House of Commons, [April?] 1621); APC 1619–21, p. 55; ESRO, RYE 47/97, 47/105; KHLC, Sa/Ac7 (Sandwich Corporation Yearbook 1608–1642), fol. 133v. Their efforts to contain the Londoners largely failed, but

PROMOTING PEACE AND PLENTY

Hull, York, and Ipswich engaged in a lengthy difference with the Eastland merchants that came before the Privy Council in 1616; Hull continued the conflict for several years.[51] Southampton's corporation clashed with the Levant Company in the mid-1610s, coming before the Privy Council several times. The Levant Company convinced the king to make a proclamation in 1615 restricting the trade to members of their company, despite Southampton's right by statute to import sweet wines. The town complained to the Board in June 1618 of the "great loss and hindrance" that the proclamation caused them, and appealed for relief. They put their concerns in the language of public good – the duty on their importation of sweet wines went toward the repair of the sea walls, which could not be maintained without the revenue now jeopardized by the Levant Company's monopoly.[52] Pitting their liberties of trade and powers of governance against those of the London trading companies, provincial borough corporations attempted to stake a claim as critical contributors to the peace and prosperity of the realm in the face of London's power.

The crown's response to provincial pleas for protection against London varied, but amidst the debates over free trade the Privy Council evidenced some sympathy for the outports. In adjudicating a conflict between Hull and the Muscovy Company in 1618, the Lords declared their care for the subsistence of the Londoners, but "so have we the like of you and your town [of Hull], whose welfare and benefit we shall assuredly respect in this kind, so far as either in justice or equity you may expect the same."[53] The Board's decisions do not suggest a rigid policy stance on the openness of trade, or provincial towns vs. London; rather, they were often persuaded by whomever stood before them at the moment, and Londoners usually got there first. In July 1617, London merchants trading into Spain and Portugal convinced the Privy Council of the benefits of incorporating them, which they argued would not hinder free trade but simply resolve the "confusion" and "disorder" of it. The Board agreed in principle, believing it would promote good government and cause no harm. Nevertheless, they notified the magistrates of Southampton, Dorchester, Plymouth, Poole, Exeter, Barnstaple, Weymouth, Bridgewater, and Bristol, soliciting comment. Unsurprisingly, the western ports declared that the charter would be "full of inconveniences and very prejudicial" to them. After hearing both parties, the Council changed direction, determining that it would

---

Charles I finally granted a charter confirmation to the Cinque Ports in 1634. HMC, *13th Report, Appendix*, pt. 3 (London, 1892), p. 355.

[51] APC *1615–16*, pp. 417–18, *1618–19*, pp. 2; CSPD *1619–23*, p. 559; HHC, BRL 173 (John Lister *et al.* to mayor and aldermen of Hull, 9 May 162[1?]), BRL 197 (John Lister *et al.* to Mayor and aldermen of Hull, 17 April 1623).

[52] Larkin and Hughes (eds), *Stuart Royal Proclamations*, vol. 1, pp. 338–40; *Statutes of the Realm*, vol. 4, pt. 2, pp. 1149–50 (4 Jac.1, c. 10); APC *1618–19*, pp. 165. Southampton's troubles over sweet wines and their sea walls continued well into the 1630s. TNA, SP16/303, fol. 154, SP16/307, fol. 167.

[53] APC *1618–19*, p. 2.

159

URBAN GOVERNMENT AND THE EARLY STUART STATE

be "neither fit nor convenient" to grant the Londoners a charter, and the trade would be left free.[54] Similarly, when the Merchant Adventurers persuaded the Board to grant their members exclusionary rights over trade in lead and other goods to Germany in January 1619, Hull's corporation protested, claiming it crossed the town's privileges and impoverished its people. Concerted efforts by Hull's mayor, John Lister (himself a merchant involved in the lead trade) resulted in extensive accommodations on the part of the Merchant Adventurers. When Lister felt these were not enough, he "prevailed upon" the Council for further hearing. By December 1619, the Board had reversed the original decision from January, enabling Hull's merchants to continue in the trade.[55] Londoners spoke loudly, but provincial voices could also be persuasive, particularly in light of the Board's reactive decision-making.

The outcry during James's reign against patents and monopolies of all sorts, in which the struggles between provincial corporations and London trading companies played a part, resounded in the 1621 Parliament.[56] Members excoriated monopolists, customs farmers, and patentees, and the king's government backed away from the policies of the 1610s that had used patents to enhance royal revenues and that tended to increase the London companies' power. King James's proclamation of 10 July 1621 addressed these grievances. In addition to suppressing excessive fees and revoking various patents, licenses, and warrants, it secured more open trade throughout the realm.[57] In particular, the king took "into his Princely care the trade of the Outports of this Realm," giving freedom for the inhabitants of provincial ports to "henceforth participate with the Merchant Adventurers freely and indifferently" in the New Draperies, and also in any commodities in which they had traded in the time of Queen Elizabeth.[58] The proclamation thus had particular resonance for provincial towns, whose government and trade had been deeply affected by the patents and monopolies at the heart of the grievances. The king's proclamation did not stop London trading companies from pressing their monopolistic interests, but it did indicate a shift in the crown's stance. The bitter failure of schemes like

---

[54] *APC 1616–17*, pp. 292, 342, 350, 353. The Council referred the London merchants to parliament for redress of any disorders in the government of their trade. An earlier statute, 3 Jac. I, c. 6, had made trade into Spain, Portugal, and France free.

[55] *APC 1618–19*, pp. 351-2, 482-3, *1619–21*, pp. 90-1; "Lister, John (1587–1640)," *HoP 1604-1629*, www.historyofparliamentonline.org/volume/1604-1629/member/lister-john-1587-1640.

[56] See Ashton, *The City and the Court*, pp. 108-9; E.R. Foster, "The Procedure in the House of Commons against Patents and Monopolies, 1621-4," in W. Aiken and B.D. Henning (eds), *Conflict in Stuart England* (New York, 1960), pp. 57-85; Robert Zaller, *The Parliament of 1621: A Study in Constitutional Conflict* (Berkeley, CA, 1971); Conrad Russell, *Parliaments and English Politics, 1621–1629* (Oxford, 1979).

[57] Notestein, *et al.* (eds), *Commons Debates 1621*; TNA, SP14/121, fol. 234; Larkin and Hughes (eds), *Stuart Royal Proclamations*, vol. 1, pp. 511-19.

[58] Larkin and Hughes (eds), *Stuart Royal Proclamations*, vol. 1, p. 516.

Cockayne's and the lobbying of the outports encouraged the crown's integration of provincial viewpoints into national policy.

Debate over free trade and the role of the outports in England's economy continued, though perhaps with less political heat, under Charles. The war with Spain and then France turned attention of both central and local authorities to war finance and defense. The new king's government also showed less enthusiasm for promoting the interests of at least some of the great London companies. Rupali Mishra argues that in the late 1620s and 1630s, the connection between the East India Company and the Privy Council became increasingly tenuous, loosening links forged under James.[59] Changing royal attitudes may have given provincial tradesmen greater hope in the face of metropolitan clout, as towns made a case for their own commitment to the good government of trade. When London merchants in 1631 attempted once again to obtain an incorporated trading company for Spain and Portugal, western ports including Plymouth, Dartmouth, Totnes, and Exeter joined in appealing to the Privy Council.[60] Dartmouth's mayor spoke for the other towns in highlighting the base motivations of Londoners. Dismissing as mere pretense metropolitan claims that a chartered company would regulate disorder in the trade, he complained that the London merchants "aim at nothing more than their own private gain," while harming "many thousands" in western ports, to the "great prejudice of the whole common wealth."[61] The JPs of both Cornwall and Devon joined the mayors of the ports in objecting, stressing that the merchants of their counties would be undone and, of significance to the state, the king's customs revenues would fall. In the end, provincial voices prevailed.[62] Exeter, in the late 1630s, can be found resisting the Merchants Adventurers' claim that all Spanish cloths must be shipped from London. Perhaps having learned lessons from Cockayne's scheme, the Council explicitly denied a metropolitan monopoly, "being not willing to shut up the trade of the outports altogether."[63] London's undeniable economic might could not silence the voice of provincial towns in defense of their trade. The Caroline regime did not equate good governance of trade with London's monopolization if it, and provincial towns successfully employed arguments for order and public good in appealing to the crown for redress against metropolitan interests.

---

[59] Mishra, *Business of State*, pp. 264, 270, 273-4, 286, 301. See also Jason White, "Royal Authority versus Corporate Sovereignty: the Levant Company and the Ambiguities of Early Stuart Statecraft," *The Seventeenth Century* 32 (2017), 234-5 on changing relationships of the crown with the Levant Company in the 1620s and 1630s.

[60] Worth (ed.), *Plymouth Municipal Records*, p. 152; Chanter and Wainwright (eds), *Reprint of the Barnstaple Records*, vol. 2, p. 135; TNA, SP16/198, fol. 79, SP16/204, fol. 71, PC2/43, p. 586.

[61] TNA, SP16/198, fol. 79.

[62] TNA, SP16/201, fol. 20, SP16/202, fol. 98, SP16/204, fol. 71.

[63] TNA, SP16/378, fol. 230, SP16/379, fol. 142, SP16/380, fols 126-8.

URBAN GOVERNMENT AND THE EARLY STUART STATE

Towns and trading infrastructure

While all corporate boroughs worked to protect their economic well-being and vigilantly held off others who might damage privileges and profit, at the same time they were very much part of a larger state on which they depended to facilitate that profit. Townsmen relied heavily on the infrastructure of the realm – roads, bridges, havens, ports – to conduct the trade that constituted their livelihoods. Within borough boundaries, urban governments raised rates to pay for things like marketplaces, roads, quays, piers, and town halls that benefited the public good and prosperity of a town.[64] Responsibility for activities like bridge maintenance typically fell to the corporation of the borough in which a bridge was located; corporate charters regularly included privileges to collect tolls or other duties for that purpose. Boston's corporation, for instance, admitted responsibility to maintain the town's great bridge, piers and seawalls while also claiming to have, since time out of mind, the right to take tolls to support the cost.[65] But some works were simply too large for one town to support, requiring engagement with the state to accomplish. Borough governors made regular appeals to the Privy Council and parliament that the cost of these public goods should be shared more widely; infrastructure served the state and not just the locality, facilitating trade as well as defense in the realm. Such projects represented an important means of connection between provincial towns and the state, as borough governors negotiated the extent – and the limitations – of shared responsibility for public assets that fostered commerce.

For towns along the coast, the perpetual battle with the sea to keep their piers and havens in repair led many of them to seek external support, arguing for the larger importance of their small-town projects. Places like Whitby in Yorkshire or Dunwich, Walberswick, and Southwold in Suffolk struggled to maintain the havens on which their largely seagoing economies rested. Dunwich, which in Saxon times served as an important port, was by its own account in 1628 almost entirely "swallowed up of the sea." A major inundation in March 1609 wiped out the road from the town down to the sea, necessitating repairs. The corporation's minutes identified this as the state's problem, not just the town's; "neither the king's majesty," they said, "nor the inhabitants could pass.[66] Throughout the first decades of the seventeenth century, ports like Dunwich called on king,

---

[64] On town halls, see Robert Tittler, *Architecture and Power: The Town Hall and the English Urban Community, c. 1500–1640* (Oxford, 1991); Tittler, *Townspeople and Nation: English Urban Experiences 1540–1640* (Stanford, CA, 2001), pp. 60–80.

[65] W. Turrentine Jackman, *The Development of Transportation in Modern England*, 2nd edn (London, 1962), pp. 148–9, 151; GA, GBR B3/1, fol. 210v; TNA, SP14/190, fol. 22–3. The statute 22 Henry VIII, c.5 declared that repairs to bridges that were within a city or corporate town were the responsibility of the inhabitants of that town.

[66] TNA, PC2/42, p. 546, SP16/100, fol. 60; SA/I, EE6/1144/10 (Dunwich Minute Book, 1596–1619), fol. 187v.

162

PROMOTING PEACE AND PLENTY

Privy Council, and parliament to bolster the commonwealth by securing their town's infrastructure.

The leaders of Dunwich made regular attempts to obtain help in their cause, sometimes banding together with neighboring coastal towns. Early in 1604, shortly after James I summoned his first parliament, Dunwich, Southwold, and Walberswick corresponded to petition parliament for a "general help" from parishes throughout England for making new piers for the haven at Dunwich and improving the channel to Southwold quay. This, they alleged, would benefit the three towns, but also the general good of the region.[67] Unfortunately, their suit failed, and parliament never took up the matter of Dunwich's harbor.[68] Again in 1611, the towns collaborated, this time petitioning the king himself. They agreed to send their man of business to Sir Edward Coke to gain his help in preferring their suit.[69] This attempt proved fruitless, as did another – to both the king and the parliament – in 1614.[70] Finally, in 1618, the towns successfully petitioned James for support in rebuilding the piers and haven. Letters patent, issued in February 1619, authorized a general collection throughout England for the repairs.[71] With war looming on the Continent, James's government began to recognize the importance of Suffolk harbors to national security.

While townsmen and Privy Council alike could agree that infrastructure existed for the public good of commerce and commonwealth, not just the private benefit of a particular corporation, the question of how to pay for it remained. In some cases, the crown used its own resources. Berwick-upon-Tweed received grants eventually totaling £15,000 from King James to replace the bridge there; the project of fostering trade and communication between England and Scotland lay close to the king's heart.[72] More often, however, the Privy Council authorized a corporation to take voluntary collections in surrounding areas or even nationwide. The city of Lincoln, "which heretofore was one of the chiefest in the kingdom, but now decayed for want of trade, and

---

[67] SA/I, EE6/1144/10, fols 130v–131, 132; HMC, *Report on Manuscripts in Various Collections*, vol. 7 (London, 1914), p. 89. Dunwich was the sole parliamentary borough among them. Each town remained jealous of its own interests and profits; collaboration proved difficult. When Southwold asked Dunwich for aid in digging out their harbor, Dunwich's assembly agreed that "the said town of Dunwich is not minded to send any help to dig any haven in any other place so long as this which they already have do run." SA/I, EE6/1144/10, fol. 211v.
[68] Dunwich Constituency Report, *HoP 1604-29*, www.historyofparliamentonline.org/volume/1604-1629/constituencies/dunwich.
[69] SA/I, EE6/1144/10, fol. 216.
[70] HMC, *Various*, vol. 7, p. 93.
[71] HMC, *Various*, vol. 7, p. 94–5; TNA, SP14/105, fol. 144.
[72] Jackman, *Development of Transportation*, pp. 152-3; *CSPD 1603–1610*, pp. 358, 431, 1619-23, p. 412; Janine van Vliet, "From a 'Strong Town of War' to 'the Very Heart of the Country': The English Border Town of Berwick-upon-Tweed, 1558-1625" (PhD dissertation, University of Pennsylvania, 2017), pp. 233-42. Van Vliet's work shows both the king's interest in the project and the corporation's eagerness to prove its competence in undertaking such an important and expensive endeavor.

URBAN GOVERNMENT AND THE EARLY STUART STATE

become poor, and one of the meanest," received the Council's warrant in 1615 to collect throughout Lincolnshire to scour the Fosse, enhancing navigation from the city to the maritime towns.[73] When the town of Whitby appealed to the Board about its damaged piers, the Council authorized a general collection for repairs, seeing it as of "great service" and "great consequence" to the king and his subjects, because it did "much concern the public."[74] Sadly, these collections did not always have the desired effect, despite the Privy Council's urging. Hastings received letters patent in 1621 to make a nationwide collection for repairing its piers, but had to lobby the Privy Council to get the collections paid in, suggesting that other localities were less sanguine about the importance of Hastings's haven to the commonwealth.[75] In the case of Dunwich, the Board sent letters to the assize judges as well as JPs, mayors, and other principal officers throughout England and Wales, requiring them to "move and exhort all his Majesty's loving subjects to contribute cheerfully." All should support "a work so profitable to the commonwealth."[76] Despite the exhortations, contributions lagged. At one point, Dunwich reported receiving only £33 3s 9d, having already expended £17 3s 6d to obtain and promote the contribution.[77] The infrastructure of commerce constituted a public good, but the early Stuart state lacked the fiscal means to provide consistently for this common good, and not all of the king's subjects believed it their duty to "contribute cheerfully" to such work.

Appeals through parliament met with similarly mixed results. Rye attempted parliamentary bills to authorize increased toll revenue to go toward repair of their harbor in the parliaments of 1604-10, 1621, and 1624, all to no avail.[78] Colchester's corporation, operating through their long-serving MP Edward Alford, promoted a bill in 1621 to allow the town to raise revenues through impositions on shipping to repave its streets and repair its silted-up haven. Alford argued that failure to take care of these matters would damage the king's customs revenues, not just the local economy. Opponents complained that there were already too many impositions, that paving the streets was an unworthy thing for the greatness of the House to consider, and that "divers places were to beare the charge which showld have noe parte of the benefitt." The bill faltered in 1621, but passed when reintroduced in the 1624 Parliament.[79] These attempts show that port towns saw themselves as important parts of a wider

---

[73] APC 1615-16, p. 415.
[74] TNA, PC2/42, p. 546.
[75] Anthony Fletcher, A County Community in Peace and War: Sussex, 1600-1660 (London and New York, 1975), p. 20; VCH Sussex, vol. 9, ed. L.F. Salzman (London, 1937), p. 10; HMC, 13th Report, Appendix, pt. 4 (London, 1892); APC 1619-21, pp. 346-7, 1621-23, p. 136.
[76] APC 1617-19, p. 378.
[77] APC 1619-21, p. 245; HMC, Various, vol. 7, p. 95.
[78] Rye Constituency Report, HoP 1604-29, www.historyofparliamentonline.org/volume/1604-1629/constituencies/rye; see also Fletcher, County Community, pp. 20-1, 237-8, 246.
[79] Notestein et al. (eds), Commons Debates 1621, vol. 2, p. 111, vol. 4, p. 83; Colchester

PROMOTING PEACE AND PLENTY

commonwealth; their economies and infrastructure contributed to the realm as a whole, and therefore the financial burden should not rest on one town alone. The varying success of the efforts, however, suggests no universal acceptance of shared burden for projects such as these in the early seventeenth century, even when the king himself promoted them.

For some provincial towns, dominance over a particular trade or commodity made the case for sharing the expense of its infrastructure compelling. Great Yarmouth, the center of the herring fishery, successfully lobbied for significant resources from the wider realm to support its haven on the basis of its importance to the public good of the commonwealth. Townsmen spent significantly on maintaining the piers and the haven, vital infrastructure for their valuable fishing trade. According to the bailiffs' accounts, they laid out on average £570 per year from 1600 to 1640, just on the haven.[80] This was a difficult cost to bear alone, and the town tried various means of raising revenues, including special export licenses, the profit from which went to haven repair. They also "adventured" £25 in the lottery for Virginia in 1615. (The official motto for the adventure: "Great Yarmouth's Haven now in great distress/Expects by Lottery some Good Success.")[81] Finally, in 1621 King James established a commission, headed by the bishop of Norwich, to inquire into the repair of the Great Yarmouth haven and how to pay for it.[82] The commissioners found that the town had spent, since the beginning of Queen Elizabeth's reign, over £30,000 on the haven, and the corporation was £23,000 in debt for it. In response, the Privy Council ordered a collection to be made throughout the realm in support of Great Yarmouth's haven. The cost of repairs, the Board said, was "too heavy if not impossible" for Yarmouth to bear alone, but the work was "nevertheless of such importance to the public that it cannot be deferred or passed over but with extreme prejudice to the commonwealth."[83] The king's letters patent for the collection reiterated the same theme of shared public good: "The haven and piers there are of great necessity and importance, as well for our service, defence, and commodity, as also for the generall good and benefit not onely of those parts, but also the whole kingdome."[84] In addition, the crown granted Yarmouth's corporation a license to export 4,000 tons of beer customs-free, the profit from which was to go toward haven repairs.[85] The corporation, the commissioners, the Council, and the king all shared the view that the haven was not a private responsibility of the corporation in whose jurisdiction it sat,

---

Constituency Report, *HoP 1604–29*, www.historyofparliamentonline.org/volume/1604-1629/constituencies/colchester.

[80] Swinden, *Great Yarmouth*, pp. 944-8.

[81] NRO, Y/C19/5, fol. 150.

[82] Swinden, *Great Yarmouth*, pp. 458-9, n. (n).

[83] TNA, SP14/123, fols 166-9, 170; *APC 1621–23*, p. 172.

[84] Swinden, *Great Yarmouth*, p. 459, n. (o).

[85] *CSPD 1619–23*, p. 426; NRO, Y/C19/5, fol. 263v, Y/C18/6, fol. 85v.

URBAN GOVERNMENT AND THE EARLY STUART STATE

but rather a public good that should be supported by the state.[86] Yet the lack of the king's own "skin in the game" suggests the precariousness of royal finance, a point that became clearer as external threats assaulted the realm's trade and security.

Piracy, war, and trade in provincial towns

Like infrastructure, establishing the safety of trade on the seas was a key component of the communication and interaction between provincial ports and central authorities in the early Stuart period. The dangers to shipping – particularly from piracy – formed a constant threat to all merchants who plied the seas. It should be remembered that Penzance's charter specifically noted piracy and defense in its preamble as reasons for the town's incorporation in 1614.[87] While merchants might band together for mutual protection, they increasingly relied on the state to provide resources and organization to secure their trade. No single port town could fully safeguard local business, as the expense was great and the authority of magistrates ran only as far as their own jurisdictions. Borough magistrates played a critical role as advocates for their communities in facing threats against trade and in soliciting the power of the crown to provide protection. Interactions between central and local authorities over trade raised questions over the extent of responsibility of the state and the role that local communities had in crafting the state's policies.

The problem of piracy loomed large in early Stuart England. In addition to interlopers and home-grown pirates,[88] the early seventeenth century saw persistent onslaughts of sea rovers including Dunkirkers and "Turks," Barbary pirates from Tunis and Algiers. The depredations of pirates took a tremendous toll, both economic and human, on port towns, in ships and cargoes lost and seamen killed or captured; financial ruin threatened the families and communities of those taken by pirates, from those losses and from the cost of redeeming captives. Thomas Cogswell has illuminated how significantly the Dunkirkers harmed towns like Aldeburgh, Suffolk, and how assiduously local communities worked to try to address the problem.[89] Merchants throughout the

---

[86] Lagging contributions led a Yarmouth alderman to grumble in October 1622 that nearby gentry voiced forwardness yet committed nothing, while the citizens of Norwich gave only 100 marks. The Privy Council urged the bishop, lord lieutenant, and JPs of Norfolk in February 1623 to proceed against the refractory. NRO, Y/C19/5, fol. 268; APC 1621–23, pp. 419–20.

[87] Pool, History of Penzance, p. 214.

[88] The East India Company, for instance, complained of English interlopers out of Portsmouth whose "purpose is rather to behave themselves as pirates than merchants, to the great scandal of the whole nation." APC 1615–16, p. 154.

[89] Thomas Cogswell, "Ten Demi-Culverins for Aldeburgh: Whitehall, the Dunkirkers, and a Suffolk Fishing Community, 1625–1630," Journal of British Studies 58 (2019), 315–37.

PROMOTING PEACE AND PLENTY

realm, in the outports as well as the metropolis, faced the scourge of piracy, and they accepted some responsibility to suppress it. But piracy touched on national defense and international politics, and it could only be confronted through coordinated efforts by central government and local communities. Those efforts were in evidence from the mid-1610s into the 1630s, as local actors begged central authorities to address the problem with naval force, and merchants, mayors, and Privy Council negotiated who would pay, and how much. The nature of these interactions changed as the focus and policy priorities of the crown evolved across the reigns of James and Charles, provoking regular inter-action between port towns and the crown over financial responsibility and the severity of the threat. In facing the problem of piracy, provincial towns helped shape the crown's policy and negotiated the boundaries of the state's responsi-bility for protecting the profit of the realm.

By the late 1610s, communities all around England's coasts felt the economic impact of pirates from Algiers and Tunis, and the merchants and port towns suffered. In response to repeated petitions, largely from the London trading companies, King James resolved in 1617 to extirpate the menace.[90] The crown dictated the means of proceeding as a matter of state, but the merchants whose trade was affected would bear the charge.[91] The essentially medieval naval finance system that the Stuarts inherited assumed that the particular beneficiaries of the state's protection should pay for their own defense. But as David Hebb has shown in his work on piracy, the increasingly integrated and specialized economy of the seventeenth century made it more difficult to identify just who benefitted from naval defense against piracy. The merchants directly involved in international trade, whose ships came under attack by pirates, obviously benefitted, but what about ship owners, or merchants involved in inland trade, or residents of port towns, or people who consumed the products being traded? No clear bureaucracy existed either to sort out the answers to these questions or to collect the money which, though typically called "contributions," were not really voluntary.[92] In London, the Board held the governors of the major trading companies responsible for collection, but in the provincial ports, the chief officers of the borough corporations found themselves at the center of this complexity. They negotiated the collections with the Privy Council and with the merchants and inhabitants of their towns. Aware of their duty as the king's officers to carry out the crown's orders, they were also borough officers called upon to advocate for corporate privileges and local concerns.

Interaction between town governments and the crown in the 1610s and early 1620s frequently revolved around paying the cost of suppressing the pirates. The Council first required contributions totaling £40,000 from the major trading

---

[90] *APC 1616–17*, pp. 181–2, 219, 263.
[91] *APC 1617–19*, pp. 358–9.
[92] David D. Hebb, *Piracy and the English Government, 1616–1642* (Aldershot, 1994), pp. 33–5.

167

URBAN GOVERNMENT AND THE EARLY STUART STATE

companies of London.[93] Soon thereafter, the Board wrote to the mayors or bailiffs of some of the outports, calling on their merchants to contribute, as well.[94] An abortive attempt in 1617 was followed by a more concerted effort at collection by the Privy Council in 1618-19. King James, for "reasons best known to himself," then postponed the expedition against pirates in 1619, after the collection had been made. An expedition finally departed in 1620, but only after another contentious round of contributions.[95] All of this put provincial corporations in a difficult position. The Privy Council held them responsible to collect the contribution from the merchants, but the authority on which borough officers did so was vague. The Board left much unspecified, leaving local magistrates to sort out whom to rate and how. Many merchants dragged their feet or refused, and town officers looked to the Council for guidance, authority, and perhaps sympathy - which they rarely received.

The Council required contributions from seventeen outports in 1619, and controversy over how to pay for the expedition dominated communications between center and localities. The magistrates of nearly all of the ports wrote to the Board with reasons why they could not raise the amounts assessed for their towns. Some, like the mayors of Plymouth, Southampton, and Bristol, advocated for reduction of the levies due to the decay of their trade or the heavy charges they were already at from lost ships or redeeming kidnapped townsmen.[96] Others sought reinforcement of their authority from the Privy Council. Hull's mayor asked the Board for additional warrant to levy the contribution only on merchants in his town who traded to the south, or else on all the inhabitants generally, indicating some confusion as to whether the burden should be borne by the narrowest definition of trade or the broadest. The mayor of Barnstaple

---

[93] APC 1616-17, pp. 218-19, 263-4, 1618-19, pp. 345-6. The outports were little consulted in the 1617 discussions; they complained they were over-assessed relative to Londoners, whose portion was inadequate considering their "infinite treasures" and command of the "trade of the whole world." TNA, SP14/92, fol. 215 (F. Gorges to Privy Council, 16 July 1617).

[94] APC 1616-17, pp. 218-19, 1618-19, pp. 358-60. The total from the provincial ports was to be £9,000, ranging from £2,500 (Bristol) to £100 (Poole). Major northern ports like Newcastle and Hull were included, but small, distant ports, like Cardiff, Carlisle, and Berwick, were not, suggesting, as Hebb noted, that the southern ports were considered to be most affected. Hebb, Piracy, p. 31.

[95] APC 1616-17, pp. 263-4, 1617-19, pp. 358-60, 1619-21, pp. 62, 105, 239, 379. See also Hebb, Piracy, pp. 77-104 for details of the expedition itself. These collections offered precedents for later Ship Money, but not clear ones. Gardiner stated that the Council resurrected "the old tax of ship-money" in this piracy levy, but that language was never used by the Board (S.R. Gardiner, The History of England from the Accession of James I to the Outbreak of the Civil War, 1603-1642, vol. 3 (London, 1890), p. 288; A.A.M. Gill, "Ship Money during the Personal Rule of Charles I: Politics, Ideology and the Law 1634 to 1640" (PhD dissertation, University of Sheffield, 1990), p. 43; Robin Swales, "The Ship Money Levy of 1628," Bulletin of the Institute of Historical Research 50 (1977), 166).

[96] TNA, SP14/108, fol. 69, SP14/107, fols 6, 80, SP14/113, fol. 51.

168

PROMOTING PEACE AND PLENTY

reported that he could only collect less than half of what was required because the merchants of Barnstaple, "not being incorporated, are subject to no government." Newcastle's mayor likewise found his town's merchants reluctant, contributing only £150 of the £300 assessment. The mayor asked the Board for further license to compel the backward to pay.[97] Mayors and bailiffs were pulled between their obligations as officers of the crown and their role as local governors in negotiating these contributions.

Trading rivalries and a strong sense of corporate privileges often mingled with excuses of poverty and lack of authority in borough governors' correspondence with the Board. The London companies debated among themselves and with the outports over rating, and the provincial ports also argued among themselves. Lyme Regis's mayor begged the Council to shift the burden off his town and onto Bristol and Exeter, whose merchants had the main trade in Lyme. Exeter's mayor played down his city's trade, alleging the small number of merchants whose ships encountered pirates. The mayor of Hull claimed that four-sevenths of the amount levied on his town should be paid by York's merchants, who denied responsibility. Great Yarmouth's bailiffs stated their inability to raise the £200 required of them, both because of their great charges for repairing their haven and piers and because of the refusal of nearby small ports to join in Yarmouth's charge (though they would contribute a small amount independently). Dartmouth's mayor complained to the Board that, while merchants in his town would willingly contribute, the merchants of Totnes refused because they were not specifically named in the Council's order; Totnes's mayor countered that they would contribute £500, but on condition that they might be freed from interference from Dartmouth.[98] All of the ports accepted responsibility for protection of their trade, but the levy brought out both economic rivalries and skirmishes over corporate liberties, none of which conduced to expeditious collection of the amount the crown expected.

The Council took firm measures to ensure that local magistrates made the collections in full, but they showed flexibility in response to some concerns. The Board made clear that the towns must submit their required amounts to support "a matter so much importing the public and the security of their private trades." To the mayor of Southampton's letter forwarding £92, the Lords replied thanking him for his readiness, but noted that since the town owed £150 this year, the amount was £58 short. The mayor must go back to the merchants for the remainder. When that failed, the Board sent a second, more forceful letter, scolding the townsmen for their "coldness and backwardness," demanding full payment, and ordering the mayor and two aldermen to appear before the Council.[99] Mayors of other towns received similar sharp letters.[100] At the same

[97] TNA, SP14/105, fol. 201, SP14/107, fols 17, 31, 79, SP14/108, fol. 67.
[98] TNA, SP14/105, fols 145, 215, SP14/107, fols 65, 17, 12, 33, 47, SP14/109, fol. 171.
[99] APC 1618–19, pp. 380, 392–3.
[100] APC 1618–19, pp. 388, 408, 409, 410.

169

URBAN GOVERNMENT AND THE EARLY STUART STATE

time, the Privy Council did take local circumstances into consideration. They supported mayors in rating disputes, requiring York to contribute with Hull and the small ports to contribute with Yarmouth; all were "equally interested in the security of common and free trade."[101] Totnes, on the other hand, was allowed to rate itself separately from Dartmouth, as long as they sent up £500.[102] The Board authorized the mayors of Colchester and Poole to collect not only from merchants and ship owners in their towns, but also other "traders of ability ... taking benefit of that port," thus making it easier to raise the full sum.[103] Towns also had leeway in how they raised the money. Newcastle, by its own choice, rated each merchant and ship owner individually. Exeter, in contrast, chose to rate commodities traded through the port; the Board ordered the customs officials not to seal imports or exports without a "ticket" under the hand and seal of Exeter's mayor, in order to assure the collection.[104] These negotiations over the funding of anti-piracy efforts show the extent to which shared interest in "the security of common and free trade" required provincial towns to engage with each other and the state, but also the necessity of the center to lead and coordinate.

The state's inability to provide an effective response colored the experience of the port towns as war with Spain and France loomed in Charles's reign. While under James, rating questions dominated the dialog about piracy between provincial ports and the crown, the focus later shifted to vocal pleas for help. "Turks" and Dunkirkers plied the coasts of England and Ireland, stealing cargoes, taking captives, and sinking ships.[105] Provincial ports assiduously alerted the crown to the danger to trade and national security, seeking engagement with the state to address the problem. Mayors, bailiffs, and aldermen of port towns all over England complained pitifully and frequently to central authorities of pirate depredations. Coastal towns like Aldeburgh, as Cogswell has shown, suffered immeasurable harm from the Dunkirkers, who stole ships, captured and killed townsmen, and threatened the very safety of the town itself; the danger moved borough governors to invoke the crown's aid to protect their towns.[106] In 1625 and 1626, mayors or bailiffs of Plymouth, Weymouth, Barnstaple, Poole, Bristol, Newcastle, Aldeburgh, Scarborough, Dartmouth, and Great Yarmouth all wrote to the Privy Council (often multiple times) about the danger of pirates harrying ships along the coasts and the need for relief.[107] Ireland, too, fell victim. The

---

[101] *APC 1618–19*, pp. 400, 410–11.
[102] *APC 1618–19*, p. 456.
[103] *APC 1618–19*, pp. 374, 409.
[104] *APC 1618–19*, p. 414; TNA, SP14/107, fol. 79.
[105] In general, Barbary pirates were more troubling to the western ports, while Dunkirkers harried the east coast ports.
[106] Cogswell, "Ten Demi-Culverins for Aldeburgh," pp. 315–37; Worth (ed.), *Plymouth Municipal Records*, p. 154.
[107] TNA, SP16/1, fol. 97, SP16/2, fols 82, 150, SP16/3, fol. 115, SP16/5, fols 12, 39, 163, SP16/8, fol. 91, SP16/19, fol. 233, SP16/22, fol. 77, SP16/25, fol. 105, SP16/33, fol. 69.

170

PROMOTING PEACE AND PLENTY

mayor of Limerick complained in 1626 to Lord Deputy Falkland of Dunkirkers, Spaniards, and Turks who had taken six ships from the town and enslaved the sailors in Barbary.[108] Piracy had a profound effect on specific towns, but borough governors lobbied hard to raise the problem to national attention and to engage the state as the only way to resolve it.

Pirates endangered the safety of particular merchants, but more worryingly they had the potential to decimate the trade of the realm as a whole, a connection which many provincial ports made to the crown. The mayor of Plymouth, after rehearsing to the Privy Council the losses suffered by Plymouth and Looe in the last year, raised the fear that all ships coming back from Virginia and the Newfoundland fisheries would be endangered. The mayor of Bristol informed the Council in August 1625 that the depredations of the Turkish pirates imperiled the valuable trade with Ireland, and he also raised worries about the Newfoundland fleet, soon to return to England.[109] Petitions from merchants and masters of ships from Ipswich, signed with the borough corporation's seal, begged the Council for defense of the coast from Dunkirkers, whose presence ruined trade, kept ships in port, and stopped the fisheries to Iceland and the North Sea. The bailiffs of Aldeburgh, Dunwich, Southwold, and Walberswick sent a similar petition to the duke of Buckingham.[110] Newcastle's mayor lamented the pirates' spoil of shipping and the ruination of "many thousand laboring people" due to the inability to "vent" coals.[111] Local officials sought to bring attention to the particular devastation of their own business, but they understood it as a larger problem, the effects of which went far beyond their town or region, requiring a national solution.

Despite repeated attempts to bring the issue of piracy to the attention of Caroline government in the first years of the reign, provincial pleas sparked only intermittent central action. For townsmen, the present danger to lives and livelihoods posed by the Turks and Dunkirkers required a strong response from the state, but the interest of King Charles and Buckingham largely lay elsewhere, on the war with Spain, and later France. Buckingham, as lord admiral, had some concern for protection of the Narrow Seas, deploying a modest number of ships to fight the pirates and escort merchant and fishing fleets. But he kept his focus on the deployment of soldiers for Spain, targeting ships, men, and money there.[112] The naval resources that were aimed at the pirate menace did

---

[108] *CSP Ireland, 1625-32*, p. 170 (Mayor of Limerick to Lord Falkland, 14 October 1626).

[109] TNA, SP16/5, fols 78 (Mayor of Plymouth to Privy Council, 12 August 1625), 109 (Mayor of Bristol to Privy Council, 18 August 1625).

[110] TNA, SP16/34, fols 126-7; SA/I, EE1/O1/1 (Aldeburgh Corporation Letter Book 1625-1663), fols 22v-23.

[111] TNA, SP16/24, fol. 28 (Mayor and aldermen of Newcastle to Privy Council, 4 April 1626).

[112] TNA, SP16/1, fol. 59, SP16/5, fol. 180, SP16/6, fol. 29, SP16/24, fol. 92, SP16/25, fol. 30. See also Thomas Cogswell, "The Lord Admiral, The Parliament-Men, and the Narrow Seas, 1625-27," in C. Kyle and J. Peacey (eds), *Connecting Centre and Locality: Political Communication in Early Modern England* (Manchester, 2020), pp. 45, 49-50.

URBAN GOVERNMENT AND THE EARLY STUART STATE

not always inspire confidence. The mayor of Plymouth complained that five naval ships under Sir Francis Stewart went out against the Turks, but the Turks out-sailed the Englishmen; Stewart's ships returned to Falmouth after only three days.[113] Complaints in parliament amplified petitions to the Council. MPs from a number of towns spoke out in both 1626 and 1628 about the Dunkirkers, and the issue played a part in the duke of Buckingham's impeachment inquiry.[114] Thomas Sherwill, representing Plymouth, was particularly outspoken about the navy's inadequacies in protecting trade.[115] It must have been a painful irony to receive King Charles's proclamation of October 1628 protecting ships and goods of Tunis, Algiers, and Sallee from English hostility when ships from those same places caused devastation to English merchants and sailors.[116] For many coastal towns, the crown's inability (or unwillingness) to adequately respond to the pirate menace and protect merchants and trade added to a sense of grievance that resonated throughout the war years in Charles's reign.[117]

The pirate threat forced coastal towns all around England to engage with central government to preserve their peace and prosperity, as did the threat of the war itself. The outbreak of war interrupted trade with Spain and France for many towns, as the crown issued a number of proclamations banning or limiting exchange.[118] War thrust the leading men of important provincial trading centers like Bristol and Exeter, and even of smaller towns, onto the front lines of international trade. The mayor and inhabitants of Poole complained in 1627 of their heavy losses due to the Spanish embargo and the stay of goods at Bordeaux, in addition to the general decay of trade.[119] William Whiteway of Dorchester recorded in his diary the impact on his town's economy of increasing conflict with France. His entry for 21 May 1627 notes that trade between England and France was "quite shut up upon former quarrels" that month, and that many French ships were brought into English ports by letters of marque and made prizes.[120] He felt the impact on his own finances of decisions on international

---

[113] TNA, SP16/5, fol. 78.

[114] *CSPD 1625–26*, p. 82; *P in P 1626*, 2:122, 137, 142–3, 262, 361, *1628*, 3:45, 47, 308, 310–11; 4:201–3, 205–6, 208–9. See also Cogswell, "Ten Demi-Culverins for Aldeburgh," pp. 322–3.

[115] *P in P 1626*, 2:122, 361; "Sherwill, Thomas (c. 1571–1631)," *HoP 1604–29*, www.historyofparliamentonline.org/volume/1604-1629/member/sherwill-thomas-1571-1631.

[116] Larkin (ed.), *Stuart Royal Proclamations*, vol. 2, pp. 209–10.

[117] See Chapter 6 for more on this point.

[118] These included "A Proclamation to forbid the Subjects of Realme of England, to have any Trade or Commerce with any of the Dominions of the King of Spaine or the Archduchesse" (24 December 1625) and several other less comprehensive proclamations. Larkin (ed.), *Stuart Royal Proclamations*, vol. 2, pp. 66–7, 72–5, 131–5, 141–2, 153–4, 165–7, 207–9.

[119] TNA, SP16/50, fol. 137; Robert Brenner, *Merchants and Revolution: Commercial Change, Political Conflict, and London's Overseas Traders, 1550–1653* (Princeton, NJ, 1993), p. 223. Brenner notes the severe damage to overseas merchants in trade disruption and loss of goods caused by the crown's war policy.

[120] William Whiteway, *William Whiteway of Dorchester: His Diary 1618 to 1635*, ed. S. Bridges,

trade made by the highest levels of royal government. Among the items he mentioned regarding the 1626 Parliament was the duke of Buckingham's mismanagement of the fleet and the "general seasure of all English goods in france, which happened at this time, by meanes of a French ship of Newhaven, value £40000, detained by the Duke." Some of Whiteway's own goods were caught up in this seizure, and he and a cousin joined with merchants from Exeter to petition Buckingham to give them as much in seized French goods as the French had "arrested" from them. Their loss of trade due to international politics meant that they could no longer give work to the poor weavers and craftsmen abounding in their region.[121]

Outliving the wars with Spain and France, piracy continued to damage commerce into the 1630s, again driving townsmen to try to elevate their local or regional concerns to a matter of state. The grievous injuries to trade perpetrated by the Turkish pirates drove John Delbridge, the inveterate "parliament man" of Barnstaple, to appeal in early 1633 to the magistrates of other western ports to make a joint effort to request help from the crown.[122] Delbridge hoped the merchants of the kingdom would combine to urge the king to take vigorous steps to suppress the Turks, or "they will fall upon our fishing shipes both att Newfoundland and Virginea, for they desire both our shippes and men." The mayor of Exeter, John Hakewill, sympathized with Delbridge, reiterating the "greate danger threatned by those mercieless Turkes to this State, especially to these westerne partes thereof." Eventually a "general meeting of the deputyes" of Exeter, Plymouth, Barnstaple, Dartmouth, Weymouth and Melcombe Regis gathered in late February. They agreed that for the "suppression of the Turkes of Argire and Tunnis" the coastal cities and towns would petition the king and Privy Council about piracy, "thereby to manifest their grievance in that behalf" and to request aid in suppressing pirates and redeeming captives.[123] Common interest in protection of trade, and a clear sense that the problem of piracy was a national one that transcended any local boundaries, encouraged the western ports to engage with the state for relief.

The pleas of merchants like these would support the crown's justification for the charge of Ship Money beginning in 1634. After years of frustration

---

trans. B. Bates, Dorset Record Society, vol. 12 (Dorchester, 1991), p. 89.

[121] Whiteway, *Diary*, pp. 79, 88; *CSPD 1627-28*, pp. 95 (Petition of French merchants of Exeter, Lyme Regis, and Dorchester to Buckingham, 14 March 1627), 576 (Petition of French merchants of Exeter, William Whiteway, *et al.* to Buckingham, 21 February 1628).

[122] Chanter and Wainwright (eds), *Reprint of the Barnstaple Records*, p. 136; "Delbridge, John (1564-1639)," *HoP 1604-29*, www.historyofparliamentonline.org/volume/1604-1629/member/delbridge-john-1564-1639. Delbridge, a cloth merchant of puritan views, served as MP for Barnstaple in 1614, 1621, 1624, 1625, 1626, and 1628, where he was an active and often vocal participant.

[123] Worth (ed.), *Plymouth Municipal Records*, pp. 219-20 (John Delbridge to [mayor of Exeter and other mayors], February 1633; John Hakewill of Exeter to mayor of Plymouth, 14 April 1633; Statement of resolutions from meeting of deputies, 28 February 1633).

in not always finding the crown's response to piracy sufficient to meet the challenge, the port towns now discovered their endangered trade raised to the level of national policy. The king had other motivations than simply addressing the ports' concerns about protecting trade. As A.A.M. Gill has shown, Charles had strategic plans to raise a strong fleet as part of an agreement with Spain to contain the Dutch; deterrence of piracy was a pretext for the king's larger aim.[124] But piracy was portrayed as a national problem requiring broad taxation to address. If the port towns could appreciate the protection of their trade, whatever its true motivation, the issue of the cost once again raised questions about who should pay and how. The idea that those merchants who benefitted should pay still lingered, but the notion that the costs of the state should be shared also had purchase. Charles's decision to use the prerogative method of Ship Money to pay for his fleet, and eventually to spread the charge to his whole realm and not just the ports that traditionally paid it, moved the matter into a new arena of political interaction, which will be discussed in the next chapter.

The significant stoppage of trade that resulted from the of onslaughts of piracy, combined in the later 1620s with war with Spain and France, placed corporate boroughs at the center of national conversations on foreign policy, public safety, and economic survival. And it should be remembered that even as they faced serious challenges to their livelihoods, in the 1620s many of these towns also felt the burden of billeting soldiers for the war, ship money, and the Forced Loan, as well as local rates for plague and poor relief.[125] When the magistrates of provincial towns, particularly those along the coasts, pleaded poverty and inability during these difficult war years, they were not simply whining.[126] Protecting their interests and pocketbooks in light of the serious disruptions to trade in the period certainly motivated borough governors. But the magistrates of towns large and small were well aware of their connection to the state. In bringing their particular concerns to central authority, provincial towns connected their own interest to a national interest and helped shape the policies of the state. They also frequently found that the state could not adequately meet their needs.

---

[124] A.A.M. Gill, "Ship Money during the Personal Rule of Charles I: Politics, Ideology and the Law, 1634 to 1640" (PhD dissertation, University of Sheffield, 1990), p. 34.

[125] See Chapter 6.

[126] See, for instance, TNA, SP16/61, fols 113, 114, 115, 116, 121, 122, 123, petitions from the mayors or bailiffs of Colchester, Ipswich, King's Lynn, Norwich, and Great Yarmouth, as well as the inhabitants of Leeds, Halifax, and Wakefield, about their serious decays and asking relief from paying their allotted ship charges in April 1627.

Navigating interests: Great Yarmouth, the herring license, and the Council

The importance of provincial towns in shaping policy, and the reactive nature of the Privy Council's policy on trade, can be traced across the early Stuart period in the experience of Great Yarmouth and its herring fishery. An important small port that dominated an industry crucial to the realm's economic health, Great Yarmouth engaged regularly with crown and Privy Council to promote its interests. Townsmen saw the good of their industry and local economy as constitutive of the good of the state as a whole, regularly representing their town as a nursery of seamen and a bastion of England's maritime might.[127] Yarmouth's persistent lobbying at the Board for favorable treatment put the town at odds with various London trading companies, and its interests at points also conflicted with royal policy and law regarding foreign trade. While the townsmen's position remained largely the same, advocating for special privileges to the benefit of their trade, the response of the Privy Council changed over time as the international situation and the vehemence of London lobbying reframed the issues. Throughout it all, the men of Great Yarmouth managed, mostly successfully, to convince central authorities that the good of their town's trade promoted the peace and prosperity of the realm.

Yarmouth, "a place of great resort of all the Herring fishermen of England," was, according to one commentator, a town "very well-gouerned by wise and ciuell Magistrates." The annual herring fair there marketed most of the herring caught by fishermen from the Cinque Ports, the southeast and northeast coasts, and the West Country, as well as the Dutch herring fleet.[128] Herring were so important to Yarmouth that the town's authoritative corporate seal, the St. Nicholas Seal, showed the image of "three half linges and three half herrings."[129] During the autumn free fair from Michaelmas to Martinmas, herring dominated civic life, and the bailiffs of Yarmouth, joined by ancient charters with representatives from the Cinque Ports, had extraordinary powers to maintain the market and keep the peace.[130] Yet for all their market authority, Yarmouth's magistrates did not control the trade on their own. They operated within a network of governance connecting them to central authorities as well as merchants and tradesmen of other provincial towns, London, and foreign nations. Subject to the crown's trade policies and the vagaries of international relations, Yarmouth's corporation exhibited a keen awareness of their town as part of the larger state;

---

[127] For an early seventeenth-century resident's view of the town's importance, see Henry Manship, *The History of Great Yarmouth*, ed. Charles John Palmer (Great Yarmouth, 1854).

[128] Tobias Gentleman, *England's Way to Win Wealth* (London, 1614), pp. 26–7.

[129] NRO, Y/C19/6, fol. 129.

[130] Robert Tittler, "The English Fishing Industry in the Sixteenth Century: The Case of Great Yarmouth," *Albion* 9 (1977), 49; David M. Dean, "Parliament, Privy Council, and Local Politics in Elizabethan England: The Yarmouth-Lowestoft Fishing Dispute," *Albion* 22 (1990), 41.

URBAN GOVERNMENT AND THE EARLY STUART STATE

the corporate body expended significant time and resources lobbying powerful men in London and keeping tabs on the machinations of London merchants. Townsmen regularly appealed to central government to maximize their own influence over the herring fishery, connecting their own profit to that of the commonwealth.

Yarmouth had a long history of advocacy for local business with the crown, stressing their orderly management of the herring fishery and its benefit to the realm. The corporation regularly sent its magistrates and men of business to London and used its parliamentary burgesses, at least one of whom was always an alderman, to good effect, as well.[131] Despite ongoing tensions with other towns over the fishery in Elizabeth's reign, Yarmouth managed to assert its interests and obtain a significant privilege. The corporation obtained a license that allowed Yarmouth men to export hundreds of lasts of red herrings in "strangers' bottoms" (foreign ships), a practice normally prohibited.[132] Their arguments were pragmatic, emphasizing the good that would come to the town, the queen, and the state at large: it would not harm English trade, the sales would enlarge the queen's customs revenue, and the profits would go directly toward the repair and maintenance of Yarmouth's haven and piers.[133] The corporation sought to renew the license every year, deeply intertwining the town's trade with the power of central authority.

Routine under Elizabeth, the annual grant of the license became less certain under James and Charles, as metropolitan interests and changing foreign policy priorities challenged Yarmouth's claim. In the first years of James's reign, the crown renewed the herring license annually through 1610.[134] But things soon changed. The king, for "restraining all disordered, and loose manner of traffique," had chartered the Company of French Merchants of London, granting it exclusive rights of carriage into France. The French Company, along with London's Fishmonger's Company, had a strong interest in thwarting Yarmouth's license to export herrings in foreign shipping.[135] King and Privy Council also sought new policies for enhancing trade and bolstering royal revenues in the 1610s. As John Cramsie has shown in his work on crown finance in James's reign, a succession of the king's key advisors sought to stabilize and

---

[131] Great Yarmouth Constituency Report, *HoP 1604–29*, https://www.historyofparliament online.org/volume/1604-1629/constituencies/great-yarmouth.

[132] Swinden, *Great Yarmouth*, pp. 450–1. See Dean, "Yarmouth-Lowestoft Fishing Dispute," for the Elizabethan context.

[133] Swinden, *Great Yarmouth*, pp. 450–4.

[134] Swinden, *Great Yarmouth*, p. 454.

[135] Ashton, "Parliamentary Agitation for Free Trade," p. 41; Charles Arnold-Baker, *Companion to British History*, ed. H. von Blumenthal (Oxford, 2015), p. 285; Swinden, *Great Yarmouth*, p. 455. The creation of the French Company was unpopular in provincial ports; the merchants of Bristol and Lyme Regis refused to join, condemning the "politic devices" of the Londoners, TNA, SP14/45, fol. 157, SP14/47, fol. 115.

PROMOTING PEACE AND PLENTY

grow the king's finances through projectors and private economic endeavors.[136] One result was a period of fluidity in England's trade policy in the 1610s. This gave local actors scope to push their own agendas, but it also overturned long-standing arrangements. James's Privy Council would waver on granting the herring license throughout the 1610s and 1620s, as local actors sought to align central policy with their own interests.

Debates over the herring fishery unfolded before the Privy Council numerous times across the early Stuart period. In 1611, aggressive lobbying by London interests succeeded in challenging the legality of Yarmouth's herring license and gaining the ear of the Board as they reconsidered the king's priorities and needs. Opponents of Yarmouth's license argued that it broke the law and decayed English fishing, convincing the earl of Salisbury to order that no Yarmouth herrings could be transported abroad except in English ships. The men of Yarmouth countered that the "common good and behoofe of that corporation and the better encouragement of the poor fishermen" would be overthrown. Their argument succeeded. Salisbury reversed himself, renewing the license and ordering customs officials to allow the shipping. "It was never intended," Salisbury said, "that by the erecting of the said [French] Company, the town should receive any prejudice."[137] That is a somewhat confounding statement, since creating an exclusive trade for the Company of French Merchants by definition had the potential to prejudice Yarmouth. Regardless, this scuffle in 1611 presaged many more, wherein the provincial port advocated its own interests by refuting the claims of the London merchants and educating the government on what best served the commonwealth.

For the next several years, the provincial port and the London companies vied for the Council's approbation. Yarmouth's advocates stressed the necessity of the license to prevent the economic ruin of their important port, a "great nursery for the supply of navigation." Having always been, in their words, "incouraged with many favours of the State" for their fishery, they repeatedly petitioned for renewal of their accustomed license.[138] The Londoners countered that transport in foreign ships contradicted law and led to the decay of shipping and sea-faring men throughout the kingdom.[139] In 1615, the Londoners' argument triumphed; after a lengthy hearing of the parties, the Council prohibited Yarmouth's license henceforth.[140] This seemingly decisive order did not stick, however,

---

[136] John Cramsie, *Kingship and Crown Finance under James VI and I, 1603–1625* (Woodbridge, 2002), p. 10, 131–2; J. Cramsie, "Commercial Projects and the Fiscal Policy of James VI and I," *Historical Journal* 43 (2000), 345–64. See also Joan Thirsk, *Economic Policy and Projects: The Development of a Consumer Society in Early Modern England* (Oxford, 1978), esp. chap. 4.
[137] Swinden, *Great Yarmouth*, pp. 455–6; NRO, Y/C18/6, fol. 195v.
[138] *APC 1613–14*, pp. 207, 232.
[139] *APC 1613–14*, p. 595, *1615–16*, p. 317.
[140] NRO, Y/C19/5, fol. 158; *APC 1615–16*, pp. 317–8, 328. It should be noted that Yarmouth's struggle over the license in 1615 coincided with broader trade debates through public pamphlets, implicating the East India Company among others. See Gentleman,

177

URBAN GOVERNMENT AND THE EARLY STUART STATE

as by 1617 the Board reversed its course after hearing Yarmouth's plea that the restrictions seriously harmed their fishery and thus the state.[141] Yarmouth again obtained the herring license each year from 1618 to 1623.[142] It was in this same period that the town managed to convince the Privy Council of the dire need to repair the haven and approve kingdom-wide collections to support the repairs.[143] Cultivating "town Friends" at court and making a strong case for its economic importance, Yarmouth retained its favorable position in the eyes of the Council.[144]

International war and tense domestic politics in the mid-1620s gave the London merchants an opening to contest Yarmouth's position, and the Council looked less favorably on Great Yarmouth's license. The depression in international trade in 1624 troubled parliament and Privy Council, and the Londoners used this as a wedge to complain against what they saw as Yarmouth's flaunting of the laws of trade.[145] A group of merchants and ship owners petitioned the Board against Yarmouth's exportation of fish in foreign ships, emphasizing that it went against the laws of the realm and resulted in the "impoverishing and decaying of our own navigation."[146] The Council, concerned to protect English shipping, discontinued Yarmouth's license and ordered the town to observe the laws of navigation, "without all fraud or evasion."[147] Ascribing the situation to the "envious malice" of the London merchants, Yarmouth attempted to make common cause with Dover and the Cinque Ports. The bailiffs solicited the mayor of Dover to join in petitioning the duke of Buckingham, imploring the men of the Cinque Ports "to join hearts and hands, with willing minds to sue for relief" or "otherwise both you and we shall be miserable spectators at our own miseries."[148] Enlistment of powerful friends like Buckingham, the earl of Arundel, and Sir John Suckling availed them nothing, and the order stood.[149] With Charles's accession and the outbreak of war, Yarmouth continued to press the necessity of the license for export in foreign bottoms, but it became more difficult to convince the Board that this was in the interest of the realm. In a November 1626 hearing, the Privy Council refused to renew Yarmouth's

---

England's Way to Win Wealth; E.S., *England's Busse* (1615); Robert Kayll, *The Trade's Increase* (1615); and Dudley Carleton, *The Defense of Trade* (1615).

[141] *APC 1616–17*, pp. 350–1.

[142] Swinden, *Great Yarmouth*, p. 458; NRO, Y/C19/5, fols 232, 249, 272v.

[143] *APC 1619–21*, pp. 166–7, 194–5, 230–1, 272, 411–12, *1621–23*, pp. 86, 172–3, 193–4, 419–20.

[144] NRO, Y/C19/5, fols 232, 249, 272v. See Catherine F. Patterson, *Urban Patronage in Early Modern England: Corporate Boroughs, the Landed Elite, and the Crown, 1590–1640* (Stanford, CA, 1999), pp. 115–17, 172, 189, 284, for Yarmouth's patronage connections.

[145] Thomas Cogswell, *The Blessed Revolution: English Politics and the Coming of War, 1621–1624* (Cambridge, 1989), provides political context of this period.

[146] *APC 1623–25*, pp. 298, 308; NRO, Y/C19/5, fol. 299.

[147] *APC 1623–25*, pp. 321–2.

[148] Swinden, *Great Yarmouth*, p. 467, n. (q).

[149] NRO, Y/C19/5, fols 308, 312, 312v; *APC 1623–25*, pp. 345, 367–8.

PROMOTING PEACE AND PLENTY

license. But the Board went farther, using the occasion to issue a clear statement of policy: herring and other fish were not to be exported in foreign ships, and this order applied not just to Yarmouth, but to all English ports, and perhaps Irish ones, too. The benefits – preservation of navigation and encouragement of merchants – provided by domestic shipping were "verie considerable in reason of State."[150] In time of war and contentious international relationships, the Board took a stance firmly in favor of English law and English shipping, a stance that Yarmouth, even with its host of "great friends," could not sway.

Yet in the long run, the Board appeared to admit the importance of Yarmouth's interests to the realm. The Lords acknowledged the town's strategic position "nearest to Dunkirk" and ensured that Yarmouth obtained ordnance, strengthened its fortifications, and procured naval protection against piracy for its fishing fleet in the 1620s and 1630s. Wavering from their clear policy statement in 1626, the Council also granted Yarmouth a license to export between 400 and 1,000 lasts of herring in strangers' bottoms numerous times from 1628 through 1638, despite protests from London companies.[151] Strikingly, the corporation managed to get positive action from the Board in 1629, 1630, and 1631, while deeply embroiled in fractious internal politics that provoked direct intervention by King Charles and the Council into borough government. It seems that Yarmouth's critical place in England's trade outweighed its divisive politics in the eyes of the Privy Council; the lords could distinguish their support for the town's economic interests, which impacted the realm's fortunes as a whole, from their unhappiness with the corporation's leaders. The support of patrons like Viscount Dorchester and the earl of Dorset certainly aided the town in weathering this difficult period.[152] Great Yarmouth's purposeful association of itself and its trade with the good of the commonwealth and the benefit of the state, through the advancement of "navigation" and the generation of customs duties, convinced central authority to align state policy with the interests of this provincial town.

While Great Yarmouth had a particularly important role in a significant industry, the story of Great Yarmouth and its herring license exemplifies many of the elements that characterized provincial towns' concerns over trade and the connections of borough corporations with each other and with the center. Competition compelled them to preserve and extend their trade. For many provincial towns, including Yarmouth, the merchants of the great London companies were the enemy, monopolizers of all trade. Only central government

---

[150] APC 1626, p. 363.
[151] APC 1628–29, pp. 206, 265–6; CSPD 1629–31, pp. 73, 89, 385; APC 1629–30, p. 179, 1630–31, pp. 83–4, 92–3, 141; CSPD 1631–33, p. 123, 174; Swinden, Great Yarmouth, pp. 471–2; CSPD 1637, pp. 573–4; CSPD 1637–8, p. 20; TNA, PC2/49, pp. 110–11, 255; NRO, Y/C19/6, fols 178v, 223v, Y/C18/6, fol. 131v. Swinden states that the license was granted every year from 1628–38, though evidence from State Papers is lacking for certain years and Swinden (unusually) does not cite his source for the information for each year.
[152] NRO, Y/C19/6, fols 141v–142, 145, 170v, 212v; Swinden, Great Yarmouth, pp. 502, 505.

URBAN GOVERNMENT AND THE EARLY STUART STATE

could prevent this monopolization, so provincial towns regularly sought the state's help to protect them. In Yarmouth's case, the town also needed a particular trading privilege that could only be obtained directly from the crown. This positioned Yarmouth's governors to be perpetual petitioners for the license to export herring in foreign ships, but many other provincial towns had needs or interests that required reaching beyond their own boundaries to support or advance. The complicated nature of trade, which crossed jurisdictions both domestic and international, meant that townsmen could not accomplish their business without this connection to and action from central authority. The relationship was not static; the crown's response fluctuated with events, the composition of the Council, and the lobbying of provincial and metropolitan actors. Central government under both James and Charles emphasized order and governance in trade, but the prosperity of borough communities, and the potential for disorder if local economies floundered, helped construct what the center's understanding of "order" meant. Just as agents from Yarmouth and London influenced the Privy Council's views of the fishing and shipping industries, so too did other towns regarding the governance of local and international trade, the infrastructure that facilitated trade, and the dangers to trade posed by piracy and war. Their advocacy of local interests collectively helped build a national interest, giving provincial towns a key role in the development of the state.[153] But the state's fiscal weakness also made the towns' national aspirations for infrastructure and defense difficult to realize.

---

[153] See Robert Ashton, "Jacobean Free Trade Again," *Past & Present* No. 43 (1969), p. 155 for more on links between provincial interests and national interest.

6

Paying the Price: Corporate Towns and the Burdens of the State

Securing the "financial, administrative and military resources" to preserve social order, enforce religion, and protect the territory and trade of the realm was, according to Michael Braddick, a fundamental activity of the early modern state.[1] Individuals and communities bore a wide array of fiscal and military duties that supported the crown's needs. Parliamentary subsidies, training and outfitting militia bands, supplying soldiers and sailors for the king's forces, customs, privy seal and other prerogative loans, billeting, and Ship Money, among many other exactions, lightened the pockets of the king's subjects and placed an administrative burden on collectors. These were in addition to other duties required by statute, like poor rates, or ordered by the Privy Council, such as collections to relieve plague sufferers or other urgent needs. Communities also had duties toward local government, and corporate towns in particular had the privilege of collecting rates toward purposes within their jurisdiction enshrined in their charters of incorporation. Other responsibilities were still under negotiation as to whether they were national or local, such as piers and havens, fortifications, and defense of merchant shipping. Contributing resources toward the king's government constituted a basic duty of the subject. Yet the cost of running the state and the proliferation of financial exactions under the early Stuarts raised new questions about these responsibilities. For England's provincial towns, the state's demands tested both pocketbooks and liberties.

The early Stuart state's relative fiscal weakness made royal finance a significant issue and drove much of the crown's policy in the period. Historians have long identified the crown's exactions as contributors to its political woes. Whig narratives emphasized what were seen as the constitutional problems raised by prerogative taxation and the arguments for the liberties of the subject arising out of debates over the Forced Loan and Ship Money. Revisionists also saw the importance of crown finance, but focused more on the practical problems generated by the fiscal weakness of the crown and the unhappiness of ratepayers to pay taxes in general. Conrad Russell identified the poverty of the crown as an important contributor to the civil war, in that it prevented the crown from succeeding at war, among other things. Kevin Sharpe, while acknowledging some tensions between center and locality over Ship Money, concluded that it was largely a success. Others, like Richard Cust writing about the Forced

---

[1] Michael Braddick, *State Formation in Early Modern England c. 1550–1700* (Cambridge, 2000), p. 48.

URBAN GOVERNMENT AND THE EARLY STUART STATE

Loan, have countered that view, redirecting attention to the ideological impact of such levies; responses varied widely, from rapid and supportive payment to principled resistance and non-payment on legal grounds.[2] The crown's policies to provide for defense and its other needs were critical to the politics of the period, however interpreted.

This chapter investigates how financial and military exactions of the state affected provincial towns and shaped relations between local and central government in a period when war, piracy, and general fiscal weakness placed increasing pressures on government at all levels. While the burdens were many and varied, here the focus is on military training and cost; the multiple financial burdens of the war years of the 1620s; and the Ship Money rate of the 1630s, all of which resonated in distinctive ways in corporate towns. The crown's increasingly vigorous stance toward local governance and revenue generation provoked frequent, dynamic interaction between towns and the crown, demonstrating both the vital connection between center and locality and the hardship and frustration that central policy could engender. Strong bonds of interest linked borough corporations to the crown, and national concerns penetrated deeply into local governance. Yet when royal policy rubbed up against chartered liberties, or when the needs of the towns seemed to be ignored, it touched off tensions within corporations, between towns and their neighbors, and at times between borough corporations and central government itself.

The mounting cost of government and the security of the state across the early Stuart period intensified communication between corporations and the crown, as central authorities enforced new policies and exactions while town officials petitioned for relief. Militia training and outfitting, billeting, Ship Money, and other exactions placed especially heavy burdens on already struggling towns, stressed by the economic ills that depressed trade and exacerbated problems of community order. The increasing requirements of the state also raised the administrative load on borough magistrates, who were expected to carry out royal policy even in the face of local intransigence. The crown's policies, especially in the 1620s and 1630s, challenged corporate liberties as well as their finances, stirring unhappiness that the crown often interpreted as disobedience and "popularity." Borough governors had strong incentives to support the crown's military, administrative, and financial needs, connecting their corporations with the broader state. But the tension between the crown's needs and the security of local liberties and interests also generated misunderstanding, and in some instances conflict, between provincial towns and central authority.

---

[2] S.R. Gardiner, *The Fall of the Monarchy of Charles I, 1637–1649*, vol. 1 (London, 1882), pp. 56-7, 327; Conrad Russell, *The Causes of the English Civil War* (Oxford, 1990), pp. 161-84; C. Russell, *Parliaments and English Politics, 1621–1629* (Oxford, 1979); Kevin Sharpe, *The Personal Rule of Charles I* (New Haven, CT and London, 1992); Richard Cust, *The Forced Loan and English Politics 1626–1628* (Oxford, 1987).

PAYING THE PRICE

Militias, musters, and borough liberties

The militia formed a fundamental part of early modern governance. In the absence of a standing army, local military units underpinned peace and order in an era that saw international war as well as fear of domestic turmoil. The lieutenancy, a critical element of administration throughout the realm, originated and grew in the sixteenth century, but the early Stuart period saw its development as both James and Charles recognized its importance for security and government. The expansion of the militia and its oversight became key aspects of early Stuart administration, and as such raised questions over who had authority and how it would be exercised. Historians of the militia as part of local governance have focused primarily on the county gentry and the impact of the crown's attempt to create a "perfect" or "exact" militia had on them and on their relations with the crown.[3] But increased central interest in military training and oversight had particular effects on corporate boroughs, as they sought to use the militia both to strengthen borough privileges and dignity, and to connect with the crown that conveyed those privileges. A shared interest in defense allowed many corporate towns to enhance their own militias with the blessing of central government in this period. At the same time, questions over jurisdiction, privileges, and cost, made more pressing by the onset of war in the 1620s, also fostered tensions between towns and the larger state over musters and training.

For many corporate towns, having a militia unit over which borough officials had authority signaled legitimacy and prestige. Oversight of a town's trained band, the naming of borough officers as deputy lieutenants for the town's militia, and the liberty to exercise that militia within its own borders formed part of corporate identity. Townsmen saw trained bands as hallmarks of corporate integrity and jurisdiction, confirmed to them by statute. The final clause of the Act for Taking of Musters (4 & 5 Philip and Mary, c.3) provided that no persons residing in a city or corporate town that had JPs by charter should be compelled to appear in musters outside that borough's liberties, nor under commission by any unless the mayor of the town was in the commission.[4] The burst of incorporation in the sixteenth and early seventeenth centuries allowed many towns to claim this privilege. From the crown's perspective, the need to maintain security and defense made extending such privileges to corporate towns a reasonable trade-off.

---

[3] Anthony Fletcher, *Reform in the Provinces: The Government of Stuart England* (New Haven, CT and London, 1986), pp. 282-4, 286-7; Lindsay Boynton, *The Elizabethan Militia, 1558-1638* (London, 1967); Thomas G. Barnes, *Somerset 1625-1640: A County's Government During the "Personal Rule"* (Cambridge, MA, 1961), pp. 68-123. An exception is Thomas Cogswell, *Home Divisions: Aristocracy, the State, and Provincial Conflict* (Stanford, CA, 1998), which examines the earl of Huntingdon's militia interactions with both the county and town of Leicester.

[4] *Statutes of the Realm*, vol. 4, pt. 1, p. 322.

URBAN GOVERNMENT AND THE EARLY STUART STATE

The largely pacific first fifteen years of James's reign saw little exercise of local militias. Relatively lax oversight prevailed, and much depended on the zeal of particular lord lieutenants and their deputies.[5] The muster of 1613, the first in over five years, revealed Jacobean government's willingness to support corporate liberties on this count. The corporations of both Dartmouth and Northampton appealed to the Board that their "pretended" privilege of exercising their own militia had been questioned by county deputy lieutenants. In both cases, the Council supported the boroughs' privileges, stressing their ancientness and utility, and stated they deserved "as much favor and liberty as may be graunted unto them without inconvenience or prejudice to his Majestie's service ..."[6] As war on the Continent eventually impinged on royal policy, central oversight became tighter and corporations less likely to have a free hand in mustering and training. The intensifying rigor of military preparedness promoted by central authority required increased engagement by borough officers with deputy lieutenants, lord lieutenants, and the Privy Council.[7] They accepted the duties of military training as a means of enhancing corporate honor and privilege while serving the state, but borough governors quickly defended local liberties when questioned. These interests were not inherently opposed, but the heightened demands of the state, which impinged on corporate liberties, created opportunities for discord.

The most secure way to ensure oversight of their own militia was for a corporation to obtain it by charter, giving them clear authority. Great Yarmouth, whose 1608 charter failed to specify the privilege of mustering, spent much of the 1610s and beyond lobbying to gain corporate authority to muster themselves.[8] The 1626 charter of the small Kent town of Queenborough confirmed that no inhabitants could be compelled to muster outside the borough, "for they be well prepared and armed for the defense of the said borough."[9] The men of Truro, when challenged by deputy lieutenants in 1626 for refusing to march the trained band out of their borough to the county muster five miles away, boldly claimed that their charter of 31 Elizabeth, as well as the statute of 4 & 5 Philip and Mary, gave them the right not to be drawn out of their corporation for musters.[10] Tewkesbury's corporation had the privilege confirmed in their

---

[5] Fletcher, *Reform in the Provinces*, pp. 286–7, 292–4. Fletcher's study focuses exclusively on county government and does not discuss civic militias.

[6] *APC 1613–14*, pp. 47–8, 67.

[7] On efforts to enhance the militia, see Henrik Langelüddecke, "'The chiefest strength and glory of this kingdom': Arming and Training the 'Perfect Militia' in the 1630s," *English Historical Review* 118 (2003), 1264–303; Boynton, *Elizabethan Militia*. On the lieutenancy more broadly, see Victor Stater, *Noble Government: The Stuart Lord Lieutenancy and the Transformation of English Politics* (Athens, GA, 1994); Cogswell, *Home Divisions*, offers a detailed study of a lord lieutenant and his dealings with the militia in the early Stuart period.

[8] NRO, Y/C19/5, fols 149, 152, 158, 172v, 174v, 177, 200v, 201v, 206v, 222v.

[9] TNA, C233/3, fol. 113.

[10] *APC 1626*, pp. 332–3. The deputy lieutenants complained that Truro's bad example caused other towns to follow suit. *CSPD 1625–26*, p. 387.

184

1610 charter. In 1618, Lord Chandos, the lord lieutenant, complained to the Privy Council that the men of Tewkesbury "pretended" an exemption from the county and "utterly refuse to be mustered and trained, or to be conformable to such precepts and directions as the deputy lieutenants of that county have addressed unto them." The Council referred the matter to the king's attorney and solicitor general, to determine if the town's refusal was "justifiable" or not.[11] Likely to Lord Chandos's chagrin, the king's lawyers found that the 1610 charter contained "an express clause" authorizing the bailiffs of the town to muster and train the inhabitants of the town and parish, and excluding any Gloucestershire lieutenants or commissioners from "intermeddling." Tewkesbury's refusal had legal warrant.[12] This finding may have prompted central authorities to think twice about granting such privileges, but in the face of a solid legal case, Chandos and his deputies gave way to the corporation.

Balancing the desire to uphold local rights and privileges while obeying the crown's orders and appeasing a powerful lord could prove tricky, but borough officials steadfastly promoted their chartered liberties. Coventry's corporation negotiated with their long-time lord lieutenant, Lord Compton, over the city's privileges. In 1608, the corporation scrupled to muster because Coventry had not been specifically named in the commission for Warwickshire. Compton required them to muster anyway.[13] By the late 1610s, Coventry pressed its right to muster separately from the county, believing the corporate charter secured the privilege. Compton, now earl of Northampton, had doubts. He required them to send him a copy of their charter, "for my better satisfaction, not meaning to oppose any thing against the honor and privilege or your city." They sent up documents and proved their privileges.[14] Similarly, the city of Canterbury sought to protect its chartered rights in the face of a challenge from the lieutenancy. A 1620 petition to King James from the mayor and aldermen of Canterbury claimed that the city, its own county separate from Kent, had the authority to muster itself by right of their charter granted by King Henry VI and confirmed by James. Unfortunately, the city's petition stretched the truth here, as the Jacobean charter had not explicitly defined that privilege. While previous lord lieutenants had honored Canterbury's autonomy in musters, the new lieutenant, James's cousin the duke of Lennox, appointed Kentish gentlemen as his deputies for the city, omitting the mayor of Canterbury. Treading lightly, the citizens attributed the lapse to Lennox's newness and unfamiliarity with local practice (though in fact the city's recent failure to select the duke's secretary as burgess for parliament likely contributed). Still, the mayor and aldermen complained of the trouble that would arise if "strangers" held these critical

[11] APC 1617–19, p. 252.
[12] TNA, SP 14/104, fol. 3 (H. Yelverton and T. Coventry to Privy Council, 2 December 1618).
[13] CovA, BA/H/Q/A79/120.
[14] CovA, BA/H/Q/A79/124, 123, BA/H/C/17/1, fol. 230.

URBAN GOVERNMENT AND THE EARLY STUART STATE

positions.[15] In claiming their privileges over military matters, borough governors portrayed themselves as those best prepared to fulfill the king's service. While borough corporations eagerly promoted their privilege to muster themselves, and with some regularity tangled with lord and deputy lieutenants, this did not signal withdrawal from their duty to the state. Taking on the responsibilities of the state through military training served as a means of enhancing corporate prestige, reinforcing the authority of mayors and other civic leaders, and forming a strong, connection between borough governors and the crown. It had the added advantage of cost savings, as trainings took place in the town, eliminating travel costs. Many towns showed their enthusiasm for the service, and made a case for their own oversight of it, by increasing the number of men or the level of training beyond minimum requirements. Dartmouth did just that in 1613. The townsmen promised to raise the number of trained men in the town from sixteen to one hundred if the earl of Bath, lord lieutenant, would allow the mayor of Dartmouth to serve as deputy lieutenant and muster the town trained band at home. Bath apparently hesitated, as the Privy Council ordered him to allow it, for the benefit of the state. The lords "doe thinke that nomber ready alwaies within the towne much more expedient for the advauncement of his Majestie's service, then those 16 sent out to the publike musters."[16] While Bath and his gentry deputies may not have appreciated it, the Board's action manifested the shared interests of the town's leadership and central government.

Demonstrations of zeal, embodied in requests to the Privy Council for military yards and more training of townsmen, became increasingly common in corporate boroughs across the period, and they received enthusiastic approval from central authorities. Between 1616 and 1622, the corporations of Coventry, Colchester, and Bury St. Edmund's petitioned the Privy Council to allow them to raise companies of men and train them to military discipline, as the Londoners did in their Artillery Yard.[17] In 1616, Coventry's citizens wrote to their lord lieutenant, Lord Compton, expressing their keenness to correct defects in training their men and asking permission to raise a voluntary band and establish a place to train them. To increase their odds, they made sure a copy of their letter made its way to the Privy Council. Swayed by the earnestness of the city's

---

[15] Canterbury Cathedral Archives, CCA-CC-Woodruff 52/21 (Petition of mayor and aldermen of Canterbury to the king, [1620]); Canterbury Constituency Report, *HoP 1604–1629*, www.historyofparliamentonline.org/volume/1604-1629/constituencies/canterbury; HMC, *The Manuscripts of the Earl Cowper, KG, Preserved at Melbourne Hall, Derbyshire*, vol. 1 (London, 1888), p. 148; Thomas Cogswell, "The Canterbury Election of 1626 and Parliamentary Selection Revisited," *Historical Journal* 63 (2020), 297.

[16] APC 1613–14, pp. 47–8, 625.

[17] APC 1616–17, p. 102; CovA, BA/H/Q/A79/121 (Lord Compton to mayor of Coventry, 20 March 1617); APC 1619–21, pp. 406–7, 1621–23, p. 344. The petitions of Colchester and Bury were nearly identical, suggesting that agents representing towns may have shared information about what would convince the Privy Council.

PAYING THE PRICE

request to provide so useful a service, the Council required Compton to allow a band of one hundred "able and sufficient" citizens to train and exercise arms in Coventry.[18] The Board encouraged the city's endeavor and instructed the lord lieutenant to support it, too.

Such requests became more frequent as hostilities with Spain broke out and towns around the realm prepared. Norwich, Bristol, Gloucester, Chester, Great Yarmouth, Ipswich, and Nottingham all proposed military yards and expanded trained bands between 1625 and 1629.[19] Gloucester's, like most of the others, was a project of the city's government, and the Council approved it with the condition that the mayor and aldermen have oversight. In Chester, William Dutton, son of an alderman, offered to build the artillery yard at his own expense, provided he could captain it. Dutton had the backing of the city as well as the lord lieutenant, and the Council granted permission, so long as Dutton worked in concert with city magistrates.[20] The mayor and aldermen of Barnstaple, concerned with the threat of Spanish attack in 1626, asked permission to raise a troop of one hundred armed men in the town, above the sixty-five they had previously raised, with the privilege of electing a captain and officers themselves. Some enterprising young men of Derby, ostensibly for the sake of exercise and to avoid resort to taverns, wished to arm and train themselves, and the bailiffs of the town asked the Privy Council for warrant to license them. The Council approved both petitions.[21]

All of these proposals had the dual purpose of demonstrating the loyalty and competence of borough governors as part of the state while also reinforcing local privileges and the personal dignity of the leading townsmen. Autonomy over military troops, while enhancing corporate honor and authority, displayed not insularity, but fulfillment of the shared goals of order in the state. Phil Withington has argued that increased interest in military training in cities and towns formed part of a wider "civic renaissance" with humanist foundations, going back well before the later seventeenth century.[22] Such "civic militarism" may well have helped shape the concerns of the leading men of cities and towns who promoted expanded military efforts. But it did not require a grounding in humanism to see the advantages of well-trained troops with corporate oversight. Aware of the world around them and the increasing need for defense, the mayors, bailiffs, and aldermen who organized these efforts saw opportunity to

---

[18] CovA, BA/H/Q/A79/117, 121; *APC 1616–17*, p. 102 (Council to Lord Compton, 30 December 1616).
[19] *APC 1623–25*, p. 482, *1625–26*, pp. 211, 309–10, 464–5, 477–8, *1629–30*, pp. 145, 223.
[20] *APC 1625–26*, pp. 464–5, 477–8; TNA, SP16/27, fol. 11; GA, GBR B3/1, fol. 512; BL, Harl. MS 2125, fol. 58v.
[21] TNA, SP16/30, fol. 126; *APC 1626*, p. 32, SP16/78, fol. 51; *APC 1628–29*, p. 407; TNA, PC2/43, p. 661.
[22] Phil Withington, "Introduction – Citizens and Soldiers: The Renaissance Context," *Journal of Early Modern History* 15 (2011), 3–30.

URBAN GOVERNMENT AND THE EARLY STUART STATE

strengthen their own governance by promoting a goal desired by the crown. The Privy Council's consistent support for military training in the hands of borough governments indicates the extent to which the center approved this local initiative.

The bond between borough government and the crown forged by military training reinforced shared concerns for security and order, but it was not uncomplicated. Corporate boroughs existed as part of a composite state with overlapping authorities; even when they believed they had power over their trained bands, they could not simply ignore other authorities. The threat, and eventual reality, of war in the 1620s offered more opportunities for tension, as the pressing needs of the state brought greater burdens for money and men, as well as increased interactions with the lieutenancy. The dangers of the times also made military authorities less sympathetic to local concerns, requiring obedience to central orders regardless of customs or privileges to the contrary. Borough magistrates found themselves having to navigate these changing circumstances, as on one hand the Privy Council continued to promote corporate initiatives for military training and on the other hand expected ever more compliance to its demands.

The crown's sometimes mixed message to corporate boroughs on military privileges could sow confusion. Regular approval of artillery yards and volunteer trained bands in many towns seems to have prompted Dorchester's corporation to include more control over the trained band among the new privileges they requested in 1628-29. In reviewing the corporation's charter petition, Attorney General Robert Heath approved most of the requested items, but he wrote "I like not this" next to the clause requesting liberty to nominate and elect the captain of their trained band and assess their own arms. Only if the county's lord lieutenant consented should it be approved.[23] This was not to be. William Whiteway of Dorchester recorded in his diary that when the corporation appealed to their lord lieutenant, he referred the question to his deputies, who "shewed so much coldness and unwillingness in it, especially Sir Thomas freke, that it came to nothing."[24] Clearly, not all of the king's officers saw the benefit of enhancing corporate military privileges.

The small Suffolk town of Aldeburgh likewise found itself frustrated by the state's seeming inconsistency over the borough's trained band. In 1631, the magistrates felt the ire of the earl of Suffolk, lord lieutenant, for having appointed their own captain to the trained men of the town. Demanding acknowledgment of their error in making such an appointment, Suffolk required

---

[23] TNA, SP16/146, fol. 97. Theophilus Howard, earl of Suffolk, was lord lieutenant of Dorset, Suffolk, and Cambridgeshire. Victor Stater, "Howard, Theophilus, second earl of Suffolk (1584-1640), Courtier and Politician," *ODNB*, accessed 31 Jul. 2020, www-oxforddnb-com.ezproxy.lib.uh.edu/view/10.1093/ref:odnb/9780198614128.001.0001/odnb-9780198614128-e-13938.

[24] William Whiteway, *William Whiteway of Dorchester: His Diary 1618 to 1635*, ed. S. Bridges, trans. B. Bates, Dorset Record Society, vol. 12 (Dorchester, 1991), p. 107.

PAYING THE PRICE

a personal appearance and submission by the bailiffs for having used the king's power illicitly. If the townsmen would make suit to him for a military company and nominate a captain for him to appoint, he deigned to consider that proposition, if it benefited the king's service.[25] The townsmen's aggrievement at this is revealed in the hand of town clerk Marmaduke Moore. Moore wrote the details of the exchange in the corporation's official records and made marginal notes to other documents, including letters from the Privy Council giving the town orders to see to their own defense and establish a perpetual guard for the town.[26] Suffolk's missive rankled, as it turned back the practice and the privilege that they believed had been established by the Privy Council some years before, during their struggle to procure ordnance to defend their town.[27] Seeing themselves as the king's officers, Aldeburgh's magistrates tried to execute that authority directly to protect their town, but the varied interests within the early modern state could make that difficult.

Corporations came under increased pressure to conform to the lieutenancy's orders as central government stepped up efforts to strengthen the militia when facing war with Spain and France.[28] The townsmen of Southampton wrote to Lord Conway in 1625 that the deputy lieutenants of Hampshire had required them to send men to Winchester for military service, at significant expense, despite the fact that their militia had always been trained within the town's liberties. When they complained of this abuse of their "ancient liberties," the Privy Council scolded them for making trouble over what the Board saw as a slight matter.[29] Leicester's corporation faced similar difficulty when their lord lieutenant, the earl of Huntingdon, called them to muster their trained men in Lutterworth, fifteen miles away.[30] The townsmen balked, claiming the privilege to muster within their own liberties, and asked the earl to rescind his order. Huntingdon, declaring that he must do what was best for the king's service, declined to change his mind. Rather than simply comply, the corporation rounded up support from the chancellor of the Duchy of Lancaster and wrote to the earl once again, quoting the statute and trying to convince him to respect

[25] SA/I, EE1/O1/1 (Aldeburgh Letter Book, 1625–1663), fol. 63.

[26] SA/I, EE1/O1/1, fols 63, 38v.

[27] See Thomas Cogswell, "Ten Demi-Culverins for Aldeburgh: Whitehall, the Dunkirkers, and a Suffolk Fishing Community, 1625–1630," *Journal of British Studies* 58 (2019), 315–337, for the saga of the ordnance. While the corporation accepted the check to their authority in 1631, they gladly received a warrant from Parliament in 1642 for the bailiffs and burgesses to muster, train, and command the trained band for the town. SA/I, EE1/O1/1, fol. 84v.

[28] Fletcher, *Reform in the Provinces*, pp. 287, 292, 301–8; Langelüddecke, "'The Chiefest Strength and Glory,'" p. 1265.

[29] TNA, SP16/521, fol. 174; APC 1625–26, p. 42.

[30] Huntingdon took particular pride in his role as leader of Leicestershire's militia; he also had a complex relationship with the corporation of Leicester. See Cogswell, *Home Divisions*, passim, but especially pp. 60–3, 129–33; and Catherine F. Patterson, *Urban Patronage in Early Modern England: Corporate Boroughs, the Landed Elite, and the Crown, 1580–1640* (Stanford, CA, 1999), pp. 194–231.

URBAN GOVERNMENT AND THE EARLY STUART STATE

their liberties. For the town's leaders, honoring their oath to uphold borough privileges and mustering the men in Leicester best forwarded the king's service.[31] In this instance, Huntingdon eventually backed away, but throughout England, the potential for friction remained, resurfacing with the outbreak of war with Scotland.

The crown's growing attention to training and mustering led inevitably to increased costs, which also became a bone of contention and a focus for negotiation between corporations, the lieutenancy, and the Privy Council. In the era of peace that characterized James's first decade and more on the throne, training rarely occurred. Attempts at widespread mustering in 1608 and 1613 largely demonstrated disorganization and low performance. The main result of the 1613 musters in Tewkesbury was that the £25 assessed for the muster was never properly accounted for, and "general offense" was taken in the town.[32] As Continental war loomed, militia activities quickened. From 1618 onward, and especially during the period 1625-29, mustering and training of town trained bands, providing powder and match, raising coat and conduct money to fit and transport pressed soldiers for service, and the pressing of local men to serve all placed financial and administrative burdens on borough governments throughout the realm.[33] The constant pressure for men, material, and money put significant strains on urban communities at a time when economic pressures from depressed and disrupted trade and many other exactions by the state weighed heavily on them, leading to complaints and hesitancy to pay.

The increased burden led in many cases to debates over corporate authority and how towns would meet the demands for men and money. Gloucester's magistrates sparred with county deputy lieutenants over the number of men they should be required to send for military service abroad and complained about the heavy taxation they paid for setting forth soldiers. Hull, already heavily in debt, struggled to arrange for the "constant" training of men in the town while also paying for soldiers, ordnance, and ships.[34] Corporate boroughs had the power by their charters to raise assessments on their inhabitants to pay for these exactions, but assessments could cause grumbling when many other costs lay upon heavily burdened taxpayers. Maidstone's magistrates in 1628 made an order that any freeman willfully refusing to pay the "cesses" and taxes imposed by their burghmote should lose their benefits as freemen until they paid; the corporation would also not protect these refusers from any "foreign service to His Majesty" - a serious threat in time of war.[35] Increased military

---

[31] ROLLR, BRII/18/15, fols 567, 575, 576, 578, 580, 581.

[32] GA, TBR A1/1, fol. 30v; RBL, vol. 4, pp. 76, 98.

[33] See A. Hassell Smith, "Militia Rates and Militia Statutes 1558-1663," in P. Clark, A.G.R. Smith, and N. Tyacke (eds), The English Commonwealth 1547-1640: Essays in Politics and Society Presented to Joel Hurstfield (Leicester, 1979), pp. 93-110 for the legal and administrative debates over military rates generally. See also Cogswell, Home Divisions, pp. 14-16.

[34] GA, GBR H2/2, pp. 18, 67; HHC, BRB3, pp. 136, 146, 180, 181, 195, 196.

[35] KHLC, Sa/Ac7, fols 136, 137, Md/ACm1/2, pp. 220, 223.

PAYING THE PRICE

costs affected all communities in this difficult period, but they posed particular challenges for corporate towns in both their internal governance and their connections with the broader state. The corporation of Leicester's experience of this change demonstrates the impact of war on the town's finances as well as its interactions with the lieutenancy. Thomas Cogswell has shown how Leicester went from supporting the occasional militia duties before 1618 largely with revenues from corporation rents to requiring regular and sometimes heavy local taxation in the 1620s, leading to tension within the borough and with Lord Lieutenant Huntingdon.[36] The years 1625 to 1627 brought trouble and charge. Militia costs grew, and Huntingdon, obedient to the increased exactions of the state at war, required the corporation to raise £50 toward military provision in the summer of 1626. This taxation came amidst an arduous plague outbreak, which also compelled significant local rates and expenditure of corporate revenues, even as disease restricted the town's trade.[37] The mayor and his brethren found themselves faced with recalcitrant townsmen, dozens of whom refused to pay. The corporation asked the earl to reduce their rate in light of their extraordinary charges.[38] With no reduction forthcoming, the magistrates faced ongoing difficulty in collecting. By the summer of 1627, discontent over the rating was such that the governing body censured its own members; the common hall agreed that if any of its company or any officer of the borough fell behind in assessments for mustering and training, or refused to pay when commanded, that person would be distrained or committed to ward. In the midst of these strains over military exactions, commissioners for the Forced Loan announced their visit to assess the townsmen in January 1627.[39] Facing high expenditures, Leicester's magistrates did all they could to protect themselves and the corporation from fiscal disaster and reduction of liberties. Arguing that the town's militia should train at home was one way both to promote the town's privileges and to save money at a time when the state's demands rose to unprecedented heights.[40]

Even within the context of heightened discipline and enforcement by the state, corporate boroughs could manage to assert their liberties while forwarding the aims of the crown. They had something valuable to offer – more trained men – and this gave them leverage to negotiate for local concerns. When the deputy lieutenants of Essex required Colchester to provide light horse to the county's militia, the town's bailiffs objected. As tradesmen and town dwellers, even their men of "best ability" might not have horses available for the service. The corporation offered an alternative; they would add thirty more foot soldiers to the company of two hundred already being raised there. In return,

[36] Cogswell, *Home Divisions*, p. 118.
[37] ROLLR, BRII/18/16, pp. 125, 131, 132; *RBL*, vol. 4, p. 224. See also Patterson, *Urban Patronage*, p. 217.
[38] ROLLR, BRII/18/16, pp. 131, 132, 135.
[39] ROLLR, BRII/18/16, pp. 193, 197, 202, 208, 209, 219, 233.
[40] Cogswell, *Home Divisions*, pp. 118–19.

URBAN GOVERNMENT AND THE EARLY STUART STATE

they asked for more authority over the town's militia company. The deputy lieutenants agreed, and Alderman John Norton was named to command the company.[41] Townsmen and deputy lieutenants alike could see the advantage of this arrangement, as it both forwarded the king's service and enhanced the borough governors' authority and profile. Totnes's corporation petitioned the Privy Council in 1635 that their trained band, after mustering in their own precincts for many years according to the statute of Philip and Mary, had now been called to muster outside the town, leaving the town open to "eminent danger" from foreign enemies and "ill-disposed" persons at home. They asked to be allowed to muster in town while increasing the number of trained soldiers they would provide from sixty to one hundred. The Council referred it to the earl of Bedford, lord lieutenant of Devon, who accepted the trade-off.[42] Local and central interests aligned, and borough corporations could find ways to both foster their privileges and further the needs of the state.

Throughout the reigns of James and Charles, compliance to the orders of lord lieutenants and the Privy Council prevailed in most towns, and borough governors viewed themselves as part of the machinery of royal government, responsible to fulfill the king's service. But tensions between borough liberties and central policies did arise, most apparently in the reign of Charles, created by the fallout from war and the more rigorous administrative regime. In Norwich, Alderman Thomas Atkin refused to attend a 1635 muster in person, saying that the statute of Philip and Mary meant he could not be compelled, since no civic officer sat on the lieutenancy commission.[43] Joint lord lieutenants Lord Maltravers and the earl of Arundel imprisoned Atkin and demanded that the corporation renounce the notion that they held this privilege by right. Most of his fellow magistrates quickly walked back from Atkin's public stand, but Atkin himself remained adamant and suffered punishment. Arundel dismantled Atkin's statutory argument, proclaiming that the powers of lieutenancy came from the king under the Broad Seal "through his absolute and undoubted power of his prerogative royal for the safety and good of the kingdom." The Privy Council likewise stated that that "the king's authority employed for the safety of the kingdom should be vigorously upheld without disputing."[44] King

---

[41] B.W. Quintrell (ed.), *The Maynard Lieutenancy Book, 1608–1639*, Essex Historical Documents No. 3 (Chelmsford, 1993), p. 69 (Deputies Maynard, Barrington, and Deane to bailiffs of Colchester, 13 July 1624).

[42] TNA, PC2/45, pp. 284, 371, SP16/311, fol. 126 (Earl of Bedford to Privy Council, [18 January] 1636).

[43] TNA, PC2/45, pp. 69; 4 & 5 Philip and Mary, c. 3 (*Statutes of the Realm*, vol. 4, pt. 1, p. 322). One other alderman initially joined Atkin in refusing, but quickly relented. On Atkin, see Keith Lindley, "Atkins, Thomas [created Sir Thomas Atkins under the protectorate] (c. 1589–1668/9), Local Politician," *ODNB*, accessed 27 Jun. 2019, www-oxforddnb-com.ezproxy.lib.uh.edu/view/10.1093/ref:odnb/9780198614128.001.0001/odnb-9780198614128-e-66500. Atkin would later serve in the Short and Long Parliaments.

[44] TNA, PC2/45, pp. 69–70; Bodl. Lib., MS Bankes 19, fols 48–9 ("The Examination of

PAYING THE PRICE

Charles, incensed by Atkin's disobedience, pronounced that no city or town corporate was exempt from the power of the lieutenancy, period. Disputing the lieutenancy's power would be punished by calling in the charter.[45] It was a sharp reminder of the subordination of corporate liberties to the prerogative authority of the king in the national state. Atkin may have been on the extreme end of political and religious views among his fellow aldermen in Norwich,[46] but his actions regarding the 1635 muster overtly confronted a Caroline policy that pressed against what he believed to be a civic right defined by statute. The willingness of most of Norwich's magistrates to conciliate with the crown and leave Atkin to fend for himself indicates that the bond of obedience was strong. Nevertheless, these events in Norwich also show that for some urban magistrates, rigid Caroline policy over musters raised grave concerns about rights and privileges.

The Atkin case in Norwich was particularly stark, but it exposes the complexity the crown's relationship with provincial towns over militia matters. With a strong sense of their own privileges, borough corporations worked to affirm their authority by gaining control over trained bands and training. In doing so, they reinforced their own dignity, but they also fulfilled the goals of the crown, often increasing the numbers of trained soldiers to further the king's service. Shared interests bound crown and corporations. Yet this connection stood in tension with points of difference, exacerbated by the stresses of war in the 1620s. Towns were hard-pressed both financially and in terms of their privileges as fiscal and military obligations ballooned. The rigor of Caroline policy made many corporations sensitive to protecting both pocketbooks and privileges. Borough corporations, as integral components of the king's government, negotiated this tension throughout the early seventeenth century.

Borough corporations, royal finance, and the costs of war

Like militia matters, taxation and other financial obligations of the state provided an important focus for negotiation between borough corporations and the early Stuart crown, as the towns carried increasing burdens, particularly in the war years of the 1620s. War's extraordinary demands necessarily altered the ways center and localities interacted. Questions about jurisdiction, ability to

---

Thomas Atkin Alderman of the City of Norwich taken the 29th of August in the 11th year of his Majesty's reign before Sir John Bankes, kt., his Majesty's Attorney General").
[45] TNA, PC2/45, p. 101.
[46] The godly Atkin objected strongly to Bishop Wren's campaign against preaching, which began not long after the events over the muster. Atkin left Norwich for London in 1637, reportedly due to his imprisonment for not attending the muster, and for Wren's strict ecclesiastical regime in Norwich. TNA, SP16/361, fol. 176. See J.T. Evans, *Seventeenth-Century Norwich: Politics, Religion, and Government 1620–1690* (Oxford, 1979), pp. 63–104, on Norwich's political and religious alignments in this period.

URBAN GOVERNMENT AND THE EARLY STUART STATE

pay, chartered privileges, and in some cases legal rights shaped relations between borough governments, the Privy Council, and other elements in the state in this period. As will be shown, in most cases, borough governors proved obedient to the crown's demands and did their best to collect what was required. As deputies of the king, designated by royal charters to govern their localities in the king's name, the leaders of borough corporations had a duty to support the king's needs and obey his commands. They had strong incentives to maintain good relations with central government, on which borough governors relied for reinforcement of their authority as well as for attainment of local needs. But they also had a duty to uphold borough liberties and defend local interests, which the collection of such exactions could challenge. Heavy financial duties to the crown, often coming one on top of another, stressed urban communities already feeling the effects of economic downturn and decay of trade. The increasing demands of the crown (in men, ships, and money), and its inability to readily pay costs incurred by towns that they saw as shared concerns of the realm (such as fortifications and billeting) weighed especially heavily on corporate towns. This prompted many of them to engage even more assiduously with the crown in pursuit of protection and favor, but it also resulted in tension and even alienation.

Not all of the state's exactions generated anxiety. Parliamentary taxation caused little grumbling among most towns and offered a clear opportunity for demonstrations of obedience and order. The legitimacy conveyed by parliamentary approval made compliance straightforward, even in the face of near-universal dislike of paying taxes. Corporate towns generally assessed themselves, with the mayor and magistrates serving as commissioners. This avoided friction between borough and county officials, though conflicts over rating of special liberties like suburbs or cathedral closes could arise.[47] The downward direction in the amounts charged in the subsidies also likely made them easy to swallow. As Michael Braddick showed in his close study of parliamentary taxation in Norfolk and Cheshire, the amounts paid in subsidies by Norwich, King's Lynn, Great Yarmouth, Thetford, and Chester trended upward in the first years of James's reign, but moved downward after 1610 until 1641 for each subsidy; the 1620s, a period of war and hardship for most towns, saw particular declines.[48] These cases indicate that corporate towns may have had little to complain about regarding parliamentary taxation across the period from a financial point of view, and ready payment demonstrated obedience to authority in fulfilling this obligation to the state.

But the early seventeenth century saw an increasing burden of other financial exactions largely based on royal prerogative – loans of various sorts, special

---

[47] Michael Braddick, *Parliamentary Taxation in Seventeenth-Century England: Local Administration and Response*, Royal Historical Society Studies in History, vol. 70 (Woodbridge, 1994), pp. 70, 43–5.
[48] Braddick, *Parliamentary Taxation*, Appendix 2, pp. 304–7, 309–11.

PAYING THE PRICE

collections, billeting charges, Ship Money – that were more complicated for corporate towns to negotiate. In the reign of James, the prerogative exactions of the 1610s and the various contributions for the Palatinate in the early 1620s generally resulted in compliance in borough corporations, but they generated discussion and some hesitancy to pay. Town magistrates had strong reasons to support the needs of the crown, as the source of their corporate authority, but not all townsmen felt the same. Many provincial corporations responded promptly to the Privy Seal Loans of 1612, though some, like Chester, tried to avoid or reduce the charge; Chester's magistrates reasoned that many of those charged in this loan had paid on Privy Seals in Queen Elizabeth's time, but were not yet repaid.[49] Reading readily paid £64 16s 6d for the 1614 Benevolence, but labeled it "the free gift required of them voluntarily," suggesting the ambiguity of the levy. Ludlow paid the Benevolence promptly and Cambridge paid out of "great love" and "dutiful affection," while the Council reprimanded Taunton for backwardness. Wealthy merchants there excused themselves from paying by saying that they already paid customs on their merchandise, intimating that this was a sufficient contribution to the king's revenues. The Board lambasted the "absurdness" of the merchants' answer and ordered the mayor to rectify it.[50] In several towns, magistrates found contributions falling short of expectations, and they used funds from corporate coffers to make up the difference, in some cases more than 50 percent of what was originally assessed.[51] There may have been principled resistance among some townsmen; it was in a letter to the mayor of Marlborough that Oliver St. John made his case for the illegality of the 1614 Benevolence.[52] But borough governors understood the importance to their personal and corporate interests of maintaining a position of dutiful submission, in hopes of gaining benefit in return.

The voluntary contribution toward defense of the Palatinate in 1622, coming as it did during a period of deep economic depression, posed more of a problem.[53] The Privy Council sent out letters on 31 March to the counties and to eighty-five towns and cities, asking for a "liberal and speedy supply." That is not what most delivered. Many had already contributed toward Bohemia in

---

[49] YCA, B.33 (York House Book 1605–1612), fols 287–7; WAAS, A.14 Box I (Worcester Chamber Order Book 1602–1650), fols 30v, 31v; CCRO, ML/6/83, 87.

[50] J.M. Guilding (ed.), *Reading Records: Diary of the Corporation of Reading*, vol. 2 (London, 1895), p. 63; SRRC, LB2/1/1 (Ludlow Minute Book, 1590–1628), fols 105v, 107; C.H. Cooper (ed.), *Annals of Cambridge*, vol. 3 (Cambridge, 1845), p. 63; APC 1615–16, p. 49.

[51] WAAS, A.14 Box 1, fols 43, 44v; HHC, BRB3, p. 39; KLTH, KL/C7/9 (Chamber Act Book 1611–1637), fols 58v, 66v.

[52] Cust, *Forced Loan*, pp. 153–5; APC 1613–14, pp. 635, 647; TNA, SP14/78, fols 38–9. St. John was reported to the Privy Council, tried in Star Chamber, fined £5,000, and imprisoned. APC 1613–14, pp. 635, 647; *Cobbett's Complete Collection of State Trials*, vol. 2 (London, 1809), p. 900.

[53] B.E. Supple, *Commercial Crisis and Change in England 1600–1642: A Study in the Instability of a Mercantile Economy* (Cambridge, 1959), pp. 53–8.

URBAN GOVERNMENT AND THE EARLY STUART STATE

various collections between 1620 and 1621, making the 1622 levy more diffi-cult.[54] Magistrates responding to the Board's orders in 1622 almost universally apologized for the small offering. They frequently cited poverty, decay of trade, the burden of supporting poor inhabitants, and heavy contributions to other levies as reasons why more generous contributions for the Palatinate were impos-sible, despite keenness for the cause.[55] Leicester proved an exception, promising nearly £95 without excuses.[56] Responses from several towns indicate that some inhabitants refused to contribute. Norwich's mayor notified the Board of refusers and "too small givers," attributing the backwardness to poverty but also to "disaffection." The unparliamentary nature of the levy may have spurred some of the recalcitrance; Richard Cust found that a few gentlemen and lords refused or showed reluctance on these grounds in 1622.[57] Various towns simply did not contribute, a tactic that would come back to bite them nearly a decade later when a patentee discovered the omission and forced several unhappy corporations to pay up.[58] Whether the issues were pragmatic or principled, frustration over heavy costs during a time of economic strain characterized this service. Yet the overall response to the exactions of James's reign was compliance and engagement, as corporations negotiated for favor with central authorities.

If prerogative levies caused some friction in James's reign, the costs generated by war in the 1620s seriously challenged the complex web of finance, juris-diction, and authority connecting provincial towns to the state.[59] The war years created a sort of perfect storm of trials for provincial towns. Rising demands by the state for men and military funding, fortifications and ships, were joined with depressed markets, trade embargoes, and economic downturn, as well as new challenges to both local finances and local authority in the form of billeting. While all of these outgrowths of war had nationwide impacts, towns felt them especially keenly. Townsmen - from merchants and craftsmen to laborers

---

[54] *RBNott*, vol. 4, p. 382; J.F. Bailey (ed.), *Transcription of the Minutes of the Corporation of Boston*, vol. 2 (Boston, 1981), p. 329; GA, GBR B3/1, fol. 476, G3/SO/1, fol. 90, F1/9; HHC, BRL 172 (John Lister to mayor and aldermen, 3 May 1621); KLTH, KL/C7/9, fol. 172; ROLLR, BRIII/2/78, fol. 65; YCA, B.34 (House Book 1613-1625), fol. 206v; Chanter and Wainwright (eds), *Reprint of the Barnstaple Records*, vol. 2, p. 149.

[55] TNA, SP14/130, fols 29, 46, 47, 52, 54, 55, 56, 63, 65, 78, 80, 100, 114, 124, 141, 142, 156, 157, SP14/131, fols 19, 20, 91, 102, 107, 113, SP14/132, fols 3, 5, 17, 41, 53, SP14/133, fol. 106; HHC, BRB3, p. 101. Piracy levies were particularly noted.

[56] TNA, SP14/130, fol. 89.

[57] TNA, SP14/130, fols 145 (Northampton), 155 (Ripon), SP14/133, fol. 19 (Norwich); Cust, *Forced Loan*, p. 157.

[58] *APC 1629-30*, p. 235, *1630-31*, pp. 34-5; TNA, SP16/171, fol. 5, SP16/202, fol. 79, SP16/204, fols 34, 42, 87, 89, 158, SP16/211, fol. 28; SA/I, EE1/O1/1, fols 66v-67; NRO, NCR Case 16d, Book 5, fol. 267, Y/C19/6, fols 225, 229, 235v-236, 236v-237v; Y/C18/6, fols 132, 134v.

[59] For a discussion of one aspect of war's impact, see Victor Stater, "War and the Structure of Politics: Lieutenancy and the Campaign of 1628," in M.C. Fissell (ed.), *War and Government in Britain, 1598-1650* (Manchester and New York, 1991), pp. 87-109.

196

PAYING THE PRICE

– experienced the direct impact of disruptions to trade from embargoes as well as piracy. William Whiteway of Dorchester noted in his diary the trade stoppage with France and the lack of protection for the Narrow Sea. A petition from Poole claimed trade losses of £8,500 in the town from the Spanish and French embargoes.[60] Pressure on corporations to supply the crown's demands, whether for benevolences, ships, or loans, put new burdens on townsmen already struggling with unemployment and poverty. Coastal towns, more than most other communities, faced the financial burden, as well as the danger to orderly government and borough liberties, of billeting large numbers of soldiers moving to and from the king's service. They also bore regular impressment of mariners for the king's ships. Managing the many obligations tested borough government and raised questions about chartered liberties. In voicing concern over policies such as billeting or the Forced Loan, townsmen at times placed their views in the context of their corporate status and privileges of self-government, turning arguments over rating into debates over liberties.

As war loomed, military expenditure rose drastically, and defense and fortification added to the military burdens of towns in the war era. As with military exercises, attention to fortifications and defenses changed radically across the first two decades of the seventeenth century. Fortifications had been allowed to decay, or in the case of border towns like Berwick, actively de-fortified, in the long era of peace under James I. When warfare and piracy threatened in the mid-1620s, many towns found themselves without defense.[61] Townsmen accepted their responsibility to protect themselves and the realm, and corporations like Weymouth and Melcombe Regis, Hull, and Aldeburgh used the ability granted to them by charter to tax their own inhabitants for provision of defense.[62] But a provincial town rarely had sufficient resources for the fortifications and munitions necessary to fend off attacks, and they hoped for assistance from the state. In the absence of any clear policy or program from the crown, individual localities reached out to the Council to beg for the means to provide for the common defense. Cogswell's close study of Aldeburgh's lengthy quest to obtain ordnance for their exposed coastal town shows how determined

[60] Whiteway, *Diary*, pp. 79, 81, 89; TNA, SP16/50, fol. 137.
[61] Quintrell (ed.), *Maynard Lieutenancy Book*, p. 99 (Earl of Warwick to Privy Council, 18 September 1625); Janine van Vliet, "From a 'Strong Town of War' to the 'Very Heart of the Country': The English Border Town of Berwick-upon-Tweed, 1558-1625" (PhD dissertation, University of Pennsylvania, 2017), pp. 196-246; TNA, SP16/6, fols 15, 16, SP16/8, fols 26, 30; M. Weinstock (ed.), *Weymouth and Melcombe Regis Minute Book 1625-1660*, Dorset Record Society, vol. 1 (Dorchester, 1964), p. 10; HHC, BRM (Hull Borough Miscellaneous) 146; Cogswell, "Ten Demi-Culverins for Aldeburgh," p. 333. According to one study, Berwick, Hull, Plymouth, and Portsmouth had "modernized, permanent defensive systems" in 1642. Peter Courtney, "Armies, Militias and Urban Landscapes: England, France and the Low Countries 1500-1900," in A. Green and R. Leech (eds), *Cities in the World, 1500-2000* (Leeds, 2006), p. 169. These fortifications were, however, poorly maintained in the 1620s.
[62] Weinstock (ed.), *Weymouth and Melcombe Regis Minute Book*, p. 10; HHC, BRM 146; Cogswell, "Ten Demi-Culverins for Aldeburgh," p. 333.

URBAN GOVERNMENT AND THE EARLY STUART STATE

local leaders could be, even those of a small and relatively poor borough. The townsmen of Aldeburgh doggedly pursued their cause for two years, from 1626 to 1628, to gain the ordnance they sought.[63] And Aldeburgh was hardly alone.[64] Unfortunately for many towns, however, central authorities acknowledged the national necessity of good defenses but lacked the wherewithal to support local needs. The earl of Totnes, master of the ordnance, declined or delayed requests from some towns for ordnance due to scarcity.[65] Given the difficult state of royal finances, the crown largely laid the financial burden of defenses and fortifications on the towns themselves, with vague promises of future reward for local "forwardness." With fear of a Spanish invasion high in July 1626, the Privy Council wrote to fourteen port towns all around the coasts, noting their present weakness of defense and urging them to fortify themselves. Yet there was no promise of assistance, just expressions of "due care" for their safety.[66] The lack of help for the port towns became a point of debate in the 1626 Parliament, as Sir Walter Erle, burgess for Lyme Regis, called out the failure to protect the Narrow Sea, fortify the coasts, or provide ordnance and ammunition as "evils" of the time; he affirmed that the forts of the kingdom were "never in so ill case as now."[67] The problem continued throughout the war years, exacerbating the financial pressures on these towns as well as their fears of invasion and depredation.

Borough governors understood the vital connection between the safety of their own localities and the safety of the realm. They called on central authority to help them financially with defense or to mitigate their burden. At the same time, the crown's fiscal weakness dictated a high level of dependence on town authorities and locally raised funds to undertake national defense. Cogswell concluded that the fact that Aldeburgh ultimately received the ten demi-culverins it requested from the crown testifies against a "functional breakdown" in the early Stuart state. Certainly, the central government's ability to carry out its functions was not entirely broken, but it was hampered by lack of resources and bureaucratic insufficiency. The inability, or at best extreme slowness, of central authorities to meet needs for basic defense put town governments in a difficult position in terms of both their safety and their pocketbooks. The resourcefulness of borough governors, like those of Aldeburgh, demonstrates the ability of provincial authorities to navigate relations with the crown and to express pressing needs of the localities, but central government's lack of support frayed relations between towns and the crown.

[63] Cogswell, "Ten Demi-Culverins for Aldeburgh," pp. 315–37.
[64] Quintrell (ed.), *Maynard Lieutenancy Book*, p. 111; TNA, SP16/14, fol. 71, SP16/23, fol. 171, SP16/24, fol. 40, SP16/32, fol. 120.
[65] TNA, SP16/24, fol. 40, SP16/25, fol. 80.
[66] APC 1626, p. 60.
[67] *P in P 1626*, 2:132. Erle served for Lyme Regis in 1626, having served for Poole in 1614, 1621, and 1624. "Earle [Erle], Walter (1586–1665)," *HoP 1604–29*, www.historyofparliament online.org/volume/1604-1629/member/earle-walter-1586-1-665.

Demands for men, munitions, and defenses placed troublesome burdens on most towns, leading to complicated relations between localities and crown. The heaviness of the costs gave rise to frustration that central authorities expected the localities to support the work of the state without understanding the pressures under which they operated. A 1628 petition from the tiny, poor town of Dunwich begged Lord Admiral Buckingham not to press any more of their men, or they would "utterly perish through want of men to follow their trade of fishing," having fewer than sixty able men left.[68] The ineffectualness of the war effort under Buckingham was widely known in the provinces, as testified to by both parliamentary debates in 1626 and 1628 and the diary of Dorchester townsman William Whiteway. Whiteway noted that the Commons spent much time in 1626 on the "Late fleete that went out, and of the causes of the bad successe, which they could not enter into without fastening upon the Duke."[69] The focus on Buckingham's ineptitude in the war raised the related point that central government exacted a high price from the localities – towns in particular – but did not consistently support local interests. This rising frustration would reach its zenith over billeting.

Billeting's burdens

Billeting, between 1625 and 1628, fell heavily on England's towns, especially (though not exclusively) those on the coasts, in or near ports from which soldiers shipped. With their concentration of population as well as goods, services, and hostelries, towns made logical sites for billeting troops. But for towns already suffering from economic woes, soldiers in their midst accentuated the misery. The numbers of troops billeted varied widely between towns and over time. In June 1625, as the first soldiers moved to the port towns to embark for the service, the mayor of Plymouth found himself grappling with billeting 10,000 men through his town. Not all were billeted in the borough itself, but this profound influx of people required clothing, food, accommodation, and minding, amidst complaints over lack of pay and insubordination of soldiers.[70] Towns like Colchester, Harwich, Maldon, Cirencester, Gloucester, Reading, and Great Yarmouth were responsible for billeting scores, and sometimes hundreds,

---

[68] TNA, SP16/100, fol. 60.
[69] *P in P 1626*, 1:465–6, 2:335, 359, 360, *1628*, 3:310; Whiteway, *Diary*, pp. 79, 81. See also Thomas Cogswell, "The Lord Admiral, The Parliament-Men, and the Narrow Seas, 1625–27," in Chris Kyle and Jason Peacey (eds), *Connecting Centre and Locality: Political Communication in Early Modern England* (Manchester, 2020), pp. 44–65.
[70] TNA, SP16/3, fol. 38. On billeting, see also George Spencer Stivers, "'A Most Grievous and Insupportable Vexation': Billeting in Early Seventeenth Century England" (PhD dissertation, University of California-Riverside, 2009); Paul Christianson, "Arguments on Billeting and Martial Law in the Parliament of 1628," *Historical Journal* 37 (1994), 539–67.

URBAN GOVERNMENT AND THE EARLY STUART STATE

of soldiers at a time.[71] The Privy Council in March 1627 ordered Hull to billet 1350 soldiers; Hull's town clerk noted that a portion of these moved on to Beverley, and some were billeted in the county of the city of Hull, but the city itself had to absorb most of them. Canterbury complained of billeting four companies in April 1628, while Whiteway recorded that a whole regiment was billeted in Dorchester in October 1626 and two dozen soldiers in April 1628.[72] These towns and many others absorbed large numbers of unwanted "guests," draining local resources and placing a significant burden on local government to manage both the financial and the order-keeping aspects of billeting in their towns.

Not just the cost of these soldiers but their behavior and impact on government and quality of life exercised borough governors. Central authorities understood the dangers of unruly soldiers, but also placed responsibility for order in the hands of local officials. The commissioners for billeting chided the mayor of Dover for housing soldiers in poor alehouses, "commonly houses of disorder and places of liberty ... to vices." The mayor was instead to find lodging in private homes, a move that might satisfy the Privy Council but likely not Dover's inhabitants.[73] Complaints from mayors and townsmen focused on the abusive and disorderly behavior of the soldiers.[74] In Hereford, residents reported that soldiers abused and solicited women, spoke dangerous words about the king, and made threats against the city and its governors. "I care not for Mr. Mayor this crust of bread," one allegedly said.[75] Controversy rose in Reading between billeted soldiers there and "divers young men" of the town, leading to the town boys disobeying the constables and being required to find sureties.[76] In Norwich, when required to billet Irish soldiers, the city's governing assembly moved that the soldiers, who committed many outrages, should be disarmed except when actually doing maneuvers.[77] Many Banbury residents believed that unruly billeted soldiers had purposely started the fire that burned down a third of the town in 1628.[78] The inhabitants of Maldon complained bitterly of the

---

[71] Quintrell (ed.), *Maynard Lieutenancy Book*, p. 102 (Earl of Warwick to bailiffs of Colchester, 15 September 1625), p. 125 (Note of proposed distribution of regiments, [n.d., but 1626]); GA, GBR H2/2 (Letter Book, 1619-39), pp. 113, 119, 127; Guilding (ed.), *Reading Records*, vol. 2, pp. 320-21, 329, 384; BL, Egerton MS 2087, fols 20, 45; NRO, Y/C19/6, fols 91v, 92v, 93.

[72] HHC, BRB3, p. 162; TNA, SP16/102, fol. 93; Whiteway, *Diary*, pp. 85, 96.

[73] BL, Egerton MS 2087, fol. 26. The commissioners for billeting in Plymouth complained to the Council that the "rich" avoided taking soldiers, so they were imposed on the "meaner sort" who were "ill able" to feed and house them. TNA, SP16/18, fol. 16v.

[74] BL, Egerton MS 2087, fols 30, 43; TNA, SP16/3, fol. 48, SP16/92, fol. 116; Quintrell (ed.), *Maynard Lieutenancy Book*, pp. 171, 231.

[75] Herefordshire Archive and Records Centre, Hereford, O/U 123 (Miscellaneous Papers 1600-1644), #68, #73, #74 (Depositions before Mayor Richard Weaver).

[76] Guilding (ed.), *Reading Records*, vol. 2, p. 392.

[77] NRO, NCR Case 16d, Book 5, fols 239, 247v.

[78] Barton John Blankenfeld, "Puritans in the Provinces: Banbury, Oxfordshire, 1554-1660"

PAYING THE PRICE

Irish soldiers billeted there. "They command in our houses, as if they were our lords, and we their slaves, enforcing us and ours to attend them at their pleasure, and to do the basest offices for them." Some residents claimed they had to stay in their houses to protect their homes and women-folk from the soldiers' depredations.[79] Canterbury's magistrates likewise faced unruly and discontented soldiers, disgruntled with both their lodging and their diet, who threatened to make mischief and refused to attend church.[80] The presence of large numbers of armed men grieved inhabitants and undermined normal borough governance.

Adding to the misery, disease arrived with the soldiers in several towns. The mayor of Dartmouth reported the general sickness among the mariners on the ships transporting soldiers, while the master of the almshouse of Dover kept accounts of the winding sheets he purchased and burials he conducted for soldiers who died there while billeted in the town.[81] Plymouth suffered greatly from infection in 1626, spurring the town to petition the duke of Buckingham early in 1627, pleading for relief from the misery spread by plague-ridden soldiers. When they again faced the possibility of receiving soldiers back from La Rochelle in 1628, the mayor and aldermen wrote to the Privy Council reminding the Board that 1,600 inhabitants of Plymouth had died when the ships from Cadiz and Ré returned with sick soldiers.[82] Townspeople and their magistrates bore a weighty burden from billeting, which became a source of grievance between towns and central authorities.

While the crown saw urban magistrates as extensions of state authority in their localities, borough governors often found themselves squeezed between their role as crown officers, charged with carrying out the king's service, and the unhappiness of townspeople over the execution of billeting orders. Epiphany

---

(PhD dissertation, Yale University, 1985), p. 227.

[79] TNA, SP16/92, fol. 116. A deputy lieutenant of Essex questioned the truthfulness of Maldon's complaints. SP16/92, fol. 82. See also Gerald Aylmer, "St. Patrick's Day 1628 in Witham, Essex," *Past & Present* No. 61 (1973), 139-48; B.W. Quintrell, "Gentry Factions and the Witham Affray, 1628," *Essex Archaeology and History* 10 (1978), 118-26. Quintrell shows the complex local politics behind billeting in Maldon, involving members of the local gentry, parliamentary patronage, and frequent communication with the Council.

[80] TNA, SP16/101, fol. 60 (Mayor and aldermen of Canterbury to Privy Council, 17 April 1628), 62 (Mayor and aldermen of Canterbury to earl of Montgomery, 17 April 1628).

[81] TNA, SP16/18, fol. 18 (Mayor of Dartmouth to commissioners for soldiers at Plymouth, 3 January 1626); BL, Egerton MS 2087, fols 7-13. At least twenty soldiers died in the almshouse between January and April 1625.

[82] TNA, SP16/29, fol. 61 (Commissioners for soldiers at Plymouth to Privy Council, 8 June 1626), SP16/31, fol. 32 (Mayor of Plymouth to Privy Council, 6 July 1626), SP16/34, fol. 35 (Commissioners for soldiers at Plymouth to Privy Council, 24 August 1626), SP16/53, fol. 79 (Petition of mayor and commonalty of Plymouth to duke of Buckingham, 9 February 1627), SP16/118, fol. 106 (Mayor *et al.* of Plymouth to Privy Council, 16 October 1628). Plague could sometimes allow a town to avoid billeting, as when the Privy Council sent 1,000 soldiers bound for Bridport and Blandford elsewhere when infection was "great" in those boroughs. *APC 1626*, p. 261.

URBAN GOVERNMENT AND THE EARLY STUART STATE

Hill, a Banbury magistrate, faced legal action by an inhabitant for billeting a soldier on him, forcing Hill to appeal to the Privy Council for redress.[83] Much of the difficulty stemmed from the slowness and inefficiency of the state to meet the financial burdens incurred through billeting. Townsmen bore the immediate brunt of billeting the soldiers in their homes, though the charges were generally to be shared more widely. Town governors regularly found themselves pleading with the Privy Council, county deputy lieutenants and other officials to provide more prompt payment and to remove the soldiers. The mayor of Southampton, when faced with more charges and no payment in sight, resisted further billeting unless the townsmen received payment for what they had already provided.[84] In Basingstoke, the two bailiffs pleaded for assistance when the billeters in their town went unpaid and the inhabitants refused to contribute any further, having already paid £180 out of their own pockets; the bailiffs tried to persuade the town's neighbors to help bear the cost, but the neighbors refuted the bailiffs' authority to compel them.[85] Gloucester's mayor appealed to the Privy Council in the summer of 1628, providing his accounts for soldiers billeted and notifying the Board how much stood unpaid to billeters, who are "daily and importunate suitors" for recompense.[86] This refrain could be repeated in almost every town that billeted soldiers: the crown fell far behind in paying what was promised.[87]

In addition to the many practical problems that billeting caused for urban dwellers and their governors, it also presented challenges to the jurisdiction of corporate boroughs. Mayors and bailiffs were pressed to protect chartered privileges and local interests while also remaining obedient to royal authority, from which their charters sprang. Corporate charters generally excluded county JPs from intruding in borough business, but the deputy lieutenants who managed military matters had authority superseding corporate jurisdiction. As scholars like Lindsay Boynton and Paul Christianson have shown, billeting also raised serious questions of jurisdiction between common law and martial law.[88] These found their way into parliamentary debates, but the practical concern for order and jurisdictional privilege played out daily in the towns.

---

[83] TNA, PC2/41, p. 428. Hill, mayor in 1627–8, was involved in a billeting dispute that came before the House of Lords in the 1628 Parliament, where he was required to testify. *P in P 1628*, 5:104, 137.

[84] TNA, SO1/1, fol. 123 (Council to Viscount Conway, 25 March 1628).

[85] TNA, SP16/103, fol. 197 (Bailiffs of Basingstoke to Sir T. Jervoise, 14 May 1628); APC 1627–28, p. 434; Francis Baigent and James Millard, *A History of the Ancient Town and Manor of Basingstoke in the County of Southampton, with a Brief Account of the Siege of Basing House, AD 1643–1645*, vol. 1 (Basingstoke and London, 1889), p. 410.

[86] GA, GBR H2/2, p. 155.

[87] Similar letters asking for payment of charges spent on billeting came from Plymouth, Chichester, Canterbury, Wokingham, Barnstaple, and Exeter. *CSPD 1627–28*, p. 50, 508–9, *1628–29*, pp. 279, 280, 376, 433.

[88] Christianson, "Arguments on Billeting," *passim*; Lindsay Boynton, "Martial Law and the Petition of Right," *English Historical Review* 79 (1964), 258.

202

Some deputy lieutenants were sensitive to corporate privileges. Sir Edward Hales wrote to the mayor of Dover about billeting early in 1627, conceding the "just complaints" of the town, and acknowledging Dover's separate jurisdiction in legal action against disorderly soldiers.[89] In other instances, the lieutenancy pressed against borough liberties in managing billeting, and boroughs pushed back against them. Brightlingsea, a "member" of the borough of Sandwich, complained in 1626 that Essex deputy lieutenants billeted soldiers on them, infringing on their liberties as part of the Cinque Ports.[90] The city of Gloucester, a county unto itself, engaged in a protracted debate with Gloucestershire deputy lieutenants and the Privy Council regarding their share in the billeting. While not refusing to billet, even though the county of the city was not explicitly mentioned in the Privy Council's order, civic officials contested the proportion of soldiers the deputy lieutenants assigned them.[91] The corporation appealed to the Privy Council, which determined that Gloucester should bear only one-tenth of the soldiers to be billeted and reduced the burden on the shire as a whole.[92] Corporate boroughs did not reject their responsibility to contribute to billeting as part of a national war effort, but at the same time they actively sought to maintain privileges they saw as critical to their prosperity, if not their existence. The Council displayed some sensitivity to local privileges, as long as the town in question was otherwise obedient and contributing to the king's service.

Not all townsmen contributed obediently, however, and refusal posed a troubling conundrum for borough magistrates. Some had sympathy with billeting resisters, for the true hardships and dangers the service caused. But as deputies to the king, magistrates were obligated to carry out royal policy in their towns. When confronted with refractory residents, town governors often appealed to lord lieutenants or privy councilors to bring the force of central authority to bear. The mayor and aldermen of Canterbury wrote to the earl of Montgomery, lord lieutenant of Kent, and to the Privy Council in April 1628 complaining of billeting refusers. Thomas Scott, a freeman of Canterbury and parliamentary burgess in 1624 and 1628, utterly refused to billet any soldiers or contribute toward it, and his example spread the contagion of refusal in the town. The magistrates (with whom Scott had ongoing political quarrels) requested a "speedy order" from Montgomery to force conformity to the billeting service among Canterbury's refusers, and they did their best to enforce the king's service on the citizens.[93] At the same time, they repeatedly begged the

---

[89] BL, Egerton MS 2087, fol. 43.
[90] TNA, SP16/21, fol. 8 (Petition of Brightlingsea to duke of Buckingham, 12 February 1626); Quintrell (ed.), *Maynard Lieutenancy Book*, pp. 125 (billeting order to Brightlingsea, 1626), 126 (Buckingham to earls of Sussex and Warwick, 9 March 1626). Brightlingsea's exemption was ultimately confirmed.
[91] *CSPD 1627–28*, p. 586; GA, GBR H2/2, pp. 119, 124, 126.
[92] GA, GBR H2/2, pp. 133-4, 140, 141; APC 1627–28, pp. 333, 341.
[93] TNA, SP16/101, fol. 154, SP16/102, fol. 93. On Scott's differences with Canterbury's

URBAN GOVERNMENT AND THE EARLY STUART STATE

Privy Council to relieve the city of the heavy burden. They painted a terrible picture of the depredations of the soldiers and of the sorry state of the city – markets decayed, trading spoiled, and poor tradesmen "undone."[94] The mayor of Plymouth, petitioning the duke of Buckingham on behalf of his beleaguered town in 1627, put the burden of billeting in the context of a multitude of miseries coinciding in the town as a result of the war. These woes included losses amounting to £44,000 due to pirates and embargoes, and sickness that was so severe they had to crave assistance from their neighbors to support their own poor, in addition to the weight of billeting, for which they were still owed £6,000.[95] Their situation untenable, magistrates like the mayors of Canterbury and Plymouth could only appeal to higher authorities for relief.

Relief was not always forthcoming. The Privy Council expected obedience to orders, whatever the local burden might be. Magistrates of corporate towns with billeted soldiers were held strictly accountable to fulfill Council directives and maintain local order. The mayor and aldermen of Southampton felt the admonition of the Board several times, when inhabitants resisted billeting. In June 1626, the mayor and his fellows complained to the deputy lieutenants of the difficulties of keeping peace when the payments for billeted soldiers fell behind. The Privy Council reproved them for not obeying the deputies' orders for where to billet the men (which the Board believed should be in the private homes of the "principal men" of the town) and for their failure to maintain order despite the lack of pay, which other communities had been able to do.[96] Two years later, when faced with an order to billet an additional four hundred soldiers in April 1628, the townsmen of Southampton, claiming poverty due to loss of trade and fifteen weeks of arrears for billeting money, balked unless they received immediate payment for this burdensome service. The king swiftly rebuked this behavior, ordering the billeting of the soldiers without delay, "it being very strange that they [the mayor and aldermen] should propose unto us conditions in a business of this nature." Secretary Conway, to whom the corporation had also appealed directly, replied to them somewhat less sternly, but he made clear the soldiers were to be billeted in the town, saying the Board would do its best to procure the money.[97] One imagines the struggling townsmen

---

magistrates, see Cogswell, "The Canterbury Election of 1626." See also Peter Clark, "Scott, Thomas (c. 1566–1635), Landowner and Politician," *ODNB*, accessed 24 Jul. 2020, www-oxforddnb-com.ezproxy.lib.uh.edu/view/10.1093/ref:odnb/9780198614128.001.0001/odnb-9780198614128-e-37945. According to the mayor of Canterbury, over 100 residents refused, left town, or failed to pay. TNA, SP16/104, fol. 88.
[94] TNA, SP16/102, fol. 93, SP16/104, fols 86, 88.
[95] TNA, SP16/53, fol. 79.
[96] *APC 1626*, p. 26.
[97] TNA, SP16/101, fol. 152 (Conway to Hampshire billeting commissioners, 23 April 1628), SP16/102, fol. 82 (Mayor of Southampton to Conway, 28 April 1628), SP16/103, fols 201 (Francis Knowles *et al.* of Southampton to Conway, 15 May 1628), 203 (Conway to mayor *et al.* of Southampton, and other commissioners in Hants., 15 May 1628), SO1/1, fol. 123 (King to Viscount Conway, 25 May 1628).

took little solace in Conway's letter. The state's inability to meet its obligations regarding billeting provided an opportunity for distrust to grow.[98]

The serious hardships created by billeting prompted resistance in some townsmen that expressed political views on the legality of the service, not simply unhappiness with practical matters of payment and trouble. The Privy Council heard in 1628 that the "bayliffs and magistrates of Dorchester have obstinately refused to billet" soldiers. Richard Bushrod (twice parliamentary burgess for the town) allegedly refused to contribute toward billeting and was examined "as an agent in [deterring] other men from billeting." The allegations "came to nothing" when a commission of local gentlemen determined his refusal rested on insufficient authority of the billeting warrants.[99] In Chichester, where the inhabitants threatened "opposition," two burgesses allegedly told the mayor that by law there could be no billeting, and advised the mayor to take heed what he did or parliament would call him to account for it.[100] The earl of Banbury reported to Lord President Manchester in February 1628 that the town of Banbury stubbornly refused to contribute to billeting and set a bad example to others. He also intimated that the town's neighbor, Lord Saye, a godly Protestant and Forced Loan refuser, incited the townsmen's refusal.[101] Local complaints over billeting became more vociferous as parliamentary debates over it gained speed.

Billeting's deep unpopularity and arguable illegality made it a key grievance in the 1628 Parliament and the debates leading to the Petition of Right. Many members decried the corrosive impact of the billeted soldiers on the peace and prosperity of the commonwealth; in the countryside, tenants gave up their farms out of fear of the soldiers, and in towns the tradesmen left off their trades in order to protect family and property. Both houses grappled with billeting's evils. An affray between local officials and billeted soldiers in Banbury became a focus of debate in the House of Lords in April.[102] The House of Commons in the same month petitioned the king specifically about billeting, restating the

---

[98] Michael B. Young, "Charles I and the Erosion of Trust, 1625–1628," *Albion* 22 (1990), 217–35, argues that Charles I himself was the focus of and agent for distrust in the period 1625–28, which was displayed in Parliament. The view from the towns in this period suggests not a distrust in the king himself but a distrust in the state's ability to honor its obligations and respond effectively to local problems.

[99] Whiteway, *Diary*, pp. 57, 96; *APC 1627–28*, p. 427; TNA, SP16/103, fol. 58 (T. Fryer to Buckingham, 5 May 1628), SP16/105, fol. 62 (T. Trenchard *et al.* to Privy Council, 28 May 1628).

[100] TNA, PC2/38, p. 506 (Privy Council to mayor of Chichester, 5 October 1628).

[101] *CSPD 1627–28*, p. 589 (Earl of Banbury to earl of Manchester, 28 February 1628); David L. Smith, "Fiennes, William, first Viscount Saye and Sele (1582–1662), Politician," *ODNB*, accessed 25 July 2020, www-oxforddnb-com.ezproxy.lib.uh.edu/view/10.1093/ref:odnb/9780198614128.001.0001/odnb-9780198614128-e-9415. According to one study, Banbury "proved much more troublesome than most towns" in its resistance to billeting as well as the Forced Loan. Blankenfeld, "Puritans in Banbury," p. 212.

[102] *P in P 1628*, 2:56, 253, 5:137–44; Christianson, "Arguments on Billeting," p. 544.

URBAN GOVERNMENT AND THE EARLY STUART STATE

"fundamental law" of a free man's "absolute propriety" in his estate, making billeting in men's houses against their will "directly contrary" to this ancient and undoubted law.[103] The debates and petition around billeting in April became a crucial foundation, along with those over martial law and the Forced Loan, for the Petition of Right in the summer. The grievance of billeting appears as Article VI of the Petition, and the supplication to the king to remove billeted soldiers and mariners in Article X.

While the great landed gentlemen and lawyers dominated the debates over liberties in parliament in this session, townsman members had direct experience of billeting and its impact. George Gollop, one of Southampton's parliamentary burgesses and an alderman and former mayor there, complained of the 160 soldiers from Ré, and then another 200, recently billeted in his town. Christopher Sherland, recorder of Northampton and a resident there, spoke vehemently against billeting on April 8: "It is not only against law, but in a transcendent manner." The fact that soldiers were placed in Northampton (under an officer who had fought on the Continent against the king and queen of Bohemia, no less) just as the 1628 parliament was called seemed ominous. "What was this," he asked, "but to frustrate the hope of this parliament?" For George Browne, member for Taunton as well as recorder of the town, billeting became very personal. He declared in the debates on April 2 that deputy lieutenants had billeted 100 men in Taunton "by force," including some in his own home, driving his wife and children to abandon it. He declared, "Every man knows there is no law for this. We know our houses are our castles, and to have such guests put upon us, our wives, and children, is a violating of the laws."[104] Men like Sir Robert Phelips and Sir Edward Coke led the charge for securing the liberties of the subject in this Parliament and the Petition of Right, but the arguments and examples from townsmen played a critical role in this constitutional conflict.

Outside of parliament, the writings of Thomas Scott of Canterbury offer rare insight into the political views on billeting of one urban dweller. Guided by a fervent brand of evangelical Protestantism, Scott deeply opposed billeting as illegal. "It is against the liberty of a free Englishman and Gentleman & of a Parliament man. And intended by the Duke to do us a mischief." Scott thought Canterbury's magistrates "over diligent and partial" in their execution of the billeting orders, suggesting they were "fools and slaves" to carry out what he viewed as an illegal "Dukish device."[105] Accused of being the "principal occasion" of a campaign against billeting in Canterbury, Scott ended up before

---

[103] *P in P 1628*, 2:451-2.
[104] *P in P 1628*, 4:159, 2:361-2, 254, 264. See also Thomas G. Barnes, "Deputies not Principals, Lieutenants not Captains: The Institutional Failure of the Lieutenancy in the 1620s," in Fissel (ed.), *War and Government in Britain*, pp. 69-75. It was alleged that the deputy lieutenant who placed the soldiers in Browne's home did so for political reasons, not liking the outcome of the recent election. *P in P 1628*, 2:570.
[105] KHLC, U951/Z9, pp. 5, 7, 8.

the Privy Council and ultimately imprisoned for his opinions in 1628.[106] Scott was likely an outlier for the intensity and radicalism of his views, but he testifies to the fact that for at least some townsmen, billeting was a matter of principle, not just of pocketbook.[107] Protecting their homes from billeting had a clear connection with broader issues of law and national politics.

The Council saw the dangers to the state of the resistance to billeting like that in Canterbury and other towns, and it made clear the subordination of corporate towns to central authority. In October 1628, the Board wrote sharply to the mayor of Chichester regarding opposition to billeting there. The earl of Dorset told the Board that some inhabitants had threatened to shut the town gates against the soldiers, "as if you assumed to be a free state, and give law to yourselves," which "seem to us strange and unheard of from persons living under a civil government."[108] This striking assertion, condemning the corporation as a "free state," reveals the crown's fear of resistance in general, but about corporate governance in particular, which produced the dangerous idea that townsmen could control their own business.[109] The specter of popularity that often seemed to glimmer around the edges of corporate towns became manifest in actions like those in Chichester. Given that this exchange occurred in the wake of the Petition of Right and the debates in parliament over billeting, the Council swiftly squashed such thinking, but it left a lingering question about the relationship between corporation and sovereign state as well as the liberties of the subject.

It seems unlikely that the people of Chichester truly saw their town as a "free state" disconnected from or unbound by the law of the land and the authority of king and Council. At the same time, the crisis of billeting along

---

[106] *P in P 1628*, 4:229; *APC 1628-29*, pp. 1, 10. See Peter Clark, "Thomas Scott and the Growth of Urban Opposition to the Early Stuart Regime," *Historical Journal* 21 (1978), 1-26; Cesare Cuttica, "Thomas Scott of Canterbury (1566-1635): Patriot, Civic Radical, Puritan," *History of European Ideas* 34 (2008), 475-89; Thomas Cogswell, "The Canterbury Election of 1626 and Parliamentary Selection Revisited," *Historical Journal* 63 (2020), 291-315; and Cust, *Forced Loan*, pp. 175-85 for discussions of Thomas Scott and his political views and activity.

[107] Scott himself said that "many Canterbury men" came to him to complain "how the soldiers were forced upon them." KHLC, U951/Z9, p. 7. Cust argues that in regard to the Forced Loan (which Scott protested but paid in full), Scott espoused singularly extreme views, but he was not simply "out on his own" in the direction of some of his positions. Cust, *Forced Loan*, pp. 182-4. See also "Scott, Thomas (c. 1566/7-1635)," *HoP 1604-29*, www.historyof parliamentonline.org/volume/1604-1629/member/scott-thomas-15667-1635.

[108] TNA, PC2/38, p. 506 (Privy Council to mayor of Chichester, 5 October 1628).

[109] Daniel Beaver has noted the use of language of a "free state" in reference to violence in Massachusetts between rival fishing settlements in the mid-1620s. Beaver sees such ideologically charged conflict on the Atlantic margins, but relatively absent in England, "where the Stuart dynastic state maintained its effective monopoly of the organized use of force." Daniel C. Beaver, "'Fruits of Unrulie Multitudes': Liberty, Popularity, and Meanings of Violence in the English Atlantic, 1623-1625," *Journal of British Studies* 59 (2020), 39. This Chichester incident, however, suggests that fear of such conflict resonated in England itself, well before the early 1640s.

URBAN GOVERNMENT AND THE EARLY STUART STATE

the coasts did expose the tensions that existed for towns as both corporate entities with some powers of self-governance and integrated parts of the early modern state.[110] Mayors and bailiffs found themselves in the difficult position of serving as deputies of the king, charged with carrying out the policies of the crown, while also grappling with the profound impact of these policies on their own authority, on their towns' economic well-being, and on borough liberties and public order. The frequent communication of town officials to the Privy Council on billeting and its seemingly existential threat testifies to billeting's impact and the expectation of redress from the crown. The Council took some actions to mitigate the burden, by shifting soldiers to other areas or finding funds to remunerate costs. But the inability of the state to solve either the crisis of funding or the crisis of order created by billeting over the course of multiple years caused serious frustration in many towns that for some raised questions of law and right. For those most affected, billeting created a profound sense of grievance that found voice in the halls of parliament as well as in the streets of the towns and in letters and petitions to the Privy Council.

Paying for war: the Forced Loan and ship charges

Corporate boroughs, while bearing a heavy burden of billeting and all the other costs associated with war and defense, were also called on to pay for the prosecution of the war through national taxation. The king's well-known difficulties with the parliament of 1626 resulted in insufficient subsidies, leading to other, prerogative methods – principally ship charges and the Forced Loan. Set against the backdrop of war, piracy, plague, and trade downturn, these exactions taxed already overburdened towns and squeezed borough governors between demands from the crown and the concerns of their communities.

Evidence from towns for the Forced Loan suggests that most magistrates collected it vigorously, obeying the crown's orders and maintaining strong relations with the Privy Council, though not all inhabitants shared the enthusiasm. Cities and towns as diverse as York, Hull, Chester, Hadleigh, Harwich, Poole, Lincoln, Derby, Bath, Monmouth, Thetford, Canterbury, and Windsor reported zeal in collecting or few if any defaults.[111] Other places – like Exeter and Shrewsbury – reported general payment, but with defaults and slowness. The bailiffs of Bridport expressed obedience, but sought remission of payment

---

[110] See Philip J. Stern, "'Bundles of Hyphens': Corporations as Legal Communities in the Early Modern British Empire," in L. Benton and R. Ross (eds), *Legal Pluralism and Empires, 1500–1850* (New York, 2013), pp. 21–47, for an extended discussion of corporations within a pluralistic early modern state.
[111] TNA, SP16/53, fols 38, 95, SP16/55, fol. 16, SP16/65, fol. 43, SP16/66, fols 41, 69, SP16/70, fol. 134, SP16/71, fol. 26, SP16/76, fols 3, 15, 24, SP16/77, fol. 25; HHC, BRB3, p. 159; APC 1627, p. 114. See also Cust, *Forced Loan*, pp. 127–35.

208

PAYING THE PRICE

due to their "desolation" from a twenty-week visitation of plague.[112] There were also signs of resistance. The mayor and one of the aldermen of Boston refused outright, though at a meeting of the town council the borough governors had agreed that the mayor should "yeald and assent" to the loan on behalf of the corporation. In Leicester, some scrupled to subscribe their names for the Loan, though they would give the sum demanded; others nominated to be collectors refused to take up the office.[113] Northampton indicated a significant amount of defaulting among those rated. Several members of Banbury's corporation refused, and Secretary of State Dudley Carleton suggested that billeting more soldiers on the town might be a fitting chastisement. Gloucester's magistrates received a sharp message from the Board for their neglect in collecting the levy, such that those "whoe stande in contempt and refuse to lende fare better then those whoe are the lenders." Nottingham's received the same. King's Lynn's mayor complained of his town's inability to pay the Loan and also notified the Council of a paper found in the town's streets, directed to English freeholders from a "well-wisher," intended to draw people away from paying the levy.[114] On the whole, borough magistrates collected all or most of what was required of them, but the collection stirred up unhappiness, and in some cases refusal.

If collection of the Loan varied but was largely accepted, ship charges caused more trouble. Despite the fact that the obligation to provide ships had long precedents, the port towns charged with ships almost universally attempted to avoid, decrease, or redistribute payment. Magistrates seem to have felt on firmer ground in protesting this charge, or at least pleading poverty, than for the Loan. The first levy in 1626 elicited complaints and petitions for relief from Lyme Regis, Bristol, Norwich, Exeter, Truro, Hull and York, Aldeburgh, and Ipswich, among others. Boston's corporation agreed that the mayor should write to "any person or persons" who could help them discharge or mitigate Ship Money.[115] In the first half of 1627, no fewer than twenty-two towns and cities petitioned the Board asking for relief from payment.[116] Nearly all lamented their desperate conditions: the decay of trade – cloth towns unable to trade with France and

---

[112] TNA, SP16/76, fol. 22 (Exeter), SP16/81, fol. 136 (Shrewsbury), SP16/40, fol. 92 (Bridport). See also Wallace MacCaffrey, *Exeter, 1540–1640: The Growth of an English County Town* (Cambridge, MA, 1958), p. 243.
[113] TNA, SP16/56, fol. 54; Bailey (ed.), *Minutes of Boston*, vol. 2, p. 519; ROLLR, BRII/1/3, p. 506.
[114] TNA, SP16/75, fol. 53, SP16/50, fol. 49, SP16/77, fol. 43; Blankenfeld, "Puritans in Banbury," p. 216; HMC, *12th Report, Appendix*, pt. 9 (London, 1891), pp. 478-9; *RBNott*, vol. 5, pp. 125-7; TNA, SP16/50, fol. 122, SP16/54, fol. 145, SP16/73, fol. 82. Lynn did eventually pay in the Loan, though some defaulted.
[115] TNA, SP16/30, fol. 138, SP16/33, fol. 152, SP16/34, fols 1, 6, SP16/37, fol. 63, SP16/42, fol. 185; HHC, BRL 217A; YCA, B.35, fols 12, 13, 17v-18; SA/I, C6/1/5, fols 76v, 77v; KHLC, Sa/Ac7, fols 136v-37, 138; KLTH, KL/C7/9, fols 255v, 263v; SA/I, EE1/O1/1, fols 10-10v, 11, 12-12v; Bailey (ed.), *Minutes of Boston*, vol. 2, p. 506.
[116] *CSPD 1627-28*, pp. 27, 28, 29, 31, 32, 33, 34, 36, 37, 39, 46, 50, 66, 118, 128, 130, 133, 141, 146, 149, 156, 157.

URBAN GOVERNMENT AND THE EARLY STUART STATE

Spain, fishing towns unable to set out for Iceland – due to war and piracy, bouts of plague, their loss of ships, their burden of poor, their costs of men, military training, billeting, and fortifications. Perhaps the most heart-rending came from Plymouth. In addition to pirates, embargoes, and decay of trade, the town bore the expense of housing and clothing the king's army on its way to and from Cadiz (for which they were not properly repaid) and suffered a terrible outbreak of plague, "which turned many out of their lives, more out of their means, and all out of their trades and employments."[117] The tone of these petitions is of desperation and near-disbelief: How can we be expected to provide ships on top of everything else?

In addition to the intense petitioning effort, there was also some outright refusal. William Whiteway recorded that the "outports were commanded to furnish ships of war to defend the coasts at ther owne charges. Weymouth, Poole, and Lie were to set out 2 but they refused." York's corporation reported that "the commoners and other subsidymen being called to pay an assessment [for ships] have all refused and denied so to do." Fearful that their citizens would prove unwilling, the magistrates of York appealed to the Council, through the offices of their high steward, Lord Keeper Coventry, requesting relief for their "overpressed" citizens.[118] While the ship charges themselves caused some distress, the perfect storm of many burdens thrown at them all at the same time drove many of these towns to seek redress from a crown that did not seem to understand the depth of their suffering.

Amid the deep frustration and even anguish experienced by the port towns, borough governors continued to reach out to central authorities to seek relief and effect change. In some ways, the hardships they experienced caused them to interact with the crown ever more strenuously, petitioning for relief while also paying much of what the crown demanded. As noted above, collection of the Forced Loan was relatively robust in many towns, and borough magistrates were among the more vigorous collectors, because it gave them leverage regarding other local concerns. Richard Cust, in his detailed study of the Forced Loan, has convincingly shown how the Council and borough magistrates played a delicate balancing game regarding ship charges and the Loan.[119] To get cooperation of the towns for the Loan, the Council used its power over borough magistrates, who needed the crown's backing both to maintain authority over their own citizens and to protect local commercial interests, under intense pressure from piracy, embargoes, and a general reduction of trade in wartime. The Privy Council also needed the cooperation of the towns to stabilize the crown's finances, and either pressed or remitted collection for ships to influence towns into cooperation on the Loan. Interactions between town governments and the Council over the Forced Loan and ships in the 1620s demonstrate the

---

[117] TNA, SP16/51, fol. 18 (Mayor et al. of Plymouth to Privy Council, 24 January 1627).
[118] Whiteway, Diary, p. 88; YCA, B.34, fols 33v–34v.
[119] Cust, Forced Loan, pp. 126–34.

PAYING THE PRICE

intertwined interests of center and locality.[120] These complex negotiations show that leverage lay not only with the Council. Exeter's mayor explained to the Council his difficulties in setting forth ships, but in the same letter noted he had received the commission for the Loan and hoped to give the king satisfaction. Norwich likewise stated bluntly to the Council that "the noise of this taxation [for ships] hindereth the payment of the Loan."[121] Both the cities and the Privy Council saw the Ship Money exactions of the 1620s as a bargaining chip for collection of the Loan. Even within the context of unpopular taxation, urban governors remained engaged with the state.

While it is difficult to know just how alienating the Forced Loan in particular was for corporate towns, the combined troubles of the war years were unquestionably demoralizing. The burden fell very hard upon the beleaguered towns, most especially the ports. They had real reason to complain of the burdens placed upon them. If county gentlemen felt some amount of alienation from central authority due to the Forced Loan and billeting, then how much more did townsmen of the ports feel, directly facing the Forced Loan, Ship Money, billeting, naval impressment, and the costs of fortifications, compounded by trade embargoes, poverty, piracy, and plague? The stresses of war intensified engagement and forged new connections between borough corporations and central authority, but it also laid bare some of the weaknesses of the state and raised mistrust between towns and the crown. The war not only put significant financial strains on provincial towns, it also provoked questions of law and constitutional liberties in some, as the debates in the 1628 Parliament and the Petition of Right, as well as the writings of Thomas Scott, demonstrate.

Towns, taxation, and the Personal Rule

While the end of the war in 1630 relieved many of the pressures that affected towns so heavily, the peace of the Personal Rule raised new questions over royal finance and local duty to the state. The collection of Ship Money in the 1630s brought tensions regarding jurisdiction, local control, Privy Council oversight, and concerns about liberties into high relief. Communities of all sorts felt these strains; as a number of historians have shown, the Privy Council's vigorous enforcement in the 1630s made it more difficult for individuals and communities to slip through the cracks or avoid payment.[122] But for corporate

[120] Cust, *Forced Loan*, p. 128.
[121] TNA, SP16/51, fol. 62, SP16/61, fol. 12.
[122] On Ship Money in the 1630s, see A.A.M. Gill, "Ship Money during the Personal Rule of Charles I: Politics, Ideology and the Law 1634 to 1640" (PhD dissertation, University of Sheffield, 1990); Kevin Sharpe, *The Personal Rule of Charles I* (New Haven, CT and London, 1992), pp. 643; Henrik Langelüddecke, "'I finde all men & my officers all soe unwilling': The Collection of Ship Money, 1635-1640," *Journal of British Studies* 46 (2007), 509-42; S.P. Salt, "Sir Symonds D'Ewes and the Levying of Ship Money, 1635-40," *Historical Journal* 37 (1994),

boroughs, it raised particular challenges to chartered liberties in the process of assessment and collection, as well as concerns about the legality of the levy itself. On one hand, many of England's corporate boroughs were port towns, liable for centuries to support the crown through maritime levies of this sort. They experienced first-hand the dangers of piracy that Ship Money in the 1630s purported to address. Just as they had a decade earlier, merchants, fishermen, and sailors shipping out of the ports faced significant risk of capture, loss of goods, and even enslavement by Dunkirkers and Barbary pirates. For them the Ship Money levy had the potential to offer a direct benefit. On the other hand, inland boroughs found paying Ship Money novel and unprecedented, and it provided no direct benefit. The responses of borough governors differed due to these varying circumstances, but in all cases, the protection of jurisdiction and privileges laid out in charters shaped their reaction. For its part, the Privy Council applied enforcement that frequently disregarded the concerns of borough magistrates (and inhabitants) in their effort to maximize financial returns and to impose obedience to central dictates.

Of all the many administrative and fiscal projects of the Personal Rule, Ship Money stands as the most controversial, both at the time and among historians. Charles's use of prerogative taxation to fund the demands of the state met a significant fiscal need but also created a firestorm of disputes over rating, collection, and liberties. Historians have diverged widely in their interpretations of the service. Whiggish views saw Ship Money and the refusal to pay it as a critical constitutional conflict that led to civil war. Revisionists turned that view on its head, interpreting the conflicts arising out of the service as largely rating disputes and opportunities to carry out local political wrangling; some of the disputes might be cover for ideological disagreement, but Ship Money itself did not create a constitutional crisis.[123] Kevin Sharpe's thoroughly revisionist view painted Ship Money in the 1630s as "one of the most successful taxes, indeed government enterprises, in early modern history."[124] Other recent scholarship has questioned that pacific view, seeing more substantive and ideological conflict emerging from the imposition.[125] Any discussion of central and local relations in the 1630s must grapple with this key interpretive question. How did the experience of the towns fit into this complex and contested story? The great diversity of interests, circumstances, and attitudes among provincial boroughs means that no single model or pattern can encompass their responses. Serious

---

253-87; Peter Lake, "The Collection of Ship Money in Cheshire in the 1630s: A Case Study of Relations between Central and Local Government," *Northern History* 17 (1981), 44-71.

[123] S.R. Gardiner, *History of England from the Accession of James I to the Outbreak of the Civil War, 1603-1642*, vol. 8 (London, 1884), pp. 80-5; Lake, "The Collection of Ship Money in Cheshire"; Kevin Sharpe, *The Personal Rule of Charles I* (New Haven, CT and London, 1992), pp. 545-600, 614-17.

[124] Sharpe, *Personal Rule*, p. 588.

[125] Gill, "Ship Money"; Salt, "Sir Symonds D'Ewes," pp. 253-87; Langelüddecke, "The Collection of Ship Money," pp. 509-42.

PAYING THE PRICE

foot-dragging, if not outright refusal, can be found, but so can fairly enthusiastic collection and payment. As with the many burdens of the state during the war years of the 1620s, the crown's policy of Ship Money in the 1630s affected corporations, their liberties, and their populations in particular ways. The Privy Council's effort to enforce the levy, while not altogether ignoring local concerns, tended to press against corporate jurisdiction and dismiss local considerations. It raised challenges to chartered liberties in the process of assessment and collection, impinged on patterns of borough governance, and at times strained the trust between townsmen and the crown. For some, its perceived danger to local government and broader ideas of liberty represented a serious grievance.

From the start, the crown identified the importance of corporations and their officers to the administration, and the success, of Ship Money. It should be remembered that before making it a nationwide levy, the Council launched the service in 1634 as a test run in the maritime towns traditionally liable to providing ships. Lord Keeper Coventry told the king in July 1634 that the committee studying the issue thought it "safest to begin with the towns," though they also predicted squabbling and appeals.[126] Memories of the hardships and difficulties experienced in the late 1620s were still fresh in the minds of many townsmen. At the same time, port towns saw the direct benefit of supporting a royal fleet to dissuade pirates and foreign powers, something they had been requesting for over a decade. While Privy Councilors likely expected to receive rafts of petitions from the towns asking for mitigation – just as they had in the 1620s – past experience suggested that most towns would pay. The Council thought strategically about how best to make the collection. One option, favored by Attorney General Noy, would have made county sheriffs responsible for the whole assessment and collection, avoiding logistical problems and "unnecessary disputes" among the towns. Another placed the responsibility in the hands of the mayors who, it was thought, would view a sheriff's powers as an encroachment on corporate jurisdiction and "trouble them as much as the payment itself." In the end, a middle way prevailed, proposed by Lord Keeper Coventry. This gave mayors first authority to decide the assessment among themselves; only if they failed did the sheriff intervene.[127] This demonstrates sensitivity on the Council's part to borough magistrates' concern for corporate liberties and a willingness to rely on them to conduct the service.

This judgment paid off, as nearly 95 percent of the levy came in promptly.[128] But the levy also raised many questions that would continue into successive

---

[126] TNA, SP16/272, fols 72-3 (Coventry to King Charles, 22 July 1634). An attempt by the Privy Council to expand the charge for ships to all counties, not just coastal towns, in February of 1628 had been quickly aborted, seemingly for practical and political reasons. Robin Swales, "The Ship Money Levy of 1628," *Bulletin of the Institute of Historical Research* 50 (1977), 164-76.
[127] TNA, SP16/272, fol. 72v; Gill, "Ship Money," pp. 50-1. The writs, dated 20 October 1634, are in TNA, SP16/276, fols 1ff.
[128] Gill, "Ship Money," pp. 353, 596.

213

URBAN GOVERNMENT AND THE EARLY STUART STATE

years and create a flurry of communication between borough officers, sheriffs, and the Privy Council. Confusion about how to proceed and disagreements among mayors over meetings and assessments proliferated. Dover's magistrates found the logistics of assessment so perplexing that they claimed not to know where to begin or what to do. King's Lynn complained that Norwich, in league with the sheriff of Norfolk, caused Lynn to be rated high and Norwich "so mean and short of their value" that the Privy Council reprimanded the sheriff for his partiality. Bristol's complaint of "unequal proceeding" by the sheriff of Gloucestershire in the assessment likewise resulted in the sheriff's chastisement; indeed, the Council intervened to assign a new assessment themselves, the "unfair dealing" being so egregious.[129] Towns like Maldon, rated at £200, and Colchester, rated at £1,000, complained to the Council of their overcharge relative to neighbors and inability to pay the amounts assessed.[130] Challenges to corporate jurisdiction also arose. In Canterbury, the city sparred with the cathedral clergy over authority to assess residents in the close, while in Southampton and Barnstaple, friction grew between their mayors and the sheriffs of their respective counties.[131] A constant stream of communication between the governors of the towns and the Privy Council flowed, as towns petitioned for relief.

The Council served as the source of hoped-for aid, but also as the stern hand of central authority when borough officials failed to meet expectations. Several mayors were chided for backwardness; "instead of real efforts we find only verbal shows with excuses and complaints with which we are in no sort satisfied."[132] Numerous sharp letters to the mayor of Norwich likely reveal that city's ambivalence about the service. When the mayor wrote to ask how to proceed against refusers, the Council faulted him, saying he had "exceedingly failed" in his duty; rather than writing the Board, he should be out collecting the money. The Council sent three further letters to Norwich, reproving the city's slowness and their attempts to "thrust upon others" their assessment.[133] The Board curbed any moves on the part of borough officials that appeared to hinder full and prompt collection of the 1634 levy.[134]

---

[129] TNA, PC2/44, pp. 298, 327, 387, SP16/277, fol. 109, SP16/283, fol. 184, SP16/285, fol. 162; Canterbury Cathedral Archives, AC4 (Burghmote Book, 1630-58), fol. 95; KHLC, Sa/Ac7, fols 245v, 259.

[130] TNA, PC2/44, pp. 327, 333, 390, 565, 589, 629.

[131] TNA, PC2/44, pp. 328, 337, 348, 41, SP16/283, fol. 184, SP16/285, fol. 164.

[132] TNA, PC2/44, pp. 314, 473, 492-3, 498, 500, 517. The Board upbraided Barnstaple's magistrates twice.

[133] TNA, PC2/44, pp. 389, 464, 497, 553; Evans, *Seventeenth Century Norwich*, pp. 79-80. Evans says the first writ "generated considerable consternation."

[134] TNA, PC2/44, pp. 565, 589. When Newcastle asked that the Council spread the levy to nearby maritime places, the Lords declined to ease the town of its burden, but did promise to take the matter into consideration for the future. TNA, PC2/44, p. 629.

PAYING THE PRICE

Lessons learned in the first levy continued to shape the service when it became a national, annual tax. While beginning in 1635 sheriffs bore final responsibility for assessing and collecting the levy, the Privy Council tasked borough officers with collecting within their jurisdictions as well as confirming the amounts each town in a county should pay. The Council recommended amounts in their instructions, but the group could alter those values as local circumstances merited. Even small towns made sure to send representatives to defend their interests. Dunwich's assembly "elected" their two bailiffs to meet with the sheriff and the other Suffolk corporations in 1637, "there to propound for the benefit of the township aforesaid for the charge of setting forth of the ship."[135] The Council's orders imply that mayors were not entirely to be trusted. The sheriff was to be of quorum for proportioning the assessment, in case any mayor "desiring the ease of your own towns beyond that which is meet, should make a major part and plurality of vote and therefore lay or leave a greater burden on any other of the corporate towns or upon the body of the county than is fit."[136] Despite any doubts about mayoral behavior, these meetings gave borough magistrates some power to affect their towns' assessments, but more importantly they signaled the Council's expectation that these officers, as the king's deputies, should come together to conduct the work of the state.

The chief officers of towns and cities took seriously their role as deputies of the king and in most cases advanced the service, particularly in the first years. Their interests as local governors intertwined deeply with those of the crown that gave them their authority in the first place. But part of their duty was also to be advocates for their localities, defending local interests and protecting jurisdiction and liberties. A belief (or at least a hope) that the Privy Council would solve problems and appreciate local circumstances within the larger concerns of the state led borough magistrates to petition frequently for relief or resolution. The Board received volumes of letters and petitions from borough officials every year, making a case for how their town was rated disproportionately or impossibly high.[137] Plague, particularly bad in 1636–38, brought economic devastation to many towns, affecting their ability to pay. St. Albans, King's Lynn, Derby, and Newcastle, among others, begged for relief due to plague.[138] The Board did occasionally reapportion and mitigate. Charles himself, sitting in Council, took pity on King's Lynn in 1636 for its impoverishment due to infection and losses by shipwrecks, ordering the sheriff of Norfolk to redo the apportionment so as

---

[135] SA/I, EE6/1144/10, fol. 89.
[136] KHLC, Sa/C5/4.
[137] See, for example, *CSPD 1635*, pp. 372, 515, *1635–36*, pp. 9, 10, 12, 213, 308–9, *1637*, pp. 45, 221–2.
[138] TNA, SP16/347, fols 100, 78, SP16/354, fol. 323, SP16/379, fol. 101, SP16/386, fol. 146; HHC, BRM 163; TNA, PC2/48, pp. 72, 101, PC2/49, p. 512. On Newcastle's 1636 plague outbreak, see Keith Wrightson, *Ralph Tailor's Summer: A Scrivener, His City, and the Plague* (New Haven, CT, 2011).

URBAN GOVERNMENT AND THE EARLY STUART STATE

to ease Lynn in its levy.[139] The connection between town and crown could bring relief to the localities.

But the Council's priority on maximum return meant that no mayor could be confident of success, no matter how good the case might be. Bristol claimed to be over-rated, the equivalent of eighteen subsidies, in the early years of the service, but the Board first dismissed the claims and later said they would consider a reduction in future. While acknowledging that both Shrewsbury and Haverfordwest had been significantly over-rated in 1635, the Council required the bailiffs of those towns to collect the full amount anyway. Bedford claimed poverty when the richest men in the town moved away, but they, too, got no relief. Even towns devastated by plague could not be sure the Board would relieve their plight. Poor Hadleigh, having been allowed to postpone payment while in the grips of the visitation, petitioned to have its charge for 1637 remitted entirely; the Council responded that they took it ill that the townsmen would take advantage of the favor done earlier, and adjured them to pay with cheerfulness and alacrity.[140] Borough magistrates turned to king and Council for help in solving local problems, but just as in the 1620s, central government's priorities gave short shrift to satisfying local interests.

Central authorities expected borough magistrates to carry out their duties, even in the face of resistance, but they were willing to reinforce mayors and other officers confronted with recalcitrant townspeople, in order to fulfill the service. When the mayor of Banbury appealed to the Board that he was threatened with lawsuits for distraining refusers, the Council (with the king present) declared that any such suits would be removed to Westminster and taken on by the attorney general.[141] Anything smacking of popularity was quickly quashed. The Board (again with the king present) heard Henry Rawson's complaint that the mayor of Windsor had over-rated him and then imprisoned him for non-payment. Unsympathetic to complaints by inhabitants against magistrates, the king ordered Rawson to pay what the mayor assessed him and also the mayor's costs for this "frivolous" suit.[142] In Barnstaple, a group of burgesses complained to the Privy Council that the magistrates enforced unlawful ordinances to bring in unqualified tradesmen, solely in order to rate them for the king's service and recoup excess money. The "overplus" allegedly went to the magistrates' private quarrels. If the burgesses expected a positive response, they were disappointed. The Council held it "very unfit in any measure or matter to countenance any Inferiors in their complaints against their Governors," and ordered referees to resolve it in a way "so as may not impeach government nor give encouragement to any to oppose or impugn it."[143] While not condoning corruption, the Board

[139] TNA, PC2/47, p. 38. See also PC2/45, p. 437, PC2/46, pp. 446, 460, PC2/48, p. 344.
[140] TNA, PC2/44, p. 266, PC2/46, pp. 41–2, 233, PC2/49, pp. 512, 541, SP16/379, fol. 101, SP16/399, fols 24, 26.
[141] TNA, PC2/48, p. 221.
[142] TNA, PC2/47, p. 63.
[143] TNA, PC2/47, pp. 450, 480.

PAYING THE PRICE

condemned popularity and focused attention on the king's service. Borough magistrates could expect the backing of central authority as long as they ensured the collection of the assessments.

Collection was not guaranteed, however. Evidence survives for several towns of failure to carry out the service to the Council's standards, as well as outright failure to comply, from borough magistrates and inhabitants. This became most dramatic beginning in 1638, but it can be found from the early days of the service. William Whiteway noted that the 1635 levy in Dorchester was paid with "much grudging." Conflicts arose over amounts, proportions, juris-diction, and privileges. Numerous towns complained to the Board of charges beyond their "just proportion" within their county.[144] In others, like Colchester and Northampton, mayors declined to pay what they collected to the sheriffs, judging it to be an intrusion on corporate privileges.[145] Mayors, annually elected typically in the autumn, often complained of inability to collect due to questionable authority; incoming mayors had not themselves received the writ, while those who left office no longer had mayoral authority. The Council had no patience for this excuse, expecting mayors to make the collection, whether in office or out.[146] The Board aimed their ire at borough magistrates in Winchester, Andover, Basingstoke, Newbury, Hereford, Newcastle, Southampton, Wenlock, Arundel, and Chichester, among others, for failing to collect and pay the annual levy and leaving arrears unpaid.[147] The mayor of Banbury in 1636 received a strongly worded letter from the Privy Council for "refusing" to pay Ship Money; his successor in 1637, Nathaniel Wheatley, complained of extreme difficulty to collect, commenting that the last mayor still had "many parcels of goods that lie rotting by him" for last year's arrears. Wheatley reported that while he personally endeavored his best, the constables collected slowly and "absolutely refuse" to distrain. Wheatley complained, "I am not only opposed by many by shutting up their doors against me, but also am threatened to be sued by such a multitude, that I think my estate is not sufficient to defend me."[148] By the 1639 assessment, the Council increasingly faced outright refusal to pay the current year's assessment and extensive arrears for 1637 and 1638, despite attempts at strong enforcement by the Board. Borough officers across England found themselves unable to collect from unwilling townsmen and facing intense scrutiny from the Council.[149] Each town had its own circumstances

---

[144] Whiteway, *Diary*, p. 156; TNA, SP16/302, fols 262, 263, 264, SP16/311, fol. 158, SP16/338, fol. 18, SP16/355, fol. 239, PC2/46, pp. 439, 444, PC2/47, p. 109.
[145] TNA, PC2/46, pp. 177, 191.
[146] TNA, SP16/304, fol. 5, SP16/304, fol. 150, SP16/305, fol. 85, PC2/45, p. 304, PC2/46, pp. 285, 338.
[147] TNA, PC2/47, pp. 19, 79, 353, PC2/48, pp. 33, 219, 311, 312, 382, 525, 557-8.
[148] TNA, PC2/46, p. 296, SP16/361, fol. 54; J.S.W. Gibson and E.R.C. Brinkworth (eds), *Banbury Corporation Records, Tudor and Stuart*, Banbury Historical Society, vol. 15 (Banbury, 1977), pp. 163-4.
[149] CSPD 1639, pp. 133, 134, 177, 191-2, 235, 317, 429, 461, 512; TNA, PC2/50, pp. 50, 68,

URBAN GOVERNMENT AND THE EARLY STUART STATE

surrounding the non-payment – Chichester was involved in a rating dispute with the cathedral, while Banbury's inhabitants seem to have been deeply opposed to the service – but it would be difficult to argue that the outcome of the Ship Money legal case in 1638 or the outbreak of the Scottish war initiated the resistance to the service. They exacerbated it, but did not create it. Ship Money presented challenges in some, though not all, towns from the start to the end of its collection.

Ship Money also posed a threat to corporate towns in the way its assessment and collection fitted into a larger set of policies and actions that affected corporate liberties. This can be seen most clearly in cathedral cities, where disputes over rating between civic and ecclesiastical officials deeply challenged corporate authority and jurisdiction and opened the cities' governing bodies to greater scrutiny, often by King Charles himself. This phenomenon will be discussed more fully in the next chapter, but suffice it to say here that Ship Money prompted or exacerbated questions over authority and jurisdiction in Canterbury, Chichester, Durham, Exeter, Lichfield, Norwich, Salisbury, Winchester, Worcester, and York.[150] As noted in Chapter 2, jurisdictional conflict over Ship Money also played into quo warranto and charter controversies for a number of cities. At the same time, the state's increased demands for soldiers and training, discussed earlier in this chapter, exhibited central government's greater willingness to alter traditional patterns, for instance training soldiers outside borough boundaries and raising the numbers of soldiers required. The stringent enforcement of Ship Money collection by the Caroline state, coupled with an unpopular religious policy and more aggressive military requirements, placed particular strains on towns and pressed on borough liberties in ways that troubled town governors and inhabitants alike.

Borough magistrates felt intense pressure in implementing the king's policy of Ship Money. As the king's officers, they were obliged to fulfill the orders of central government. In addition to simple duty, they also saw the benefit to themselves and their localities of maintaining a strong link to the Privy Council and the king, the source of resolution for many of their problems. Yet as the service progressed, some magistrates felt this obligation less strongly than others, focusing more on the considerations of their own inhabitants and proving more willing to ignore the orders of the state. In *The Personal Rule of Charles I*, Kevin Sharpe provided two case studies, of Bristol and York, to illustrate his view of relatively harmonious relations between cities and the crown in the 1630s.[151] It is certainly true that towns continued to reach out to the Privy Council and the king as the best means of trying to resolve their many problems, yet had Sharpe chosen to look at Banbury or Northampton, he might have told a somewhat

---

74, 105, 132, 147, 204, 313, 361, 392, 395, 435, 440, 576, 596, 600, 635, 680.
[150] TNA, PC2/44, p. 348; Canterbury Cathedral Archives, AC4, fol. 96; TNA, PC2/45, pp. 335, 372, PC2/46, pp. 245-7, PC2/47, pp. 238, 380, 432-3, PC2/48, pp. 340, 383, PC2/49, pp. 28, 168, 492.
[151] Sharpe, *Personal Rule*, pp. 636-43.

different story. And even York and Bristol had reasons to grumble. While some towns paid promptly and with seemingly little anguish, the levy brought out concerns about jurisdiction, corporate liberties, and basic problems of economic welfare that challenged borough governments. The level of uncooperativeness, pushback, and refusal among inhabitants, and sometimes borough governors, varied widely among towns, but it suggests resistance to the service that went beyond simple rating disputes or dislike of taxes in general. The story of Ship Money and the towns cannot be seen as a simple dichotomy between harmonious connection and stark alienation. It was rather an ongoing negotiation, characterized by both engagement and estrangement, that by 1639–40 had not entirely broken down, but was certainly under stress.

The interpenetration of national and local concerns, and the complex network of authority within the early modern state, are clearly borne out in the dynamic relationship linking the towns and the crown as they negotiated fiscal and military burdens. Corporate towns played an increasingly important role in the state for the revenue they generated, but also for their critical functions in national defense and security. The interests of borough governments and central authority often meshed, as town magistrates found ways to associate their own authority, as well as borough liberties, to central concerns. The success of many provincial towns in gaining their own militia bands by bargaining with additional trained soldiers for the king's defense exemplifies this connection. But the crown's increasing demands, exacerbated by war in the 1620s, placed especially heavy obligations on the towns, which in many cases were already grappling with disrupted trade, increased poverty, and epidemic disease. The extraordinary costs (financial and otherwise) of billeting for many towns raised frustrations and distrust in the face of the state's failure to meet what the towns saw as its obligations. The towns' distress resounded loudly in parliament and helped inform the Petition of Right. Prerogative exactions like the Forced Loan and Ship Money also exercised many townsmen, even as borough magistrates largely fulfilled their duties as royal officers and collected what was owed to the crown. Corporate towns were not fundamentally antagonistic to the fiscal and military demands of the state, but many of the crown's actions and policies in the 1620s and 1630s raised frustrations that could not be negotiated away.

7

Defining Church and Corporation: Corporate Towns and Religious Policy

In 1603, the mayor, aldermen, and commonalty of Salisbury petitioned King James, then passing through the city on his way to assume the English throne, for a royal charter of incorporation. The unincorporated city fell under the bishop's authority, a condition city fathers disliked. They conceived themselves to be the king's immediate deputies in that place, not the bishop's, and they wished Salisbury to "be your highness's city and so called." The magistrates sought an immediate connection to the monarch, unmediated by the bishop. It took years of petitioning, but in 1612 James granted Salisbury its charter of incorporation, redrawing civil and ecclesiastical boundaries and removing church officials from authority over the city.[1] In 1632-33, the magistrates of Salisbury found themselves once again petitioning the monarch, this time King Charles, to plead for their city's liberties. The bishop, dean, and chapter sought to undo parts of the 1612 charter and restore ecclesiastical authority to the city. Desperate to stave off this reversal, but seriously hampered by charges of iconoclasm against their recorder, the mayor and aldermen appealed to the king to ignore "aspersions of inconformity" against them and keep the city's liberties as they were. Charles, however, advancing a vision of order that privileged ceremonialism in the church and ecclesiastical authority in government, reshaped the city's liberties and inserted the bishop, dean, and other ecclesiastical officials as justices of peace of Salisbury.[2]

Salisbury's experience provides a useful window into relations between towns and the crown on the fraught subject of religion in the early Stuart period. Questions of jurisdiction as well as belief were central to the experience of religion in many towns, and the changing nature of royal policy produced new answers to those questions. Historians have increasingly come to see religion as a (if not the) key disruptor of order in this period, as beliefs fragmented and the monarchs attempted to impose their own constructs of belief and

---

[1] WSHC, G23/1/3, fol. 174–174v; Catherine Patterson, "Whose City? Civic Government and Episcopal Power in Early Modern Salisbury, c. 1590–1640," *Historical Research* 90 (2017), 496–9.
[2] WSHC, G23/1/226 ("The Demands of the Clergy"), G23/1/223 (petition of mayor and commonalty of Salisbury to King Charles); TNA, SP16/232, fol. 100 (Sec. Windebank to Bishop Davenant, 16 February 1633); TNA, PC2/47, p. 404. For a full discussion of the relations between city, bishops, and king from 1590 to 1640, see Patterson, "Whose City," pp. 486–505.

220

DEFINING CHURCH AND CORPORATION

conformity, less flexible under Charles than under James.[3] The extent to which the crown's religious regime was disruptive has long been a point of debate among historians. Studies of puritanism as a revolutionary force have given way to a focus on the impact of Caroline religious policy as a cause of conflict. While differing significantly on whether Arminian theology or Laudian (or "Caroline") ceremonial practice was a more significant factor in religious conflict across the period, historians like Nicholas Tyacke, Kenneth Fincham, Julian Davies, and Peter Lake make the case that the 1630s experienced a change in religious emphasis and direction from the crown that alienated the godly and some moderates, as well.[4] Others, such as Peter White, G.W. Bernard, and Kevin Sharpe, have argued that the 1630s did not mark so significant a change in direction or source of conflict.[5] Regardless of the interpretive frame, the importance of religious policy to politics and governance in the early Stuart period is undeniable. For corporate towns like Salisbury, religious matters created points of both connection and tension with the crown, as boundaries of corporate and ecclesiastical authority within the state were renegotiated, and changes in policy and perspective affected both religious practice and civic liberties.

This chapter investigates relations between towns and the crown through the lens of religion, focusing on the intersection of religious authority with borough government and corporate liberties. While not attempting to answer the question of whether urban places were especially disposed to a particular brand of religion, it does explore how magistrates in many towns built their authority around godly ideals of order, and how changing policies and patterns from the first years of James's reign through the Personal Rule of Charles affected towns specifically.[6] In corporate towns, where ecclesiastical and corporate authority rubbed against each other every day, belief and practice regularly intertwined

---

[3] John Morrill, "The Religious Context of the English Civil War," *Transactions of the Royal Historical Society*, 5th Ser., 34 (1984), 155–78.
[4] Nicholas Tyacke, *Anti-Calvinists: The Rise of English Arminianism c. 1590–1640* (Oxford, 1987); Kenneth Fincham and Nicholas Tyacke, *Altars Restored: The Changing Face of English Religious Worship, 1547–c. 1700* (Oxford, 2007); Peter Lake, "The Laudian Style: Order, Uniformity and the Pursuit of the Beauty of Holiness in the 1630s," in K. Fincham (ed.), *The Early Stuart Church* (Stanford, CA, 1993), pp. 161–85; Julian Davies, *The Caroline Captivity of the Church: Charles I and the Remoulding of Anglicanism* (Oxford, 1992).
[5] Peter White, "The Via Media in the Early Stuart Church," in Fincham (ed.), *The Early Stuart Church*, pp. 211–30; G.W. Bernard, "The Church of England c. 1529–c.1642," *History* 75 (1990), 183–206; Kevin Sharpe, *The Personal Rule of Charles I* (New Haven, CT, 1992), pp. 275–402.
[6] On the question of puritanism and the urban context in the early Stuart period, see Phil Withington, *The Politics of Commonwealth: Citizens and Freemen in Early Modern England* (Cambridge, 2005) pp. 230–47; Paul Seaver, *The Puritan Lectureships: The Politics of Religious Dissent 1560–1662* (Stanford, CA, 1970), pp. 89–91; Christopher Hill, *Economic Problems of the Church* (Oxford, 1956), p. 57. The present analysis does not support the notion that towns were inherently puritan by culture, but there is no question that godly ideals of order and belief resonated among many urban magistrates and inhabitants.

221

URBAN GOVERNMENT AND THE EARLY STUART STATE

with questions over the boundaries of church and civic jurisdiction within the state. The pervasiveness of lectureships sponsored by and in corporate towns generated questions over control and pay, as well as religious conformity, stirring frequent engagement between borough governors and the crown. Symbols of authority, precedence, jurisdiction, and liberties were regularly renegotiated across the period between ecclesiastical and corporate officials. This can be seen most clearly in cathedral cities, but it was true in all sorts of towns. Borough governors, as representatives of the king's authority, had to balance their duty to carry out the crown's policies with their interest in protecting both local religious practices and the liberties of their towns.

This balancing act became more difficult over the course of the early Stuart period, as this chapter will show. The crown's changing religious policies had a direct impact on many borough corporations, as the intense concern of the Caroline state about popularity and religious irregularity put towns in the cross-hairs of royal policy.[7] During the first years of James's reign, religious policy was flexible enough to allow corporations to extend their authority in various ways over the religious life of their towns. In contrast, the Personal Rule of Charles saw the vigorous application of policies that promoted a ceremonial style of worship and an elevation of ecclesiastical authority that challenged jurisdiction as well as beliefs in many towns and cities. This led to tensions over the appointment of corporate lecturers, struggles between corporate and ecclesiastical authorities over spaces, and in some cases loss of chartered privileges in the face of ecclesiastical challenges. The Caroline state increasingly empowered church officials over borough magistrates, implementing a vision of order that upset the previous status quo, overturning precedents laid down under James. While Charles and Laud's religious changes applied to the whole realm, elements of it created, in effect, an urban policy that stirred up contention and colored the relationship between corporate towns and the crown.

Corporate boroughs and religious governance

The close association of ecclesiastical and civil governance within the English state meant that borough magistrates frequently grappled with matters of religion.[8] All borough officials were, of course, required to be conformable members of the established church and to attend divine service at their parish church (and in cathedral cities, at the cathedral, as well). As the king's deputies in the towns, mayors and their brethren enforced statutes on church attendance,

---

[7] See Richard Cust, "Charles I and Popularity," in T. Cogswell, R. Cust and P. Lake (eds), *Politics, Religion and Popularity in Early Stuart Britain: Essays in Honour of Conrad Russell* (Cambridge, 2002), pp. 247–51.
[8] Charles Prior, *A Confusion of Tongues: Britain's Wars of Reformation, 1625–42* (Oxford, 2012) argues that the sovereignty of the church was still an open question in this period, as was the precise definition of church and secular liberties and the crown's responsibility to them.

222

DEFINING CHURCH AND CORPORATION

recusancy, separatism, and the like. The commercial and busy nature of towns attracted all manner of people, including those attempting to spread illegal religious messages. Central authorities expected borough magistrates to seek out and punish those who engaged in Protestant conventicles as well as both home-grown recusants and suspected "papists" and priests passing through their towns. Not all were as enthusiastic as Thomas Chettle, mayor of Leicester, who searched an alehouse looking for lewd persons and discovered a "spie" with "dyvers papisticall books, Picktures, [and] Crusyfixes," but the crown relied heavily on borough magistrates to protect the realm against religious danger.[9]

While dependent on town authorities to patrol and report such activity, the Privy Council did not entirely trust local magistrates to enforce the rules rigorously on their own inhabitants. Central authorities suspected that godly magistrates in some towns were too cozy with "schismatics" and separatists. King Charles was reportedly "not only informed but incensed against" the magistrates of Great Yarmouth "for conniving at and tolerating a company of Brownists amongst you," while James's Privy Council admonished the mayor of Sandwich for being "too remisse and carelesse, if otherwise not a mayntainer and favorer of such ill affected persons."[10] On the other end of the spectrum, the Council sharply reprimanded the mayor and aldermen of Newcastle for remissness in executing recusancy laws in his jurisdiction, leading to the "unsufferable evil" of increasing popery. The Board admonished the magistrates to make an exact enquiry, "as you tender the good of Religion and the happy government of this Common-wealth."[11] The religious complexion of towns and cities in Ireland also worried central authorities. As shown in Chapter 1, the crown's concern to have trustworthy - meaning Protestant - leadership in Ireland led to policies attempting to assure Protestant magistracy in towns and cities. The problem of corporations continuing to elect magistrates who refused to conform to the Protestant church posed serious political problems, and from early in James's reign, the Council mandated Protestant church attendance for all mayors and aldermen.[12] While they may have turned a blind eye to some level of religious irregularity, either out of sympathy for those views or a desire not to stir trouble for inhabitants, magistrates in English and Welsh towns generally carried out the policies of the crown. Yet suspicions lingered about the scrupulousness with which they did so in towns that were viewed as potentially untrustworthy in religion, at one end of the spectrum or the other, but particularly on the godly end.

Questions over the reliability of borough magistrates on matters of religion fostered tensions between the crown and the towns across the early Stuart

[9] *CSPD 1603–1610*, p. 502, *1619–23*, p. 311, *1623–25*, pp. 184–5, *1625–26*, p. 310; *RBL*, vol. 4, pp. 23, 271–2.
[10] NRO, Y/C18/6, fol. 256 (Earl of Dorset to bailiffs of Great Yarmouth, August 1630); *APC 1613–14*, p. 614.
[11] *APC 1628–29*, pp. 383–4.
[12] *CSP Ireland, 1603–1606*, p. 242.

223

period, which heightened during the 1630s. The presumption (sometimes well-founded) of puritan tendencies among the governors of many towns made them suspect, even as the crown relied ever more heavily on them to maintain order and contribute to the needs of the state. Both James and Charles called out magistrates in places like Coventry, Exeter, Salisbury, and Great Yarmouth for their puritan or even schismatic views.[13] As Peter Lake has shown, puritanism came increasingly to be associated with popularity and therefore disorder, a trend reaching its height in the 1630s with Laudian polemicists who justified the religious regime of the Personal Rule.[14] The predisposition on the part of central authority to doubt the obedience of the godly posed a problem for borough magistrates who had to defend themselves from such suspicions. The mayor of Boston, for instance, came under close scrutiny in 1621 for complicity in cutting off the crosses from the town's official maces. Boston's reputation for puritanism inclined the Privy Council to believe the mayor's responsibility for this act of iconoclasm.[15] Yet borough magistrates, even the godliest of them, viewed themselves as bastions of order within their towns and generally eschewed "popularity." At some level, the crown appreciated the orderly government often associated with godly magistrates. As noted above, central authorities praised the magistrates of both Dorchester and Ipswich for their careful attention to maintaining order and good government.[16] Differing definitions of precisely what constituted order would have a significant effect on relations between towns and the crown across the period. The reciprocal dependence of central authority and borough governors for maintaining order and proper governance necessitated some flexibility, a trait more frequently exhibited in James's reign than in Charles's.[17]

---

[13] TNA, SP14/90, fol. 28 (N. Brent to [D. Carleton], 14 January 1617); DALS, ECA Letter 242 (John Prowse to mayor of Exeter, 17 April 1623); WSHC, G23/1/223 (Petition of mayor and commonalty of Salisbury to King Charles); TNA, SP16/148, fol. 122 (Sir Robert Heath to Viscount Dorchester, 16 August 1629). Despite the characterization, magistrates varied in their beliefs; Robert Woodford noted critically that Arminian views were propounded at a dinner by some members of Coventry's corporation, while Stoyle has shown that not all of Exeter's corporation shared Ignatius Jurdain's puritan zeal. J. Fielding (ed.), *The Diary of Robert Woodford, 1637–1641*, Camden 5th Ser., vol. 42 (Cambridge, 2013), p. 254; Mark Stoyle, *From Deliverance to Destruction: Rebellion and Civil War in an English City* (Exeter, 1996), p. 27.

[14] Peter Lake, "Anti-puritanism as Political Discourse: the Laudian Critique of Puritan 'Popularity'," in Cesare Cuttica and Markku Peltonen (eds), *Democracy and Anti-democracy in Early Modern England, 1603–1689* (Leiden and Boston, MA, 2019), pp. 152–73.

[15] TNA, SP14/120, fols 115–18 (Certificate and examinations by Anthony Irby and Leonard Bawtry, April 1621); APC 1619–21, p. 385, 386. The mayor was eventually exonerated.

[16] TNA, SP16/146, fol. 43; APC 1619–21, pp. 122–3; BL, Lansdowne MS 162, fol. 195.

[17] This point will be further explored below. See also David Cressy, "Conflict, Consensus, and the Willingness to Wink: The Erosion of Community in Charles I's England," *Huntingdon Library Quarterly* 61 (1998), 131–49.

DEFINING CHURCH AND CORPORATION

In the context of local governance, matters of church and state regularly intersected in the spaces shared by town and ecclesiastical officials. Church buildings functioned as important civic spaces where mayors and aldermen and their wives attended in state wearing their official gowns. Though a sacred space, the church also served various purposes in many towns, intermingling parish and corporate business. According to one scholar, Maldon's borough government permeated parish authority, treating two of the town's parish churches almost as corporate properties and managing various aspects of the town's religious life. Leicester had a library in St. Martin's church by the 1620s, available for the use of ministers and magistrates. Great Yarmouth, and likely other corporations, kept some of its records in the parish church's vestry.[18] In addition to claiming space, corporations at times assumed tasks related to the church. Borough corporations often managed poor relief functions that properly belonged to a parish, as noted in Chapter 4, and some intervened in parish business such as churchyard maintenance and seating arrangements. Many corporate towns elected their own lecturers (discussed later in this chapter) and in some cases acquired the advowson of the parish church in the process of the Reformation.[19] Thus in many different ways, corporate authority mingled with ecclesiastical structures, reinforcing the authority of borough governors in the community. In the first years of James's reign, central authority tolerated or even promoted this connection, but patterns shifted in the 1620s and especially the 1630s, as Caroline government attempted increasingly to separate, and elevate, ecclesiastical authority.

The gradual inroads of corporate authority over ecclesiastical structures and the reversal of that pattern in the 1620s and 1630s can be seen clearly in the experience of Maidstone in Kent. Maidstone, an early stronghold of Protestantism, benefitted from the Reformation's dissolution of the collegiate establishment there, and the collegiate church of All Saints became the parish church of the town. By the early decades of Elizabeth's reign, the mayor, jurats, and commonalty gradually assumed authority over tasks like pew assignments on behalf of the parish. While the archbishop of Canterbury selected the ministers, town officials made nominations and aimed for able preaching ministers. The corporation paid regular stipends, and at least some of the

---

[18] W.J. Petchey, "The Borough of Maldon, Essex, 1500-1688: A Study in Sixteenth and Seventeenth Century Urban History" (PhD dissertation, University of Leicester, 1972), pp. 213-23; *RBL*, vol. 4, pp. 246, 270-1; Bodl. Lib., Tanner MS 68, fol. 323; NRO, Y/C19/6, fols 166, 197v.

[19] "Hull in the 16th and 17th Centuries," in K.J. Allison (ed.), *VCH York East Riding*, vol. 1, *The City of Kingston Upon Hull* (London, 1969), pp. 90-171. *British History Online*, accessed 9 June 2021, www.british-history.ac.uk/vch/yorks/east/vol1/pp90-171. See Robert Tittler, *The Reformation and the Towns in England: Politics and Political Culture, c. 1540-1640* (Oxford, 1998), pp. 110-36, on the pattern of corporate acquisition of church lands and privileges in the sixteenth century, and pp. 185-6 for a brief discussion of the changing relationship between parish and corporate authority.

URBAN GOVERNMENT AND THE EARLY STUART STATE

curates and preachers became freemen of the town. Robert Carr, who served the cure for thirty years under Elizabeth and James enjoyed good relations with the magistrates.[20] King James officially granted All Saints church and churchyard to the corporation in its 1604 charter.[21] The corporation increasingly became the decision-making body for certain church matters in the course of James's reign. In 1613, the vestry referred a dispute regarding church fees to the burghmote (the corporation's governing council), which drew up an approved list of fees. The corporation ordered this to be written into the burghmote book as an official record, and hung a table of fees in the church for all to see.[22] They also made orders regarding burials in the churchyard and requested from diocesan officials a commission for placing and displacing inhabitants in church pews.[23] From the 1560s to the early 1620s, a norm of corporate authority in the ecclesiastical life of the town emerged.

This norm would be challenged in the course of the 1620s and 1630s, due to the temperament of a new minister in concert with the crown's changing policy. Rev. Robert Barrell held a very different view than the corporation regarding their authority over the parish church. In 1625, Barrell refused to abide by the table of fees established by the corporation in 1613 and reported townsmen who refused his demands to the ecclesiastical court. Incensed, the mayor and jurats ordered a new table of fees to be drawn up and displayed prominently in the church. Controversies over the appointment of parish clerks and lecturers also brewed in the late 1620s, but the main combustion began in 1634, when Barrell's sense of personal primacy connected with Archbishop William Laud's push to enhance ecclesiastical authority.[24] Aiming at the corporation's interest in church business, Barrell took shots in both Maidstone and London. Contrary to "ancient custom," Barrell refused to announce upcoming meetings of the burghmote in the church; in response, the corporation made elaborate orders for such announcements in the town, "as if the same had been published in the Church."[25] Simultaneously, Barrell reported borough leaders to the High Commission for their invasion of ecclesiastical jurisdiction.

Between October 1634 and May 1636, seven members of the corporation's burghmote appeared before the High Commission Court on charges that "they

[20] Walter B. Gilbert, *Memorials of the Collegiate and Parish Church of All Saints in the King's Town and Parish of Maidstone* (Maidstone, 1866), pp. 58, 68, 82, 84–5, 86–7, 91. As noted in Chapter 2, Maidstone lost its charter under Mary for participating in Wyatt's rebellion. See Peter Clark, *English Provincial Society from the Reformation to the Revolution: Religion, Politics, and Society in Kent 1500–1640* (Hassocks, 1977), pp. 76–7.
[21] Gilbert, *Memorials*, pp. 89–90; Martin Weinbaum, *British Borough Charters, 1307–1660* (Cambridge, 1943), p. 62.
[22] Maidstone, *Records of Maidstone: Being Selections from Documents in the Possession of the Corporation* (Maidstone, 1926), pp. 68–70; Gilbert, *Memorials*, p. 91–3.
[23] *Records of Maidstone*, pp. 80, 82, 84; Gilbert, *Memorials*, pp. 95–7, 100.
[24] *Records of Maidstone*, pp. 90, 95–7; KHLC, Md/ACm1/2, p. 260; Gilbert, *Memorials*, pp. 99–106. See also Clark, *English Provincial Society*, p. 326.
[25] KHLC, Md/ACm1/2, p. 294.

DEFINING CHURCH AND CORPORATION

being lay persons and having no jurisdiction ecclesiastical" had exercised ecclesiastical authority. The central complaint involved the table of fees, dating back to 1613 and reconfirmed in 1625, and its placement in the church as well as in the records of the burghmote. The burghmote book itself became an object of contention, as the High Commission demanded that it be brought to the court and left with its officers. The recorder and fellow magistrates, justifiably uncomfortable with giving up this powerful symbol of corporate authority and history, refused to do so and were attached for contempt. Eventually the townsmen left the book with commissioners, who perused its contents for offending entries.[26] After lengthy deliberations, the court ruled in May 1636 that the mayor, jurats, and common council of Maidstone had illegally exercised ecclesiastical authority in numerous ways: drawing up and enforcing the table of fees, choosing the parish clerk, disposing church pews, and using corporation funds to defend freemen against suits brought against them by Barrell in the ecclesiastical courts. The court excommunicated seven borough governors and also fined jurats Ambrose Beale and Caleb Banckes (considered "more faulty" than the others) £50 each. The table of fees and all other orders written into the burghmote book that concerned ecclesiastical affairs were to be "rased and obliterated."[27] Dismayed at the fact that Beale and Banckes suffered this harsh penalty "chiefly for making or enacting or else for executing of orders made in the Court of Burghmote," the corporation petitioned – unsuccessfully – to have the fines mitigated and agreed to contribute toward their charges. Beale himself crossed through all of the offending entries in the burghmote book in compliance with the court's order.[28] The slighting of corporate authority in the face of a resurgent church – in both locality and center – was made manifest in the record of the corporate body as well as on the bodies of members of the corporation.

To be sure, there was more to Maidstone's story than jurisdictional wrangling. A strong impulse toward godly religion ran among many magistrates as well as inhabitants, chafing against Laudian religious changes. Some disliked Rev. Barrell's brand of worship enough to travel four miles to Otham, where jurat Robert Swinnock held the presentation and installed Thomas Wilson, a godly preaching minister. The High Commission accused the town of harboring conventicles and alleged the mayors forbade the ringing of bells on Sundays and other formalities.[29] In his visitation reports to the king in 1634 and 1635, Laud labeled Maidstone a center of nonconformity. The Privy Council also censured Mayor Caleb Banckes and other magistrates in 1634 for arresting several young townsmen for trespass when they danced in a field on a Sunday afternoon, a

---

[26] *CSPD 1634–35*, pp. 262, 266, 317, 324, 334, 496. The court eventually agreed to return the book if the townsmen would provide registered copies of all the "acts or constitutions" concerning church matters.

[27] *CSPD 1635–36*, pp. 508–10.

[28] KHLC, Md/ACm1/2, p. 316; *Records of Maidstone*, p. 68n.

[29] KHLC, Md/ACm1/2, p. 260; George Swinnock, *The Life and Death of Mr. Tho. Wilson, Minister of Maidstone, in the County of Kent* (London, 1672), p. 11; *CSPD 1635–36*, p. 509.

227

URBAN GOVERNMENT AND THE EARLY STUART STATE

"lawful recreation" allowed by the Book of Sports.[30] Theology and liturgy clearly played an important part in Maidstone's troubles, as religious policy shifted in the 1630s, but these issues cannot be divorced from the jurisdictional tensions that also defined religious practice in the corporate town.[31] Maidstone's story was specific to its circumstances, yet it paralleled the experiences of towns and cities across the period. Corporate symbols, jurisdiction, and authority, which had largely been allowed to build in the early years of James's reign, faced a significant reversal, most especially in the 1630s during Laud's period of ascendancy. Intertwined questions of belief and jurisdiction complicated relations between borough government and the crown over religious matters. For borough governors, the involvement of the corporation in all aspects of community life added to the good government and order the crown expected them to provide. But this concept of order could not easily stand in the face of stronger measures by central authority to define the boundaries of religious practice.

Controlling the word: borough government and town lectureships

The complicated relationship between religious practice, borough government, and central authority manifested itself in a variety of dimensions, but the strains between local and central ideas of good governance and control can be seen clearly in the appointment and oversight of town lectureships. While not a part of borough government *per se*, the lectures established in many towns and cities connected deeply with corporate authority. As Paul Seaver has shown, these lectures originated to provide more preaching to the populace at a time when suppressing Roman Catholic beliefs was considered critical to the success of the state. From their start in the sixteenth century, these lectures nearly always propounded thoroughly reformed, if not actively puritan, theology appealing to many of those who governed England's corporate towns. Institutionally, the lectures were divorced from control of the church hierarchy, as corporations selected and paid borough lecturers themselves.[32] Lecturers often became important men in their towns, highly esteemed by borough governors as well as inhabitants generally. The brand of theology preached by many of these men – not always conforming strictly to the church's established teaching – as well as the institutional structure more connected to borough government than

---

[30] William, Laud, *The Works of the Reverend Father in God William Laud*, vol. 5, pt. 2 (Oxford, 1853), pp. 323, 331; TNA, PC2/44, pp. 198, 272.

[31] Notably, after the harsh High Commission sentence against the magistrates in 1636, Maidstone no longer appears in Laud's visitation reports as troublesome. But in 1640, the townsmen petitioned the Long Parliament against Barrell; Barrell was ejected and Thomas Wilson replaced him. L.B. Larking (ed.), *Proceedings, Principally in the County of Kent, In Connection with the Parliaments Called in 1640* (London, 1862), pp. 19n, 202–5.

[32] Seaver, *Puritan Lectureships*, pp. 5–6, 16–17, 22, 91, 93–4.

228

DEFINING CHURCH AND CORPORATION

the ecclesiastical hierarchy raised questions around lectureships across the early Stuart period.[33] But tensions rose in the 1630s over approval and suspension, as Caroline government promoted policies that pushed back against both the theological viewpoints and the lay authority that characterized borough lectureships.

Lectureships became a critical element of corporate governance in many towns. Corporations valued the control that a lectureship afforded; lecturers served at the pleasure of the corporation, at least in their preaching capacity. The corporate body could hire and fire, as long as their choice had the bishop's license to preach. The structure of lectureships meant that borough governors had a great deal of responsibility over them, both financially and administratively. Some towns paid lecturers as much as £100 per annum, collected by voluntary contribution or assessment on inhabitants, making a lectureship a significant item in a town's annual budget. A lecturer's death or departure led to careful deliberation in the corporation to choose a successor and ensure his licensing. The suspension of a lecturer by ecclesiastical authorities presented the corporate body with the practical problem of either attempting reinstatement or finding another to fill the position.[34] This meant time and expense in going to the bishop to appeal or seeking out candidates for a new preacher. In some cases, as will be shown below, it might mean financially supporting a suspended lecturer while also paying others to preach. In addition, lectureships in a number of towns provoked disagreements between clergy holding regular benefices and lecturers hired by the corporation; tensions over the theological content of preaching as well as pay, respect, and discipline led to conflict and even lawsuits in towns like Great Yarmouth, Coventry, Newcastle, and Stratford-upon-Avon that their corporations had to manage.[35] Pragmatic considerations of control and administration, as well as religious ones, surrounded borough lectureships.

---

[33] The suspicions the crown harbored about town lectureships in England was not an indictment of preaching ministry generally; in the quite different context of Ireland, early efforts were made to appoint preachers in every city and corporate town and to support "learned and paynfull ministers" to secure a Protestant regime there. CSP Ireland, 1603–1606, p. 242; APC 1615–16, pp. 447–54.

[34] KLTH, KL/C7/9, fols 315v, 329v, 334v; J.R. Chanter and Thomas Wainwright (eds), Reprint of the Barnstaple Records, vol. 2 (Barnstaple, 1900), p. 100; CSPD 1623–25, p. 236; J.M. Guilding (ed.), Reading Records: Diary of the Corporation of Reading, vol. 2 (London, 1895), p. 250; RBNott, vol. 5, p. 153; YCA, B.33, fol. 111, B.34, fols 77–77v; HHC, BRB3 (Hull Bench Book 5), fols 38, 141; GA, GBR B3/1 (Corporation Minute Book, 1565–1632), fol. 466, B3/2, fols 50, 136.

[35] NRO, Y/C19/5, fols 96, 311, Y/C19/6, fols 275v–76; TNA, PC2/41, pp. 364, 379–80, 481–4; CovA, BA/H/C/17/1, fols 313v, 318–318v; CSPD 1639–40, p. 169; Roger Howell, Newcastle upon Tyne and the Puritan Revolution: A Study of the Civil War in North England (Oxford, 1967), pp. 87, 89; Shakespeare Birthplace Trust, Stratford upon Avon, BRU2/3, p. 14, 34, 88. See also Ann Hughes, "Religion and Society in Stratford upon Avon, 1619–1638," Midland History 19 (1994), 58–84.

URBAN GOVERNMENT AND THE EARLY STUART STATE

While forming a regular element of civic life and business for many towns, lectureships also could be points of discord between borough government and the structures of ecclesiastical and royal authority that bound them. In the first decade or two of James's reign, lectures and godly preaching had been allowed to grow under Archbishop George Abbott, a moderate Calvinist, and evangelical-friendly bishops like John Jegon of Norwich. As Matthew Reynolds has shown, under Jegon's tenure in Norwich (1603-18), that city's lectureships, and the strong bond between magistrates and minsters in civic business, solidified.[36] A shift in direction began in the 1620s, as bishops like Samuel Harsnett took aim at preaching and lectures in key towns like Norwich and Ipswich.[37] William Laud's appointment as bishop of London in 1628 and his translation to the archbishopric of Canterbury in 1633 intensified scrutiny of town lecturers and preaching. He believed lecturers encouraged schism and faction, threatening the church's beliefs and structure. Their basis on voluntary financial support of laymen rather than the official institutions of the church made them inherently disorderly. Laud thought that lecturers "by reason of their pay are the people's creatures and blow the bellows their way."[38] Although the strictness of the enforcement depended on the views and rigor of the local bishop, Laud and his royal master charted a clear policy that the lectures, which fomented popularity, must be contained.

In 1629, King Charles sent instructions to then-archbishop Abbott requiring reforms in the church, including particular notice of lecturers. Bishops were to "take great care concerning the lecturers," requiring that afternoon sermons be turned into catechizing, that lecturers read divine service before their lecture, and that lecturers be "grave and orthodox divines." The king also ordered that "if a corporation maintain a single lecturer, he be not suffered to preach, till he profess his willingness to take upon himself a living with cure of souls within that corporation."[39] Laud reinforced these orders upon becoming primate, cracking down sternly on preachers lacking the required benefice and urging bishops to enforce standards of conformity and licensing. The archbishop concerned himself with all lectures, but he had a particular antipathy to lectures in towns, where popularity and unorthodox ideas could readily spread.

Reports of Laud's metropolitical visitations from 1634 to 1639 indicate clearly his program of suppressing lectures in corporate boroughs. In his first

---

[36] Matthew Reynolds, *Godly Reformers and Their Opponents in Early Modern England: Religion in Norwich, c. 1510-1643* (Woodbridge, 2005), p. 84.

[37] *CSPD 1619-23*, p. 431; Reynolds, *Godly Reformers*, p. 116; Noah Millstone, "Space, Place and Laudianism in Early Stuart Ipswich," in C. Kyle and J. Peacey (eds), *Connecting Centre and Locality: Political Communication in Early Modern England* (Manchester, 2020), pp. 69-70.

[38] Seaver, *Puritan Lectureships*, pp. 71, 243; Peter Heylyn, *Cyprianus Anglicus* (London, 1671), p. 188; William Prynne, *Canterburies Doome* (London, 1646), p. 368. While both Heylyn and Prynne appear to provide the full text of Laud's "Considerations," only Prynne's version contains the language about lecturers being "the people's creatures."

[39] Laud, *Works*, vol. 5, pp. 307-8.

DEFINING CHURCH AND CORPORATION

report as archbishop, he writes approvingly of the bishop of Bath and Wells's efforts to "put down divers Lecturers in Market-Towns." The report from that diocese two years later remarks with appreciation that "there is not a single Lecturer in any Town Corporate, but grave Divines Preach by course."[40] In 1637, the bishop of Peterborough reported that Daventry maintained a lecturer by contributions of the town, to which Laud replied that he must "take care of" that irregularity.[41] Finding that the Mercers of London had established a lecture in Huntingdon for which they claimed the power to appoint and remove, without resort to the bishop of the diocese, Laud solicited the king's support in suppressing this disorderly arrangement. "My most humble suit to your Majesty is, that no Lay-Man whatsoever, and least of all Companies or Corporations, may under any Pretence of giving to the Church or otherwise, have Power to put in or put out any Lecturer or Minister." The archbishop clearly had corporate towns, as well as livery companies, in mind in lodging his complaint with the king. Charles's marginal notes on the report reflect his full approval: "Certainlie I cannot hould fitt that anie Lay-Person or Corporation whatsoever, should have the Power these Men would take to themselves. For I will have no Preest have anie Necessitie of a Lay Dependencie. Wherefore I command you show me the way to overthrow this, and to hinder the performance in tyme, to all such Intentions."[42] Charles disliked lay dependency generally, but its root as a policy seems clearly tied to the corporate lectureships. The increasingly strict policy regarding lecturers, while not aimed exclusively at corporate towns, certainly had a differential impact upon them. As will be seen below, it heightened tensions between corporations and ecclesiastical authorities, and thus the crown, over both their beliefs and their authority to regulate themselves.

Differences over the definition of order in reference to lectures emerged in a number of towns. Ipswich saw the maintenance of their lecturer as key to the regulation of the town, while ecclesiastical authorities increasingly viewed it as disorderly and divisive. Known for its godliness as well as the generally good order of borough government, Ipswich had a "common preacher" as early as 1551, and the corporation elected lecturers throughout Elizabeth's reign and into James's.[43] In 1605, they chose Samuel Ward, one of the great puritan preachers of the era. Ward was a towering figure in the town, well connected with the town's magistracy and known for the excellence and influence of his

---

[40] William Laud, *The History of the Troubles and Tryal of ... William Laud* (London, 1695), pp. 526, 535.
[41] Laud, *Troubles and Tryal*, p. 548.
[42] Laud, *Troubles and Tryal*, p. 527. On London companies' establishment of provincial lectures, see Newton E. Key and Joseph P. Ward, "Metropolitan Puritans and the Varieties of Godly Reform in Interregnum Monmouth," *The Welsh History Review* 22 (December 2005), 646–72 and Joseph P. Ward, *Culture, Faith and Philanthropy: Londoners and Provincial Reform in Early Modern England* (New York, 2013).
[43] Nathaniel Bacon, *The Annalls of Ipsw'che*, ed. W. Richardson (Ipswich, 1884), pp. 235, 332, 341, 364, 419.

URBAN GOVERNMENT AND THE EARLY STUART STATE

preaching. The townsmen supported Ward handsomely with a stipend that by the 1630s had grown to £100 per annum, plus a house.[44] His influence was well known to church authorities who came to believe he contributed to religious irregularity in Ipswich. In his visitation for the archbishop of 1635, Nathaniel Brent found that "the Towne is exceeding facious, and yet the better part are Conformable in a reasonable good measure. Mr. Samuel Ward is thought to be the chiefe author of their nonconformity."[45] Ward's brand of preaching clearly pleased many Ipswich magistrates and inhabitants, but it also brought negative scrutiny to the governance of the town.

For more than fifteen years, Ward's lecturing proceeded without incident, and the corporation rewarded his emphasis on improving the town's moral order with increasing remuneration and respect. But changing religious winds brought Ward to the attention of ecclesiastical officials for touching on controversial topics. In 1622, as conflict between Protestants and Catholics on the Continent raged, King James commanded that the corporation require Ward to "surcease the preaching of his lecture." Ward had allegedly exercised his artistic abilities by drawing caricatures against Spain and Rome, for which he was suspended and briefly imprisoned. The move against Ward was part of Bishop Harsnett's program against sole lectureships, which he believed stemmed from "pride, singularity and faction" not "piety and devotion." At the king's request, Harsnett set aside Ipswich's lecturer and licensed five or six "learned conformable preachers, having benefices with cure of souls" to preach the lecture and the Sunday sermon. Two years of lobbying and petitioning (at an expense of over £200) by the corporation and Ward himself eventually resulted in his restoration to the lecture in 1624.[46] In the 1630s, with Laud's programs for conformity and against lecturers in full swing, Ward again fell afoul of religious authorities. High Commission convened Ward in 1634, and the many articles against him included preaching against set prayer and his alleged contention that ministers should be elected by the people. Ward eventually submitted, but not before he made numerous trips to London and spent time in prison.[47]

[44] SA/I, C6/3, fols 196v, 197v, 220; J.M. Blatchly, "Ward, Samuel (1577-1640)," *ODNB*, accessed 30 June 2020, ed. David Cannadine, January 2008, www.oxforddnb.com/view/article/28704.

[45] *CSPD 1635*, p. xxxii. Tyacke attributes the first Paul's Cross sermon to mention Arminianism to Ward in 1617, when he spoke about the Pelagian danger of Arminius. Tyacke, *Anti-Calvinists*, p. 257.

[46] TNA, SP14/120, fol. 20v (Chamberlain to Carleton, 10 March 1621); SA/I, C5/14/1 (Ipswich Great Court Book), fol. 325; Bacon, *Annalls of Ipsw'che*, p. 479n.; TNA, SP14/130, fol. 127 ("The Humble Petition of Samuel Ward ..."); Bodl. Lib., Tanner MS 265, fol. 28; SA/I, C6/1/5, fols 35v, 42, 43v, 44, 54, C9/2(2), fols 305v-8v; Blatchly, "Ward, Samuel (1577-1640)." See also Millstone, "Space, Place," pp. 69-70.

[47] *CSPD 1634-35*, pp. 321, 361-2, 490, *1635*, pp. 184, 198, 207, 476, 504-5, 613, *1635-6*, pp. 130, 478, 496. A lengthy recitation of Ward's interactions with the authorities in the 1620s and 1630s can be found in *CSPD 1635-36*, pp. xxxi-lx.

232

DEFINING CHURCH AND CORPORATION

Ward's troubles became the corporation's. Not only deprived of their minister, the townsmen also grappled with multiple threats to corporate authority that stemmed from Ward's case. Corporation members went to the bishop of Norwich (anti-Calvinist Matthew Wren) and the archbishop of Canterbury in 1635 and 1636 to lobby on behalf of Ward and the town. Their pleas failed to move Wren and Laud, who viewed the townsmen's behavior as defiance. According to Laud, Wren would have allowed them a different lecturer, but "they resolve to have Mr. Ward or none, and that (as is conceived) in despite of the censure of the court."[48] Ward's suspension also led to a broader questioning of how ministers in Ipswich were paid. The corporation sent agents to Cambridge, Norwich, and Chelmsford to consult on the matter, but nevertheless could not make their case. The king heard the suit in Council, where, after listening to his solicitor general and the bailiffs and portmen of Ipswich, he determined that the nomination of stipendiary ministers lay wholly in the king, not the townsmen.[49] At the same time, the town suffered strong challenges against chartered liberties from Lady Blount and Sir John Hayes, who likely timed their existential threat against the corporation to capitalize on the negative attention already drawn by the advocacy of Ward.[50] Forceful application of ecclesiastical policy by Bishop Wren and Archbishop Laud not only affected the preaching heard in the town, but it had a significant impact on the authority of the corporation and the security of its liberties, as well. Ward's suspension made clear that the town was out of step with the crown's views, making Ipswich vulnerable to further scrutiny. The townsmen's frustration with Wren's policies would become clear several months later, with an alleged riot against the bishop's authority.[51]

The increasing concern on the part of anti-Calvinist ecclesiastical authorities about lecturers put magistrates in a number of towns in the difficult position of upholding corporate privileges that conflicted with central policy. Richard Cust has shown how Great Yarmouth's divisions over its charter in the late 1620s and early 1630s were intimately connected with the crown's new direction in religious policy. Much of the conflict had specifically to do with the corporation's appointment of lecturers. Rev. John Brinsley, a moderate puritan beloved by the town's godly, served as the main lecturer; though supported by many aldermen, a more conservative, conformist faction in the corporation opposed him.[52] The corporation claimed the privilege of appointment, a position increasingly challenged by the dean and chapter of Norwich in the latter

---

[48] SA/I, C9/2(2) (Ipswich Treasurer's and Chamberlain's Accounts 1635–6), C6/1/5 (Ipswich Assembly Book), fol. 132v; Blatchly, "Ward, Samuel"; Laud, *Works*, vol. 5, pt. 2, p 340.
[49] SA/I, C9/2(2), fols 405, 409; TNA, SP16/351, fol. 69. See Millstone, "Space, Place," pp. 68–9 on the unusual parish organization in Ipswich.
[50] SA/I, C5/14/3, fols 274v–75.
[51] See below, p. 252.
[52] Richard Cust, "Anti-puritanism and Urban Politics: Charles I and Great Yarmouth,"

233

URBAN GOVERNMENT AND THE EARLY STUART STATE

1620s.[53] By 1631-32, with the corporation still tangled in the quo warranto suit against its charter, the curate of St. Nicholas church, Matthew Brooks, protested both against Brinsley's religious views and the corporation's governance. He addressed what the corporation called a "clamorous petition full of foul and false aspersions" to the king in the name of the dean and chapter. The petition's fifteen articles fulminated "against the present government of the town touching faction and misgovernment."[54] Brooks's petition resulted in an appearance before the Privy Council by several magistrates in March 1632. King Charles, present in person, declaring "how sensible and careful he is of the countenancing and maintenance aswell of Ecclesiastical authority and discipline as of civil order and Government," denounced division and restricted Brinsley from preaching anywhere in Great Yarmouth. The king also ordered the imprisonment of four aldermen thought to be puritan abettors of faction.[55] Promoting peace and precluding popularity, the Council ordered that the corporation could no longer choose the town lecturer, but instead would present names to the Board. The townsmen complied, stating they desired a lecturer "who may be a person of quiet disposition inclined to peace and concord." William Laud, assigned by the Board to make the choice, selected George Burdette, who, ironically, turned out to be far from quiet. Burdette stirred trouble with other ministers and proved unconformable; the High Commission suspended him for schismatic doctrine and ordered him removed from the Yarmouth lectureship.[56] The dispute over lecturers questioned both the religious complexion of the town and the privileges and government of the corporation.

For Great Yarmouth, the lectureship served as a focal point for negotiation between center and locality, and within the town itself, as boundaries between corporate and ecclesiastical authority were redrawn. The controversy over lecturers was entwined with the great struggle over the charter of incorporation that nearly destroyed the corporation in the late 1620s and early 1630s.[57] The expansion of ecclesiastical authority at the expense of corporate authority was a bitter pill, and one that was being swallowed by many corporations in the 1630s. From the perspective of Archbishop Laud, the suppression of the lecture led to peace and order. His visitation report for 1636 stated, "At Yarmouth,

---

Historical Journal 35 (1992), 1-26; Richard Cust, "Brinsley, John (1600-1665)," *ODNB*, accessed 4 July 2020, www.oxforddnb.com/view/article/3441.

[53] TNA, C2/ChasI/N15/23 (Bill of Complaint by dean and chapter of Norwich against bailiffs *et al.* of Great Yarmouth, with Answers, 23 May 1625); NRO, Y/C19/6, fols 74, 83v; Y/C18/6, fols 215, 238, 238v.

[54] NRO, Y/C18/6, fol. 130, Y/C19/6, fols 217v, 223v, 228v.

[55] TNA, PC2/41, pp. 581-4. Brinsley, with Sir John Wentworth's patronage, continued his preaching in nearby Lound, but did not return to Yarmouth for over a decade. Cust, "Brinsley, John".

[56] TNA, PC2/42, pp. 144, 337-8, 428-9; NRO, Y/C19/6, fols 245v, 254, 254v, 255v, 262, 275-275v, 308v, 318v; *CSPD 1634-35*, pp. 115, 125, 537-9, 547. Presumably Laud was unaware of Burdette's true character and regretted his choice.

[57] See above, pp. 67-71, for the struggle over the charter.

DEFINING CHURCH AND CORPORATION

where there was great division heretofore for many Years, their Lecturer being Censured in the High Commission about two Years since, went into New England, since which time there hath been no Lecture, and very much peace in the Town, and all Ecclesiastical Orders well observed."[58] The corporation, in contrast, bemoaned both the loss of "painful" preaching and the challenge to corporate rights of nomination that the suppression of the lecture represented. Religious viewpoints and notions of civic authority were inextricably connected, complicating the relationship between center and locality over these matters.

The corporation of Gloucester likewise found its corporate authority challenged due to its advocacy for its lecturer. While Gloucester had a long history as a godly city, the corporation formally established a public preaching lecture in 1620, devoting twenty marks out of civic revenues to support a minister to preach twice a week, "forever."[59] The corporation established another lecture in 1632 for the benefit of the poor "and others who will resort to it."[60] Gloucester expressed a firm commitment to godly preaching, establishing and continuing the lectureships despite serious economic hardship.[61] This commitment offered a sense of identity to town and corporation, but it also exposed Gloucester to scrutiny when local views did not align with national policy. The city's main lecturer, John Workman, preached a forthrightly godly message. He managed to retain his post in the early 1620s during the episcopacy of Calvinist Miles Smith, but ran afoul of Smith's less sympathetic successor, Godfrey Goodman, for his "scandalous" words. Among other things, he allegedly preached that "how many paces a man made in dancing so many paces he made to hell," and that the election of ministers properly belonged to the people. He was suspended and sent before the High Commission. Despite the suspension, the corporation of Gloucester agreed to provide Workman with an annual stipend of £20 as long as he lived in the city "whether he preach or not."[62] This act of resistance resulted in the mayor and town clerk being convented before the High Commission for supporting their suspended minister. The court found Workman guilty and banned him from preaching – or even teaching school – due to his "schismatical" views. While the magistrates of Gloucester acknowledged their error

---

[58] Laud, *Troubles and Tryal*, p. 541.
[59] GA, GBR B3/1, fol. 466.
[60] GA, GBR B3/1, fol. 560.
[61] See Peter Clark, "'The Ramoth-Gilead of the Good': Urban Change and Political Radicalism at Gloucester 1540-1640," in P. Clark, A.G.R. Smith, and N. Tyacke (eds), *The English Commonwealth 1547-1640: Essays in Politics and Society Presented to Joel Hurstfield* (Leicester, 1979), pp. 167-87.
[62] J. Foster, *Alumni Oxonienses: The Members of the University of Oxford 1500-1714*, vol. 4 (Oxford, 1891), p. 1680; J.N. Langston, "John Workman, Puritan Lecturer in Gloucester," *Transactions of the Bristol and Gloucestershire Archaeological Society* 66 (1945), 222-3; John Tiller, "Smith, Miles (d. 1624)," *ODNB*, accessed 2 June 2020, https://doi-org.ezproxy.lib.uh.edu/10.1093/ref:odnb/25879; Nicholas W.S. Cranfield, "Goodman, Godfrey (1583-1656)," *ODNB*, accessed 2 June 2020, https://doi-org.ezproxy.lib.uh.edu/10.1093/ref:odnb/10977; TNA, PC2/43, p. 405; GA, GBR B3/2, p. 23.

URBAN GOVERNMENT AND THE EARLY STUART STATE

and were dismissed from High Commission, the sense of grievance over this episode continued to fester, and it would reappear when the tables were turned on the ecclesiastical authorities after 1640.[63]

Tensions over corporate lectureships affected many towns, as church officials became increasingly concerned with the impact of preaching in the urban context. This anxiety showed itself clearly in the case of the feoffees for impropriations, a group of London-based ministers, lawyers, and merchants, who endeavored to improve the preaching ministry. Pooling their money, they purchased lay impropriations, using the proceeds to support lectureships and enhance the stipends of preaching ministers. A similar group, including Alderman Thomas Atkin and lawyer Miles Corbett, emerged in Norwich and Norfolk.[64] While much of the money of the London feoffees went toward lecturers in the metropolis, a number of provincial towns, like Bridgenorth, Hertford, Cirencester, Haverfordwest, and Shrewsbury, were also involved. Peter Heylyn, the leading foe of the feoffees, called them the "Chief Patrons of Faction" and opposers of church and government. He saw them as promoters of a conspiracy to circumvent the king's authority and to plant dangerous doctrine in the pulpits of towns and cities where it would have the most destructive impact.[65] William Laud, as bishop of London, likewise viewed the feoffees as a threat; he referred the issue to Attorney General William Noy, who initiated an Exchequer action against them in 1632.[66] The case put both the legality of the feoffees and the dangers of urban preaching in the spotlight.

Of the various wrongs ascribed to the feoffees, two stand out in the context of the present discussion. First was the allegation that the feoffees purposely targeted towns that had the parliamentary franchise, with the implication that lectures and preaching would stir hearers to choose burgesses unsympathetic to the ecclesiastical hierarchy and thus – in the eyes of their accusers – the monarchy.[67] Central authorities clearly believed that town lectures had a political motivation, whether or not those funding them intended this. Second, the crown viewed the organization of the feoffees as dangerous. Unlike a borough or trading corporation, the feoffees had no royal charter or official imprimatur from the king, yet they functioned in many ways like a corporation. In effect, they usurped the king's prerogative authority to conduct their

---

[63] *CSPD 1634–5*, pp. 49, 51, 110, 262, 268, 273, 317, 490, *1635*, pp. 182, 194–5, 222, 233; GA, GBR G3/2, pp. 23, 25.

[64] On the feoffees, see Ethyn Kirby, "The Lay Feoffees: A Study in Militant Puritanism," *Journal of Modern History* 14 (1942), 1–25; Seaver, *Puritan Lectureships*, pp. 88–92, 235–8, 253–4, 289–90; Vivienne Larminie, "Feoffees for Impropriations," *ODNB*, accessed 20 June 2020, https://doi.org/10.1093/ref:odnb/10732. On the Norwich feoffees, see Reynolds, *Godly Reformers*, pp. 160–5 and J.T. Evans, *Seventeenth-Century Norwich* (Oxford, 1979), p. 87.

[65] Quoted in Kirby, "Lay Feoffees," p. 13.

[66] Larminie, "Feoffees."

[67] Kirby, "Lay Feoffees," p. 15; Seaver, *Puritan Lectureships*, p. 88; Larminie, "Feoffees."

DEFINING CHURCH AND CORPORATION

business, bypassing official structures of the church to gain secular control over ecclesiastical livings. With Charles's well-evidenced dislike of lay control in the church, his high regard for his own prerogative, and his sensitivity to the politics of parliament, it is unsurprising that the feoffees for impropriations met with royal disdain and eventual legal suppression, with an Exchequer decree against them in February 1633.[68]

Controversies over preaching and lecturers formed one part of the larger concerns in many towns over religious practice, but they are important for a number of reasons. Laud's assault on lectureships can be identified as an element of urban policy under Charles. While it had a broader thrust regarding conformity and "lay dependency," the policy aimed most pointedly at lectures in corporate towns. For corporations, these controversies went beyond matters of belief. Disputes over lecturers posed challenges to privileges of nomination and appointment, as the boundaries of civic and ecclesiastical authority within the state were renegotiated. Towns subjected to scrutiny over their lecturers often found themselves vulnerable to other questions over corporate privileges and order, as well. The controversies over preaching would return as key points of contention in 1640.

Cathedral cities and the boundaries of authority

The conflicts over lecturers highlight the ways that corporate liberties could be exposed and curtailed as religious policy evolved. This tension was particularly acute for England's cathedral cities, where corporation and church came in constant contact, both in physical space and legal authority. Over the centuries, cathedral clergy and civic governors sparred regularly over jurisdiction and control in matters of taxation, law, and precedence. Citizens gradually carved out rights and privileges separate from those of ecclesiastical officials.[69] In the wake of the Reformation many cathedral cities sought royal incorporation, and by the early seventeenth century the corporate governments of most important cathedral cities had enhanced their jurisdiction and could even display the

---

[68] Larminie, "Feoffees."
[69] On cathedrals in this period, see Ian Atherton, "Cathedrals, Laudianism, and the British Churches," *Historical Journal* 53 (2010), 895-916; Carl Estabrook, "Ritual, Space, and Authority in Seventeenth-Century English Cathedral Cities," *Journal of Interdisciplinary History* 32 (2002), 593-620; Carl Estabrook, "In the Mist of Ceremony: Cathedral and Community in Seventeenth-Century Wells," in S. Amussen and M. Kishlansky (eds), *Political Culture and Cultural Politics in Early Modern England* (New York, 1995), pp. 133-61; Stanford Lehmberg, *Cathedrals under Siege: Cathedrals in English Society, 1600-1700* (University Park, PA, 1996), pp. 202-14; Claire Cross, "'Dens of Loitering Lubbers': Protest against Cathedral Foundations, 1540-1640," *Studies in Church History* 9 (1972), 231-7. See also Catherine F. Patterson, "Corporations, Cathedrals, and the Crown: Local Dispute and Royal Interest in Early Stuart England," *History* 85 (2000), 546-71.

URBAN GOVERNMENT AND THE EARLY STUART STATE

insigniae of civic authority within the cathedral close.[70] The development of Caroline policies promoting church authority and casting suspicion on the motives of allegedly puritan townsmen encouraged churchmen in a number of cathedral cities to try to win back lost ground. Local infighting came quickly to the attention of the Privy Council and ultimately the king himself, resulting in challenges to the charters of a number of England's cities.

The boundaries of jurisdiction and authority between cathedral chapter and corporation came under frequent dispute in most cathedral cities. Some proceeded by law, contesting the powers and properties granted by charters going back into the distant past.[71] But they also were carried out through symbol and precedence in the cathedral and its precincts. As representatives of the king's government, mayors and aldermen in these cities understood that their own authority and honor were tied to the great ecclesiastical edifices in their midst. They took care to reinforce their own dignity through public displays of corporate splendor in the cathedral and close. The corporation of Canterbury admonished its members to attend service at the cathedral dressed not just in their cloaks, but in their official gowns of office, in order to make a clear show of their status to churchmen and citizens alike. York's lord mayor and his brethren, noting the unseemliness of corporation members coming into the cathedral "scatteringly," agreed that they should henceforward "come orderly together into the quire"; all others were to be kept out of the seating to preserve the dignity of the corporation.[72] At the same time, they felt keenly the churchmen's use of the cathedral's symbolic power to diminish the status of the corporation in relation to their own. The location and ordering of seating, the attendance and comportment of members of the civic corporation at divine service, and the carrying of civic symbols – mace or sword – into the cathedral precincts were important emblems of corporate authority vis-à-vis the cathedral clergy. Churchmen in cathedral cities took advantage of changing royal policies in the 1630s to assert their dominance over these symbols, attempting to press back any inroads civic governments had made in previous decades.[73]

Seating arrangements could be highly politicized in any church, as the order and location of seats symbolically represented the hierarchical order of the community.[74] In a cathedral church, the political ramifications were even more apparent, as the space displayed multiple authorities. The dean and

---

[70] Patterson, "Corporations, Cathedrals, and the Crown," pp. 550-3.

[71] See, e.g., WSHC, G23/1/226 (Papers in city's disputes with bishop, dean and chapter of Salisbury, uncatalogued); Muriel Curtis, *Some Disputes between the City and Cathedral Authorities of Exeter* (Manchester, 1932).

[72] Canterbury Cathedral Archives, AC4 (Canterbury Burghmote Book 1630-1658), fol. 102v; YCA, B.35 (York House Book 1625-1637), fol. 186v.

[73] See Daniel C. Beaver, *Parish Communities and Religious Conflict in the Vale of Gloucester, 1590-1690* (Cambridge, MA, 1998) for a theoretical approach to understanding symbols and boundaries in the parish setting in this period.

[74] See Christopher Marsh, "Order and Place in England, 1580-1640: The View from the

DEFINING CHURCH AND CORPORATION

chapter, who were resident, had certain seats; the bishop, when in residence, had another. The members of the city's government, expected to attend divine service at the cathedral and their local parish churches, had prominent seats, as did their wives. Also in this mix sat members of the local gentry who worshipped at the cathedral and the regular citizens who attended. Potential for competition over marks of status abounded. The crown's emerging policy emphasizing the "beauty of holiness" and the protection of ecclesiastical privileges shook up this potent social mixture.[75] Emboldened, churchmen at a number of cathedrals initiated seating disputes with the intention of slighting civic government.

In Salisbury, a seating dispute erupted in 1632, exacerbating a struggle between the corporation and the bishop over the city's charter. The churchmen took the opportunity to assert their authority symbolically. They turned over part of the common council's seats to gentlemen, "abused" the wives of the mayor and the aldermen regarding their seating, and displaced some aldermen from their accustomed seats. The city's leaders believed that the churchmen intentionally dishonored the corporation to diminish civic government and appealed to Bishop John Davenant hoping for redress. Davenant had his own differences with the dean and chapter, but on this issue he showed no sympathy to the citizens, perhaps because of the legal troubles already brewing between them. When told of the churchmen's dishonor of the citizens, Davenant responded that "he was not acquainted or privy thereunto, and it did not in any way concern him." Finding no help there, the corporation sent three of its members to London to consult with legal counsel, hoping to counter this disgrace.[76] The seating dispute mirrored the larger struggle over jurisdiction between the corporation of Salisbury and the church, an important visual and physical manifestation of the conflict.[77]

The translation of William Laud to the archbishopric of Canterbury in 1633 formalized a pattern regarding seating that was already in motion.[78] Laud began a program to beautify and order cathedrals throughout his archdiocese; Archbishop of York Richard Neile would apply it in the north, as well. Beginning with his own metropolitan church of Canterbury, Laud ordered more attention to the choir, organ, decorations, and altar. He decried the "exorbitant seats" where the mayor of Canterbury and other local dignitaries sat and ordered that they be pulled down. Patrick Collinson has contended that Laud had a

---

Pew," *Journal of British Studies* 44 (2005), 3-26, for a discussion of the political nature of church seating.

[75] Lake, "The Laudian Style," pp. 161-86.

[76] WSHC, G23/1/3, fols 368, 369, 369v; R.C. Hoare, *History of Modern Wiltshire*, vol. 6, *The City of Salisbury*, by Robert Benson and Henry Hatcher (London, 1843), p. 379.

[77] For the broader context of the Salisbury corporation's relationship with the cathedral, see Patterson, "Whose City?"

[78] Laud's interest in re-establishing the majesty of cathedral churches began well before his accession to the archiepiscopate. Ian Atherton, "Cathedrals, Laudianism, and the British Churches," *Historical Journal* 53 (2010), 900-2.

URBAN GOVERNMENT AND THE EARLY STUART STATE

"comprehensive plan both for the Cathedral and its internal arrangements and liturgical function, and for the surrounding Precincts as a space which Laud was determined to make not only decent but sacred." This stirred up antagonism between the citizens of Canterbury and the cathedral clergy, making the citizens intruders in the cathedral, to be allowed only within the bounds set by the clergy.[79] Seating arrangements symbolized larger questions over jurisdiction and control, and Laud's policies pushed these to the fore.

Laud's program in Canterbury shaped practices in other cathedrals, leading to more instances of discord between civic and church officials over seating and attendance. Visitation records for the 1630s indicate Laud's concern that cathedrals were "pestered" with too many seats, resulting in orders to eliminate them.[80] In Worcester, Laud ordered the pulling down of all fixed seats, including those of the mayor and aldermen, and replacement with moveable seats, "according to the discretion of the dean," while in Gloucester the seats of the aldermen's wives were entirely removed from the cathedral.[81] This new policy upended customary practices of seating and created opportunities for conflict. In his visitation of Chichester cathedral in 1635, Nathaniel Brent instituted a number of orders that beautified the church and reframed the relationship of the citizens of Chichester to it. The "many" seats in the cathedral required reformation, though Brent noted the difficulty of fitting seats for the bishop, the dean and chapter, and the mayor and aldermen into the space.[82] By 1636, the corporation was at loggerheads with the churchmen over the relegation of civic leaders to less prominent seats, among other things. The corporation perceived the changed arrangements as a purposeful affront to the honor and status of the city by the dean and chapter. A hearing before the Privy Council to stop the squabbling shows the crown's preference for order that reinforced ecclesiastical authority. The king, present in Council, ordered that the mayor and aldermen, "for some special reasons alleged to his Majesty by the said Dean," must sit in their present seats until Michaelmas next. After that, they might be placed in better seats ("where the knights now sit"), but only on condition that the mayor agree in writing, on behalf of the corporation, that "neither he nor his successors will disturb or affront the dean" as they had lately done.[83] The seating dispute encapsulated the desire of both the churchmen and the corporation to assert authority and maintain dignity, but the king's response shows his will to give greater precedence to the churchmen.

---

[79] Patrick Collinson, "The Protestant Cathedral, 1541–1660," in P. Collinson, N. Ramsay, and M. Sparks (eds), A History of Canterbury Cathedral (Oxford, 1995), pp. 188–90.

[80] Laud, Troubles and Tryal, p. 530; CSPD 1635, p. xxxvi.

[81] Laud, Works, vol. 5, pp. 480, 491.

[82] CSPD 1635, p. xlii.

[83] TNA, PC2/46, p. 245. On relations between the city and the cathedral clergy in Chichester, see also Anthony Fletcher, A County Community in Peace and War: Sussex 1600–1660 (London and New York, 1975), pp. 235–7.

DEFINING CHURCH AND CORPORATION

The civic leaders of York likewise found that the new policies resulted in perceived slights to their corporate dignity. In September 1633, the corporation agreed to consult Justice Hutton about precedence in the cathedral. The archdeacon of York, Henry Wickham, had on the previous Sunday taken a seat in the minster a number of stalls above the mayor, "which as yet was never seen before by any man living." The seating in the minster was in flux, since at the recent visit of King Charles to York, he had expressly ordered the removal of a number of seats. In the new arrangement, the corporation expected the archdeacon to sit below the mayor, as accustomed. Instead, Wickham took a higher seat, much to the corporation's dismay. This symbolic slight impugned their honor and endangered good order, since it might "tend to the contempt and disgrace" of city government. In the face of this affront, the corporation agreed to write Archbishop Neile and Lord Keeper Coventry (the city's high steward) for assistance, but they also voted by "the most voices" to "forebear going to the Minster" as a sign of their displeasure.[84]

Civic leaders suspected that Wickham acted not on his own, but rather at the behest of his superiors, to make a statement about ecclesiastical authority. The corporation agreed to ask him why he sat above the mayor, hoping he would desist in the future.[85] In response, Wickham admitted that he took the seat not intentionally to be above the lord mayor, but rather that he had been "willed" to take it by Laud and Neile. By the town clerk's account, Wickham himself inclined toward compromise, but another churchman, Dr. Hodgson, condemned the whole business, rebuking the city for asking impertinent questions. This steeled Wickham's resolve, as he then declared that the seat was his by right and he would sit in it.[86] Not willing to let it go, the corporation sent two members to London to petition the king for redress.

Lord Keeper Coventry advocated for the city in the face of this injury, but even in assisting them he knew that the king's strong views on seating and precedence in cathedrals could not be brooked. In consultation with Justice Hutton, Coventry arranged a meeting with the archbishops of Canterbury and York to accommodate differences between city and church. They agreed that some "ancient and respected persons" should be consulted to establish the precedents. But Coventry made clear that whatever the outcome of this consultation, the lord mayor could not claim his seat by right.

> Only to deal clearly with you, it will not be yielded that either you or any other (but the churchmen) have place of right in any of the prebends stalls but for conveniency, decency, and respect to the civil Magistrate and other persons of quality. And therefore I do advise that yourselves do forebear and as much as may be silence in others (especially your officers and dependents) anything tending to a challenge

---

84 YCA, B.35, fols 218v, 221.
85 YCA, B.35, fol. 220v.
86 YCA, B.35, fol. 224.

URBAN GOVERNMENT AND THE EARLY STUART STATE

of right, which will be very difficult for you to prove and will but hinder a good accommodation.[87]

Advising them not to do anything to aggravate the situation, he especially urged them to return to attendance at the minster, or it "may be very likely to be brought to his Majesty's attention in an evil sense." Finally, Coventry reminded them that the removal of seats in the minster had been done at the personal command of King Charles. He warned them, "Let no words of opposition be cast out in respect thereof, for that will be construed not as an opposition to the dean and chapter but to the king."[88] The mayor and magistrates potentially undermined their own roles as the king's deputies if they pressed against the churchmen regarding seating.

The seating dispute ended relatively amicably, but it brought into sharp relief the difficulties that corporations faced in dealing with churchmen newly energized by the policies of the 1630s. In tussling with the archdeacon over seating, the lord mayor of York was defending the honor and government of his city and himself. Indeed, the corporation was simultaneously involved in a dispute over seating in St. Mary le Belfry parish church with the vice-president of the Council of the North.[89] But in pursuing the city's interests, the magistrates opened themselves to accusations that they opposed the king's government, not just the ecclesiastical officials at the center of their complaint. Even if the corporation's boycott of services and displeasure with the changes to the interior of the cathedral church had no theological content, it was a dangerous position to take in the context of the times.

This clash over precedence between corporations and cathedral clergy played out in other symbolic ways, as well, as assertions of corporate privilege were turned back in the face of a resurgent church. This can be seen graphically in disputes over whether the symbols of civic authority could be carried upright within cathedral precincts. In the first decades of the seventeenth century, a number of cathedral city corporations, including Chester and Chichester, had asserted the privilege to bear the sword or mace upright in the cathedral precincts as a sign of honor to the civil magistrate.[90] Mayors took seriously their role as the king's deputies, and they carried that authority with them even as they crossed jurisdictional bounds into the territory of the churchmen. Ecclesiastical authorities resented this assertion of civic right. As Archbishop Neile wrote in a letter to Bishop Bridgeman of Chester, mayors in cathedral cities "carry up their Swords and Maces, as if the jurisdiction of those places belonged to them," a practice he decried and vigorously sought to end.[91] The

---

[87] YCA, B.35, fol. 225.
[88] YCA, B.35, fols 225–225v.
[89] YCA, B.35, fols 203v, 214, 219v, 220v.
[90] Patterson, "Corporations, Cathedrals, and the Crown," pp. 553, 556, 558.
[91] Cheshire Archives and Local Studies, Chester (CALS), EDA 3/1, fol. 469 (Archbishop Neile to Bishop Bridgeman, 27 August 1637).

DEFINING CHURCH AND CORPORATION

1630s witnessed a renegotiation of space and boundaries, redefining where symbols of civic authority could run and overturning older practices as Charles, Laud, and Neile sought to enhance the dignity of the church. The debate over civic insigniae broke out first in London, as the lord mayor and the dean and chapter of St. Paul's sparred over the practice of carrying the civic sword upright in the cathedral, but this metropolitan conflict presaged others in provincial cities.[92] In Chichester, a broader argument over precedency included a dispute over whether the civic mace should be carried before the mayor in the cathedral close and church. The king himself took an interest in the matter. In 1636, he proscribed the carrying of the civic mace in the choir of the cathedral. This determination went beyond Chichester itself, as the king resolved to make "a general order ... to be observed by all mayors in all Cathedral Churches" regarding civic insigniae in sacred precincts. The mayors of York, Chester, and Winchester received letters from their bishops instructing them to desist carrying their symbols in the cathedral precincts, based on the Chichester ruling.[93] The struggle over symbols renegotiated the boundaries of civic and ecclesiastical authority to the advantage of the church.

This new policy had particular impact in Winchester, where it exacerbated strains between the corporation and the cathedral and arguably the crown, as well. When the dean of Winchester cathedral informed the city's mayor about the king's order for Chichester limiting the mace in the cathedral precincts, the mayor and his brethren chose to absent themselves from the cathedral. This led to further intervention and an express command from King Charles stating that civic governors must attend divine service at the cathedral. In addition, the king placed even more restrictive rules on the corporation regarding its symbols of authority. His solution for preventing disorder and taking "special care" for the liberties of both close and city was to order that "from henceforth there shall not be borne before the mayor of that our city any maces at all within the Quire of our said cathedral church at Winchester; neither shall he make any use of these ensigns of authority in any part of the cathedral or liberties thereof but upon courtesy and permission expressly granted by the Dean and Chapter."[94] The king's command clearly subordinated the corporation to the clerics' authority in that space, overturning practices and precedents that had been in place since James's reign, if not before.

---

[92] TNA, PC2/43, p. 13. See also Derek Keene, St. Paul's: The Cathedral Church of London, 604–2004 (New Haven, CT, 2004), p. 56.

[93] TNA, PC2/46, p. 245; YCA, B.35, fol. 335v–336; CALS, EDA 3/1, fol. 469; W.R.W. Stephens and F.T. Madge (eds), Documents Relating to the History of the Cathedral Church of Winchester in the Seventeenth Century (London and Winchester, 1897), p. 10 ("The brieffe of the cause prepared for the Council of the Dean and Chapter of the Cathedral Church of Winton ... 18 June 1637"). Fletcher states that the mace continued to be carried in the cathedral in Chichester despite the king's order. Fletcher, County Community, p. 237.

[94] TNA, SO1/3, fol. 41 (King Charles to mayor and aldermen of Winchester, 2 June 1637).

243

URBAN GOVERNMENT AND THE EARLY STUART STATE

The mayor's response to this elevation of the churchmen is telling. Upon receiving the king's letter, he allegedly shoved it into his pocket and later the same day brazenly attended service at the cathedral with the mace borne up before him, without requesting permission from the dean. This was a dangerous move. It flew in the face of a direct royal command, even if the mayor's real target was the cathedral chapter, with whom the city had clashed for some time. The Privy Council sent a sharp warning of the king's displeasure and demanded immediate conformity to the orders.[95] Whether the mayor's actions constituted a political statement about the king's ecclesiastical policy or was more narrowly a poke in the eye to his rivals the dean and chapter is unclear. To some extent it makes no difference. From the crown's point of view the motivation did not matter, only the outcome – defiance of a clear command. Longstanding contentions between city and close over symbols transformed into statements about obedience and conformity in the new policy environment of the 1630s.

York and Winchester were not alone in their boycotts, as other cathedral city magistrates also chose to vote with their feet in the face of resurgent ecclesiastical power and, for some, the highly formal worship of the cathedrals. In Chester, it was reported that the mayor "in a sort abandoneth [the] cathedral church" in the context of disputes over carrying the civic symbols in the cathedral precincts.[96] Worcester's corporation shunned the cathedral services when the dean refused to allow civic preachers to use the cathedral pulpit.[97] Throughout the 1620s and 1630s, the corporation of Norwich wrangled with deans and bishops over attendance at the cathedral. Bishop Wren in particular enforced strict attendance at the cathedral on the corporation in the mid-1630s. The magistrates argued that they could not maintain their honor at the cathedral service, since their seats directly below the public galleries made them targets for books, shoes, hats, and even spittle, urine, and feces. While this concern for personal and corporate dignity was real, it was also something of a fig leaf for covering the dislike of the Laudian worship in the cathedral among some civic leaders.[98] As Evans and Reynolds have shown, Norwich's magistrates were divided in their religious views, and Wren's rigorous enforcement policies furthered divisions within the corporate body.[99] The extent to which displays of civic activism in these and

[95] TNA, PC2/48, p. 26.
[96] YCA, B.35, fol. 221; TNA, SO1/3, fol. 41; CALS, EDA 3/1, fol. 469.
[97] TNA, SP16/343, fol. 210 (Bishop Thornborough to Archbishop Laud, 13 January 1637), SP16/344, fol. 220 (C. Potter to Laud, 25 January 1637), SP17/D/12 (Petition of mayor *et al.* of Worcester to Laud, 13 March 1637); S. Bond (ed.), *The Chamber Order Book of Worcester*, Worcester Historical Society Publications, NS, vol. 8 (Worcester, 1974), pp. 45-6. See also Anthony Fletcher, "Factionalism in Town and Countryside: The Significance of Puritanism and Arminianism," *Studies in Church History* 16 (1979), 299.
[98] Ian Atherton and Victor Morgan, "Revolution and Retrenchment: The Cathedral, 1630-1720," in Ian Atherton *et al.* (eds), *Norwich Cathedral: Church, City, and Diocese, 1096-1996* (London, 1996), pp. 549-50.
[99] Evans, *Seventeenth-Century Norwich*, pp. 89-90; Reynolds, *Godly Reformers*, pp. 186-213.

DEFINING CHURCH AND CORPORATION

other cathedral cities over attendance were statements on the nature of worship at the cathedral as well as the honor of the corporation is difficult to discern, but both elements were at work in making this an important issue in this period of strong central policy enforcement.

Whatever the root cause of the absence of civic leaders from worship, the response of Charles's government was swift and uniform: Mayors and aldermen would attend divine service at the cathedral, behave themselves appropriately at all times while there, and abase the civic insigniae in the cathedral precincts. Letters went forth in the king's name to the mayors of cathedral cities throughout the realm. To the mayor and aldermen of Worcester, the monarch stated his pleasure that, for "the solemnity of God's service, as the preservation of due honor to the cathedral, being the Mother Church, as also for the maintenance of the public and outward state of the corporation," the mayor and aldermen must attend the full service at the cathedral. While there, they must adhere "in all obedience and conformity" to the canons of the church and the customs of cathedrals. So that they would not forget this royal dictate, they were to enter the king's letter into the acts of their city, as well as in the register of the dean or the cathedral.[100] The magistrates of Norwich, Winchester, and Chichester all received such letters, along with the requirement that they enter them into the acts of their respective corporations.[101] In York, the receipt of the king's letter led to soul-searching among the magistrates as to how to respond. They called a meeting of the common council to discuss whether the mayor should go to the minster on Sunday or not. After lengthy debate, the common council agreed that, whatever their previous opinion had been, now the mayor and the senior aldermen should attend at the minster, with the sword abased before him, in obedience to the king's direct command. But they also agreed that they must immediately petition King Charles to ask for relief.[102] Central policy, defined by Laud's, and the king's, views of worship, preaching, and order, was unequivocal; magistrates had little leeway to avoid attendance at services that constrained civic authority and that at least some found distasteful. The result of these tensions over symbols and space was acquiescence on the part of corporations in obedience to the king's commands, but the process was painful and left lingering resentments.

Corporate charters and ecclesiastical policy

Struggles over seating, symbols and attendance were outward manifestations of jurisdictional disputes newly politicized under the crown's ecclesiastical

[100] TNA, SP16/363, fol. 16 (King to mayor et al. of York, 2 July 1637), SO1/3, fol. 29v (King to the mayor et al. of Worcester, 13 March 1637). See also TNA, SP16/349, fol. 189.
[101] TNA, SO1/2, fol. 250 (King to mayor et al. of Norwich, 14 March 1636), SO1/3, fol. 41 (King to mayor et al. of Winchester, 2 June 1637), PC2/48, p. 26.
[102] YCA, B. 35, fol. 336–336v.

245

URBAN GOVERNMENT AND THE EARLY STUART STATE

policies of the 1630s. Even more worrisome to the corporations, especially of cathedral cities, were threats to their charters of incorporation that arose in concert with the disputes over their honor and authority. Churchmen, buoyed by the king's personal support, endeavored to claw back jurisdiction over both physical space and legal liberties they believed had been lost over the course of the unfolding Reformation. The general assessment of Ship Money created a flashpoint for disputes over authority and boundaries that ultimately challenged civic liberties.[103] Collection of the levy precipitated serious confrontations in several cathedral cities. At the base of all of them was a corporation's right to collect within the boundaries of the close, which brought out past jurisdictional disputes. But, as with conflicts over seating and insigniae, corporations saw their privileges eroded by ecclesiastical authorities with whose ceremonial and doctrinal positions many of them did not agree. In the 1630s, king and Privy Council entered disputes that previously drew only occasional royal interest. Ship Money gave central authorities a significant stake in actively managing the liberties of corporations and cathedrals. This changed stance caused serious strain for civic officials, whose duty to obey the king and protect corporate privileges stood at odds.

In Canterbury, Lichfield, Chichester, Winchester, York, Exeter, and Salisbury, rivalries escalated when civic corporations attempted to rate their respective cathedral closes for Ship Money.[104] In each case, cathedral authorities proclaimed their exclusion from civic jurisdiction. Rather than being negotiated in the locality, these disputes came directly to the attention of the Privy Council and often King Charles himself.[105] The Council assiduously defended the church's privileges, denying corporations the right to collect from anyone residing within the cathedral's jurisdiction. The Board's interest hardly surprises. By 1636 the Privy Council boasted three episcopal members, all of them active proponents of Laudian views: Laud himself, Richard Neile of York, and William Juxon, bishop of London. Charles's appointment of Juxon as lord treasurer early in 1636 must have reinforced the impression of the church's ascendancy and linked full collection of Ship Money with protecting

---

[103] A.A.M. Gill touches on how Ship Money exacerbated differences like that between the dean and chapter of Winchester and the civic corporation, and how "competing interest groups" sought to win the king's support. Gill, "Ship Money during the Personal Rule of Charles I: Politics, Ideology and the Law 1634 to 1640" (PhD dissertation, University of Sheffield, 1990), p. 198.

[104] TNA, PC2/44, p. 348, PC2/45, pp. 201, 335, PC2/47, p. 238, PC2/49, p. 221; VCH Yorkshire, The City of York, ed. P.M. Tillott (London, 1961), p. 174; TNA, PC2/46, p. 247, PC2/48, p. 340, PC2/46, p. 245, PC2/48, pp. 466–7. For Winchester, see also Stephens and Madge (eds), Winchester, pp. 1–18. In Chester, debates arose over Ship Money, as well, though unusually, the cathedral clergy chose to be rated by the city rather than the county, which had charged them higher. TNA, SP16/354, fol. 92 (T. Delves to Privy Council, 21 April 1637); Peter Lake, "The Collection of Ship Money in Cheshire during the Sixteen-thirties: A Case Study of Relations between Central and Local Government," Northern History 17 (1981), 48.

[105] TNA, PC2/46, p. 247, PC2/47, pp. 380, 432–3.

246

DEFINING CHURCH AND CORPORATION

ecclesiastical jurisdiction.[106] Clear patterns developed quickly. In January 1635 Canterbury cathedral clergy complained to the Privy Council that they had been rated by the corporation, contrary to their ancient rights and privileges. The Council quickly agreed, allowing the clergy to rate themselves.[107] In November, Lichfield's corporation received a stern warning not to rate the cathedral close, after a complaint from the clergy.[108] Early the next year, the Council, upon hearing a rumor that Chichester's corporation had tried to assess residents of the cathedral close, instructed the dean and chapter to pay their rates directly to the sheriff. The Board then firmly ordered the corporation not to collect in the close, commanding the mayor to return any money already collected there.[109] Seeing the writing on the wall, the mayor and sheriffs of Lincoln made a point of telling the Privy Council that they had left it to the dean to assess the clergy and residents of the close.[110] Unusually, Salisbury received permission from the Privy Council to rate the residents of the close, likely because the king had recently ordered the insertion of various churchmen among the magistrates of the city.[111] The Ship Money disputes as a group ended favorably for the privileges of the church.

This determination, rather than ending differences, served as a catalyst for more conflict over the balance between cathedral and corporate authority. Cathedral clergy sensed that the political winds of royal favor blew strongly in their direction. They used the opportunity to remind the crown that the privileges of the church had been under assault for years from corporate authorities, reopening old issues of governance and jurisdiction and adding to them the more novel element of religious conformity.[112] The churchmen had good hope of success because of staunch support from king and Council. As a direct result of Ship Money disputes, the Privy Council investigated corporate intrusions into the privileges of cathedrals in Lichfield, Chichester, Salisbury, York, Winchester, and Exeter, all between June 1636 and November 1637.[113] Chichester's case illustrates the pattern. A hearing before the Council concerning the mayor's assessment of Ship Money in the cathedral close led directly to more general questioning of the city's relations with the cathedral. The Council declared that

---

[106] TNA, SP16/315, fol. 137; Brian Quintrell, "The Church Triumphant? The Emergence of a Spiritual Lord Treasurer, 1635-1636," in J.F. Merritt (ed.), *The Political World of Thomas Wentworth, Earl of Strafford, 1621-1641* (Cambridge, 1996), pp. 81-108.
[107] TNA, PC2/44, p. 348.
[108] TNA, PC2/45, p. 201.
[109] TNA, PC2/45, pp. 335, 372.
[110] TNA, SP16/314, fol. 222 (Mayor of Lincoln to Privy Council, 29 February 1636). In 1628 the city had received a new charter which contained a clause expressly protecting the rights of the bishop, dean and chapter of Lincoln. Weinbaum, *British Borough Charters*, p. 73.
[111] TNA, PC2/48, pp. 466-7, PC2/47, p. 404.
[112] Peter Lake, "Puritanism, Arminianism, and a Shropshire Axe-Murder," *Midland History* 15 (1990), 50, and Cust, "Urban Politics," p. 26, show how people in different communities used the "polemical idiom current at the centre" to gain ground against their local rivals.
[113] TNA, PC2/45, pp. 201, 372, PC2/46, pp. 245, 246, 247, PC2/48, pp. 26, 340.

247

URBAN GOVERNMENT AND THE EARLY STUART STATE

the corporation could not collect the rate in the close and then commissioned the attorney general to hear all the differences the cathedral alleged against the corporation, ordering both citizens and clergy to bring in their charters and "evidences."[114] In Chichester and the other five cities, the Board decided in favor of the cathedrals and curtailed corporate privileges. King Charles's active promotion of decisions favorable to the church in these disputes is clear; he attended the Council personally to hear and decide most of them.[115]

These Ship Money cases touched off a series of inquiries into corporate charters of several cathedral cities which, as shown in Chapter 1, demonstrated the Caroline crown's willingness to challenge corporate privileges and alter charters in favor of the church. Chichester and York received commands to surrender their corporate charters, and royal promises to grant new charters did not make up for the fact that both cities lost some jurisdiction in the bargain.[116] Winchester's attempts to gain a new charter in 1637 stalled when the king stopped its passage until the privileges of the cathedral had been guaranteed.[117] For Lichfield, scrutiny of the corporation's practices in collecting Ship Money in the cathedral close led to a quo warranto against the city's charter and a determination excluding the cathedral and its precincts entirely from the corporation's authority.[118] The king wielded his authority over corporate liberties to bring them in line with his ideal of a strong, orderly, privileged church.

An equally direct challenge to corporate jurisdiction came with the Caroline crown's policy of including members of the clergy amongst the justices of the peace of cities and towns. King Charles's preference for ecclesiastical authority and distrust of corporate magistrates shows itself clearly in his directives to adjust charters in this way. The policy arose initially in response to a dispute in a cathedral city, but it was then extended to all towns corporate. King Charles ordered that bishops or chancellors be inserted as JPs in corporate charters as a matter of course. The king's strong desire to both protect ecclesiastical authority and enforce good order on towns he frequently viewed as suspect in matters of religion and government ran counter to decades of practice that had validated corporate jurisdiction.

An examination of two episodes, one in James's reign and one in Charles's, shows the change in attitude toward the expansion of ecclesiastical authority. The first involved Exeter, where efforts in 1622 attempted to place Valentine Carey, bishop of Exeter, onto the bench of JPs of the city.[119] Lord Keeper John

---

[114] TNA, PC2/45, p. 372.

[115] TNA, PC2/46, p. 245, PC2/47, pp. 380, 404, 432-3.

[116] See above, p. 44. Fletcher notes that Chichester's recorder, Christopher Lewkenor, continued to press for the city's liberties under other charters even after submitting the 1621 charter to the king. Fletcher, *County Community*, pp. 236-7.

[117] TNA, PC2/47, pp. 432-3; Stephens and Madge (eds), *Winchester*, p. 5.

[118] TNA, PC2/45, p. 201.

[119] DALS, ECA Letters 217 (William Prowse to mayor of Exeter, 4 May 1622), 218 (same to same, 7 May 1622), 219 (same to same, 18 May 1622). Tyacke identifies Carey as an

248

DEFINING CHURCH AND CORPORATION

Williams noted it was King James's "express wish" that Carey be a justice due to the city's "forward carriage" to the bishop in the past.[120] Heroic lobbying by the mayor's brother, William Prowse, managed to bring the city's charter before Attorney General Sir Thomas Coventry, who determined that it was good in law and would not admit of an additional justice.[121] Prowse nevertheless feared that the king might use his prerogative authority to get around the legal finding, granting a *non obstante* "to settle against the power of your Charter and consequently the common law of the realm, wherein every good subject hath an estate of inheritance."[122] Yet, in the end, James did not press the matter, the attorney general's legal finding held, and the bishop failed to become a JP of Exeter. In the 1630s, a similar situation reached a quite different result. The charter dispute in Salisbury between the bishop and the city offered King Charles a perfect opportunity to establish his preference for ecclesiastical oversight. Concerned with Salisbury's apparent puritanism – made manifest in Recorder Henry Sherfield's destruction of a stained-glass window in a parish church – the king determined that including churchmen among the magistrates would bring proper order to the city. After lengthy appeals and petitioning on the part of the corporation, in 1637 Attorney General Sir John Bankes and Solicitor General Edward Littleton certified their opinion that ecclesiastical officials should be added to the civic bench. The king then ordered that the bishop and several cathedral officials be made JPs, overturning the city's charter in that regard.[123]

Spurred by this precedent, Charles went on to generalize the rule to all charters of incorporation going forward. The king's personal interest shows clearly in the case of Derby. The Council made a warrant to the attorney general in January 1638 to grant a new charter, reorganizing the corporation to include a mayor rather than two bailiffs, and designating the mayor, recorder, and three aldermen as JPs. When shown this draft charter at the Council Board, Charles himself ordered the insertion into the charter of the bishop and chancellor of the diocese as justices of peace in the corporation. The king and Council then proceeded to order "that upon the granting or renewing of any Charters to Corporations for the future, the Bishops of the Diocese or their Chancellors for the time being should be inserted into the Commissions for the Peace within

---

anti-Calvinist, though it seems he was not a particularly fervent Arminian. See Tyacke, *Anti-Calvinists*, p. 193; Marc L. Schwarz, "Carey, Valentine (d. 1626), Bishop of Exeter," *ODNB*, accessed 22 Aug. 2020, www-oxforddnb-com.ezproxy.lib.uh.edu/view/10.1093/ref:odnb/9780198614128.001.0001/odnb-9780198614128-e-4844. See also Catherine F. Patterson, *Urban Patronage in Early Modern England: Corporate Boroughs, the Landed Elite and the Crown, 1580–1640* (Stanford, CA, 1999), pp. 135–7.

[120] DALS, ECA Letters 222 (William Prowse to mayor of Exeter, 29 May 1622), 226 (same to same, 28 June [1622]).

[121] DALS, ECA Letters 226, 227 (William Prowse to mayor of Exeter, 29 June 1622), 229 (same to same, 2 July [1622]), 230 (same to same, [n.d., but July 1622].

[122] DALS, ECA Letters 231 (William Prowse to mayor of Exeter, 6 July [1622]), 232 (same to same, [n.d., but July 1622]), 233 (same to same, 13 July 1622).

[123] For a detailed discussion of these events, see Patterson, "Whose City," pp. 499–504.

URBAN GOVERNMENT AND THE EARLY STUART STATE

the said Corporations respectively."[124] There is little doubt that Charles believed the surest way to establish order and obedience in potentially disorderly towns and cities was putting more authority into the hands of the churchmen.

Issues of religious belief and practice resonated through many of the disputes over civic and ecclesiastical authority, but concern for corporate honor and liberties played a crucial part, as well. The language of nonconformity and faction could be a potent weapon when used by clergy to attack their civic counterparts. If we take civic leaders at their words, however, the assault on corporate privileges by the clergy that the crown actively fostered was a significant root of their grievances. The reversal of a decades-long trend towards the extension of jurisdiction by civic government caused surprise and real distress among corporations. What had formerly been treated largely as local squabbles vaulted to the level of central government policy, with the crown enforcing a uniform set of standards that privileged churchmen and constrained corporations.

Responding to religious change

While concern for liberties and jurisdiction caused anxiety and disgruntlement in many corporate towns, the intermingling of those concerns with changes in belief and practice raised fears in many provincial towns. The new religious policies altering the interior space of churches, suppressing corporate lecturers, and redefining relations between civic and ecclesiastical authorities in cities and towns stirred tensions between many borough corporations and the crown in the 1630s. In a number of notable instances, godly urban magistrates diverged from the ecclesiastical regime in word or action, meeting with stern censure. Henry Sherfield, recorder of Salisbury, who broke a stained-glass window in his parish church, was indicted in Star Chamber, imprisoned, and fined £500. Ignatius Jurdain, stalwart puritan alderman of Exeter, wrote a letter to King Charles "expostulating with him about his setting forth" the Book of Sports in 1633; the king took deep offense, and only the bishop of Exeter's timely intervention averted serious consequences for Jurdain. John Robins, alderman of Great Yarmouth, allegedly spread "false new lies and tales" about Archbishop Neile, resulting in a Star Chamber censure and a £1,000 fine, plus damages. These episodes were well known among godly magistrates elsewhere. William Whiteway, a capital burgess of Dorchester, remarked upon all three of these incidents and the punishments laid out to the men; his diary entries display his sympathy for the offenders in the face of official chastisement.[125] These

---

[124] TNA, PC2/48, p. 512, PC2/49, pp. 249, 250.

[125] TNA, SP16/211, fols 25ff; *Cobbett's Complete Collection of State Trials*, vol. 3 (London, 1809) p. 562; F. Nicolls, *The Life and Death of Mr. Ignatius Jurdain* (London, 1654), p. iv; TNA, SP16/276, fol. 51; William Whiteway, *William Whiteway of Dorchester: His Diary 1618 to 1635*, ed. S. Bridges, trans. B. Bates, Dorset Record Society, vol. 12 (Dorchester, 1991), pp.

DEFINING CHURCH AND CORPORATION

incidents were individual acts and not official, corporate ones, yet they reflect the deep unhappiness felt by godly urban magistrates.

The ecclesiastical policies of the Caroline regime, promoting ceremonialism and ecclesiastical authority, proved objectionable and frustrating in many provincial towns, but we cannot assume they were universally detested. Opinions differed among townsmen and caused friction and discord within governing bodies of several towns. Great Yarmouth's corporation included both strong puritans and Laudian proponents. Matthew Reynolds has made the case that pro-Laudian groups existed, amidst a largely godly magistracy, in Norwich and several other cities. Even in so-called "puritan towns," religious perspectives were not monolithic.[126] The magistrates of some borough corporations supported the changes to patterns of practice. In Grantham (Lincs.), the alderman and burgesses approved of the railing-in of the communion table and its altar-wise placement as being more "convenient" than before, when boys would sit on or lean their elbows on the table "unreverently." The corporation praised the organ that had recently been set up in the parish church and vouched for the good behavior of their conformist vicar Edward Dickes, who had been accused by his detractors of suppressing preaching and moving the communion table.[127] Grantham's inhabitants clearly differed on these matters, since a local complaint to parliament in 1640 triggered the corporation's statement. But the supportive "certificate," recorded in the official minutes of the corporation, suggests that at least a majority of the town's leaders aligned themselves with Caroline religious policy.

Whether godly or not, most borough magistrates acquiesced to central dictates, whether with full-throated approval, unenthusiastic and slow compliance, or in some cases by High Commission or Privy Council order. As the king's deputies, they were expected to uphold royal authority within their jurisdiction. At the same time, many chafed against novel policies and sought to have their voices heard through petitioning and otherwise. King's Lynn, at the "special request" of the corporation and the whole parish, sent a delegation of the mayor, recorder, and several other town worthies to the bishop of Norwich in 1636, entreating him to stay proceedings in the churches and chancels of the town

---

128, 135, 151. Whiteway knew the precise amounts of fines against the men and which Privy Councilors spoke against or for the offenders.

[126] Cust, "Urban Politics"; Evans, Seventeenth-Century Norwich, pp. 89-91; Wallace MacCaffrey, Exeter 1540-1640: The Growth of an English County Town (Cambridge, MA, 1958), pp. 198-200; A.M. Johnson, "Politics in Chester during the Civil Wars and Interregnum 1640-62," in P. Clark and P. Slack (eds), Crisis and Order in English Towns 1500-1700: Essays in Urban History (Toronto, 1972), p. 204; Reynolds, Godly Reformers, pp. 255-67.

[127] LA, GRANTHAM BOROUGH/5/1 (Grantham Corporation Minute Book 1633-1704), fols 88v-89v; TNA, SP16/470, fol. 153 (Certificate of the alderman and burgesses of Grantham to the House of Commons). The organ playing the psalm reportedly took away "the confusion which sometimes heretofore hath happened in our church."

URBAN GOVERNMENT AND THE EARLY STUART STATE

ordered by the bishop's visitor on the Injunctions.[128] It has already been noted that the corporation of York's first instinct, when confronted with orders to attend the cathedral service and abase the civic mace, was to obey the royal order but petition the king for relief. In Norwich, Bishop Wren's suppression of godly lecturers and precise enforcement of high-church ceremonies in the churches in 1636 created significant turmoil among a divided magistracy. According to a Laudian partisan, the "silly puritan mayor" of Norwich wished to present a petition on behalf of the ministers to the king, though many aldermen opposed it.[129] Even in the face of division and frustration, corporations continued to try to reach out to central authorities using traditional means, hoping through this process to bring the changes they wanted.

Given the circumstances of the later 1630s, however, such petitions were unlikely to find success. In Ipswich, Wren's crackdown on preaching and institution of Laudian worship in the churches resulted in dismay among many magistrates and inhabitants. Samuel Ward, their beloved preacher, had been suspended and jailed for nonconformity, and, as Noah Millstone has detailed, the town's churches were dramatically remodeled by Wren for worship in the new ceremonial style.[130] Frustrated by these changes, the bailiffs and portmen of Ipswich petitioned the king for relief, hoping to regain some of the authority over the town's religious environment that they previously enjoyed. For the men of Ipswich, Wren's actions had overthrown an old order that had served the town well. The king was hardly receptive to such a request, particularly when a "riot" erupted at the bishop's residence in the town in the summer of 1636, allegedly fostered by certain magistrates.[131] Justification by the townsmen simply made things worse, as Wren reinforced to the king the "many outrages" and "foul passages" committed there. The bishop denounced the men of Ipswich, but he also amplified the incident as a dangerous precedent to which other towns were susceptible. He perceived that Ipswich's "ill example becomes a leading case to all your majesty's corporate towns (not within that diocese alone, but even of the whole realm) for contempt of your Majesty's most sacred authority and for obstinate disorder touching all matters ecclesiastical." Ipswich must be reduced to "obedience, peace, and good order, both civil and ecclesiastical" as

---

[128] KLTH, KL/C7/9, fol. 441.

[129] Bodl. Lib., Tanner MS 68, fol. 147 ([William Allanson] to [Bishop Wren], 8 October 1636).

[130] Millstone, "Space, Place," pp. 73-7. Millstone's analysis shows that the peculiar circumstances of Ipswich's parishes and the level of lay control over lectureships and livings in the town made it a target for Wren's intense focus on ecclesiastical discipline. Wren himself had personal connections to the town and some of its leading men.

[131] SA/I, C2/16, fols 1-5. It was alleged that the petition to the king was devised secretly by a small group of magistrates, not the whole body. SA/I, C2/16, fols 5, 10. See also Frank Grace, "'Schismaticall and Factious Humours': Opposition in Ipswich to Laudian Church Government in the 1630s," in D. Chadd (ed.), *Religious Dissent in East Anglia*, vol. 3 (Norwich, 1996), pp. 97-119.

DEFINING CHURCH AND CORPORATION

an example for the rest of the kingdom.[132] While Ipswich's failings were particularly egregious, corporate towns as a whole posed a danger to Wren's (and likely the king's) vision of order, leaving little room for negotiation.

The crown's changing policy on religion across the period, and the move toward stricter enforcement of a particular view of order, directly affected corporate towns in specific ways. In the first years of James's reign, as the crown continued to forge a strong connection with borough magistrates begun in the previous century, town governments took strength from the connection to bolster their authority. This included expanding corporate authority into areas of ecclesiastical jurisdiction left malleable in the wake of the Reformation. The Jacobean regime, particularly before 1620, largely allowed borough governments latitude in this regard. Desiring a preaching ministry but without sufficient funds to properly support its maintenance, the crown permitted the continuation and growth of lectureships, paid for directly by borough governors and inhabitants. In corporate towns and cathedral cities alike, borough corporations made inroads into ecclesiastical spaces, both literal and figurative. This was apparently a reasonable trade-off in return for strengthened government in urban localities and an expanded preaching ministry.

As puritanism came to be seen as an increasing danger to the state, however, this position became less tenable from the crown's perspective. New theological and liturgical practices took greater hold in the church, reinforced in royal policy. On one hand, the crown appreciated the strong sense of order that often accompanied godly magistracy in corporate towns. On the other, royal government condemned any hint of nonconformity or what it viewed as potential "popularity," increasingly enforcing strict obedience to new standards. The changing complexion of the church in the 1620s and especially the 1630s alienated many (though certainly not all) townsmen, but it also launched new inquiries into the boundary between corporate and ecclesiastical jurisdiction. These resulted almost exclusively in limitations on corporate liberties and the expansion of ecclesiastical authority. The frequent intervention by Charles personally in matters involving religion in towns and cities indicates the importance he attached to them and the extent to which central policy in this regard originated with the king himself. Julian Davies may overstate the case of a "Caroline Captivity of the Church," but Charles's intense concern to advance ecclesiastical authority in corporate towns is quite clear.[133] The king appeared increasingly suspicious of borough magistrates' trustworthiness to carry out the vision of order he prescribed.

The crown's policy in the 1630s, combining matters of belief and practice with those of liberties and jurisdiction, affected the sense of orderly self-government

---

[132] Bodl. Lib., MS Bankes 58, fol. 15 (Petition of [Matthew Wren] to the King, 12 March 1637).

[133] Julian Davies, *The Caroline Captivity of the Church: Charles I and the Remoulding of Anglicanism* (Oxford, 1992).

in many towns. As obedient subjects to the king, most borough governors submitted to the monarch's will. Corporations were deeply connected to the king's prerogative authority, and town leaders understood that their own authority lay in that vital connection. In the face of accusations of their collusion in the Ipswich "riot," several magistrates proclaimed they were "and ever hath been in all things obedient to his Majesty's happy government and conformable to the doctrine, discipline and ceremonies of the Church of England and the jurisdiction and government of the reverend fathers in God the bishops."[134] Corporations continued to use traditional methods – like petitions – to maintain communication with the crown on matters of liberties and governance. But new and stringent religious policies in the 1630s allowed little flexibility. Caroline policy, challenging both beliefs and liberties, bred consternation and even alienation in many corporate boroughs. Laud and his royal master may have extolled the peace and order that came to towns like Yarmouth and Chichester with the suppression of lecturers and redrawing of their liberties, but it was peace gained at a price, as many of these changes would come back as grievances once parliament returned in 1640.

[134] SA/I, C2/16, fol. 7.

Conclusion

The relationship between towns and the crown in the early seventeenth century was one of both connection and discord. Caroline policies regarding religion, taxation, and other matters affecting corporate liberties generated anxiety in many towns and reveal mistrust about "popularity" on the part of the king and his ministers. Challenges to corporate jurisdiction and borough government grew in the 1630s, altering patterns established under James. Yet those signs of friction should not obscure the many ways that the early Stuart period saw greater integration of the borough corporations into the monarchical state and the participation of urban magistrates (and to some extent townsmen more broadly) in its formation. The tension between protection of borough liberties and the drive to interact beyond borough boundaries was fundamental to urban government in the early Stuart state. The stories of connection and discord must be told in tandem.

Corporate towns had strong incentives to forge connections to the crown and the state more broadly. Their corporate charters, fundamental to their existence, provided a basis for relationship between center and locality. Charters identified borough magistrates as the king's immediate deputies and drew a clear line between the authority of the corporate body and the prerogative power of the monarch. Mayors, bailiffs, aldermen, common councilors, and other town officers stood as agents of the crown within the locality, and they wanted to be seen as such both by the inhabitants of their own towns and by others. Through appeals to the Privy Council, petitions to the king, correspondence with other towns, cultivation of patrons, use of the courts, instructions to their burgesses to parliament, and many other means, provincial corporations worked to ensure their liberties but also ensure their place within the state. Savvy local actors found ways to co-opt royal authority and central institutions to achieve their ends, whether to gain a new charter, settle local divisions, or stave off legal challenges. While protective of their liberties, borough corporations cultivated the bond between town and crown embodied in their charters.

The liberties defined in corporate charters governed political and social order in the towns, but also linked them to the broader concerns for order in the state. The increasing administrative strength of the early modern state was not simply a one-way street, with a centralizing monarchy forcing its will on reluctant and "independence"-minded towns; local actors played important roles in developing policy and initiating interaction with the crown. The towns served both themselves and the state in maintaining social order through enforcement of, and indeed development of, programs for poor relief, alehouse regulation, and a variety of other aspects of social and moral control. Trade, which animated the economies of towns, made corporations both protective of local liberties and perpetually facing outward, connecting with markets within

URBAN GOVERNMENT AND THE EARLY STUART STATE

and beyond the realm and highly sensitive to the crown's policies. Townsmen saw the interests of their own localities as tied into a larger national interest, identifying their needs for order, infrastructure, and defense with those of the prosperity and protection of the realm. Even on some of the more contentious issues that troubled early Stuart politics, such as militia training and national taxation, corporate towns found ways to engage and negotiate, understanding their role as part of the monarchical state. Corporate towns and townsmen were deeply involved in many ways with the business of state and questions of national interest. In times of trouble – serious economic downturn and war – towns often felt the pain first. As this book has endeavored to show, borough corporations, far from looking inward and trying to avoid the center's gaze frequently reached out to engage with state and crown, as local interests helped constitute national interests.

This dynamic relationship was not without its stresses. The state's ability (or inability) to meet the demands of its component parts was an ongoing point of negotiation. As this study has shown, the capacity of the early Stuart state to confront threats, preserve order, and support trade was critical to the economic and political well-being of corporate boroughs. Provincial towns, particularly those on the coasts, maintained frequent contact with central authorities in pursuit of resources needed to conduct and protect their trade, safety, and governance. Town authorities were integrally involved in the work of government and accepted responsibility to support and further the crown's business. The persistent engagement of the corporate towns helped keep the machine of state running. The crown acknowledged a broader responsibility for public goods like ports and havens, fortifications, and naval protection for shipping, but was often hard-pressed to live up to it. As Cogswell has argued, the state, while "creaky and never well-funded," was not unable to function.[1] Yet its limitations had significant impact on urban government, as the towns carried heavy burdens for the realm as a whole. Central authorities often turned the responsibility back on corporate boroughs (sometimes with help from surrounding counties) to pay for things that could be seen as national and not just local concerns, such as fortifications or plague relief. Likewise, the crown's inability, or lack of political will, to meet obligations like timely repayment of the costs of billeting or protection of merchant ships from piracy in the 1620s caused tremendous hardship in many towns, creating a sense of frustration that did not simply disappear when the immediate crises of the 1620s resolved. The towns clearly felt the centralizing strength of the early Stuart state in some ways and also suffered from its weakness in others.

---

[1] Thomas Cogswell, "Ten Demi-Culverins for Aldeburgh: Whitehall, the Dunkirkers, and a Suffolk Fishing Community, 1625–1630," *Journal of British Studies* 58 (2019), 318, 335–6; T. Cogswell, *Home Divisions: Aristocracy, the State, and Provincial Conflict* (Manchester, 1998), pp. 180–4. See also Conrad Russell, *Parliaments and English Politics, 1621–1629* (Oxford, 1979), pp. 64–70; C. Russell, *Causes of the English Civil War* (Oxford, 1990), pp. 168–84.

CONCLUSION

The crown likewise recognized the significance of the towns to the governance, economic well-being, and security of the early Stuart state, on one hand reinforcing borough liberties and corporate government, but on the other revealing mistrust. The governments of James I and Charles I, and both of these kings personally, paid close attention to corporate charters and borough governance in England as well as Ireland. The campaign in Ireland, particularly under James, to plant new corporate towns and to adjust the chartered liberties of established ones speaks to the crown's belief in the importance of well-ordered towns to the state. Central authority did not (and probably could not) micro-manage, but that said, the Privy Council involved itself in many aspects of urban governance, often doing so at the request of local actors. A significant portion of the Privy Council's business related to towns and urban issues in one way or another, especially in times of trade depression and war. While never entirely coherent nor fully formed, what may be described as an urban policy emerged across the period, as the crown attempted both to leverage the resources, financial and otherwise, of corporate towns and to control what it increasingly saw as their disorderly and popular tendencies.

Royal attitudes and policy toward corporate boroughs and their governments evolved over the course of the early seventeenth century. During James's reign, the alliance, begun long before, between borough governments and the crown grew.[2] The crown increasingly placed trust in corporations and borough magistrates to ensure the safety of the realm through governing the towns that were vital to trade but also to keeping order over a potentially volatile population. Yet even as the connection between crown and borough governors grew, central authorities became more doubtful about how towns fit into the framework of order and obedience that the crown promoted. Under the strains of war in the 1620s, the crown placed serious burdens on towns and pressed against borough liberties. King Charles's powerful concern with popularity led him to develop policies that altered charters, restricted liberties, and extended ecclesiastical authority to the detriment of corporate jurisdiction. He used quo warranto or its threat to align corporations with his ideas of order or to punish acts he found disobedient, something not typical of his father's reign. The enforcement of these policies – including the increasingly stringent crackdown on preaching and the realignment of boundaries between ecclesiastical and corporate jurisdictions in the 1630s – directly affected corporate liberties and self-government. Both James and Charles understood the importance of corporate towns to the peace and prosperity of the state, but Charles's took the more active, and even at times punitive, stance to manage borough government.

---

[2] For relations between urban governments and the crown going back to the fifteenth century, see Eliza Hartrich, *Politics and the Urban Sector in Fifteenth-Century England, 1413–1471* (Oxford, 2019). Even then, the connection between towns and the crown, particularly through charters, was strong (p. 26).

257

The evidence presented here has shown that Charles I's views on urban government, while not wholly negative, did affect relations between towns and the crown, particularly during the Personal Rule. Caroline government used a heavier hand than Jacobean on matters of interest to the towns. We can see flashes of dissent, as townsmen, occasionally even magistrates, spoke out in favor of borough liberties that connected with the broader liberties of the subject. This is apparent in the crisis over billeting in the 1620s, as people in some towns resisted and were accused of acting as a "free state," and the outspoken Canterbury citizen Thomas Scott drew a direct line between billeting and tyranny. Their grievances made their way into parliamentary debates and the Petition of Right. It also shows itself in other places: in complaints (even "riots") over preaching and ecclesiastical authority; in pushback against some prerogative taxation; in the invocation of Magna Carta by the town clerk of Stamford to defend the town's privileges; in the welcome given in Coventry and Chester to William Prynne as he journeyed to prison in 1637. Kevin Sharpe's view that "there was no breakdown in relationship between the cities and the central government" in the 1630s is essentially correct; there was much that bound towns and the crown from 1603 all the way to the outbreak of war, and obedience to the king's government was the norm throughout the period. At the same time, Sharpe perhaps underestimated the feeling of anxiety and even grievance that some Caroline policies, with their pressure on corporate liberties, engendered.[3] By the early 1640s, these policies came to be seen as attacks not just on local liberties, but illegal exercise of arbitrary authority on the part of central government.

The outbreak of war with Scotland and the subsequent return of parliament altered the political landscape, opening new streams of communication between center and localities and providing a platform for the airing of grievances from the provinces. Even as borough governors continued to carry out the work of the royal state, they worried about borough liberties. Complaints about the suppression of preaching proliferated, and in some towns Ship Money payment faltered or stopped. Boston, among other towns, petitioned the Council to keep its trained band at home and not be sent to York - a request that was promptly denied.[4] Evidence from the parliamentary elections of 1640 indicates that while traditional arrangements of patronage held in some boroughs, in others both local and national issues disrupted patterns and stirred more politicized choices. Rumors in Sandwich that Edward Nicholas was a papist tanked his candidacy for the Short Parliament, while Canterbury rejected the archbishop's nominee, as electors cried out against papists and cathedral clergy. Of the October 1640 election in Hastings, a correspondent commented that it "seems that the opinion is grown general that whoever is not Scottishly must be Popishly affected, the brethren of corporations especially being verily stiff in this opinion." This

---

[3] Kevin Sharpe, *The Personal Rule of Charles I* (New Haven, CT and London, 1992), p. 643.
[4] *CSPD 1640*, p. 538.

CONCLUSION

heated atmosphere permeated municipal elections, as well; the 1640 Hastings election for parliament reflected divisions that also split the mayoral election that year.[5] Differences between corporations and central authorities, among magistrates within corporations, and between borough governors and their inhabitants all mounted in the swirl of religious and political tensions presented by the Scottish war and its fallout.

Changes to which corporations had acquiesced in the 1620s and 1630s came back into play as parliament's return offered a platform for grievance and a venue for petitioning. The towns of Weymouth-Melcombe Regis, Boston, and Scarborough all sent petitions to parliament, the latter two complaining specifically of Ship Money.[6] A number of corporate towns used the opportunity to attempt to turn back the clock and reclaim liberties. Oxford's governors contested the encroachments of the university's 1636 charter, which had roundly subordinated the civic corporation. They petitioned the House of Lords, challenging several privileges confirmed in the university charter and claiming that Laud, as the university's chancellor, illicitly sought to assume royal power by humbling the corporation. As with a number of his interactions with corporations in the 1630s, Laud's behavior toward Oxford's civic corporation would emerge as a charge against him at his trial.[7] Canterbury, Worcester, and York were among the cathedral city corporations that sought to petition parliament regarding "agrievances" against ecclesiastical government in their respective jurisdictions. Canterbury's went on to authorize a search of records in the Tower and Exchequer to prove that the cathedral and other ecclesiastical lands were subject to taxation with the city.[8] Great Yarmouth petitioned parliament against Mr. Brooks, their curate, for causing vexation over preaching and usurping their

[5] KHLC, Sa/Ac7, fols 364v-66v; TNA, SP16/441, fol. 268 (Mayor and jurats of Sandwich to earl of Suffolk, 13 January 1640), SP16/448, fol. 66 (Mayor and jurats of Sandwich to Edward Nicholas, 19 March 1640), SP16/448, fol. 108 (earl of Northumberland to Sir John Pennington, 21 March 1640), SP16/470, fol. 124 (Francis Read to Robert Read, 26 October 1640); CSPD 1640, pp. 36, 56; Mark Kishlansky, Parliamentary Selection: Social and Political Choice in Early Modern England (Cambridge, 1986), pp. 107-13. See also Madeline V. Jones, "Election Issues and the Borough Electorates in Mid-Seventeenth Century Kent," Archaeologia Cantiana 85 (1970), 21. With the impending publication of the History of Parliament section for 1640-1660, we will know much more about how corporate towns responded electorally to the changed dynamics in 1640.
[6] Maureen Weinstock (ed.), Weymouth and Melcombe Regis Minute Book 1625-1660, Dorset Record Society, vol. 1 (Dorchester, 1964), p. 49; John Rushworth, Historical Collections, pt. 3, vol. 1 (London, 1721), p. 21.
[7] Alan Crossley, "City and University," in The History of the University of Oxford, vol. 4, Seventeenth Century Oxford, ed. N. Tyacke (Oxford, 1997), p. 115; William Laud, The History of the Troubles and Tryal of the Most Reverend Father in God, and Blessed Martyr, William Laud, Lord Archbishop of Canterbury, wrote by Himself during his Imprisonment in the Tower (London, 1695), p. 296.
[8] Canterbury Cathedral Archives, AC4 (Canterbury Burghmote Book, 1630-1658), fols 159v, 169; WAAS, A.14, Box 1/2 (Worcester Chamber Order Book 2), fols 199, 199v, 200, 203v, 204; YCA, B.36, fols 52, 53, 58. York also agreed to petition for a university.

259

URBAN GOVERNMENT AND THE EARLY STUART STATE

"ancient right" to nominate the parish clerk in the mid-1630s; they also agreed to petition to free the town from mustering outside their own boundaries.[9] Both corporate liberties and religious fears lay at the heart of many petitions.

As events unfolded in 1640–41, the impact for many towns of the crown's policy regarding preachers and preaching in the 1630s became apparent. When the corporation of Great Yarmouth met to discuss what grievances should be addressed by its parliamentary burgesses in 1640, "the want of preaching and other religious exercises which this town hath formerly enjoyed but cannot now have" topped the list, along with two matters affecting fishing.[10] Both Aldeburgh and Dunwich petitioned against their ministers for "divers abuses" and lack of satisfactory preaching.[11] Banbury petitioned parliament against their "wicked vicar" who "put downe preaching, and vexed them that weere godly who sought it elsewheere." The inhabitants of Maidstone – including the mayor and most of the corporation – made similar complaints about their minister Robert Barrell in a petition to parliament in May 1641.[12] Bishop Wren's aggressive policies in the diocese of Norwich provoked a groundswell of grievance. Norwich complained of Wren's church policies and their negative effect on the city, petitioning the Commons in both the Short and Long Parliaments.[13] Ipswich sent several members of the corporation to London in early 1641 in an attempt to gain the "free election" of the town's ministers by the townsmen, by petition to the king "and if need be to have the same confirmed by act of Parliament."[14] King's Lynn's corporation agreed to write to their parliamentary burgesses concerning the "grievances of the church which Bishop Wren caused to be done in our town."[15] The crown's ecclesiastical policies of the 1630s clearly stirred discontent in many corporate towns.

Complaints such as these should not be seen simply as special pleading from a localist perspective. In petitions to the Short and Long Parliaments and letters and instructions to parliamentary burgesses, provincial townsmen identified their grievances within a context of national politics. Petitions from Great Yarmouth and York included concerns specific to their towns (fishing in Yarmouth, a university in York), but both focused attention on national religious policy – the "innovations" brought in by Laud and others – and

---

[9] NRO, Y/C19/6, fols 474, 475.
[10] NRO, Y/C19/6, fol. 470v.
[11] SRO/I, EE1/P6/4 (draft petition to the House of Commons [n.d., but ca. 1641]), EE1/O1/1, fol. 93, EE6/1144/11, fol. 130v.
[12] Wallace Notestein (ed.), *The Journal of Sir Symonds D'Ewes* (New Haven, CT, 1923), p. 77; *Journal of the House of Lords*, vol. 4 (London, 1767–1830), p. 108, *British History Online*, accessed 15 December 2020, www.british-history.ac.uk/lords-jrnl/vol4/pp107-; L.B. Larking (ed.), *Proceedings, Principally in the County of Kent, In Connection with the Parliaments Called in 1640* (London, 1862), pp. 202–5.
[13] HMC, *4th Report*, pt. 1 (London, 1874), p. 24; J.T. Evans, *Seventeenth-Century Norwich: Politics, Religion and Government, 1620–1690* (Oxford, 1979), pp. 109, 112–13.
[14] Nathaniel Bacon, *The Annalls of Ipsw'che*, ed. W. Richardson (Ipswich, 1884), p. 526.
[15] KLTH, KL/C10/7, fol. 54v.

260

CONCLUSION

its impact. In Newcastle, some prominent merchants (who were not among the town's aldermen at the time) had clear ideas about national issues that they attempted to convey to their town's parliamentary burgesses. Anthony Errington, a warden of Newcastle's Merchant Adventurers, submitted a petition in March 1640 to the mayor of Newcastle, asking (with the "good liking" of the governing body) to give instructions to Sir Peter Riddell and Sir Thomas Riddell about the town's concerns. Errington's petition aired complaints about the soap and coal trades and customs fees, but began by urging the parliamentary burgesses to take care to maintain the "orthodox faith" of the church, oppose any innovations "both in doctrine or discipline," and stand for the liberties and freedoms of the subjects, "maintaining Magna Carta and the other fundamental parliamentary laws." "These two particulars being faithfully preserved will no doubt settle both Church and State in truth and peace, but in either if there be a sufferance of alteration we may in short time fear a loss of both." He hoped they would take note of the "grievances of the commonwealth," including the "intolerable burden" of Ship Money and monopolies.[16] While the oligarchical magistrates of Newcastle did not take up his petition (and in fact seem to have reported him to the Privy Council), Errington articulated a position that directly linked national and local concerns and identified both religion and the liberties of the subject as matters requiring parliament's attention.

National grievances arising out of specifically urban and corporate contexts emerged in the trials of William Laud, archbishop of Canterbury, and to a lesser extent that of Thomas Wentworth, earl of Strafford. In both trials, alleged attacks on chartered liberties and borough government became examples of tyranny, corruption, and the overthrow of law. Laud's trial, which only began in earnest in 1644, but for which initial charges were devised in 1641,[17] featured several accusations stemming from his intervention into corporate governance in the 1630s, especially on religious matters. In addition to the charge that he oppressed borough governors in Dedham regarding Ship Money, he was alleged to have accepted bribes from men in Chester involving a High Commission case, engaged in corruption in a legal suit involving ministers in Colchester, and persecuted Henry Sherfield, recorder of Salisbury, for breaking a window in his parish church. Laud's censure of John Workman, lecturer of Gloucester, and of members of that corporation for making an annuity to their suppressed lecturer also featured prominently in the trial. The archbishop's alleged attempt to "exempt the Clergy from the Civil Magistrate," related to his orders to submit the civic sword ("the emblem of Temporal Power") during divine service in

---

[16] TNA, SP16/449, fols 65 (Examination of A. Errington, 30 March 1640), 67 (Petition of A. Errington to the mayor of Newcastle, [March 1640]), 69–70 (Copies of Errington petition, with additions, 26 March 1640). See also Roger Howell, *Newcastle upon Tyne and the Puritan Revolution: A Study of the Civil War in North England* (Oxford, 1967), pp. 113–15 on Errington's religious affiliations.

[17] On the timing of the trial, see Nicholas R.C. Forward, "The Arrest and Trial of Archbishop Laud" (MPhil thesis, University of Birmingham, 2012), pp. 34–6, 97.

corporate cities and towns, as well as his insertion of churchmen as JPs into corporate charters were cited as examples of illegal overreach of ecclesiastical authority.

Both Laud's and Strafford's trials featured charges of overturning or threats to corporate charters and liberties. Laud allegedly prompted the quo warranto against the charter of Coventry "only for supposed favours shew'd to Mr. Pryn in his passage that way" and instigated the quo warranto against Shrewsbury's charter.[18] In Strafford's trial, among the many "treasonous" activities in Ireland cited was his arbitrary rejection of the corporate liberties of the city of Dublin. Speaking of charters granted to the city by previous English kings, Strafford allegedly said that "their Charters were nothing worth, and did bind the King no further than he pleased." Debate arose on the different context of Ireland from England, but the charge still suggests acute concern about the safety of chartered privileges.[19] In both trials, efforts to restrict or overthrow corporate liberties came to be seen as dangerous attempts against liberties of the realm more broadly. While using accusations made in 1641 to understand attitudes from some years earlier merits caution, the charges in these trials reveal anxieties that royal policies in the 1630s generated for corporate towns.

At the same time, the crown's policies toward the towns, for all the tensions they bred, cannot be said to have driven borough magistrates unequivocally into the arms of Parliament. Each town had its own motivations and interests, and these aligned (or did not align) with royal policy in varied ways. It should be remembered that magistrates in some coastal towns actively collected Ship Money even in 1640; they saw the benefit of this national policy to their economic well-being and chose to engage with it despite its unpopularity. The earl of Strafford would be impeached for treason in November 1640, yet only a few months earlier the corporations of both Hull (a town with a puritan reputation that would bar the gates against the king in 1642) and York (a future royalist garrison) chose the earl of Strafford as their high steward.[20] When civil war eventually erupted, more towns and cities can be found among the parliamentarians than the royalists,[21] yet some remained loyal to the king, even those that had experienced serious disturbances and divisions over matters of religion or taxes or participation. Shrewsbury, a target of the quo warranto push of the 1630s, had its governing constitution significantly revised by the crown amid divisions among magistrates over godly religion and popular participation. While by 1642, supporters of both parliament and the king could be

[18] Laud, *Troubles and Tryal*, pp. 153, 232-3, 244, 252, 260, 274, 287-9, 301, 307, 332-3, 334.
[19] *The Tryal of Thomas, Earl of Strafford, Lord Lieutenant of Ireland, upon and Impeachment of High Treason by the Commons Assembled in Parliament* (London, 1680), p. 156.
[20] HHC, BRB3, pp. 528, 530; YCA, B.36, fol. 39v. Strafford was impeached and imprisoned in November 1640; his trial began in March 1641. Ronald G. Asch, "Wentworth, Thomas, First Earl of Strafford (1593-1641)," *ODNB*, accessed 5 September 2020, https://doi-org.ezproxy.lib.uh.edu/10.1093/ref:odnb/29056.
[21] Anthony Fletcher, *The Outbreak of the English Civil War* (London, 1981), pp. 393-400.

CONCLUSION

found among its governors, when the crisis came, Shrewsbury held for the king. York's corporation, which had been required to submit its royal charter to King Charles for revision and suffered a painful blow to its corporate honor vis-à-vis the cathedral there, nevertheless remained in the king's camp. The city's magistrates held mixed views and certainly chafed under the royal garrison there, but royalists retained control.[22] Other towns seemed to work hard to maintain neutrality, not necessarily out of intense localism but perhaps out of pragmatic concerns to keep their options open.[23]

There is no question that all the corporate boroughs examined in this study valued their liberties and struggled in different ways with policies affecting their governance and business. It would be convenient from an explanatory point of view if towns and cities were, *tout court*, predisposed to the parliamentarian perspective. But just as the county gentry did not speak with one voice, and "county communities" have been shown to represent many different perspectives, loyalties, and agendas, so corporate towns varied in how they responded to the political crisis and often struggled with rifts within their own corporate bodies. And even after the trauma and divisions of civil war, as Paul Halliday has shown, the divided corporate bodies that emerged in England's towns regularly sought to find stability through charters of incorporation granted by the later Stuart kings, as well as through the king's courts.[24]

Royalist characterizations of England's towns and cities as "naturally malignant" or as "petty free state[s] against monarchy" have shaped understandings of urban government and the relationship of corporate towns to the crown since the seventeenth century.[25] But to accept that view is to ignore the many ways that urban governments were increasingly tied into the network of

---

[22] Hugh Owen and John Blakeway, A *History of Shrewsbury*, vol. 1 (London, 1825), pp. 415-18; "The Seventeenth Century: Politics and the Civil War," in *VCH Yorkshire, The City of York*, ed. P.M. Tillott (London, 1961), pp. 186-198, *British History Online*, accessed 23 May 2021, www.british-history.ac.uk/vch/yorks/city-of-york/pp186-198. A 1642 speech drafted for the mayor of Shrewsbury to welcome the king to the town (but never delivered) emphasized their "extasie of joy" at the king's presence, but also concern to protect borough liberties. The mayor, draper John Studely, may have felt less joy at the prospect of the royal presence than did the town clerk, Thomas Owen, or recorder, Timothy Tourneure, who likely wrote it. W.A. Leighton (ed.), "The Mayor of Shrewsbury's Intended Speech 1642," *Transactions of the Shropshire Archaeological and Natural History Society*, 1st Ser., 2 (1879), 389-9.

[23] Roger Howell, "Neutralism, Conservativism, and Political Alignment in the English Revolution: The Case of the Towns, 1642-9," in J.S. Morrill (ed.), *Reactions to the English Civil War 1642-1649* (New York, 1982), pp. 67-77; John Morrill, *The Revolt of the Provinces: Conservatives and Radicals in the English Civil War 1630-1650* (London, 1976), pp. 38-9, 167; *RBL*, vol. 4, pp. 312-13; Fletcher, *Outbreak*, pp. 397-8.

[24] Paul Halliday, *Dismembering the Body Politic: Partisan Politics in England's Towns 1650-1730* (Cambridge, 1998), pp. xii-xiii, 29-55, 151-61.

[25] Edward, Earl of Clarendon, *The History of the Rebellion and Civil Wars in England*, vol. 1 (Oxford, 1843), p. 273; William Cavendish quoted in Mark Goldie, "The Unacknowledged Republic: Officeholding in Early Modern England," in Tim Harris (ed.), *The Politics of the Excluded, c. 1500-1850* (Basingstoke, 2001), p. 155.

governance in the early seventeenth century and helped shape the early modern state. The relationship between towns and the crown was dynamic, complex, and multi-directional. Incorporated towns had an important stake in connection with the crown, and central authorities, while always somewhat dubious of them, understood their importance to the peace and prosperity of the realm. The magistrates of towns and cities were confident that they knew best how to run their localities and wished to avoid unnecessary attention of other levels of government. At the same time, their very liberties came from the hand of the monarch, necessitating engagement. In all sorts of ways – through charters, local governance, poor relief programs, alehouse regulation, trade regulation, militia companies, even ship charges and taxes – corporate towns were negotiating their relationship with the crown and trying to shape royal policy. The early Stuart monarchs sought to take advantage of what the towns had to offer, seeing them as essential for public order and defense, as well as royal revenues. That central authorities also tried to curb tendencies in towns seen to be dangerous or popular is also clear; policies targeting corporate liberties, particularly during the Personal Rule of Charles I, though never systematic, did cause friction and raise anxiety among corporate towns. Yet we should not only look at the relationship between towns and the crown through the lens of the problems that beset it. Identifying with both the town and the nation, borough corporations and the men who constituted them were pulled in multiple directions, just as were members of the gentry who governed the counties. Provincial towns were not backwaters resistant to or remote from the interests of central government, the needs of the state, or the issues and controversies of the day. They were active participants in them.

Bibliography

Manuscripts

British Library, London

Additional Manuscripts
Egerton Manuscripts
Harleian Manuscripts
Lansdowne Manuscripts
Stowe Manuscripts

The National Archives, Kew

Chancery Records
Privy Council Registers
Signet Office Registers
Star Chamber Records
State Papers

Bodleian Library, Oxford

Bankes Manuscripts
Tanner Manuscripts

Cambridge University Library, Cambridge

William Whiteway's Commonplace Book

Cambridgeshire Archives, Ely

Cambridge Borough Records

Canterbury Cathedral Archives, Canterbury

Canterbury City Archives
Thomas Scott Papers
Woodruff Letters

BIBLIOGRAPHY

Cheshire Archives and Local Studies, Chester
Cheshire Diocesan Records

Chester City Record Office
Chester City Archives

Coventry Archives
Coventry City Archives

Devon Archives and Local Studies, Exeter
Exeter City Archives

East Sussex Record Office, Brighton
Rye Borough Records

Gloucestershire Archives, Gloucester
Gloucester Borough Records
Tewkesbury Borough Records

Hampshire Record Office, Winchester
Winchester City Archives
Jervoise of Herriard MSS (Henry Sherfield papers)

Herefordshire Archive and Records Centre, Hereford
Hereford City Archives

Hertfordshire Archives and Local Studies, Hertford
Hertford Borough Records
St. Albans Borough Records

266

BIBLIOGRAPHY

Hull History Centre

Kingston-upon-Hull Borough Records

Kent History and Libraries Center, Maidstone

Dover Borough Records
Knatchbull Manuscripts (Thomas Scott of Canterbury papers)
Maidstone Borough Records
Sandwich Borough Records

King's Lynn Town Hall

King's Lynn Borough Records

Lambeth Palace Library

Shrewsbury Papers

Lincolnshire Archives, Lincoln

Lincoln City Archives
Grantham Borough Records

Norfolk Record Office, Norwich

Great Yarmouth Borough Records
Norwich City Records

Nottinghamshire Archives

Nottingham Hall Books
Newark-upon-Trent Hall Book

Record Office for Leicestershire, Leicester, and Rutland, Leicester

Leicester Borough Records

267

BIBLIOGRAPHY

Shakespeare Birthplace Trust, Stratford-upon-Avon

Stratford Borough Records

Shropshire Records and Research Centre, Shrewsbury

Bridgenorth Corporation Minutes
Ludlow Borough Records
Shrewsbury Borough Records
Wenlock Corporation Minutes

Suffolk Archives, Ipswich

Aldeburgh Borough Records
Dunwich Borough Records
Ipswich Borough Records

Wiltshire and Swindon History Centre, Chippenham

Salisbury City Archives

Worcestershire Archives and Archaeology Service, Worcester

Worcester City Archives
Coventry Docquets (Croome Collection)

York City Archives

York Hall Books

Printed primary sources

Acts of the Privy Council of England. 13 vols, 1613-1631. London, 1921-1964.
Bacon, Nathaniel. The Annalls of Ipsw'che. Ed. William Richardson. Ipswich, 1884.
Bailey, John F. (ed.). Transcription of the Minutes of the Corporation of Boston. Vol. 2, 1608-1638. Boston, 1981.
Baker, W.T. (ed.). Records of the Borough of Nottingham. Vol. 5, 1625-1702. London and Nottingham, 1900.

268

BIBLIOGRAPHY

Bateson, Mary (ed.). *Records of the Borough of Leicester*. Vol. 3, *1509–1603*. Cambridge, 1905.

Bidwell, William B. and Maija Jansson (eds). *Proceedings in Parliament 1626*. 4 vols. New Haven, CT, 1992.

Birch, Walter (ed.). *The Royal Charters of the City of Lincoln, Henry II to William III*. Cambridge, 1911.

Blackstone, William. *Commentaries on the Laws of England*. 2 vols. Philadelphia, PA, 1893.

Bond, Shelagh (ed.). *The Chamber Order Book of Worcester*. Worcestershire Historical Society Publications, NS, vol. 8. Worcester, 1974.

Boyle, J.R. and F.W. Dendy (eds). *Extracts from the Records of the Merchant Adventurers of Newcastle-upon-Tyne*. Surtees Society, vol. 93. Durham, 1895.

Broadway, Jan, Richard Cust, and Stephen K. Roberts (eds). *A Calendar of the Doquets of Lord Keeper Coventry 1625–1640, Part 1*. List and Index Society Special Series, vol. 34. London, 2004.

Bruce, John (ed.). *Original Letters, and Other Documents, Relating to the Benefactions of William Laud, Archbishop of Canterbury, to the County of Berks*. London, 1841.

Calendar of State Papers, Domestic Series, of the Reign of James I. 5 vols. London, 1857–1859.

Calendar of State Papers, Domestic Series, of the Reign of Charles I. 22 vols. London, 1858–97.

Calendar of State Papers Relating to Ireland of the Reign of James I. 5 vols. London, 1872–1880.

Calendar of State Papers Relating to Ireland of the Reign of Charles I. 2 vols. London, 1900–1901.

Challenor, Bromley (ed.). *Selections from the Municipal Chronicles of the Borough of Abingdon from A.D. 1555 to A.D. 1897*. Abingdon, 1898.

Chanter, J.R. and Thomas Wainwright (eds). *Reprint of the Barnstaple Records*. 2 vols. Barnstaple, 1900.

Cobbett's Complete Collection of State Trials. Vol. 3. London, 1809.

Colchester Borough. *The Charters and Letters Patent Granted to the Borough by Richard I and Succeeding Sovereigns*. Colchester, [1904].

Connor, W.J. (ed.). *The Southampton Mayor's Book of 1606–1608*. Southampton Records Series, vol. 21. Southampton, 1978.

Cooper, C.H. (ed.). *Annals of Cambridge*. Vol. 3. Cambridge, 1845.

Dalton, Michael. *The Countrey Justice*. London, 1635.

East, Robert (ed.). *Extracts from the Records in the Possession of the Municipal Corporation of the Borough of Portsmouth*. Portsmouth, 1891.

Fielding, John (ed.). *The Diary of Robert Woodford, 1637–1641*. Camden 5th Ser., vol. 42. Cambridge, 2013.

Gentleman, Tobias. *England's Way to Win Wealth*. London, 1614.

Gibson, J.S.W. and E.R.C. Brinkworth (eds). *Banbury Corporation Records, Tudor and Stuart*. Banbury Historical Society Publications, vol. 15. Banbury, 1977.

269

BIBLIOGRAPHY

Gidden, H.W. (ed.). *The Charters of the Borough of Southampton*. Vol. 2. Southampton, 1910.

Giuseppi, M.S. (ed.). *Calendar of the Manuscripts of the Most Honourable Marquess of Salisbury*. Vol. 19. London, 1965.

Great Britain. *The Statutes of the Realm*. 11 vols. London, 1810-1828.

Groombridge, Margaret (ed.). *Chester City Council Minutes, 1603-1642*. Lancashire and Cheshire Record Society, vol. 106. Blackpool, 1956.

Guilding, J.M. (ed.). *Reading Records: Diary of the Corporation of Reading*. Vols 2 and 3. London, 1895-1896.

Heylyn, Peter. *Cyprianus Anglicus*. London, 1671.

Historical Manuscripts Commission. *4th Report*, pt. 1. London, 1874.

——. *12th Report, Appendix*, pt. 9. London, 1891.

——. *13th Report, Appendix*, pts 3 and 4. London, 1892.

——. *The Manuscripts of the Earl Cowper, KG, Preserved at Melbourne Hall, Derbyshire*. Vol. 1. London, 1888.

——. *Report on Manuscripts in Various Collections*. Vol. 7. London, 1914.

Hobbes, Thomas. *Leviathan, or the Matter, Forme, & Power of a Common-wealth Ecclesiastical and Civill*. London, 1651.

Hobson, M.G. and H.E. Salter (eds). *Oxford Council Acts 1626-1665*. Oxford Historical Society, vol. 95. Oxford, 1933.

Hoyle, R.W. and Danae Tankard (eds). *Heard Before the King: Registers of Petitions to James I, 1603-16*. List and Index Society Special Series, vol. 38. London, 2006.

Hyde, Edward, Earl of Clarendon. *The History of the Rebellion and Civil Wars in England*. Vol. 1. Oxford, 1843.

James, William (ed.). *The Charters and Other Documents Relating to the King's Town and Parish of Maidstone*. London, 1825.

Johnson, Robert C. *et al.* (eds). *Proceedings in Parliament 1628*. 6 vols. New Haven, CT and London, 1977-1983.

Kemp, Thomas (ed.). *The Black Book of Warwick*. Warwick, 1898.

Kettle, Ann (ed.). "Matthew Cradocke's Book of Remembrance 1614-15." In *Collections for a History of Staffordshire*. Staffordshire Records Society, 4th Ser., vol. 16. Stafford, 1994, pp. 67-169.

Kingsbury, Susan M. (ed.). *The Records of the Virginia Company of London*. Vol. 4. Washington, DC, 1935.

Larkin, James (ed.). *Stuart Royal Proclamations*. Vol. 2, *Royal Proclamations of King Charles I 1625-1646*. Oxford, 1983.

Larkin, James and Paul Hughes (eds). *Stuart Royal Proclamations*. Vol. 1, *Royal Proclamations of King James I 1603-1625*. Oxford, 1973.

Larking, L.B. (ed.). *Proceedings, Principally in the County of Kent, in Connection with the Parliaments Called in 1640, and Especially with the Committee on Religion Appointed in that Year*. London, 1862.

Laud, William. *The History of the Troubles and Tryal of the Most Reverend Father in*

270

BIBLIOGRAPHY

God and Blessed Martyr William Laud, Archbishop of Canterbury, wrote by Himself during his Imprisonment in the Tower. London, 1695.

——. *The Works of the Reverend Father in God William Laud.* Vol. 5. Oxford, 1853.

Leighton, W.L. (ed.). "The Mayor of Shrewsbury's Intended Speech, 1642." *Transactions of the Shropshire Archaeological and Natural History Society* 2 (1879), 398–9.

Maidstone. *Records of Maidstone.* Maidstone, 1926.

Maitland, F.W. and Mary Bateson (eds). *The Charters of the Borough of Cambridge.* Cambridge, 1901.

Manship, Henry. *The History of Great Yarmouth.* Ed. Charles John Palmer. Great Yarmouth, 1854.

Markham, C.A. and J.C. Cox (eds). *The Records of the Borough of Northampton.* 2 vols. Northampton, 1898.

Martin, G.H. (ed.). *The Royal Charters of Grantham.* Leicester, 1963.

Mayo, Charles H. and Arthur Gould (eds). *The Municipal Records of the Borough of Dorchester Dorset.* Exeter, 1908.

McIlwain, C.H. (ed.). *The Political Works of James I.* Cambridge, MA, 1918.

Moody, W.T. (ed.). "Ulster Plantation Papers." *Analecta Hibernica* No. 8 (1938).

Newton, A. Percival (ed.). "Lord Sackville's Papers Respecting Virginia, 1613–1631." *American Historical Review* 27 (1922), 493–538.

Nicolls, Ferdinando. *The Life and Death of Mr. Ignatius Jurdain.* London, 1654.

Notestein, W., F. Relf and H. Simpson (eds). *Commons Debates 1621.* 7 vols. New Haven, CT, 1935.

Orders appointed by His Maiestie to be straitly obserued, for the preuenting and remedying of the dearth of Graine and other Victuall, Dated the 28. day of September 1630. London, 1630.

Pritchard, C. Fleetwood (ed.). *Reading Charters, Acts, and Orders 1253–1911.* Reading and London, 1913.

Prynne, William. *Canterburies Doome.* London, 1646.

Quintrell, B.W. (ed.). *The Maynard Lieutenancy Book, 1608–1639.* Essex Historical Documents 3. Chelmsford, 1993.

Rushworth, John. *Historical Collections.* Pt. 3, vol. 1. London, 1721.

Scott, Thomas. "A Discourse of Polletique and Civill Honor." In G.D. Scull (ed.), *Dorothea Scott, otherwise Gotherson and Hogben of Egerton House, Kent, 1611–1680.* Oxford, 1883, pp. 145–98.

Sheppard, Steve (ed.). *The Selected Writings and Speeches of Sir Edward Coke.* Vol. 1. Indianapolis, IN, 2003.

Sheppard, William. *Of Corporations, Fraternities, and Guilds ... With Forms and Presidents of Charters of Corporation.* London, 1659.

Slack, Paul (ed.). *Poverty in Early-Stuart Salisbury.* Wiltshire Record Society, vol. 31. Devizes, 1975.

Spalding, Ruth (ed.). *The Diary of Bulstrode Whitelocke 1605–1675.* Oxford, 1990.

Stephens, W.R.W. and F.T. Madge (eds). *Documents Relating to the History of*

271

BIBLIOGRAPHY

the Cathedral Church of Winchester in the Seventeenth Century. London and Winchester, 1897.

Stevenson, W.H. and James Raine (eds). Records of the Borough of Nottingham. Vol. 4, 1547–1625. London and Nottingham, 1889.

Stocks, Helen and W.H. Stevenson (eds). Records of the Borough of Leicester. Vol. 4, 1603–1688. Cambridge, 1923.

Studley, Peter. The Looking-Glases of Schisme. London, 1634.

Swinnock, George. The Life and Death of Mr. Tho. Wilson, Minister of Maidstone, in the County of Kent. London, 1672.

Webb, John (ed.). Poor Relief in Elizabethan Ipswich. Suffolk Records Society, vol. 9. Ipswich, 1966.

Weinstock, Maureen (ed.). Weymouth and Melcombe Regis Minute Book 1625–1660. Dorset Record Society, vol. 1. Dorchester, 1964.

Whiteway, William. William Whiteway of Dorchester His Diary 1618 to 1635. Ed. Sarah Bridges, trans. Brian Bates. Dorset Record Society, vol. 12. Dorchester, 1991.

Worth, R.N. (ed.). Calendar of the Plymouth Municipal Records. Plymouth, 1893.

Published secondary works

Ashton, Robert. The City and the Court, 1603–1643. Cambridge, 1979.

——. "The Parliamentary Agitation for Free Trade in the Opening Years of the Reign of James I." Past & Present No. 38 (1967), 40-55.

——. "Jacobean Free Trade Again," Past & Present No. 43 (1969), 151-7.

Atherton, Ian. "Cathedrals, Laudianism, and the British Churches." Historical Journal 53 (2010), 895-918.

Atherton, Ian and Victor Morgan. "Revolution and Retrenchment: The Cathedral, 1630–1720." In Ian Atherton et al. (eds). Norwich Cathedral: Church, City, and Diocese, 1096–1996. London, 1996.

Aylmer, Gerald. "St. Patrick's Day 1628 in Witham, Essex." Past & Present No. 61 (1973), 139-48.

Baigent, Francis and James Millard. A History of the Ancient Town and Manor of Basingstoke in the County of Southampton, with a Brief Account of the Siege of Basing House, AD 1643–1645. Vol. 1. Basingstoke and London, 1889.

Baker, J.H. An Introduction to English Legal History. 3rd edn. London, 1990.

Barnes, Thomas G. "Deputies not Principals, Lieutenants not Captains: The Institutional Failure of Lieutenancy in the 1620s." In M.C. Fissel (ed.), War and Government in Britain, 1598–1650. Manchester and New York, 1991, pp. 58-86.

——. Somerset 1625–1640: A County's Government During the "Personal Rule." Cambridge, MA, 1961.

Beaver, Daniel C. "'Fruits of Unrulie Multitudes': Liberty, Popularity, and Meanings of Violence in the English Atlantic, 1623–1625." Journal of British Studies 59 (2020), 372-95.

BIBLIOGRAPHY

——. *Parish Communities and Religious Conflict in the Vale of Gloucester, 1590–1690.* Cambridge, MA, 1998.

——. "Sovereignty by the Book: English Corporations, Atlantic Plantations and Literate Order, 1557–1650." In Chris Kyle and Jason Peacey (eds), *Connecting Centre and Locality: Political Communication in Early Modern England.* Manchester, 2020, pp. 157–73.

Beier, A.L. "Poverty and Progress in Early Modern England." In A.L. Beier, David Cannadine and James Rosenheim (eds), *The First Modern Society: Essays in English History in Honour of Lawrence Stone.* Cambridge and New York, 1989, pp. 201–39.

Bellany, Alistair. "'The Brightness of the Noble Lieutenants Action': An Intellectual Ponders Buckingham's Assassination." *English Historical Review* 118 (2003), 1242–63.

Bennett, Judith. *Ale, Beer, and Brewers: Women's Work in a Changing World, 1300–1600.* Oxford and New York, 1996.

Bernard, G.W. "The Church of England c. 1529–c.1642." *History* 75 (1990), 183–206.

Bilder, Mary Sarah. "The Corporate Origins of Judicial Review." *Yale Law Journal* 116 (2006), 502–66.

——. "English Settlement and Local Government." In Michael Grossberg and Christopher Tomlins (eds), *The Cambridge History of Law in America,* vol. 1, *Early America (1580–1815).* Cambridge, 2008.

Bond, Shelagh and Norman Evans. "The Process of Granting Charters to English Boroughs, 1547–1649." *English Historical Review* 91 (1976), 102–20.

Boothroyd, Benjamin. *The History of the Ancient Borough of Pontefract.* Pontefract, 1807.

Bower, Jacqueline. "Kent Towns, 1540–1640." In Michael Zell (ed.), *Early Modern Kent, 1540–1640.* Woodbridge, 2000, pp. 141–76.

Boynton, Lindsay. *The Elizabethan Militia, 1558–1638.* London, 1967.

——. "Martial Law and the Petition of Right." *English Historical Review* 79 (1964), 255–84.

Braddick, Michael J. *The Nerves of State: Taxation and the Financing of the English State, 1558–1714.* Manchester and New York, 1996.

——. *Parliamentary Taxation in Seventeenth-Century England: Local Administration and Response.* Woodbridge, 1994.

——. *State Formation in Early Modern England c. 1550–1700.* Cambridge, 2000.

Brown, Cornelius. *The Annals of Newark-upon-Trent.* London, 1879.

Brown, James. "Alehouse Licensing and State Formation in Early Modern England." In Jonathan Herring *et al.* (eds), *Intoxication and Society: Problematic Pleasures of Drugs and Alcohol.* Basingstoke, 2013, pp. 110–32.

Canny, Nicholas. *Making Ireland British, 1580–1650.* Oxford, 2001.

Carruthers, Robert. *The History of Huntingdon, from the Earliest to the Present Times.* Huntingdon, 1824.

BIBLIOGRAPHY

Chauncey, Henry. *The Historical Antiquities of Hertfordshire*. Vol. 2. London, 1826.

Christianson, Paul. "Arguments on Billeting and Martial Law in the Parliament of 1628." *Historical Journal* 37 (1994), 539-67.

Clark, Peter. *The English Alehouse: A Social History 1200-1830*. London and New York, 1983.

——. *English Provincial Society from the Reformation to the Revolution: Religion, Politics and Society in Kent 1500-1640*. Hassocks, 1977.

——. "'The Ramoth-Gilead of the Good': Urban Change and Political Radicalism at Gloucester 1540-1640." In Peter Clark, A.G.R. Smith and Nicholas Tyacke (eds), *The English Commonwealth 1547-1640: Essays in Politics and Society Presented to Joel Hurstfield*. Leicester, 1979, pp. 167-87.

——. "Thomas Scott and the Growth of Urban Opposition to the Early Stuart Regime." *Historical Journal* 21 (1978), 1-26.

Clark, Peter and Lyn Murfin. *A History of Maidstone: The Making of a County Town*. Stroud, 1995.

Clark, Peter and Paul Slack (eds). *Crisis and Order in English Towns: Essays in Urban History*. Toronto, 1972.

——. *English Towns in Transition, 1500-1700*. Oxford, 1976.

Cogswell, Thomas. *The Blessed Revolution: English Politics and the Coming of War, 1621-1624*. Cambridge, 1989.

——. "The Canterbury Election of 1626 and *Parliamentary Selection* Revisited." *Historical Journal* 63 (2020), 291-315.

——. *Home Divisions: Aristocracy, the State and Provincial Conflict*. Manchester, 1998.

——. "The Lord Admiral, the Parliament-Men, and the Narrow Seas, 1625-27." In Chris Kyle and Jason Peacey (eds), *Connecting Centre and Locality: Political Communication in Early Modern England*. Manchester, 2020, pp. 44-65.

——. "Ten Demi-Culverins for Aldeburgh: Whitehall, the Dunkirkers, and a Suffolk Fishing Community, 1625-1630." *Journal of British Studies* 58 (2019), 315-37.

Cokayne, G.E. *Some Account of the Lord Mayors and Sheriffs of the City of London during the First Quarter of the Seventeenth Century*. London, 1897.

Collinson, Patrick. "The Monarchical Republic of Queen Elizabeth I." *Bulletin of the John Rylands Library* 69 (1987), 394-424.

Collinson, Patrick, Nigel Ramsay and Margaret Sparks (eds). *A History of Canterbury Cathedral*. Oxford, 1995.

Coulton, Barbara. "Rivalry and Religion: The Borough of Shrewsbury in the Early Stuart Period." *Midland History* 28 (2003), 28-50.

Courtney, Paul. "Armies, Militias and Urban Landscapes: England, France and the Low Countries 1500-1900." In A. Green and R. Leech (eds), *Cities in the World, 1500-2000*. Leeds, 2006, pp. 167-94.

Cramsie, John. "Commercial Projects and the Fiscal Policy of James VI and I." *Historical Journal* 43 (2000), 345-64.

BIBLIOGRAPHY

——. *Kingship and Crown Finance under James VI and I, 1603–1625.* Woodbridge, 2002.

Cressy, David. "Conflict, Consensus, and the Willingness to Wink: The Erosion of Community in Charles I's England." *Huntingdon Library Quarterly* 61 (1998), 131–49.

Cross, Claire. *Urban Magistrates and Ministers: Religion in Hull and Leeds from the Reformation to the Civil War.* Borthwick Papers, No. 67. York, 1985.

Crossley, Alan. "City and University." In *The History of the University of Oxford. Vol. 4, Seventeenth Century Oxford.* Ed. N. Tyacke. Oxford, 1997, pp. 105–34.

Curtis, Muriel. *Some Disputes between the City and Cathedral Authorities of Exeter.* Manchester, 1932.

Cust, Richard. "Anti-Puritanism and Urban Politics: Charles I and Great Yarmouth." *Historical Journal* 35 (1992), 1–26.

——. "Charles I and Popularity." In Thomas Cogswell, Richard Cust and Peter Lake (eds), *Politics, Religion, and Popularity in Early Stuart Britain: Essays in Honour of Conrad Russell.* Cambridge, 2002, pp. 235–58.

——. *The Forced Loan and English Politics, 1626–28.* Oxford, 1987.

——. "'Patriots' and 'Popular Spirits': Narratives of Conflict in Early Stuart Politics." In N. Tyacke (ed.), *The English Revolution, c. 1590–1720: Politics. Religion, and Communities.* Manchester and New York, 2007, pp. 43–61.

——. "Reading for Magistracy: The Mental World of Sir John Newdigate." In John F. McDiarmid (ed.), *The Monarchical Republic of Early Modern England: Essays in Response to Patrick Collinson.* Farnham, 2007, pp. 181–200.

Cuttica, Cesare. "Thomas Scott of Canterbury (1566–1635): Patriot, Civic Radical, Puritan." *History of European Ideas* 34 (2008), 475–89.

Cuttica, Cesare and Markku Peltonen (eds). *Democracy and Anti-democracy in Early Modern England, 1603–1689.* Leiden and Boston, MA, 2019.

Davies, Julian. *The Caroline Captivity of the Church: Charles I and the Remoulding of Anglicanism.* Oxford, 1992.

Dean, David M. "Parliament, Privy Council, and Local Politics in Elizabethan England: The Yarmouth-Lowestoft Fishing Dispute." *Albion* 22 (1990), 39–64.

Dickinson, William. *The History and Antiquities of the Town of Newark.* London, 1819.

Drakard, John. *The History of Stamford in the County of Lincoln.* Stamford, 1822.

Dyer, Alan. "Warwickshire Towns under the Tudors and Stuarts." *Warwickshire History* 3 (1976–77), 122–35.

Eales, Jacqueline. *Puritans and Roundheads: The Harleys of Brampton Bryan and the Outbreak of the English Civil War.* Cambridge, 1990.

——. "The Rise of Ideological Politics in Kent, 1558–1640." In Michael Zell (ed.), *Early Modern Kent, 1540–1640.* Woodbridge, 2000, pp. 279–314.

Ellis, George Alfred. *The History and Antiquities of the Borough and Town of Weymouth and Melcombe Regis.* Weymouth and London, 1829.

Estabrook, Carl. "In the Mist of Ceremony: Cathedral and Community in

BIBLIOGRAPHY

Seventeenth-Century Wells." In Susan Amussen and Mark Kishlansky (eds), *Political Culture and Cultural Politics in Early Modern England.* Manchester and New York, 1995, pp. 133-61.

——. "Ritual, Space, and Authority in Seventeenth-Century English Cathedral Cities." *Journal of Interdisciplinary History* 32 (2002), 593-620.

Evans, Connie S. "'An Echo of the Multitude': The Intersection of Governmental and Private Poverty Initiatives in Early Modern Exeter." *Albion* 32 (2000), 408-28.

Evans, J.T. "The Decline of Oligarchy in Seventeenth Century Norwich." *Journal of British Studies* 14 (1974), 46-77.

——. *Seventeenth-Century Norwich: Politics, Religion and Government, 1620-1690.* Oxford, 1979.

Everitt, Alan. *The Community of Kent and the Great Rebellion.* Leicester, 1966.

Fincham, Kenneth and Nicholas Tyacke. *Altars Restored: The Changing Face of English Religious Worship, 1547-c. 1700.* Oxford, 2007.

Fletcher, Anthony. *A County Community in Peace and War: Sussex 1600-1660.* London and New York, 1975.

——. "Factionalism in Town and Countryside: The Significance of Puritanism and Arminianism." *Studies in Church History* 16 (1979), 291-300.

——. *The Outbreak of the English Civil War.* London, 1981.

——. *Reform in the Provinces: The Government of Stuart England.* New Haven, CT and London, 1986.

Friis, Astrid. *Alderman Cockayne's Project and the Cloth Trade.* London, 1927.

Foster, Andrew. "Church Policies of the 1630s." In R. Cust and A. Hughes (eds), *Conflict in Early Stuart England.* London, 1989, pp. 193-223.

Foster, E.R. "The Procedure in the House of Commons against Patents and Monopolies, 1621-4." In W. Aiken and B.D. Henning (eds), *Conflict in Stuart England.* New York, 1960.

Foster, J. *Alumni Oxonienses: The Members of the University of Oxford 1500-1714.* Vol. 4. Oxford, 1891.

Friedrichs, Christopher. *The Early Modern City 1450-1750.* London, 1995.

Fuller, John. *The History of Berwick upon Tweed.* Edinburgh, 1799.

Gardiner, S.R. *The Fall of the Monarchy of Charles I, 1637-1649.* Vol. 1. London, 1882.

——. *History of England from the Accession of James I to the Outbreak of the Civil War, 1603-1642.* Vol. 8. London, 1884.

Garrett-Goodyear, Harold. "The Tudor Revival of *Quo Warranto* and Local Contributions to State-Building." In Morris Arnold *et al.* (eds), *On the Laws and Customs of England: Essays in Honor of Samuel E. Thorne.* Chapel Hill, NC, 1981, pp. 231-95.

Gilbert, Walter. *Memorials of the Collegiate and Parish Church of All Saints, in the King's Parish and Town of Maidstone.* Maidstone, 1866.

Gillespie, Raymond. *Colonial Ulster: The Settlement of East Ulster 1600-1641.* Cork, 1985.

276

BIBLIOGRAPHY

Goldie, Mark. "The Unacknowledged Republic: Officeholding in Early Modern England." In Tim Harris (ed.), *The Politics of the Excluded, c. 1500–1850*. Basingstoke, 2001, pp. 153–94.

Goose, Nigel. "The Rise and Decline of Philanthropy in Early Modern Colchester: The Unacceptable Face of Mercantilism?" *Social History* 31 (2006), 469–87.

Grace, Frank. "'Schismaticall and Factious Humours': Opposition in Ipswich to Laudian Church Government in the 1630s." In D. Chadd (ed.), *Religious Dissent in East Anglia*. Vol. 3. Norwich, 1996, pp. 97–119.

Gruenfelder, John. *Influence in Early Stuart Elections*. Columbus, OH, 1981.

—. "Yorkshire Borough Elections, 1603–1640." *Yorkshire Archaeological Journal* 49 (1977), 101–14.

Hailwood, Mark. *Alehouses and Good Fellowship in Early Modern England*. Woodbridge, 2014.

Halliday, Paul. *Dismembering the Body Politic: Partisan Politics in England's Towns 1650–1730*. Cambridge, 1998.

Halliday, Paul, Eleanor Hubbard and Scott Sowerby (eds). *Revolutionising Politics: Culture and Conflict in England, 1620–60*. Manchester, 2021.

Hanawalt, Barbara. *Ceremony and Civility: Civic Culture in Late Medieval London*. Oxford, 2017.

Hartrich, Eliza. *Politics and the Urban Sector in Fifteenth-Century England, 1413–1471*. Oxford, 2019.

Hebb, David Delison. *Piracy and the English Government, 1616–1642*. Aldershot, 1994.

Henderson, Edith. *Foundations of English Administrative Law: Certiorari and Mandamus in the Seventeenth Century*. Cambridge, MA, 1963.

Hill, Christopher. *Economic Problems of the Church*. Oxford, 1956.

Hill, J.W.F. *Tudor and Stuart Lincoln*. Cambridge, 1956.

Hindle, Steve. *On the Parish? The Micro-Politics of Poor Relief in Rural England c. 1550–1750*. Oxford, 2004.

—. *The State and Social Change in Early Modern England, c. 1550–1640*. Basingstoke, 2000.

Hirst, Derek. *The Representative of the People? Voters and Voting in England under the Early Stuarts*. Cambridge, 1975.

Hoare, R.C. *History of Modern Wiltshire*. Vol. 6, *Old and New Sarum or Salisbury*, by Robert Benson and Henry Hatcher. London, 1843.

Holdsworth, W.S. "English Corporation Law in the 16th and 17th Centuries." *Yale Law Review* 31 (1922), 382–407.

Holmes, Clive. "The County Community in English Historiography." *Journal of British Studies* 19 (1980), 54–73.

Homeshaw, Ernest J. *The Corporation of the Borough and Foreign of Walsall*. Walsall, 1960.

Howell, Roger. "Neutralism, Conservativism, and Political Alignment in the English Revolution: The Case of the Towns, 1642-9." In J.S. Morrill

BIBLIOGRAPHY

(ed.), *Reactions to the English Civil War 1642–1649*. New York, 1982, pp. 67-87.

———. *Newcastle upon Tyne and the Puritan Revolution: A Study of the Civil War in North England*. Oxford, 1967.

Hoyle, R.W. "The Masters of Requests and the Small Change of Jacobean Patronage." *English Historical Review* 126 (2011), 544-81.

———. "The Sheffield Cutlers and the Earls of Shrewsbury: A New Interpretation." In R.W. Hoyle (ed.), *Histories of People and Landscape: Essays on the Sheffield Region in Memory of David Hey*. Hatfield, 2021, pp. 25-45.

Hughes, Ann. "Coventry and the English Revolution." In R.C. Richardson (ed.), *Town and Countryside in the English Revolution*. Manchester, 1992.

———. *Politics, Society and Civil War in Warwickshire, 1620–1660*. Cambridge, 1987.

———. "Religion and Society in Stratford upon Avon, 1619-1638." *Midland History* 19 (1994), 58-83.

Hunter, R.J. "Towns in the Ulster Plantation." *Studia Hibernica* 11 (1971), 40-79.

Jack, Sybil. *Towns in Tudor and Stuart Britain*. New York, 1996.

———. *Trade and Industry in Tudor and Stuart England*. London, 1977.

Jackman, W. Turrentine. *The Development of Transportation in Modern England*, 2nd edn. London, 1962.

Jewitt, Llewellyn. *The Corporation Plate and Insigniae of Office of the Cities and Towns of England and Wales*. Vol. 1. London, 1895.

Johnson, A.M. "Politics in Chester during the Civil Wars and Interregnum 1640-62." In P. Clark and P. Slack (eds), *Crisis and Order in English Towns 1500–1700: Essays in Urban History*. Toronto, 1972, pp. 204-36.

Johnson, Richard. *The Ancient Customs of the City of Hereford*, 2nd edn. London, 1882.

Jones, Madeline V. "Election Issues and the Borough Electorates in Mid-Seventeenth Century Kent." *Archaeologia Cantiana* 85 (1970), 19-27.

Jordan, W.K. *Philanthropy in England, 1480–1660: A Study in the Changing Pattern of English Social Aspirations*. New York, 1959.

Keene, Derek. *St. Paul's: The Cathedral Church of London, 604–2004*. New Haven, CT, 2004.

Key, Newton E. and Joseph P. Ward. "Metropolitan Puritans and the Varieties of Godly Reform in Interregnum Monmouth." *The Welsh History Review* 22 (2005), 646-72.

Kirby, Ethyn. "The Lay Feoffees: A Study in Militant Puritanism." *Journal of Modern History* 14 (1942), 1-25.

Kishlansky, Mark. *Parliamentary Selection: Social and Political Choice in Early Modern England*. Cambridge, 1986.

———. "Tyranny Denied: Charles I, Attorney General Heath, and the Five Knights' Case." *Historical Journal* 42 (1999), 53-83.

Knafla, Louis (ed.). *Law and Politics in Jacobean England: The Tracts of Lord Chancellor Ellesmere*. Cambridge, 1977.

Lake, Peter. "Anti-puritanism as Political Discourse: The Laudian Critique

BIBLIOGRAPHY

of Puritan 'Popularity'." In Cesare Cuttica and Markku Peltonen (eds), *Democracy and Anti-democracy in Early Modern England, 1603–1689*. Leiden and Boston, MA, 2019, pp. 152–73.

—. "The Collection of Ship Money in Cheshire during the 1630s." *Northern History* 17 (1981), 44–71.

—. "The Laudian Style: Order, Uniformity, and the Beauty of Holiness in the 1630s." In Kenneth Fincham (ed.), *The Early Stuart Church, 1603–1642*. Stanford, CA, 1993, pp. 161–86.

—. "Puritanism, Arminianism, and a Shropshire Axe-Murder." *Midland History* 15 (1990), 37–64.

Langelüddecke, Henrik. "'The chiefest strength and glory of this kingdom': Arming and Training the 'Perfect Militia' in the 1630s." *English Historical Review* 118 (2003), 1264–1303.

—. "'I finde all men & my officers all soe unwilling': The Collection of Ship Money, 1635–1640." *Journal of British Studies* 46 (2007), 509–42.

—. "'Patchy and Spasmodic'? The Response of Justices of the Peace to Charles I's Book of Orders." *English Historical Review* 113 (1998), 1231–48.

Langston, J.N. "John Workman, Puritan Lecturer in Gloucester." *Transactions of the Bristol and Gloucestershire Archaeological Society* 66 (1945), 219–32.

Laski, Harold. "The Early History of the Corporation in England." *Harvard Law Review* 30 (1917), 561–88.

Lehmberg, Stanford. *Cathedrals under Siege: Cathedrals in English Society, 1600–1700*. University Park, PA, 1996.

Levin, Jennifer. *The Charter Controversy in the City of London, 1660–1688, and Its Consequences*. London, 1960.

Lynch, William. *The Law of Election in the Ancient Cities and Towns of Ireland as Traced from Original Records*. London, 1831.

MacCaffrey, Wallace. *Exeter, 1540–1640: The Growth of an English County Town*. Cambridge, MA, 1958.

Maitland, Frederick. *Township and Borough*. Cambridge, 1897.

Marcombe, David. *English Small Town Life: Retford, 1520–1642*. Oxford, 1993.

Marsh, Christopher. "Order and Place in England, 1580–1640: The View from the Pew." *Journal of British Studies* 44 (2005), 3–26.

Mendenhall, T.C. *The Shrewsbury Drapers and the Welsh Wool Trade in the XVI and XVII Centuries*. London, 1953.

Merewether, Henry and Archibald Stephens. *The History of the Boroughs and Municipal Corporations of the United Kingdom from the Earliest to the Present Time*. London, 1835.

McClendon, Muriel. *The Quiet Reformation: Magistrates and the Emergence of Protestantism in Tudor Norwich*. Stanford, CA, 1999.

McDiarmid, John F. (ed.). *The Monarchical Republic of Early Modern England: Essays in Response to Patrick Collinson*. Farnham, 2007.

McIntosh, Marjorie K. *Poor Relief and Community in Hadleigh, Suffolk, 1547–1600*. Hatfield, 2013.

BIBLIOGRAPHY

——. *Poor Relief in England 1350–1600.* Cambridge, 2011.

Miller, John. "The Crown and the Borough Charters in the Reign of Charles II." *English Historical Review* 100 (1985), 53–84.

Millstone, Noah. "Space, Place and Laudianism in Early Stuart Ipswich." In C. Kyle and J. Peacey (eds), *Connecting Centre and Locality: Political Communication in Early Modern England.* Manchester, 2020, pp. 66–93.

Mishra, Rupali. *A Business of State: Commerce, Politics, and the Birth of the East India Company.* Cambridge, MA, 2018.

Moody, T.W., F.X. Martin and F.J. Byrne (eds). *A New History of Ireland.* Vol. 3, *Early Modern Ireland.* Oxford, 1978.

Morrill, John. "The Attack on the Church of England in the Long Parliament, 1640–1642." In D. Beales and G. Best (eds), *History, Society, and the Churches: Essays in Honour of Owen Chadwick.* Cambridge, 1985, pp. 105–24.

——. "The Making of Oliver Cromwell." In J.S. Morrill (ed.), *Oliver Cromwell and the English Revolution.* London and New York, 1990, pp. 19–48.

——. (ed.). *Reactions to the English Civil War 1642–1649.* New York, 1982.

——. "The Religious Context of the English Civil War." *Transactions of the Royal Historical Society.* 5th Ser., 34 (1984), 155–78.

——. *The Revolt of the Provinces: Conservatives and Radicals in the English Civil War, 1630–1650.* London, 1976.

Musselwhite, Paul. "'This Infant Borough': The Corporate Political Identity of Eighteenth-Century Norfolk." *Early American Studies* 15 (2017), 801–34.

——. *Urban Dreams, Rural Commonwealth: The Rise of Plantation Society in the Chesapeake.* Chicago, IL and London, 2019.

Nicholls, John. *History of Leicestershire.* Vol. 1, pt. 2. London, 1815.

O'Day, Rosemary. "The Triumph of Civic Oligarchy in Seventeenth Century England." In R. O'Day *et al.* (eds), *The Traditional Community under Stress.* Milton Keynes, 1977, pp. 103–36.

Ohlmeyer, Jane. "'Civilizinge of Those Rude Partes': Colonization within Britain and Ireland, 1580s–1640s." In N. Canny (ed.), *The Origins of Empire: British Overseas Enterprise to the Close of the Seventeenth Century.* Oxford, 1998, pp. 124–47.

O'Siochru, Micheal. "Civil Autonomy and Military Power in Early Modern Ireland." *Journal of Early Modern History* 15 (2011), 31–57.

Overall, W.H. and H.C. Overall. *Analytical Index to the Series of Records Known as the Remembrancia, 1579–1664.* London, 1878.

Owen, Hugh and John Blakeway. *A History of Shrewsbury.* Vol. 1. London, 1825.

Palliser, D.M. *Towns and Local Communities in Medieval and Early Modern England.* Aldershot, 2006.

Patterson, Catherine. "Consensus, Division and Voting in Early Stuart Towns." In P. Halliday, E. Hubbard and S. Sowerby (eds), *Revolutionising Politics: Culture and Conflict in England, 1620–60.* Manchester, 2021, pp. 145–63.

——. "Corporations, Cathedrals, and the Crown: Local Dispute and Royal Interest in Early Stuart England." *History* 85 (2000), 546–71.

BIBLIOGRAPHY

——. "Quo Warranto and Borough Corporations in Early Stuart England: Royal Prerogative and Local Privileges in the Central Courts." *English Historical Review* 120 (2005), 879–906.

——. *Urban Patronage in Early Modern England: Corporate Boroughs, the Landed Elite, and the Crown, 1590–1640.* Stanford, CA, 1999.

——. "Whose City? Civic Government and Episcopal Power in Early Modern Salisbury, c. 1590–1640." *Historical Research* 90 (2017), 486–505.

Pawlisch, Hans. *Sir John Davies and the Conquest of Ireland: A Study in Legal Imperialism.* Cambridge, 2002.

Pearl, Valerie. *London and the Outbreak of the Puritan Revolution: City Government and National Politics 1625–43.* London, 1961.

Perceval-Maxwell, M. "Ireland and the Monarchy in the Early Stuart Multiple Kingdom." *Historical Journal* 34 (1991), 279–95.

Pool, P.A.S. *The History of the Town and Borough of Penzance.* Penzance, 1974.

Potter, Matthew. "The Greatest Gerrymander in Irish History? James I's 40 Boroughs of 1612–13." *History Ireland* 21 (2013), 14–17.

Pound, John. "The Social and Trade Structure of Norwich, 1525–1575." *Past & Present* No. 39 (1966), 49–69.

Quintrell, B.W. "The Church Triumphant? The Emergence of a Spiritual Lord Treasurer, 1635–1636." In J.F. Merritt (ed.), *The Political World of Thomas Wentworth, Earl of Strafford, 1621–1641.* Cambridge, 1996, pp. 81–108.

——. "Gentry Factions and the Witham Affray, 1628." *Essex Archaeology and History* 10 (1978), 118–26.

——. "Government in Perspective: Lancashire and the Privy Council, 1570–1649." *Transactions of the Historical Society of Lancashire and Cheshire* 131 (1981), 35–62.

——. "The Making of Charles I's Book of Orders." *English Historical Review* 95 (1980), 553–72.

Rawcliffe, Carole and Richard Wilson (eds). *Norwich since 1550.* London and New York, 2004.

Reynolds, Matthew. *Godly Reformers and Their Opponents in Early Modern England: Religion in Norwich, c. 1560–1643.* Woodbridge, 2005.

Roberts, S.K. "Alehouses, Brewing, and Government under the Early Stuarts." *Southern History* 2 (1980), 45–71.

Russell, Conrad. *The Causes of the English Civil War.* Oxford, 1990.

——. *Parliaments and English Politics 1621–1629.* Oxford, 1979.

Sacks, David Harris. *The Widening Gate: Bristol and the Atlantic, 1450–1700.* Berkeley and Los Angeles, CA, 1991.

Sacret, J.H. "The Restoration Government and Municipal Corporations." *English Historical Review* 45 (1930), 232–59.

Salt, S.P. "Sir Symonds D'Ewes and the Levying of Ship Money, 1635–40." *Historical Journal* 37 (1994), 253–87.

Scott, John. *Berwick-upon-Tweed: The History of the Town and Guild.* London, 1888.

Seaver, Paul. *The Puritan Lectureships: The Politics of Religious Dissent 1560–1662.* Stanford, CA, 1970.

BIBLIOGRAPHY

Shagan, Ethan. "The Two Republics: Conflicting Views of Participatory Local Government in Early Tudor England." In John F. McDiarmid (ed.), *The Monarchical Republic of Early Modern England: Essays in Response to Patrick Collinson*. Farnham, 2007, pp. 19–36.

Sharpe, Kevin. *The Personal Rule of Charles I*. New Haven, CT and London, 1992.

Shaw, William. *A History of the English Church during the Civil Wars and under the Commonwealth, 1640–1660*. 2 vols. London, New York, and Bombay, 1900.

Sheehan, A.J. "The Recusancy Revolt of 1603: A Reinterpretation." *Archivium Hibernicum* 38 (1983), 3–13.

Sheehan, Anthony. "Irish Towns in a Period of Change, 1558–1625." In Ciaran Brady and Raymond Gillespie (eds), *Natives and Newcomers: Essays on the Making of Irish Colonial Society 1534–1641*. Newbridge, 1986, pp. 93–119.

Simon, Joan. "The Two John Angels." *Transactions of the Leicestershire Archaeological and Historical Society* 31 (1955), 37–40.

Simpson, Robert. *A Collection of Fragments Illustrative of the History and Antiquities of Derby*. Vol. 1. Derby, 1826.

Slack, Paul. "Books of Orders: The Making of English Social Policy, 1577–1631." *Transactions of the Royal Historical Society* 30 (1980), 1–22.

—. "Dearth and Social Policy in Early Modern England." *Social History of Medicine* 5 (1992), 1–17.

—. *From Reformation to Improvement: Public Welfare in Early Modern England*. Oxford, 1999.

—. *The Impact of Plague in Tudor and Stuart England*. London, 1985.

—. *Poverty and Policy in Tudor and Early Stuart England*. London, 1988.

—. "Poverty and Politics in Salisbury, 1597–1666." In P. Clark and P. Slack (eds), *Crisis and Order in English Towns, 1500–1700*. Toronto, 1972, pp. 164–203.

Smith, A. Hassell. "Militia Rates and Militia Statutes 1558–1663." In P. Clark, A.G.R. Smith and N. Tyacke (eds), *The English Commonwealth 1547–1640: Essays in Politics and Society Presented to Joel Hurstfield*. Leicester, 1979, pp. 93–110.

Smith, Brendan. "Late Medieval Ireland and the English Connection: Waterford and Bristol, ca. 1360–1460." *Journal of British Studies* 50 (2011), 546–65.

Smith, David Chan. *Sir Edward Coke and the Reformation of the Laws: Religion, Politics, and Jurisprudence, 1578–1616*. Cambridge, 2014.

Smith, Edmond. "Governance." In W. Pettigrew and D. Veevers (eds), *The Corporation as a Protagonist in Global History, 1550–1750*. Leiden and Boston, MA, 2019.

Spufford, Margaret. "Puritanism and Social Control?" In A. Fletcher and J. Stevenson (eds), *Order and Disorder in Early Modern England*. Cambridge, 1985, pp. 41–57.

Stater, Victor. *Noble Government: The Stuart Lord Lieutenancy and the Transformation of English Politics*. Athens, GA, 1994.

—. "War and the Structure of Politics: Lieutenancy and the Campaign of 1628."

BIBLIOGRAPHY

In M.C. Fissel (ed.), *War and Government in Britain, 1598–1650*. Manchester and New York, 1991, pp. 87–109.

Stern, Philip J. "'Bundles of Hyphens": Corporations as Legal Communities in the Early Modern British Empire." In L. Benton and R. Ross (eds), *Legal Pluralism and Empires, 1500–1850*. New York, 2015, pp. 21–47.

——. *The Company-State: Corporate Sovereignty and the Early Modern Foundations of the British Empire in India*. Oxford, 2011.

——. "The Corporation and the Global Seventeenth-Century English Empire: A Tale of Three Cities." *Early American Studies* 16 (2018), 41–63.

Stoyle, Mark. *From Deliverance to Destruction: Rebellion and Civil War in an English City*. Exeter, 1996.

Supple, B.E. *Commercial Crisis and Change in England 1600–1642: A Study in the Instability of a Mercantile Economy*. Cambridge, 1959.

Sutherland, Donald. *Quo Warranto Proceedings in the Reign of Edward I, 1278–1294*. Oxford, 1963.

Swinden, Henry. *The History and Antiquities of the Ancient Burgh of Great Yarmouth in the County of Norfolk*. Norwich, 1772.

Taylor, J.K.G. "The Civil Government of Gloucester, 1640-6." *Transactions of the Bristol & Gloucestershire Archaeological Society* 67 (1946–48), 59–118.

Tittler, Robert. *Architecture and Power: The Town Hall and the English Urban Community, c. 1500–1640*. Oxford, 1991.

——. "The English Fishing Industry in the Sixteenth Century: The Case of Great Yarmouth." *Albion* 9 (1977), 40–60.

——. "The Incorporation of Boroughs, 1540–1558." *History* 62 (1977), 24–42.

——. *The Reformation and the Towns in England: Politics and Political Culture, c. 1540–1640*. Oxford, 1998.

——. *Townspeople and Nation: English Urban Experiences 1540–1640*. Stanford, CA, 2001.

Treadwell, Victor. "The Establishment of the Farm of the Irish Customs, 1603-10." *English Historical Review* 93 (1978), 580–602.

Tronrud, Thorold. "Dispelling the Gloom: The Extent of Poverty in Tudor and Early Stuart Towns, Some Kentish Evidence." *Canadian Journal of History/ Annales Canadiennes d'Histoire* 20 (1985), 1–21.

Tyacke, Nicholas. *Anti-Calvinists: The Rise of English Arminianism c. 1590–1640*. Oxford, 1987.

Underdown, David. *Fire from Heaven: Life in an English Town in the Seventeenth Century*. New Haven, CT, 1992.

——. *Somerset in the Civil War and Interregnum*. Newton Abbott, 1973.

Victoria County History of Cheshire. Vol. 5, Pt. 1, *The City of Chester*. Eds. Chris Lewis and Alan Thacker. London, 2003.

Victoria County History of Essex. Vol. 9, *The Borough of Colchester*. Eds. Janet Cooper and C.R. Elrington. London, 1994.

Victoria County History of Gloucestershire. Vol. 4, *The City of Gloucester*. Ed. Nicholas Herbert. London, 1988.

BIBLIOGRAPHY

Victoria County History of Sussex. Vol. 3. Ed. L.F. Salzman. London, 1935.

Victoria County History of Sussex. Vol. 9. Ed. L.F. Salzman. London, 1937.

Victoria County History of Shropshire. Vol. 6, Pt. 1, *Shrewsbury: General History and Topography.* Eds. W.A. Champion and A.T. Thacker. London, 2014.

Victoria County History of Yorkshire, East Riding. Vol. 1, *The City of Kingston upon Hull.* Ed. K.J. Allison. London, 1969.

Victoria County History of Yorkshire, The City of York. Ed. P.M. Tillott. London, 1961.

Walter, John. "Grain Riots and Popular Attitudes to the Law: Maldon and the Crisis of 1629." In John Brewer and John Styles (eds), *An Ungovernable People: The English and Their Law in the Seventeenth and Eighteenth Centuries.* New Brunswick, NJ, 1980, pp. 47–84.

——. *Understanding Popular Violence in the English Revolution: The Colchester Plunderers.* Cambridge, 1999.

Ward, Joseph P. *Culture, Faith and Philanthropy: Londoners and Provincial Reform in Early Modern England.* New York, 2013.

——. *Metropolitan Communities: Trade Guilds, Identity, and Change in Early Modern London.* Stanford, CA, 1997.

Warmington, A.R. "The Corporation of York in Peace and War, 1638–1645." *York Historian* 9 (1990), 16–26.

Weinbaum, Martin. *British Borough Charters, 1307–1660.* Cambridge, 1943.

Welford, Richard. *History of Newcastle and Gateshead.* Vol. 3. London, 1887.

White, Jason. "Royal Authority versus Corporate Sovereignty: The Levant Company and the Ambiguities of Early Stuart Statecraft." *The Seventeenth Century* 32 (2017), 231–55.

White, Peter. "The Via Media in the Early Stuart Church." In Kenneth Fincham (ed.), *The Early Stuart Church.* Stanford, CA, 1993, pp. 211–30.

White, Stephen D. *Sir Edward Coke and the Grievances of the Commonwealth.* Chapel Hill, NC, 1979.

Williams, Ian. "Edward Coke." In D.J. Galligan (ed.), *Constitutions and the Classics: Patterns of Constitutional Thought from Fortescue to Bentham.* Oxford, 2014, pp. 86–107.

Williamson, Fiona. "When 'Commoners Were Made Slaves by the Magistrates': The 1627 Election and Political Culture in Norwich." *Journal of Urban History* 43 (2017), 3–17.

——. *Social Relations and Urban Space: Norwich, 1600–1700.* Woodbridge, 2014.

Withington, Phil. "An 'Aristotelian Moment': Democracy in Early Modern England." In M. Braddick and P. Withington (eds), *Popular Culture and Political Agency in Early Modern England and Ireland: Essays in Honour of John Walter.* Woodbridge, 2017, pp. 203–22.

——. "Introduction – Citizens and Soldiers: The Renaissance Context." *Journal of Early Modern History* 15 (2011), 3–30.

——. *The Politics of Commonwealth: Citizens and Freemen in Early Modern England.* Cambridge, 2005.

BIBLIOGRAPHY

Wood, Anthony. *Alumni Atheniensis*. 3rd edn, facsimile of London 1817 edn. The Sources of Science, no. 55. New York and London, 1967.

Wrightson, Keith. "Alehouses, Order, and Reformation in Rural England, 1590-1660." In Eileen Yeo and Stephen Yeo (eds), *Popular Culture and Class Conflict 1590-1914: Explorations in the History of Labour and Leisure*. Brighton, 1981.

——. *Earthly Necessities: Economic Lives in Early Modern England*. New Haven, CT, 2002.

——. *Ralph Tailor's Summer: A Scrivener, His City, and the Plague*. New Haven, CT, 2011.

Wrightson, Keith and David Levine. *Poverty and Piety in an English Village: Terling, 1525-1700*, rev. edn. Oxford, 1995.

Wrigley, E.A. "Urban Growth and Agricultural Change: England and the Continent in the Early Modern Period." *Journal of Interdisciplinary History* 15 (1985), 683-728.

——. "Urban Growth in Early Modern England: Food, Fuel, and Transport." *Past & Present* No. 225 (2014), 79-112.

Young, Michael B. "Charles I and the Erosion of Trust, 1625-1628." *Albion* 22 (1990), 217-35.

Zaller, Robert. *The Parliament of 1621: A Study in Constitutional Conflict*. Berkeley, CA, 1971.

Zaret, David. *Origins of Democratic Culture: Printing, Petitions, and the Public Sphere in Early-Modern England*. Princeton, NJ, 2000.

Unpublished dissertations and theses

Baron, Sabrina Alcorn. "'The Board Did Think Fit and Order': The Structure and Function of the Privy Council of Charles I, c. 1625-41, with Special Reference to the Personal Rule." PhD dissertation, University of Chicago, 1995.

Blankenfeld, Barton John. "Puritans in the Provinces: Banbury, Oxfordshire, 1554-1660." PhD dissertation, Yale University, 1985.

Davis, James R. "Colchester, 1600-1662: Politics, Religion, and Officeholding in an English Provincial Town." PhD dissertation, Brandeis University, 1980.

Forward, Nicholas R.C. "The Arrest and Trial of Archbishop William Laud." MPhil thesis, University of Birmingham, 2012.

Gill, A.A.M. "Ship Money during the Personal Rule of Charles I: Politics, Ideology and the Law 1634 to 1640." PhD dissertation, University of Sheffield, 1990.

Knowles, Philip. "Continuity and Change in Urban Culture: A Case Study of Two Provincial Towns, Chester and Coventry, c. 1600-1750." PhD dissertation, University of Leicester, 2001.

BIBLIOGRAPHY

Marlowe, Nicholas. "Government and Politics in the West Country Incorporated Boroughs, 1642–1662." PhD dissertation, University of Cambridge, 1986.

Metters, G.A. "The Rulers and Merchants of King's Lynn in the Early Seventeenth Century." PhD dissertation, University of East Anglia, 1982.

Musselwhite, Paul. "Towns in Mind: Urban Plans, Political Culture, and Empire in the Colonial Chesapeake, 1607–1722." PhD dissertation, College of William and Mary, 2011.

Petchey, W.J. "The Borough of Maldon, Essex, 1500–1688: A Study in Sixteenth and Seventeenth Century Urban History." PhD dissertation, University of Leicester, 1972.

Roberts, John. "Parliamentary Representation in Dorset and Devon 1559–1601." MA thesis, University of London, 1958.

Schilling, W.A.H. "The Central Government and the Municipal Corporations in England, 1642–1663." PhD dissertation, Vanderbilt University, 1970.

Stivers, George Spencer. "'A Most Grievous and Insupportable Vexation': Billeting in Early Seventeenth Century England." PhD dissertation, University of California-Riverside, 2009.

Van Vliet, Janine. "From a 'Strong Town of War' to the 'Very Heart of the Country': The English Border Town of Berwick-upon-Tweed, 1558–1625." PhD dissertation, University of Pennsylvania, 2017.

Web-based sources

Journal of the House of Lords. Vol. 4. London, 1767–1830. *British History Online.* www.british-history.ac.uk/lords-jrnl/vol4/pp107-8.

Oxford Dictionary of National Biography. Ed. D. Cannadine. Online edn. Oxford University Press, 2004. www.oxforddnb.com.

The History of Parliament: The House of Commons 1604–1629. Eds. Andrew Thrush and John P. Ferris. Online edn. History of Parliament, 2010. www.historyofparliamentonline.org/.

Victoria County History of Yorkshire, The City of York. Ed. P.M. Tillott. London, 1961. *British History Online.* www.british-history.ac.uk/vch/yorks/city-of-york/.

Index

Maps and Tables are indicated by *italic* page numbers.

Abbott, George, archbishop of
  Canterbury   93, 94 n.58, 230
Abingdon
  municipal election disputes in   90-1,
    96, *106, 107*
  quo warranto challenges   57
Admiralty jurisdiction   25, 58, 67, 149
alcohol, regulating   *see* alehouses,
  brewing, and drinking
Aldeburgh
  charter of incorporation   32, 33
  housing controls in   118
  lectureships and preaching in   260
  militias, mustering and
    training   188-9
  piracy, combating   166, 170, 171
  poverty and poor relief in   112-13,
    118
  Ship Money from   209
  war, fiscal burden of   197-8
alehouses, brewing, and drinking   124-6
  billeting soldiers in alehouses   200
  Book of Orders and   129, 137, 138,
    139, 144
  common brewhouses funding poor
    relief   60-1, 116
  corporate members and officers,
    brewers and alehouse keepers
    as   42, 44, 127-8, 138-9
  crown involvement in   128-36
  disorder, association with   125
  grain, waste or dearth of   127, 128,
    129, 134-5
  licensing alehouses   65-6, 125-34
  patents and patentees   131-4
  plague and closing of alehouses   122
  poverty and   125, 126, 128, 133
  quo warranto challenges
    targeting   60-1, 65, 134
  regulation of brewing   127
  religious belief and regulation of   115,
    128

revenue enhancement, licensing used
  for   131
in Star Chamber   128, 130
urban licensing and regulation of
  alehouses and brewing   125-9
Alford, Edward (MP of Colchester)   164
Algiers
  Barbary pirates or "Turks" from   166,
    167, 170, 171, 172, 173, 212
  proclamation protecting ships and
    goods of   172
Anderson, Sir Henry   84
Andover, Ship Money from   217
anti-Calvinists   233, 249 n.119
Arminians and Arminianism   46, 68,
  102, 221, 224 n.13, 232 n.45,
  249 n.119; *see also* Laudian
  religious ideals and practice
artillery yards   186, 187, 188
Arundel, earl of   178, 192
Arundel, Ship Money from   217
Astley, Sir John   61-2, 63
Atkin, Thomas (alderman of
  Norwich)   192-3, 236
attorneys general; *see also specific attorneys
  general by name*
  granting of charter, role in   26-8
  list of early Stuart
    officeholders   26 n.39
  quo warranto challenges and   55, 61,
    62, 63, 68-71, 75, 76, 152
Ayr, Viscount   44, 98

Bacon, Sir Francis   26 n.39, 156
Bacon, Sir Nathaniel   156
Bailiffs   *see* two-bailiff versus single
  mayor government
Banbury
  billeting in   200, 202, 205
  Book of Orders in   140-1
  charter of incorporation   28
  Forced Loan and   209

287

INDEX

Banbury (*continued*)
  lectureships and preaching in   260
  Ship Money from   216. 217, 218
Banbury, earl of   205
Banckes, Caleb (jurat of Maidstone)   227
Bankes, Sir John   26, 41, 74, 249
Banks, Mr. (shipping grain out of
  Sandwich)   143
Barbary pirates or "Turks," 166, 167, 170,
  171, 172, 173, 212
Barnstaple
  militias, mustering and training   187
  piracy, combating   168-9, 170, 173
  Ship Money from   214, 216
  trade in   147, 159
Barrell, Robert (minister of
  Maidstone)   226, 227, 228 n.31,
  260
Bartholomew Fair   122
Basingstoke
  billeting in   202
  charter of incorporation   32
  Ship Money from   217
Bath, and Forced Loan   208
Bath, earl of   186
Bath and Wells, bishop of   231
Beale, Ambrose (jurat of
  Maidstone)   227
Beaver, Daniel   207 n.109, 238 n.73
Beck, Mr. (alderman of Lincoln)   95
Bedford, earl of   192
beer   see alehouses, brewing, and
  drinking
Beier, A.L.   113 n.8
Berkshire, earl of   98
Bernard, G.W.   221
Berwick-upon-Tweed
  dissolution of royal garrison, effects
    of   88, 101, 197
  incorporation by parliament   16 n.8
  municipal election disputes in   85-8,
    100-1, 106
  piracy, combating   168 n.94
  trade in   156 n.41, 163
  war, fiscal burden of   197
Beverley
  alehouses, brewing, and drinking
    in   134

billeting in   199
Bideford, charter of incorporation
  for   31
billeting   199-208
  coastal and port towns most heavily
    affected by   199
  debates in parliament over   205-6,
    207, 219, 258
  jurisdictional issues raised by   202-3
  multiple financial burdens on
    townspeople and   124, 174, 204,
    211
  payment for   202
  plague and sickness, spread of   201
  political resistance to   205-8, 258
  as punishment   206 n.104, 209
  refusals of   203-5
  social and moral order in corporate
    towns affected by   200-1
  war leading to additional burdens
    of   197
Blandford, billeting in   201 n.82
Blosse (Norwich alderman)   88
Blount, Lady   71-2, 233
Bodmin
  Book of Orders in   140
  municipal election disputes in   101-2,
    107
Bond, Shelagh   17 n.14, 21
Book of Orders (1630-31)   112, 136-44
  alehouses, brewing, and drinking
    in   129, 137, 138, 139, 144
  certificates, returns of   139-40
  enforcement issues, jurisdictional
    tensions, and conflicts of
    interest   137-41, 143-4
  grain supply and   136-7, 140-4
  impact of   136
  origins and purposes of   136-7
  plague control and   122
  poverty and the poor in   137, 138,
    140, 141, 142, 144
  religious belief and   139 n.131, 143
  vagrancy and   140
Book of Sports   228, 250
boroughs, corporate   see corporate towns
Boston
  Book of Orders in   141

288

INDEX

charter of incorporation, reading aloud
of   19 n.24
Forced Loan and   209
militias, mustering and training   258
religious governance in   224
Ship Money from   209, 259
trade in   150 n.12, 156, 156 n.41, 162
Braddick, Michael   9, 181, 194
*State Formation in Early Modern
England*   3, 5
Brenner, Robert   172 n.119
Brent, Nathaniel   232, 240
brewers and brewing   *see* alehouses,
brewing, and drinking
Bridgeman, John, bishop of
Chester   242
Bridgeman, Sir John (recorder of
Shrewsbury)   48
Bridgenorth
Book of Orders in   140
lectureships and preaching in   236
Bridgewater
Book of Orders in   139
trade in   156 n.41, 159
Bridport
billeting in   201 n.82
charter of incorporation   31, 32 n.62
Brightlingsea, billeting in   203
Brinsley, John (preacher of Great
Yarmouth)   233-4
Bristol
alehouses, brewing, and
drinking   135 n.113
bakers' company in   152
French Company, merchants refusing
to join   176 n.135
king's direct intervention in elections
in   98
Merchant Venturers' Company
of   151, 152
militias, mustering and training   187
piracy, combating   168, 169, 170
quo warranto challenges   58
Ship Money from   209, 214, 216,
218-19
trade in   4, 147, 151, 152, 156 n.41,
159, 172
Waterford, trade ties with   39

Brook, Christopher (deputy recorder of
York)   130
Brooks, Matthew (minister of Great
Yarmouth)   234, 259-60
Brown, James   125-6
Browne, George (MP of Taunton)   206
Brownists   128, 223
Buckingham, George Villiers,
duke of   66, 171-2, 173, 178,
199, 201, 204
Burdette, George (preacher of Great
Yarmouth)   234
Burton, Henry   75-6
Bury St. Edmunds
militias, mustering and training   186
plague in   123
Bushrod, Richard (bailiff of
Dorchester)   205
Butcher, Richard (town clerk of
Stamford)   138-9
Buttolphe, William (bailiff of Great
Yarmouth)   68, 70

Calvinists and Calvinism   68, 87 n.34,
94 n.58, 115, 230, 235
Cambridge
charter of incorporation   17-18, 25,
28
crown request to accept specific
nominee for town clerk   45 n.118
housing controls in   119
municipal election disputes in   92-3,
98 n.72, 99, 105, 106
plague in   123
prerogative levies in   195
Cambridge University
housing controls and poverty
management   119 n.38
objections to town's 1616
reincorporation   25, 28
St. John's College and town
of Shrewsbury, dispute
between   75 n.107
Canterbury
alehouses, brewing, and drinking
in   127-8
billeting in   199, 201, 203, 204 n.93,
206-7, 258

289

INDEX

Canterbury (*continued*)
cathedral seating disputes in   238,
   239-40
Forced Loan and   208
militias, mustering and
   training   185-6
municipal election disputes in   93-4,
   95
parliamentary elections for   258
parliamentary petition from   259
quo warranto challenges   56-7
Ship Money from   214, 218, 247
Cardiff
piracy, combating   168 n.94
trade in   149, 156 n.41
Carey, Valentine, bishop of
   Exeter   248-9
Carleton, Dudley   see Dorchester,
   Dudley Carleton, Viscount
Carlisle
charter of incorporation   30
dissolution of royal garrison, effects
   of   101
municipal election disputes in   101
piracy, combating   168 n.94
poverty and poor relief in   112
trade in   156 n.41
Carr, Robert (minister of
   Maidstone)   226
Carver, Mr. (in disputed Norwich
   election)   88
Castlekeagh, charter of incorporation
   for   39
cathedral cities   237-45
Charles I's support for ecclesiastical
   authority in   40, 43, 44, 72-4,
   238, 240, 241-2, 245
charters/incorporation, ecclesiastical
   objections to   246-8
civic attendance requirements   237,
   244-5
civic sword or mace in cathedral
   precincts, laws/disputes
   regarding   28, 43 n.113, 238,
   242-5, 252, 261-2
Ellesmere's support for civic officials
   in   28
parliamentary petitions from   259-60

quo warranto challenges   56 n.19,
   57 n.24, 72
seating and precedence arrangements
   and disputes   238-42
Ship Money disputes in   44, 73, 214,
   218, 246-8
special jurisdictional concerns of   10,
   194
Catholics
civic governance and   128, 223
Irish boroughs, Catholic governments
   in   37, 64, 92 n.55, 223
lectureships and suppression of   228
municipal election disputes
   involving   91-2, 99
parliamentary elections of 1640
   and   258
quo warranto challenges in Ireland
   and   64
Cavan, charter of incorporation for   38
Cavendish, William   263 n.25
Chancery, charters of incorporation
   through   68
Chandos, Lord   185
Charles I
alehouses, brewing, and drinking
   under   128
charters of incorporation under   14,
   20, 28-9, 39-49
ecclesiastical authority, Caroline
   protection of   43-4, 72-4,
   220, 225, 237, 238, 240, 243-4,
   248-54
housing controls initiated by   118
incorporations and reincorporations
   under   23
Irish boroughs, incorporation of   36
on lectureships and preaching   230,
   231, 233, 234, 237
legal challenges to urban government
   and corporate liberties under   9
militias, mustering and training   183,
   192-3
municipal elections and   82, 97-104
number of charters granted by   20
order and profit, on link
   between   146
piracy and   167, 170, 171-2, 174

INDEX

plague controls under 122-4
popular government, concerns
about 5, 7-8, 32, 40, 100, 104,
257
quo warranto under 51, 54, 67-76
religion and corporate towns
under 43-4, 72-4, 220-5,
229-31, 233, 234, 237, 238,
240-5, 248-54
royal policy under 5, 257-8, 263, 264
trade under 149, 156, 161, 176,
178-9, 180
trust, loss of 205 n.98
two bailiffs versus single mayor
arrangement under 32
see also Book of Orders; Civil War;
Forced Loan; Personal Rule; Ship
Money
Charles II 50
charters of incorporation 8, 13-49
appeals for inspection, confirmation,
or revision of 58
attorneys general and lord keepers/lord
chancellors, roles of 26-8
under Charles I 14, 20, 28-9, 39-49
constitutions, charters viewed as 50
customary privileges, confirming 15,
16
ecclesiastical objections to 25, 28,
220, 245-50
failure of petitions for 25
fictitious personhood granted by 13,
15
incorporations and reincorporations
under Charles I 23
incorporations and reincorporations
under James I 22
in Irish boroughs 36-9
under James I 20, 28-9, 39-40,
42 n.109, 49
language of 15-19
legal effects of 13
militia privileges in 184-5, 188
monarch, establishing town's
relationship with 15-19
monarch's personal interest in 28-9
on mutual obligations and reciprocal
governance 18

narrowing of freemen's authority
in 29-36
nature of relationship between
borough and state created
by 13-14
negotiation of interests in 24-5
number and terms of early Stuart
versus Tudor charters 20-1
petitions for 21-5
on poverty and poor relief 114-15,
116, 119-20
preambles 17-19
process of obtaining 20-9
reading aloud of 19
reincorporations versus new
incorporations 29
surrender to crown without legal
process, under Charles I 43-4
trade issues, addressing 146-7,
150
Chester
alehouses, brewing, and drinking
in 132-3
charter of incorporation 28, 31
civic sword or mace in cathedral
precincts, laws/disputes
regarding 28, 242, 243, 244
Forced Loan and 208
independent nature of town
government in 14, 97
James I's request to accept Hugh
Mainwaring as recorder, denial
of 45
Laud's trial and 261
militias, mustering and training 187
municipal election disputes in 82,
85, 97, 105
parliamentary taxation in 194
prerogative levies in 195
trade in 147, 156
Chettle, Thomas (mayor of
Leicester) 27, 223
Chetwyn, William (chamberlain of
Bristol) 98
Chichester
billeting in 205, 207
cathedral seating and attendance
requirements 240, 245

INDEX

Chichester (*continued*)
 charter of incorporation   42 n.109,
  44, 248
 civic sword or mace in cathedral
  precincts, laws/disputes
  regarding   242, 243
 disruptiveness of religious change
  in   254
 municipal election disputes in   94-5
 quo warranto challenges   57, 59
 Ship Money from   217, 218, 247, 248
 trade in   156 n.41
Chichester, Sir Arthur   37, 38
Chipping Norton
 charter of incorporation   32 n.62
 municipal election disputes in   85,
  107
Chitty, Henry (alderman of
  Chichester)   94-5
Cinque Ports
 billeting in   203
 Book of Orders and grain supply
  in   141-4
 herring fisheries in   175
 incorporation by parliament   16 n.8
 trade in   158, 178
Cirencester
 billeting in   199
 lectureships and preaching in   236
Civil War
 center/local relations and   1
 fiscal weakness of crown and   181
 historical attitudes toward corporate
  bodies and   3
 loyalties of corporate towns in   262-3
 pre-Civil War period (1639-42),
  significance of events of   10,
  255-64
 state capacity question and   8, 256
Clarendon, Edward Hyde, earl of   3
Clark, Peter   4
cloth industry
 Cockayne, William, and Cockayne
  Project   157
 collapse of   113, 120, 134, 154,
  209-10
 Ipswich, incorporation of tailors and
  clothmakers in   152-4

Welsh cloths dispute   155
Cockayne, William, and Cockayne
 Project   157, 161
Cogswell, Thomas   81, 100 n.76, 166,
 170, 183 n.3, 184 n.7, 191, 197-8,
 256
Coke, Sir Edward   15, 26-7, 158, 163,
 206
Coke, Sir John   154-5
Colchester
 alehouses, brewing, and drinking
  in   42, 44, 128, 139
 billeting in   199
 charter of incorporation   18 n.18, 20,
  32, 34, 41-2, 44
 Laud's trial and   261
 militias, mustering and training   186,
  191-2
 municipal election disputes in   99,
  100, 101, 107
 piracy, combating   170
 poverty and poor relief in   116-17,
  120
 quo warranto challenges   57, 73, 101
 Ship Money from   174 n.126, 214, 217
 trade infrastructure in   164
Colfe, Joseph (JP of Canterbury)   127-8
Collinson, Patrick   239-40
colonies, plans for corporate towns
 in   5; *see also specific colonies*
commerce   *see* trade
Compton, Lord (later earl of
  Northampton)   185, 186-7
Congleton, charter of incorporation
 for   24
constitutions, charters viewed as   50
conventicles, Protestant   223
Conway, Lord   189, 204-5
Cooper, Benjamin (bailiff of Great
 Yarmouth)   68, 69, 70, 103
Corbett, Miles   236
Cork, charter of incorporation for   37
corporate towns   1-10
 autonomy and privileges, sense of   7
 central/local relations and   1-5,
  255-64
 charters of incorporation   8, 13-49;
  see also charters of incorporation

INDEX

diversity of 10
engagement of borough governments
  with state, focus on 6-7
group action among 114, 155-6, 158,
  161, 163, 173, 178
internal order in government of 9,
  78-104; *see also* internal order in
  borough government; municipal
  elections
lobbying of 6, 147, 167, 175, 176, 180
map of English, Welsh, and Irish
  towns, *xii*
military and fiscal demands of the
  state and 9-10, 181-219;
  see also fiscal demands of the
  state; military burdens of the
  state
parliament, petitioning 258-61
popular government, royal concerns
  about 5, 7-8, 257; *see also*
  popular government/popularity
in pre-Civil War period
  (1639-42) 10, 255-64
quo warranto challenges to 8-9,
  50-77; *see also* quo warranto
  challenges
religion and 10, 220-54; *see also*
  religion and corporate towns
social and moral order in 9, 111-45;
  see also social and moral order in
  corporate towns
state capacity question and 8, 256
studies of British 1, 3-4
trade and 9, 146-80; *see also* trade
urban civic forms, early Stuart attitudes
  toward 5
corporations/trading
  companies 57 n.25, 147-54,
  158-61, 231; *see also specific
  institutions by name*
Coulton, Barbara 45 n.120
Council of the North 242
county officials, corporate towns
  interacting with 6; *see also*
  Justices of the Peace
county studies 2
courts, corporate towns interacting
  with 6, 7, 84 n.20

Coventry
  lectureships and preaching in
    229
  militias, mustering and training 185,
    186-7
  poverty and poor relief in 114
  William Prynne and 75-6, 258
  quo warranto challenges 57, 74,
    75-6, 262
  religious governance in 224
Coventry, Sir Thomas, Lord
  Coventry 24, 25, 26 n.39, 46,
    66, 93, 99, 210, 213, 241-2, 249
Coward, Mr. (mayor of Salisbury) 60
Cramsie, John 176-7
Crane, Thomas (alderman of Great
  Yarmouth) 103 n.86
Crew, Thomas (MP of
  Northampton) 66
Cromwell, Oliver 34-5
cursus honorum in municipal elections 80
Cust, Richard 46 n.124, 67, 96 n.68,
  103, 181-2, 196, 207 n.106, 210,
  233
customary liberties and privileges 15,
  16, 21, 29, 36, 150
customs duties
  government concern for 65, 148-9,
    160, 161, 179, 195
  in Ireland 38, 149

Dalton, Michael, *The Countrey Justice*
  (1635) 43
Dartmouth
  militias, mustering and training 184,
    186
  piracy, combating 169, 170, 173
  trade in 161
Davenant, John, bishop of
  Salisbury 239
Davenport, Humfrey 69
Daventry, lectureships and preaching
  in 231
Davies, Julian 221, 253
Davies, Sir John 37
Davis, James 41
Dedham, Ship Money from 261
Delbridge, John (MP of Barnstaple) 173

293

INDEX

Derby
  bishop as JP in, crown efforts to
    include 249-50
  charter of incorporation 20, 31, 32,
    33, 43, 249
  Forced Loan and 208
  militias, mustering and training 187
  plague in 215
  Ship Money from 215
  trade in 150
Dering, Sir Edward 141-3, 144
Derry (Londonderry), charter of
    incorporation for 38
Dickes, Edward (vicar of
    Grantham) 251
Digges, Sir Dudley 157 n.44
Dodington, Sir Francis 140 n.134
Doncaster
  alehouses, brewing, and drinking
    134
  required to choose Viscount Ayr as
    high steward by Charles I 44,
    45, 98
Dorchester
  billeting in 200, 205
  charter of incorporation 20, 32, 34,
    44-5
  disruptiveness of religious change
    in 250
  militias, mustering and training 188
  plague in 122
  poverty and poor relief in 116, 120,
    144-5
  religious governance in 224
  Ship Money from 217
  social and moral order, religious
    impetus for 115
  trade in 151, 159, 172-3
  war, fiscal burden of 197
Dorchester, Dudley Carleton,
    Viscount 68, 103, 179, 209
Dorset, earl of 103, 156, 179, 207
Dover
  billeting in 200, 201, 203
  grain supply and Book of Orders
    in 141-2, 143
  Ship Money from 214
  trade in 178

drink and drunkenness, regulating see
    alehouses, brewing, and drinking
Droitwich, charter of incorporation
    for 32 n.62
Dublin
  charter of incorporation 37
  Strafford's trial, arbitrary rejection of
    corporate liberties at 262
Duke, Richard (jurat of Maidstone) 83
Dunkirkers 166, 170, 171, 172, 212
Dunwich
  alehouses, brewing, and drinking
    in 126-7
  lectureships and preaching in 260
  piracy, combating 171
  poverty and poor relief in 113 n.6
  Ship Money from 215
  trade in 162-4
  war, fiscal burden of 199
Durham, Ship Money from 218
Dutch see Low Countries
Dutton, William (of Chester) 187

East India Company 150, 157 n.44, 161
East Retford, charter of incorporation
    for 32 n.62
ecclesiastical authorities see religion and
    corporate towns
Edward I 52
Edward VI 20
Egerton, Sir Thomas see Ellesmere, Sir
    Thomas Egerton, Lord
elections see municipal elections
Elizabeth I 4, 20, 27, 36, 38, 52-3, 121,
    160, 165, 176, 195, 225-6
Elizabethan Poor Law of 1601 114,
    117-18
Ellesmere, Sir Thomas Egerton,
    Lord 26 n.39, 27-8, 156
Erle, Sir Walter 198
Errington, Anthony (merchant of
    Newcastle-upon-Tyne) 261
Evans, Connie 117
Evans, John (J. T.) 4, 89, 244
Evans, Norman 17 n.14, 21
Evelyn, Sir John 61 n.41
Everitt, Alan, *The Community of Kent and
    the Great Rebellion* 2

294

INDEX

Exchequer
  Canterbury's petition to parliament
    and 259
  feoffees, decree against 236, 237
  quo warranto in *see* quo warranto
    challenges
Exeter
  alehouses, brewing, and drinking
    in 135
  bishop as JP, crown efforts to
    include 248-9
  disruptiveness of religious change
    in 250
  Forced Loan and 208, 211
  piracy, combating 169, 170, 173
  plague in 83, 121
  poverty and poor relief in 117
  religious governance in 224
  self-sufficient and semi-autonomous
    nature of 3, 16 n.12
  Ship Money from 209, 211, 218, 247
  social and moral order, religious
    impetus for 115
  trade in 147, 151, 156 n.41, 159, 161,
    172, 173
Eye, Book of Orders in 140

fairs *see* markets and fairs
Falkland, Lord Deputy 171
Farmer, Ralph 98
Faversham, Book of Orders in 142,
  143
feoffees for lay impropriations 236-7
Fermanagh, charters of incorporation
  for 38-9
Finch, John 93-4, 95
Fincham, Kenneth 221
fiscal demands of the state 181-2; *see*
  also billeting; Forced Loan; Ship
  Money; taxation
  alehouse and brewing licenses as
    revenue enhancement 131
  historians' evaluation of 181-2
  militias, mustering and
    training 190-1, 193
  multiple financial burdens on
    townspeople and 124, 174, 191,
    204, 208, 209-11

piracy, contributions to
  combat 167-70
  prerogative levies 194-6
  quo warranto challenges as means of
    revenue generation 65-6
  trade infrastructure, paying for
    163-6
  trade regulation and revenue
    generation 155-6
  war, fiscal burden of 193-4, 196-9,
    211
Fishmonger's Company 176
Fleming, Chief Justice 25
Fletcher, Anthony 2, 243 n.93
  Reform in the Provinces 2
Forced Loan 208-11
  historians' evaluation of effects
    of 181-2
  multiple financial burdens on
    townspeople and 124, 174, 191,
    208, 211
  municipal election disputes and 92,
    96 n.68
  Petition of Right and 205, 219
  resistance to/refusals of 205,
    207 n.107, 209
  Ship Money and 209-11
Forestall, Henry (mayor of
  Sandwich) 143-4
fortifications and defenses
  cost of 9, 17, 194, 198, 210, 211
  disrepair of 197
  orders for towns to maintain 38,
    198
  ordnance for 179, 189, 190, 197-8
  shared national interest in 179, 181,
    197, 256
Foster, Andrew 73
Fowles, Sir David 84
France, war with 161, 170, 172-4, 189,
  209-10
"free state" claims 207, 258, 263
free trade debate 154, 155 n.35, 157-8,
  159, 161, 170
freemen, narrowing of authority
  of 29-36
Freke, Sir Thomas 188
French Merchants 158, 176

295

INDEX

Gamull, William (alderman of
Chester) 85
Gape, Francis (town clerk of Weymouth-
Melcombe Regis) 55
Gardiner, S.R. 168 n.95
Garrett-Goodyear, Harold 53
Germany, Merchant Adventurers trading
with 160
Gill, A.A.M. 174
Gillott, Nicholas (mayor of
Leicester) 132
Gloucester
attitude toward royal government
in 4
billeting in 199, 202, 203
Forced Loan and 209
lectureships and preaching in 235-6,
261
militias, mustering and training 187,
190
poverty and poor relief in 113 n.6
social and moral order, religious
impetus for 115
trade in 156 n.41
godly towns and magistrates
charters of incorporation and 10, 42,
46, 262
civic governance and 221, 223-4,
227-8
defined 115
disruptiveness of religious change
and 250-1, 252, 253
lectureships/preaching and 230, 233,
235, 260
municipal election disputes and 91
social/moral order and 115-16,
121 n.45, 126, 128, 139 n.131,
144-5
trade and 193 n.46, 205
Godmanchester, charter of
incorporation 32 n.62
Goldie, Mark 3
Gollop, George (MP of
Southampton) 206
Goodman, Godfrey, bishop of
Gloucester 235
Gostling, Mr. (in disputed Norwich
election) 88

grain supply
alehouses/brewing, and concerns
about waste or dearth of 127,
128, 129, 134-5
Book of Orders and 136-7, 140-4
local lack of control over
transportation of 143-4
riots over 137, 141
Grantham
charter of incorporation 24
disruptiveness of religious change
in 251
plague in 123
quo warranto challenges 58
trade in 150
Gravesend, charter of incorporation 30
Great Yarmouth
billeting in 199
Book of Orders in 140
charter of incorporation 28, 31, 32,
33, 34, 234-5
disruptiveness of religious change
in 250, 251, 254
haven of 165-6, 169, 176, 178
herring trade in 147, 156, 165-6,
175-80
housing controls in 118
king's direct interventions in elections
of 95-6, 102-4
lectureships and preaching in 229,
233-5, 260
London merchants and 157-8, 175,
176
militias, mustering and training 184,
187, 260
municipal election disputes in 99,
100, 102-4, 106
parliamentary petitions from 259-61
parliamentary taxation in 194
piracy, combating 169, 170, 179
plague in 122
popular government in 46 n.124
public reading aloud of charter
in 19 n.24
quo warranto challenges 55, 58,
67-71, 234-5
religious governance in 46 n.124,
223, 224, 225

296

INDEX

Ship Money from 174 n.126
social and moral order, religious
   impetus for 115
Greene, George (mayor of
   Chichester) 94-5
Grigson, William (mayor of
   Berwick-upon-Tweed) 85-8

Hadleigh
   Forced Loan and 208
   Ship Money from, and plague in 216
Hailwood, Mark 125
Hales, Sir Edward 203
Halifax, Ship Money from 174 n.126
Halliday, Paul 26 n.39, 50, 263
Halloway, Charles (recorder of
   Abingdon) 96
Hardware, Mr. (alderman of Great
   Yarmouth) 103
Harrington, Sir Henry 27
Harsnett, Samuel, bishop of
   Norwich 230, 232
Hartlepool, municipal election disputes
   in 84-5, 91-2, 105
Harwich
   billeting in 199
   Forced Loan and 208
   king and Council ordering removal of
   town clerk from office 95
Hastings
   municipal election disputes in 107
   parliamentary elections for 258-9
   trade in 164
Haverfordwest
   lectureships and preaching in 236
   Ship Money from 216
Hayes, Sir John 233
Heath, Sir Robert
   charters of incorporation and 24, 25,
   26, 32, 33
   militias, mustering and training 188
   municipal election disputes and 102
   on poverty and poor relief 116,
   144-5
   quo warranto challenges and 61 n.41,
   62-3, 67-71
Hebb, David 167
Henry III 52

Henry VI 185
Henry VIII 43, 52, 162 n.65
Hereford
   alehouses, brewing, and drinking
   in 129
   billeting in 200
   Book of Orders in 139
   Ship Money from 217
   herring trade in Great Yarmouth 147,
   156, 165-6, 175-80
Hertford
   bylaws, seeking central review and
   confirmation of 6
   lectureships and preaching in 236
Heylyn, Peter 230 n.38, 236
High Commission 226-7, 228 n.31,
   232, 234-6, 251, 261
Higham Ferrers, municipal election
   disputes in 99 n.74, 107
Hill, Epiphany (magistrate of
   Banbury) 201-2
Hindle, Steve 112
The State and Social Change 2-3
Hobart, Sir Henry 26 n.39, 131 n.93,
   132
Hobbes, Thomas 3
Hoblyn, Thomas (of Bodmin) 101
Hodgson, Dr. (clergyman of York) 241
Holiday, William (alderman of
   London) 157 n.55
Holland *see* Low Countries
housing controls for the poor 118-20
Howard, Theophilus *See* Suffolk,
   Theophilus Howard, earl of
Hoyle, Richard 25, 28
Hughes, Ann 2
Hull
   alehouses, brewing, and drinking
   in 130, 134, 135
   billeting in 199
   Book of Orders in 140
   Forced Loan and 208
   militias, mustering and training 190
   piracy, combating 168, 169, 170
   plague in 124
   poverty and poor relief in 117 n.25
   Ship Money from 209
   Strafford, earl of, as high steward 262

INDEX

Hull (*continued*)
   trade in   151, 154, 156, 159, 160
   war, fiscal burden of   197
Huntingdon
   charter of incorporation   17, 32, 33, 34-5
   quo warranto challenges   57
Huntingdon, Henry Hastings, fifth earl of   25 n.34 27, 183 n.3, 189-90, 191
Hutton, Justice   241
Hyde, Edward, earl of Clarendon   3
Hyde, Sir Nicholas   71
Hythe, alehouses, brewing, and drinking in   129

Icelandic fisheries   171, 210
impressment   197, 199
Ince, Nicholas (mayor of Chester)   85
Ince, Thomas (common councilor of Chester)   132-3
incorporation   *see* charters of incorporation; corporate towns; corporations
infrastructure and trade   162-6
Ingram, Sir Arthur   157 n.44
internal order in borough government
   clergy as corporate officials, Caroline inclusion of   43, 248-50
   corporate liberties and hierarchical order, tensions between   93-7
   crown dictation of inclusion or exclusion of particular categories or individuals in positions of authority   44-5, 98
   crown interest in   78, 79, 90, 92-3, 97, 100
   discord and disorder, towns as sites of   78-80
   narrowing of freemen's authority in charters of incorporation   29-36
   two bailiffs versus single mayor   31-5, 68, 69, 70, 102, 103, 122 n.50
   see also municipal elections
Ipswich
   charter of incorporation   31
   disruptiveness of religious change in   252-3, 254

lectureships and preaching in   231-3
militias, mustering and training   187
poverty and poor relief in   112, 117-18, 120
quo warranto challenges   55, 57, 58, 71-2, 152-4, 233
religious governance in   224, 260
"riot" against bishop's authority in   233, 252, 254
Ship Money from   174 n.126, 209
social and moral order, religious impetus for   115
tailors and clothmakers, incorporation of   152-4
trade in   156, 156 n.41, 159
Irish boroughs
   Catholic governments in   37, 64, 92 n.55, 223
   charters of incorporation in   36-9, 257
   herring trade in   179
   lectureships and preaching in   229 n.33
   map of incorporated towns, *xii*
   municipal election disputes in   98-9, *105*
   piracy and   170-1
   quo warranto challenges in   57 n.25, 64
   trade in   149
   Ulster, towns in   5, 36, 38-9, 257
   see also specific towns by name
Ivie, John (mayor of Salisbury)   121, 126, 128

Jackson, Sir Robert   87-8
James I
   alehouses, brewing, and drinking under   128-31
   charters of incorporation under   20, 28-9, 39-40, 42 n.109, 49
   Chester requested to accept Hugh Mainwaring as recorder by   45
   dissolution of royal garrisons along Scottish border after accession of   88, 101
   fiscal demands of the state under   194-6

298

INDEX

housing controls initiated by 118
incorporations and reincorporations
  under 22
Irish boroughs, incorporation
  of 36-7
lectures and preaching under 230,
  231-2
militias, mustering and
  training 183-5, 190, 192
municipal elections and 82, 104
number of charters granted by 20
order and profit, on link
  between 146 n.2
piracy and 167, 168
plague orders under 122
popular government, concerns
  about 5, 7, 100, 104
on poverty and poor relief 120
quo warranto under 51, 53-4, 64-7
religion and corporate towns
  under 220-4, 226, 228, 230-2,
  248-9, 253
royal policy under 5, 255, 257
trade under 149, 153, 155-6, 160-1,
  163, 165, 176-7, 180
two bailiffs versus single mayor
  arrangement under 32
James II 50
Jegon, John, bishop of Norwich 230
John (king of England) 37
Jole, Robert (brewer of Salisbury) 60-1,
  128
Jones, William 57
JPs see Justices of the Peace
Jurdain, Ignatius (alderman of
  Exeter) 121, 224 n.13, 250
jurisdictional disputes 6-7, 10, 255
  charters of incorporation and
    13 n.1, 14, 16, 21, 24-5, 27, 40,
    43-4
  ecclesiastical versus corporate
    authority 6, 10, 43-4, 57 n.24,
    72, 220, 222, 223, 226-8,
    237-42, 245-8, 250, 251, 253,
    254, 257, 259
  military/fiscal burdens of the state
    and 183, 193, 196, 202-3,
    211-15, 217-19

quo warranto challenges and 50, 52,
  57 n.24, 59, 61-4, 67, 72, 73
social/moral order and 119, 123, 131,
  134, 137-41, 143-4
trade and 149, 151, 154, 165-6, 180
Justices of the Peace (JPs)
  alehouses, brewing, and drinking,
    regulation of 127, 132
  billeting and 202
  Book of Orders and 136, 137-8, 140,
    142
  clergy as 248-50, 262
  Henry VIII's statute on 43
  municipal election dispute assigned by
    Privy Council to 85
  plague and 123, 124
  poor relief and correction schemes
    instigated by 115
  quo warranto challenges and 63
  trade issues and 161, 164, 166 n.86

Kilkenny, charter of incorporation
  for 37
King's Bench
  internal order, involvement in disputes
    over 84 n.20
  quo warranto in see quo warranto
    challenges
King's Lynn
  disruptiveness of religious change
    in 251-2, 260
  Forced Loan and 209
  parliamentary taxation in 194
  plague in 215
  Ship Money from 174 n.126, 214,
    215-16
  trade in 146, 155-6
Kingston-upon-Hull see Hull
Kingston-upon-Thames, charter of
  incorporation for 28, 32 n.62,
  33
Knafla, Louis 28

Lake, Peter 71, 91 n.50, 221, 224,
  247 n.112
Lancaster, charter of incorporation
  for 24
Lancaster, Duchy of 24, 27, 189

INDEX

Langport, charter of incorporation for 32 n.62
language of charters 15-19
Laud, William, bishop of London, later archbishop of Canterbury
 on cathedral cities 237-9, 240, 241, 243, 245
 charters of incorporation and 19, 46
 civil governance of religious issues and 226, 228
 on lectureships and preaching 230-7
 quo warranto challenges and 74-6
 religious change instigated by 222, 254, 259, 260
 trial of 74, 259, 261-2
Laudian religious ideals and practice 71, 221, 224, 227, 244, 246, 251, 252
lectureships and preaching 193 n.46, 228-37, 260
Leeds
 alehouses, brewing, and drinking 134
 charter of incorporation 20
 Ship Money from 174 n.126
legal challenges to urban government and corporate liberties *see* quo warranto challenges
Leicester
 alehouses, brewing, and drinking in 126, 129, 131-2, 133, 135
 Bishop's Fee, request for extended jurisdiction over 24, 25, 27
 Book of Orders in 140
 charter of incorporation 18 n.19, 25, 27
 Forced Loan and 209
 militias, mustering and training 183 n.3, 189-90, 191
 poverty and poor relief in 113 n.6, 114
 religious governance in 223, 225
 social and moral order, religious impetus for 115
Lennox, duke of 185
letters patent, obtaining 21
Levant Company 159, 161 n.59
Ley, Sir James 25
licenses and licensing

alehouses 65-6, 125-34
 export licenses 160, 165
 grain shipments 142, 143
 herring license in Great Yarmouth 175-80
 preaching licenses 229, 230, 232
Lichfield
 Book of Orders and 137
 charter of incorporation 32 n.62, 248
 quo warranto challenges 57, 73
 Ship Money from 218, 246, 247, 248
Lifford, charter of incorporation for 38
Limerick
 charter of incorporation 37
 piracy, combating 171
Lincoln
 alehouses, brewing, and drinking in 128, 129, 135 n.113
 charter of incorporation 19
 Forced Loan and 208
 king and Council ordering reinstatement of specific aldermen 95
 quo warranto challenges 72
 religious controversy in 95, 128
 Ship Money from 247
 trade in 163-4
Lisgoole, charter of incorporation for 39
Lister, John (mayor of Hull) 160
Littleton, Edward 249
Liverpool
 alehouses, brewing, and drinking in 135
 charter of incorporation 20
London
 alehouses, brewing, and drinking in 129, 135
 Book of Orders and 137
 civic sword or mace in cathedral precincts, laws/disputes regarding 243
 Derry, patent to develop town and county of 38
 herring trade in 175-8
 lectureships and preaching in 231, 236

300

INDEX

Mercers of 231
militias, mustering and training 186
municipal election disputes in 84, 106
piracy, combating 167, 169
plague in 122
poverty and poor relief in 111
quo warranto cases heard at, expenses involved in 54-5, 71, 134
trade conflicts with provincial towns 155, 157-61, 175-8
trade in 146, 151, 155, 175-8
Londonderry *see* Derry
Long Parliament 192 n.43, 228 n.31, 258-60
Looe
piracy, combating 171
Ship Money from 210
lord keepers/lord chancellors
granting of charter, role in 26-8
list of early Stuart officeholders 26 n.39
see also specific officeholders by name
lord lieutenants and lieutenancy 6, 24 n.34, 73, 184-6, 188-9, 191-2, 202-3
lottery for Virginia (1615) 165
Low, Sir Thomas 157 n.55
Low Countries
herring fleet 175
naval plans of Charles I and 174
plague from 122
Ludlow
charter of incorporation 32 n.62, 33
prerogative levies in 195
quo warranto challenges 54, 60 n.34, 66
Lyme Regis
French Company, merchants refusing to join 176 n.135
piracy, combating 169, 173
Ship Money from 209
war, fiscal burden of 198

MacCaffrey, Wallace 3, 16 n.12
Mackworth, Humphrey (of Shrewsbury) 75 n.107
Magna Carta, appeals to 139, 258, 261

Maidstone
All Saints as parish church of 225-6
elected officials refusing to take up office in 83, 85
lectureships and preaching in 260
loss of charter under Mary I due to participation in Wyatt's rebellion 52, 226 n.20
militias, mustering and training 190
quo warranto challenges 52, 55, 57, 59, 61-4, 76
religious governance in 225-8
Mainwaring, Hugh 45
Mainwaring, Sir Randle (mayor of Chester) 133
Maldon
billeting in 199, 200
grain riots in 137, 141
religious governance in 225
Ship Money from 214
Malmesbury, charter of incorporation for 30
Maltravers, Lord 192
Manchester, earl of, lord president of the Privy Council 35, 205
markets and fairs
plague outbreaks affecting 121, 122
privilege to hold 21, 150
quo warranto challenges targeting 65, 66-7
Marlborough, prerogative levies in 195
Mary I 20, 52, 64 n.58, 76, 192, 226 n.20
Massachusetts colony 207 n.109
Mayott, Mr. (in disputed Abingdon election) 90
Medowes, Mr. (bailiff of Great Yarmouth) 103
Melcombe Regis *see* Weymouth-Melcombe Regis
Merchant Adventurers 151, 157 n.55, 158, 160, 161, 261
merchants *see* trade
Michell, Edward (of Maidstone) 85
Milford, trade in 156 n.41
military burdens of the state 9-10, 181-2; *see also* billeting; Ship Money; war

301

INDEX

military burdens of the state (*continued*)
artillery yards 186, 187, 188
dissolution of royal garrisons along
  Scottish border, effects of 88,
  101, 197
fortifications and defenses 9, 17, 179,
  181, 194, 196-8, 210, 211, 256
impressment 197, 199
militias, mustering and
  training 183-93
Millstone, Noah 252
Mishra, Rupali 161
Mompesson, Sir Giles 66
Monins, Stephan (mayor of Dover) 143
Monmouth
  Book of Orders in 140
  Forced Loan and 208
monopolies *see* patents and monopolies
Montgomery, earl of 203
Moore, Edward (alderman of
  Berwick) 85-8
Moore, Marmaduke (town clerk of
  Aldeburgh) 189
moral order *see* social and moral order
  in corporate towns
Morrill, John 2, 35
Morton, Thomas, bishop of
  Durham 86-8
Mountjoy, Lord Deputy of Ireland
  (Charles Blount, Lord
  Mountjoy) 37
municipal elections 9, 78-104
  as annual event 80
  Charles I and 82, 97-104
  corporate liberties and hierarchical
    order, tensions between 93-7,
    104
  corporate office or membership,
    Privy Council resolving
    disputes and questions
    over 83-4
  crown interest in internal order
    and 78, 79, 90, 92-3, 97, 100
  direct intervention of king/Council
    in 44-5, 95-6, 98
  disorder and discord in 81-2
  disputes heard by Privy
    Council 82-5, 87, 88, 105-7

good government and proper order as
  chief concern of Privy Council
  in 90, 92-3
James I and 82, 104
King's Bench and 84 n.20
local actors appealing to Privy Council
  regarding 88-91, 100-1
Personal Rule, increasing number of
  disputes during 97-104
plague affecting 82-3, 121
quo warranto challenges and disputes
  in 101
refusals of elected officials to take up
  office 83, 84
relations between borough and state,
  disputes revealing different ideas
  about 85-8, 104
religious frictions involved in 91-2,
  94 n.58, 95, 101, 102
rules and bylaws for 80-1
Ship Money and disputes in 100,
  101-2
Star Chamber hearings on disputes
  in 82 n.13, 98 n.72
state involvement in disputes
  over 81-2
town officials versus ordinary
  townspeople, Privy Council
  attitude toward 89-92, 100-1
Muscovy Company 159
Musselwhite, Paul 5

Narrow Sea 171, 197, 198
Neile, Richard, archbishop of York 239,
  241, 242-3, 250
Netherlands *see* Low Countries
Neve, Jeffrey (of Great Yarmouth)
  95-6
Newark-upon-Trent
  charter of incorporation 24, 28
  quo warranto challenges 57
Newburgh, Lord 99 n.74
Newbury
  Ship Money from 217
  vagrancy, regulation of 118
Newcastle-upon-Tyne
  alehouses, brewing, and drinking
    in 130

302

INDEX

Hostmen's guild 151
municipal election disputes in 78,
 89-90, 98, *105, 106*
parliamentary petitions from 261
piracy, combating 169, 170, 171
plague in 122, 215
religious governance in 223
riot over town lime kilns (1633) 89
Ship Money from 214 n.134, 215,
 217, 261
town lectureships in 229
trade in 147, 149, 151, 155-6, 158
Newfoundland fisheries 171, 173
Nicholas, Edward 25, 258
Nicholls, Thomas (bailiff of
 Shrewsbury) 45-6, 75 n.108
Nixe, Leonard (alderman of
 Nottingham) 119
non-residents, denial of town privileges or
 office to 90-1, 96
Norgatt, Mr. (bailiff of Great
 Yarmouth) 103
Northampton
 billeting in 206
 charter of incorporation 17
 Forced Loan and 209
 militias, mustering and training 184
 Ship Money from 217, 218
 trade in 150
Norton, John (alderman of
 Colchester) 192
Norwich
 billeting in 200
 cathedral seating and attendance
  requirements 244, 245
 charter of incorporation 31 n.58
 disruptiveness of religious change
  in 251, 252, 260
 lectureships and preaching in 230,
  236, 260
 militias, mustering and training 73,
  187, 192-3
 municipal election disputes in 84,
  88-9, 97, 98, 100, *105, 106*
 parliamentary taxation in 194
 plague in 123
 poor relief in 111-12
 prerogative levies in 196

quo warranto challenges 73
religious differences and election
 dispute in 46 n.124
Ship Money from 174 n.126, 209,
 211, 214, 218
trade in 147, 166 n.86
Norwich, bishop of, and town of Great
 Yarmouth 102, 165
Norwich, dean of 69, 233-4
Nottingham
 alehouses, brewing, and drinking
  in 126, 127, 132
 Book of Orders in 140
 Forced Loan and 209
 housing controls in 119
 militias, mustering and training 187
 municipal election disputes heard by
  Privy Council 105
Noy, William 26 n.39, 213, 236

oligarchy/oligarchs
 charters of incorporation, narrowing
  of freemen's authority in 29-30,
  35
 internal order in corporate towns
  and 79, 81, 89, 97
 parliamentary petitions and 261
 quo warranto challenges and 51, 53,
  60
 trend toward 5
Oswestry, trade in 155
Otham, godly preaching in 227
Owen, Thomas (town clerk of
 Shrewsbury) 46, 263 n.22
Oxford
 charter of incorporation 28
 housing controls in 118 n.31, 119
 masons' company in 152
 municipal election disputes in 98,
  105
 trade in 152
 university charter protested by
  city 259
Oxford University
 Caroline charter for 40-1, 259
 on masons' company 152
 objections to incorporation of city
  of Oxford 28

303

INDEX

Palatinate, defense contributions
for 195-6
papists *see* Catholics
Parlett, Francis (recorder of King's
Lynn) 146
parliament
billeting disputes in 202 n.83, 205-6,
258
corporate towns petitioning 258-61
elections for 80, 258-9
incorporation by 15, 16 n.8
limited involvement of 6-7
Long Parliament 192 n.43, 228 n.31,
258-60
militias, mustering and
training 189 n.27
on patents and quo warranto 66, 134
petition for charter of incorporation
requesting additional burgesses
for 28
on poverty and poor relief 114-15
Ship money complaints to 259
Short Parliament 192 n.43, 258, 260
taxation by 194
trade issues in 154, 158, 160 n.54,
163, 164, 178
patents and monopolies
alehouses, brewing, and
drinking 131-4
as grievance in 1621 Parliament 66,
132, 134, 160
parliamentary petitions regarding 261
quo warranto challenges by 65-6
trade and 155-6, 157, 160-1
Penzance
charter of incorporation 17, 166
trade in 150, 166
Perryman, John (town clerk of
Bodmin) 101
Personal Rule
central/local relations and 258, 264
charters of incorporation under 41
municipal elections during 97-104
religion and corporate towns in 221,
222, 224
urban policy under 7-8, 10
see also Ship Money
Peterborough, bishop of 231

Petition of Right 205-6, 207, 211, 258
petitioning as political strategy 6 n.14,
55, 215, 252, 259-61
petitions for incorporation 21-5
Phelips, Sir Robert 206
Philip and Mary, militia statute of 183,
184, 192
piracy and pirates 17, 166-74, 197, 204,
210, 212, 213
plague 82-3, 120-4, 126, 128, 144-5,
150, 174, 191, 201, 209, 215, 216
Plymouth
alehouses, brewing, and drinking
in 126
billeting in 199, 200 n.73, 201, 204
charter of incorporation 28
piracy, combating 168, 170, 171, 172,
173
plague in 123, 124, 201, 210
Ship Money from 210
trade in 156, 159, 161
Pool, P.A.S. 17 n.13
Poole
Forced Loan and 208
piracy, combating 168 n.94, 170
Ship Money from 209
trade in 156 n.41, 159, 172
the poor *see* poverty and poor relief
popular government/popularity
billeting, political resistance to 207
charters of incorporation, narrowing of
freemen's authority in 29-36
municipal elections and 84, 92, 95
quo warranto challenges and 74, 262
religion and 46, 224, 230, 235, 253
royal concerns about 5, 7-8, 257
Ship Money, resistance to
paying 216-17
Portsmouth
charter of incorporation 18
Elizabethan versus Caroline charters
of 18 n.19
municipal election disputes in 82-3
Portugal, London merchants trading
into 159, 161
poverty and poor relief 112-20
alehouses, brewing, and
drinking 125, 126, 128, 133

304

INDEX

Book of Orders and 137, 138, 140, 141, 142, 144
charters of incorporation addressing 114-15, 116, 119-20
common brewhouses funding poor relief 60-1, 116
economic instability in early 17th century and 111, 113-14
housing controls 118-20
in-migration of rural poor to urban areas 111, 118
management programs for 114, 116-17, 120
multiple financial burdens on townspeople and 174
national policies and programs 111-12, 114-15, 120
religious motives and solutions for 115-16
vagrancy, regulation of 112, 114, 118, 140
preaching and lectureships 193 n.46, 228-37
pre-Civil War period (1639-42) 10, 255-64
prerogative levies 194-6
prescriptive liberties see customary liberties and privileges
Prior, Charles 222 n.8
Privy Council
on alehouses, brewing, and drinking 125, 128-9, 130, 131, 133-5
on billeting 200-5, 207, 208
Book of Orders and 136-40, 143
central/local relations and 192-4, 255, 257, 261
charters of incorporation and 15, 25, 30, 31 n.58, 35, 41, 43, 45, 46-8
corporate office or membership, resolving disputes and questions over 83-4
corporate towns interacting with 6, 7, 9
Forced Loan and 208, 210-11
fortifications and 198
herring trade in Great Yarmouth and 175, 177-80

internal order in borough government and 78
Irish boroughs, incorporation of 35, 37, 39
London and provincial towns, trade rivalries between 157-61
militias, mustering and training 184-90, 192
narrowing of freemen's authority and 30
on piracy 167-72, 173
plague orders and 121, 122-4
poverty/poor relief and 113, 119
on prerogative levies 195
quo warranto challenges and 57 n.25, 60, 64, 68, 70 n.84, 73-6
Registers (1603-14) lost to fire 83
on religion and corporate towns 223, 224, 233, 234, 238, 240, 244, 246-8, 251
Ship Money and 210-11, 213-18, 246, 247
trade governance by 147, 149-50, 152-7, 180
trade infrastructure and 162-5
see also under municipal elections
Privy Seal Loans (1610) 195
provincial corporate towns see corporate towns
Prowse, William (of Exeter) 249
Prynne, William 75-6, 230 n.38, 258, 262
Purefoy, Michael (MP of Nottingham) 132
puritans and puritanism
charters of incorporation and 46
civil governance of religious matters and 221, 224, 228, 233, 249, 251, 252, 253, 262
in civic government 91, 173 n.122, 234, 250-1
municipal elections and 91
royal attitudes toward 42, 116, 224, 249, 253
social/moral order and 116, 143, 144
trade and 173 n.122
urban prevalence of 74, 115-16, 238, 262

INDEX

Pusey, Rowland (mayor of Leicester) 131-2

quartering of troops *see* billeting
Queenborough, militia in 184
Quintrell, B.W. 201 n.79
quo warranto challenges 8-9, 50-77
 alehouses and brewing targeted
  by 60-1, 65, 134
 appeals for inspection, confirmation,
  or revision of charter in response
  to 58
 under Charles I 51, 54, 67-76
 cost, time, and anxiety involved
  in 54-5, 70-1, 134
 crown use of 50-1, 53, 56, 60, 64,
  72, 76-7
 defined and described 52-6
 final legal judgments, rarity of 54,
  56-7, 77
 and Irish towns 57 n.25, 64, 77,
  105
 under James I 51, 53-4, 64-7
 Laud 1644 trial of 74-6, 262
 local peoples' use of 51, 53, 56, 60-4,
  67, 72, 75, 77
 management of 55-6
 municipal election disputes and 101
 negotiation of authority by 59-64
 number and frequency of 53-4, 65,
  72-3
 outcomes of 56-9
 by patentees 65-6
 revenue generation, as means
  of 65-6
 Ship Money disputes and 44, 72,
  73-4, 218
 surrender of town charter due to 41,
  46, 50, 73, 75
 trade issues and 152
 venire facias, issuance of 54, 65

Rawson, Henry (of Windsor) 216
Reading
 alehouses, brewing, and drinking
  in 126, 135
 billeting in 199, 200
 Book of Orders in 140

charter of incorporation 19, 31, 43,
 119-20
housing controls and poverty
 in 119-20
prerogative levies in 195
trade in 149-50
recusants *see* Catholics
reforming religion 115, 228; *see also*
 puritans and puritanism
regional councils, corporate towns
 interacting with 6, 7, 89
religion and corporate towns 10,
 220-54; *see also* cathedral cities;
 specific denominations
 alehouses, brewing, and drinking,
  regulation of 115, 128
 billeting, political resistance to 205,
  206
 Book of Orders and 139 n.131, 143
 under Charles I 43-4, 72-4, 220-5,
  229-31, 233, 234, 237, 238,
  240-5, 248-54
 civil governance of religious
  matters 222-8
 clergy as corporate officials, Caroline
  inclusion of 43, 248-50, 262
 disruptiveness of religious
  change 220-1, 250-4
 ecclesiastical authority, Caroline
  protection of 43-4, 72-4, 220,
  225, 237, 240, 243-4, 248-54
 incorporation/charters, ecclesiastical
  objections to 25, 28, 220,
  245-50
 interactions between towns and
  ecclesiastical authorities 6
 Irish boroughs, Catholic governments
  in 37, 64, 92 n.55, 223
 Irish boroughs, incorporation
  of 36-9
 under James I 220-4, 226, 228,
  230-2, 248-9, 253
 jurisdictional disputes 220, 222, 223,
  226-8, 237-42, 245-8, 250, 251,
  253, 254, 257, 259
 lectureships and preaching 193 n.46,
  228-37
 municipal elections, religious

306

INDEX

frictions in 91-2, 94 n.58, 95, 101, 102
in Personal Rule 221, 222, 224
plague controls and 121 n.45, 122
popular government/popularity and 46, 224, 230, 235, 253
poverty and poor relief 115-16
quo warranto challenges and 64, 67-8, 72-4
relations between central/local authorities and 220-1
Ship Money disputes in cathedral cities 44, 73, 214, 218, 246-8
social and moral order, impetus for 115-16, 144-5
Reynolds, Matthew 230, 244, 251
Riddell, Sir Peter 261
Riddell, Sir Thomas 261
Ridlington, Robert (mayor of Hartlepool) 91
Robins, John (alderman of Great Yarmouth) 250
Rochester
charter of incorporation 24-5
plague in 123
Roman Catholicism see Catholics
Russell, Conrad 181
Rye
Book of Orders and 137
trade infrastructure in 164

Sabin (mayor of Canterbury) 94 n.58
Sacks, David Harris 4, 98, 151
Saffron Walden, alehouses, brewing, and drinking in 131
Salisbury
alehouses, brewing, and drinking in 126, 128
bishop as JP, crown efforts to include 43, 220, 248-9
Book of Orders in 141
cathedral seating dispute in 239
charter of incorporation 16, 25, 28, 40, 43, 220, 249
disruptiveness of religious change in 250
episcopal objections to incorporation of 25, 28, 72, 220, 221

plague in 121
quo warranto challenges 55, 57, 60-1, 64, 72
religious governance in 224
Ship Money from 218, 246-7
social and moral order, religious impetus for 115
stained glass window in parish church, town recorder's destruction of 249, 250, 261
vagrancy, regulation of 118
Sallee, proclamation protecting ships and goods of 172
Salter, William (JP of Stamford) 138
Sandwich
billeting in 203
Book of Orders in 142, 143-4
municipal election disputes in 99, 106
parliamentary elections for 258
religious governance in 223
rules for municipal elections in 80 n.7, 81
trade in 156 n.41, 158 n.49
Savage, Sir Thomas 24
Saye, Lord 205
Scarborough
alehouses, brewing, and drinking 134
piracy, combating 170
Ship Money from 259
Schilling, W.A.H. 40 n.99, 48
schismatics and separatists 223, 224, 234, 235; see also Brownists
scire facias 64, 152
Scotland, war with 190, 218, 258-9
Scott, Thomas (of Canterbury) 139 n.131, 203, 206-7, 211, 258
Seaver, Paul 228
Sharpe, Kevin 181, 212, 221, 258
The Personal Rule of Charles I 218
Sheffield, failure of petitions for incorporation of 25
Sheppard, William, Of Corporations, Fraternities, and Guilds (1659) 15-16
Sherfield, Henry (recorder of Salisbury) 249, 250, 261

307

INDEX

Sherland, Christopher (recorder of Northampton) 206
Sherwill, Thomas (MP of Plymouth) 172
Ship Money 209-19
annualization and nationalization of 215
assessment and collection of 214-16, 218, 262
cathedral cities and disputes over 44, 73, 214, 218, 246-8
Forced Loan and 209-11
historians' evaluation of 181, 212-13
importance of corporate towns to success of 213
legal case (1638) 218
multiple financial burdens on townspeople and 124, 174, 208, 209-11
municipal election disputes and 100, 101-2
parliament, complaints to 259
piracy and 168 n.95, 173-4, 212
quo warranto challenges and 44, 72, 73-4, 218
resistance to/refusal to pay 210, 212-13, 216-19, 258, 259
Short Parliament 192 n.43, 258, 260
Shrewsbury
Book of Orders in 140
charter of incorporation 16 n.8, 20, 31, 32, 34, 43, 45-8, 75 n.107
civic sword or mace in cathedral precincts, laws/disputes regarding 43 n.113
in Civil War 263
Drapers' Company of 151
Forced Loan and 208
incorporation by parliament, consideration of 16 n.8
Laud's intervention in 46, 74-5, 262
lectureships and preaching in 236
municipal election disputes in 99, 100, 101, 107
quo warranto challenges 55, 57, 74-5, 101, 262
Ship Money from 216

St. Chad's, dispute over appointment of curate at 74
trade in 151, 155, 158
Slack, Paul 112 n.5, 115, 116, 120-1, 122, 136
Smith, Miles, bishop of Gloucester 235
social and moral order in corporate towns 9, 111-45; see also alehouses, brewing, and drinking; Book of Orders; poverty and poor relief
billeting and 200-1
Colchester's Caroline charter of incorporation addressing 42
common interests of state and local governments in 112
disorder, controlling potential for 111-12, 113, 125
expansion of governance and 112
plague and plague orders 120-4, 144
religious motivations for 115-16, 144-5
soldiers, billeting see billeting
Southampton
alehouses, brewing, and drinking in 126
billeting in 202, 204-5, 206
charter of incorporation 17, 43
incorporation by parliament 16 n.8
militias, mustering and training 189
piracy, combating 168, 169
quo warranto challenges 58
Ship Money from 214, 217
trade in 154, 156 n.41, 158, 159
Southwold
piracy, combating 171
trade in 162, 163
Spain
London merchants trading into 159, 161
piracy and 171
war with 92, 161, 170-4, 187, 189, 198
Spufford, Margaret 115
St. Albans
alehouses, brewing, and drinking in 127
charter of incorporation 31

308

INDEX

plague in 215
quo warranto challenges 66–7
Ship Money from 215
St. John, Oliver 195
St. Paul's cathedral (London) 243
Stafford
  Book of Orders and 137
  charter of incorporation 32, 34, 40
Stamford
  Book of Orders in 138–9
  borough liberties in 139, 258
  king and Council ordering removal of
    town clerk from office 95, 139
Stanley, Alice Spencer 27 n.45
Stapp, Otho (mayor of Bodmin) 101
Star Chamber 82 n.13, 98 n.72, 128,
    130, 195 n.52, 250
Stern, Philip 13 n.1
Stewart, Sir Francis 172
Stone, William (of Bodmin) 101
Stoyle, Mark 224 n.13
Strafford, Thomas Wentworth, earl
    of 261–2
Stratford-upon-Avon
  charter of incorporation 40
  housing controls in 119
  lectureships and preaching in 229
  poverty and poor relief in 113 n.6,
    119
Studely, John (mayor of
    Shrewsbury) 263 n.22
Sturbridge Fair 122
Suckling, Sir John 178
Suffolk, Theophilus Howard, earl of 99,
    141–2, 188–9
Sutton's Hospital case 15
sweet wine trade in Southampton 154,
    159
Swinden, Henry 179 n.151
Swinnock, Robert (jurat of
    Maidstone) 227

Tamworth, and Book of Orders 137
Tanfield, Sir Lawrence 65
Taunton
  billeting in 206
  Book of Orders in 139, 140
  charter of incorporation 20

prerogative levies in 195
taxation
  parliamentary 194
  plague controls, funding 123–4,
    174
  poor rates 111, 115, 174
  quo warranto challenges to 61–3
  see also Forced Loan; prerogative levies;
    Ship Money
Taylor, John (of Maidstone) 85
Teisdall, Thomas (of Abingdon) 96
Tenterden, Book of Orders in 142
Tewkesbury
  charter of incorporation 32 n.62
  housing controls in 118–19
  militias, mustering and
    training 184–5, 190
Thetford
  Forced Loan and 208
  parliamentary taxation in 194
Thirty Years' War 232
Tisdale, Benjamin (mayor of
    Abingdon) 90–1
Tittler, Robert 5, 13, 16 n.12, 20, 53,
    59, 79, 225 n.19
  The Reformation and the Towns 4, 51
Tiverton, charter of incorporation
    for 40
Totnes
  militias, mustering and training 192
  piracy, combating 169, 170
  quo warranto challenges 59–60, 64
  trade in 161
Totnes, earl of 198
Tourneure, Timothy (recorder of
    Shrewsbury) 263 n.22
towns, corporate see corporate towns
trade 9, 146–80; see also cloth industry;
    markets and fairs
  under Charles I 149, 156, 161, 176,
    178–9, 180
  charters of incorporation
    addressing 146–7, 150
  disputes and dispute
    settlement 152–7
  free trade debate 154, 155 n.35,
    157–8, 159, 161, 170
  governance of 148–57

309

INDEX

trade (*continued*)
grain supply, local lack of control over
transportation of   143-4
herring trade in Great Yarmouth   147,
156, 165-6, 175-80
infrastructure and   147, 162-6, 176
under James I   149, 153, 155-6,
160-1, 163, 165, 176-7, 180
London and provincial towns, conflicts
between   155, 157-61, 175-8
negotiation between local governments
and crown regarding   147-50,
155-7, 162-3, 170, 175
order and profit, link between   146
patents and patentees
affecting   155-6, 157
piracy   166-74, 210, 212
revenue generation, regulation as
means of   155-6
war affecting   172-3, 209-10
trading companies/
corporations   57 n.25, 147-54,
158-61, 231; *see also specific
institutions by name*
troops, billeting   *see* billeting
Truro
militias, mustering and training   184
Ship Money from   209
Tudor period
charters and incorporations   20-1,
32, 43
poor relief in   114
quo warranto challenges during
52-3
Tufton, Sir Humphrey   61-2
Tunis
Barbary pirates or "Turks" from   166,
167, 170, 171, 172, 173, 212
proclamation protecting ships and
goods of   172
two-bailiff versus single mayor
government   31-4, 41, 47, 68,
69, 70, 122 n.50, 249
Tyacke, Nicholas   221, 232 n.45,
248 n.119

Ulster, towns in   5, 36, 38-9, 257;
see also Irish boroughs

Underdown, David   2, 4, 116
universities
York's parliamentary petition
regarding   260
see also Cambridge University; Oxford
University
urbanization   5, 36

vagrancy, regulation of   112, 114, 117,
118, 140
van Vliet, Janine   163 n.72
Villiers, George, duke of
Buckingham   66, 171-2, 173,
178, 199, 204
Virginia colony
lottery for (1615)   165
piracy affecting   171, 173
plan for corporate towns in   5
Virginia Company   57 n.25, 157 n.44

Wakefield, Ship Money from   174 n.126
Walberswick
piracy, combating   171
trade in   162, 163
Walker, Thomas (mayor of Exeter)   83
Walsingham, Sir Thomas   25
Walter, John   41, 141
war
fiscal burden of   193-4, 196-9, 211
with France   161, 170, 172-4, 189,
209-10
impressment and   197, 199
militias, mustering and training   187,
188, 189, 190, 191
multiple financial burdens on
townspeople and   174
Palatinate, defense contributions
for   195-6
with Scotland   190, 218, 258-9
with Spain   92, 161, 170-4, 187, 189
Thirty Years' War   232
trade affected by   172-3, 209-10
see also Civil War
Ward, Samuel (preacher of
Ipswich)   115, 231-3, 252
Waterford
Bristol, trade ties with   39
charter of incorporation   37, 39

INDEX

municipal election disputes in 99
quo warranto, loss of charter
by 57 n.25, 64
Webb, Thomas (town clerk of
Harwich) 95
Wells, poverty and poor relief in 113
Welsh cloths dispute 155
Wenlock, Ship Money from 217
Wentworth, Sir John 71, 234 n.55
Wentworth, Thomas, earl of
Strafford 261-2
Westbury
charter of incorporation 40
failure of petition for
incorporation 25
Westminster, plague in 122
Westmorland, Francis Fane, earl of 62-3
Weymouth-Melcombe Regis
parliamentary petition from 259
piracy, combating 170, 173
quo warranto challenges 55-6, 58
Ship Money from 210
trade in 159
war, fiscal burden of 197
Wharton, Mr. (alderman in Lincoln) 95
Whatman, Thomas (recorder of
Chichester) 94-5
Wheatley, Nathaniel (mayor of
Banbury) 217
Whig historical interpretations 65, 181,
212
Whitby, infrastructure of trade in 162,
164
Whitchurch, trade in 155
White, John (minister of
Dorchester) 115, 116
White, Peter 221
Whitelocke, Bulstrode 90-1
Whitelocke, James 57
Whiteway, William (of
Dorchester) 34 n.72, 172-3,
188, 197, 199, 200, 210, 217, 250
Wickham, Henry, archdeacon of
York 241
Williams, John, bishop of Lincoln and
Lord Keeper 26, 248-9
Wilson, Thomas (minister of
Maidstone) 227

Winchelsea
Book of Orders in 143
municipal election disputes
in 98 n.72, 99 n.74, 105, 106
Winchester
cathedral attendance
requirements 245
charter of incorporation 248
civic sword or mace in cathedral
precincts, laws/disputes
regarding 243-4
incorporation by parliament,
consideration of 16 n.8
Ship Money from 217, 218, 247, 248
Windebank, Francis 46
Windsor
Forced Loan and 208
Ship Money from 216
Withington, Phil 5, 14, 29, 35, 40, 79,
85, 187
The Politics of Commonwealth 4
Woodford, Robert 224 n.13
Woolley, Robert (JP of St. Albans) 127
Worcester
alehouses, brewing, and drinking
in 129, 135 n.113
cathedral seating and attendance
requirements 240, 245
changing corporate order from two
bailiffs to one mayor in 32, 34
charter of incorporation 34, 57
housing controls in 118
parliamentary petition from 259
plague in 121 n.44
quo warranto challenges 57
Ship Money from 218
Shrewsbury, as model for 47
Workman, John (preacher of
Gloucester) 235, 261
Wren, Matthew, bishop of Norwich 72,
193 n.46, 233, 244, 252-3, 260
Wright, William (mayor of
Hartlepool) 91
Wrightson, Keith 138
writs of restitution 84 n.20
Wyatt's rebellion 52, 76, 226 n.20
Wycombe, alehouses, brewing, and
drinking in 135

311

INDEX

Yarmouth *see* Great Yarmouth
Yelverton, Sir Henry 17 n.15, 26 n.39
York
  alehouses, brewing, and drinking
    in 130, 134, 135
  Book of Orders in 139
  cathedral seating and attendance
    requirements 238, 241-2, 245
  charter of incorporation 44, 248
  civic sword or mace in cathedral
    precincts, laws/disputes
    regarding 243, 244, 252
  in Civil War 263
  disruptiveness of religious change
    in 252
  Forced Loan and 208

  parliamentary petitions from 259,
    260-1
  piracy, combating 169, 170
  poverty and poor relief in 117 n.25,
    120
  quo warranto challenges 57, 65, 72,
    134
  Ship Money from 209, 210, 218-19,
    247, 248
  St. Mary le Belfry parish church,
    seating in 242
  Strafford, earl of, as high steward 262
  trade in 147, 154, 158, 159
  university, petition regarding 260

Zouche, Edward, Lord 93

STUDIES IN EARLY MODERN CULTURAL,
POLITICAL AND SOCIAL HISTORY

I
Women of Quality
Accepting and Contesting Ideals of Femininity in England, 1690–1760
Ingrid H. Tague

II
Restoration Scotland, 1660–1690
Royalist Politics, Religion and Ideas
Clare Jackson

III
Britain, Hanover and the Protestant Interest, 1688–1756
Andrew C. Thompson

IV
Hanover and the British Empire, 1700–1837
Nick Harding

V
The Personal Rule of Charles II, 1681–85
Grant Tapsell

VI
Royalism, Print and Censorship in Revolutionary England
Jason McElligott

VII
The English Catholic Community, 1688–1745
Politics, Culture and Ideology
Gabriel Glickman

VIII
England and the 1641 Irish Rebellion
Joseph Cope

IX
Culture and Politics at the Court of Charles II, 1660–1685
Matthew Jenkinson

X
Commune, Country and Commonwealth
The People of Cirencester, 1117–1643
David Rollison

XI
An Enlightenment Statesman in Whig Britain
Lord Shelburne in Context, 1737–1805
Edited by Nigel Aston and Clarissa Campbell Orr

XII
London's News Press and the Thirty Years War
Jayne E.E. Boys

XIII
God, Duty and Community in English Economic Life, 1660–1720
Brodie Waddell

XIV
Remaking English Society
Social Relations and Social Change in Early Modern England
Edited by Steve Hindle, Alexandra Shepard and John Walter

XV
Common Law and Enlightenment in England, 1689–1750
Julia Rudolph

XVI
The Final Crisis of the Stuart Monarchy
The Revolutions of 1688–91 in their British, Atlantic and European Contexts
Edited by Tim Harris and Stephen Taylor

XVII
The Civil Wars after 1660
Public Remembering in Late Stuart England
Matthew Neufeld

XVIII
The Nature of the English Revolution Revisited
Essays in Honour of John Morrill
Edited by Stephen Taylor and Grant Tapsell

XIX
The King's Irishmen
The Irish in the Exiled Court of Charles II, 1649–1660
Mark R.F. Williams

XX
Scotland in the Age of Two Revolutions
Edited by Sharon Adams and Julian Goodare

XXI
Alehouses and Good Fellowship in Early Modern England
Mark Hailwood

XXII
Social Relations and Urban Space: Norwich, 1600–1700
Fiona Williamson

XXIII
British Travellers and the Encounter with Britain, 1450–1700
John Cramsie

XXIV
Domestic Culture in Early Modern England
Antony Buxton

XXV
Accidents and Violent Death in Early Modern London, 1650–1750
Craig Spence

XXVI
Popular Culture and Political Agency in Early Modern England and Ireland
Essays in Honour of John Walter
Edited by Michael J. Braddick and Phil Withington

XXVII
Commerce and Politics in Hume's History of England
Jia Wei

XXVIII
Bristol from Below: Law, Authority and Protest in a Georgian City
Steve Poole and Nicholas Rogers

XXIX
Disaffection and Everyday Life in Interregnum England
Caroline Boswell

XXX
Cromwell's House of Lords
Politics, Parliaments and Constitutional Revolution, 1642–1660
Jonathan Fitzgibbons

XXXI
Stuart Marriage Diplomacy
Dynastic Politics in their European Context, 1604–1630
Edited by Valentina Caldari and Sara J. Wolfson

XXXII
National Identity and the Anglo-Scottish Borderlands, 1552–1652
Jenna M. Schultz

XXXIII
Roguery in Print: Crime and Culture in Early Modern London
Lena Liapi

XXXIV
Politics, Religion and Ideas in Seventeenth- and Eighteenth-Century Britain
Essays in Honour of Mark Goldie
Edited by Justin Champion, John Coffey, Tim Harris and John Marshall

XXXV
The Hanoverian Succession in Great Britain and its Empire
Edited by Brent S. Sirota and Allan I. Macinnes

XXXVI
Age Relations and Cultural Change in Eighteenth-Century England
Barbara Crosbie

XXXVII
The National Covenant in Scotland, 1638–1689
Chris R. Langley

XXXVIII
Visualising Protestant Monarchy
Ceremony, Art and Politics after the Glorious Revolution (1689–1714)
Julie Farguson

XXXIX
Blood Waters
War, Disease and Race in the Eighteenth-Century British Caribbean
Nicholas Rogers

XL
The State Trials and the Politics of Justice in Later Stuart England
Edited by Brian Cowan and Scott Sowerby

XLI
Africans in East Anglia, 1467-1833
Richard C. Maguire

XLII
Royalism, Religion and Revolution: Wales, 1640-1688
Sarah Ward Clavier

XLIII
Painting for a Living in Tudor and Early Stuart England
Robert Tittler

XLIV
Scotland and the Wider World
Essays in Honour of Allan I. Macinnes
Edited by Neil McIntyre and Alison Cathcart